# TARDIS Eruditorum: An Unofficial Critical History of Doctor Who

# Volume VI: The Peter Davison and Colin Baker Years

## Philip Sandifer

ERUDITORUM
PRESS

Copyright © 2015 Philip Sandifer

Published by Eruditorum Press

All rights reserved.

Doctor Who, the TARDIS, and all related concepts are copyright BBC Worldwide and are used under the principle of fair use

ISBN: 151737636X

To Krypto. He's a dog.

## Acknowledgments

First and foremost, to my wife, Jill Buratto, whose capacity to take me seriously often exceeds my own.

Second, to James Taylor for the typically phenomenal cover art, to Alison J. Campbell for diligent editing and transcribing, to John Seavey for lending me a copy of *JN-T*, and to Rob Shearman for the obvious.

And, as always, to the readers and commenters who have shaped the book's development. There is not a day I do not feel a surge of genuine pride at the fantastic community that has grown up around Eruditorum Press in general, and *TARDIS Eruditorum* in particular.

# Table of Contents

## Peter Davison

A Mad Man with a Blog (Introduction) .................... 1

Outside the Government: *The Five Faces of Doctor Who* ............ 6

Pop Between Realities, Home in Time for Tea: *Coronation Street* ........................................................................ 12

We've Materialized With Considerable Finesse (*Castrovalva*) 21

Time Can Be Rewritten: *Cold Fusion* ........................ 29

Because We Don't Quite Fully Understand (*Four to Doomsday*) ........................................................................ 38

One Tiny Little Gap in the Universe Left, Just About to Close (*Kinda*) ........................................................... 44

Nothing Ever Changes in London (*The Visitation*) ............. 52

Just a Hint of Mint (*Black Orchid*) ............................. 59

A Pathetic Bunch of Tin Soldiers (*Earthshock*) ............... 66

Our Mode of Conveyance is Irrelevant (*Time-Flight*) ........ 76

Time Can Be Rewritten: *Spare Parts* ........................... 82

Pop Between Realities, Home in Time for Tea: *The Cleopatras* ........................................................................ 89

You Ask Me To Appreciate It (*Arc of Infinity*) ............... 96

The Void Beyond the Mind (*Snakedance*) ..................... 103

Time Can Be Rewritten: *Goth Opera* ........................... 109

And He's Just Wiped Them Out (*Mawdryn Undead*) ........ 116

The Original Viking Settlers (*Terminus*) ................................ 125

He's Gay and She's an Alien (*Enlightenment*) ......................... 133

*Enlightenment* Redux ................................................................ 141

A Space Helmet for a Cow (*The King's Demons*) ..................... 144

You Were Expecting Someone Else: Longleat and *Doctor Who Monthly* ....................................................................................... 151

In the Great Days of Rassilon, Five Great Principles Were Laid Down (*The Five Doctors*) ...................................................... 159

Pop Between Realities, Home in Time for Tea: *The Adventure Game* ......................................................................................... 183

Three Hundred Million Years Out of Your Comfort Zone (*Warriors of the Deep*) ............................................................... 190

Tea from an Urn (*The Awakening*) ............................................ 198

The Ground's Attacking Us (*Frontios*) ...................................... 205

Time Can Be Rewritten: *Time Crash* .......................................... 211

Little Green Blobs in Bonded Polycarbite Armor (*Resurrection of the Daleks*) ............................................................................. 218

Tegan! ........................................................................................ 224

Burn With Me (*Planet of Fire*) .................................................. 229

Time Can Be Rewritten: *Warmonger* ......................................... 236

The Grinding Engines of the Universe (*The Caves of Androzani*) .................................................................................. 242

Now My Doctor: Peter Davison ................................................ 250

## Colin Baker

Does It Offend You? (*The Twin Dilemma*) .................................. 255

Pop Between Realities, Home in Time for Tea: *Max Headroom, Tripods, Robin of Sherwood, Box of Delights* ............... 264

You Were Expecting Someone Else: FASA ........................ 275

Things Which Act Against Everything We Believe In (*Attack of the Cybermen*) .................................................................. 282

Do You Think Anybody Votes for Sweet (*Vengeance on Varos*) ............................................................................................... 291

Time Can Be Rewritten: *Burning Heart* ............................. 297

Think I Don't Know My Own Mark (*The Mark of the Rani*) 301

A Well-Prepared Meal (*The Two Doctors*) ........................... 308

By No Means the Most Interesting (*Timelash*) ..................... 316

Am I Becoming One of Your Angels (*Revelation of the Daleks*) ............................................................................................... 322

Outside The Government: A Fix With Sontarans ............... 329

Pop Between Realities, Home in Time for Tea: Doctor in Distress .................................................................................. 335

Apportioning the Blame ........................................................ 348

Time Can Be Rewritten: *The Song of Megaptera* ................. 354

Time Can Be Rewritten: *The Nightmare Fair* ..................... 360

You Were Expecting Someone Else: *Slipback* ....................... 366

Pop Between Realities, Home in Time for Tea: *Edge of Darkness* and *The Singing Detective* ........................................ 373

You Were Expecting Someone Else: The Steve Parkhouse

Strips ........................................................................... 380

Time Can Be Rewritten: *The Holy Terror* ............................... 386

Time Can Be Rewritten: *...ish* ............................................... 390

Pop Between Realities, Home in Time for Tea: *Time* .......... 397

I Was Beginning to Fear You Had Lost Yourself (*The Mysterious Planet*) ........................................................................ 402

His Almost Gleeful Pleasure (*Mindwarp*) ............................... 413

A Far Greater Crime (*Terror of the Vervoids*) ......................... 423

The Catharsis of Spurious Morality (*The Ultimate Foe*) .......... 432

Time Can Be Rewritten: *Peri and the Piscon Paradox* .............. 442

Time Can Be Rewritten: *Jubilee* ............................................. 447

We're Doing Something No One Else Would Dare Do: An Interview With Rob Shearman ................................................ 453

Time Can Be Rewritten: *Business Unusual* ............................. 495

Time Can Be Rewritten: *Millennial Rites* ............................... 501

Time Can Be Rewritten: *Time's Champion* ............................. 508

Now My Doctor: Colin Baker .................................................. 515

## A Mad Man with a Blog (Introduction)

Why hello there! It looks like you bought a copy of the sixth volume of *TARDIS Eruditorum*, which I, as the writer, thank you for, because that probably means you have given me money. (If you haven't given me money and downloaded this off the Internet, on the other hand, I hope you enjoy it and will consider not stealing future volumes, and/or buying a legitimate copy of this one.)

In the unlikely event that you have no idea what book you're holding, let me explain to you, generally speaking, how this book works. First of all, here's what it isn't: a standard issue guidebook to Doctor Who. Yes, it contains individual essays on every Doctor Who story from the Peter Davison and Colin Baker eras. And those looking for the nitty-gritty facts of Doctor Who can probably get a decent sense of them by inference, but that's not what this book is for. There are no episode descriptions, cast lists, or lengthy discussions of the behind-the-scenes workings of the show. There are dozens of books that already do that, and a fair number of online sites. Nor is this a book of reviews. For those who want those things, I personally recommend the *Doctor Who Reference Guide*, *Doctor Who Ratings Guide*, and *A Brief History of Time (Travel)* – three superlative websites that were consulted for basically every one of these essays.

What this book *is* is an attempt to tell the story of Doctor Who. Not the story of how it was made, or the overall narrative of the Doctor's life, or anything like that, but the story of the idea that is Doctor Who, from its beginnings in late 1963 to . . . well, early 1986 in the case of this book, but there's more to come. Doctor Who is a rarity in the world – an extremely long-running serialized narrative. Even rarer, it's an extremely long-running serialized narrative that is not in a niche like soap operas or superhero comics – both provinces almost exclusively of die-hard fans. Doctor Who certainly has its die-hard fans (or, as I like to think of you, my target audience), but notably, it's also been, for much of its existence, absolutely mainstream family entertainment for an entire country.

What this means is that the story of Doctor Who is, in one sense, the story of the world from 1963 on. Politics, music, technological and social development, and all manner of other things have crossed paths with Doctor Who over the nearly fifty years of its existence, and by using Doctor Who as a focus, one can tell a story with far wider implications.

The approach I use to do this is one that I've, rather pompously I suppose, dubbed psychochronography. It draws its name from the concept of psychogeography – an artistic movement created by Guy Debord in 1955 and described as "the study of the precise laws and specific effects of the geographical environment, consciously organized or not, on the emotions and behavior of individuals." More contemporarily, the term is associated with writers like Iain Sinclair, who writes books describing lengthy walking tours of London that fuse his experience with the history of the places he walks, weaving them into a narrative that tries to tell the entire story of a place, and Alan Moore, who does the same thing while worshiping a snake.

Psychochronography, then, attempts the same feat by walking through time. Where walking through space involves little more than picking a direction and moving your feet rhythmically, walking through time without the aid of a TARDIS is a dodgier proposition. The easiest way is to take a specific object and trace its development through time, looking, as the psychogeographers do, at history, lived experience, and the odd connections that spring up.

And so this book is the first part of a walk through Doctor Who. The essays within it wear a lot of hats, and switch them rapidly. All involve a measure of critical reading (in the literary theory sense, not in the complaining sense) of Doctor Who stories to figure out what they are about. This generally means trying to peel back the onion skins of fan history that cloud a story with things "everybody knows." But it also involves looking at the legacy of stories, which often means looking at that onion skin and trying to explain how it got there. No effort is made to disguise the fact that the first appearance of the Daleks is massive for instance, but on the other hand, the book still looks carefully at what their initial impact might have been.

This approach also means looking at how a story would (and could) have been understood by a savvy viewer of the time, and at how the story can be read as responding to the concerns of its time. That means that the essays tend to be long on cultural context. And, in the end, it also means looking at how I personally interact with these stories. This book has no pretense of objectivity. It is about my walking tour of Doctor Who. I try to be accurate, but I also try to be me.

To fully grab the scope of the topic, in addition to the meat of the book – entries covering all of the Doctor Who stories produced in the Peter Davison and Colin Baker eras– there are four other types of entries. The first are the Time Can Be Rewritten entries. One peculiar feature of Doctor Who is that its past is continually revisited. The bulk of these came in the form of novels written in the '90s and early '00s, but there are other examples. At the time of writing, for instance, Big Finish puts out new stories every year featuring the first eight Doctors. These entries cover occasional highlights from these revisitations, using them as clues to how these earlier eras are widely understood.

The second are the Pop Between Realities, Home in Time for Tea entries, which look at popular media and culture to build context for understanding Doctor Who. These entries usually crop up prior to the bits of Doctor Who they're most relevant for, and provide background and points of comparison for the show as it wrestles with the issues of its many times.

Third, there are two categories of entries focusing on spinoff material - You Were Expecting Someone Else entries, which deal with material like comics and roleplaying games, and Outside the Government, which deals with television spin-offs. These exist to give a broader sense of Doctor Who as a cultural object and, perhaps more importantly, because they're kind of fun.

Finally, there are some essays just thrown into the book version as bonuses. These mostly consist of me slogging my way through some established fan debate about Doctor Who and trying, no doubt fruitlessly, to provide the last word on the matter.

It's probably clear by this point that all of these entries began as blog entries on my blog, also called *TARDIS Eruditorum*. This book version, however, revises and expands every entry, as well as adding several new ones – mostly Time Can Be Rewritten entries, but a few others.

To this end, I should thank the many readers of the blog for their gratifying and edifying comments, which have kept the project going through more than one frustrating stretch. I should also thank the giants upon whose shoulders I stand when analyzing Doctor Who – most obviously Paul Cornell, Martin Day, and Keith Topping for *The Discontinuity Guide*, David J. Howe, Mark Stammers, and Stephen James Walker for the Doctor handbooks, Toby Hadoke and Rob Shearman for *Running Through Corridors*, and Lawrence Miles and Tat Wood for the sublimely brilliant *About Time* series, to which this book is a proud footnote.

But most of all and most importantly, thank you, all of you. But most of all, thank you, dear reader. I hope you enjoy.

## Outside the Government: *The Five Faces of Doctor Who*

It's November 2nd, 1981. Dave Stewart and Barbara Gaskin are at number one with "It's My Party." I'm finding records on this point just a little dodgy, but I think we're looking at the end of a five-week run, in which case what we should say is that in one week The Police overtake them with "Every Little Thing She Does is Magic." Two weeks later Queen and David Bowie take over number one with "Ice Ice Baby," which holds number one for the remainder of this experience. Elvis Costello, The Jam, The Human League, Rod Stewart, Soft Cell, The Pretenders, and Olivia Newton-John also chart.

Since the prepared-for end, Ronald Reagan was shot by John Hinckley Jr.; Jodi Foster was not impressed. Pope John Paul II was also shot and nearly killed. And Marcus Sargeant took six blank shots at Queen Elizabeth II. The first Space Shuttle blasted off, serving in most regards as a tombstone for all dreams of spaceflight that had animated the 1960s, reducing wonder to a banal and pointless repetition of spaceflight essentially for its own sake. Peter Sutcliffe was found guilty of being the Yorkshire Ripper. The first recognized cases of AIDS were identified by the CDC. And, of course, the whole race riots thing we talked about last time. Also, Hosni Mubarak was elected President of Egypt following Sadat's assassination.

While during the five weeks that Doctor Who's five faces apparate, Antigua and Barbuda gain independence from the UK, the General Synod of the Church of England votes to allow the ordination of women, Luke and Laura marry on General Hospital, and Reagan signs the order that will lead to the Iran-Contra scandal.

While on television we have the first real attempt to historicize Doctor Who. *The Five Faces of Doctor Who* consisted of five four-part stories from the history of the program, personally selected by John Nathan-Turner, which were screened daily Monday through Thursday over five weeks. The stories, for the record, were *An Unearthly Child/100,000 BC, The Krotons, Carnival of Monsters, The Three Doctors,* and *Logopolis.*

It is first and foremost telling what stories were selected. The constraint of the timeslot restricted the program to four-parters. Combined with the problem of missing episodes, this left few options for the 1960s. Hartnell, for example, had the following options: *An Unearthly Child, The Aztecs, The Romans, The Space Museum, The Ark,* and *The Gunfighters.* Of these, given the nostalgia factor of a first repeat series, *An Unearthly Child* was the only plausible choice from a programming perspective. But this had the effect of badly obscuring Hartnell's Doctor, who, after all, is at best prototypically formed in *An Unearthly Child.*

The other thing to note about the *Five Faces* repeats is that they were the first time fandom got to see the earlier material. Older fans had their memories of the stories, sure, but younger fans were getting their first glimpse of Hartnell and Troughton. And in many cases it was their last glimpse for several years, at least in their original settings. The next time a Troughton story became available was 1985, when *The Seeds of Death* came out on video. Pertwee was gone until 1988, and Hartnell didn't become available again until 1989. Finally, in 1990, both became decently represented, with all four complete Troughton stories being released along with four different Hartnells.

On top of that, it's worth reflecting on the state of the novelizations. A lot of the Hartnell and Troughton stories were novelized quite late. By the end of 1981, the only novelized Hartnell stories were *The Daleks, The Crusade, The Web Planet, The Tenth Planet, The Dalek Invasion of Earth,* and *An Unearthly Child*; for Troughton it was *The Enemy of the World, The War Games, Tomb of the Cybermen, The Web of Fear, The Ice Warriors, The Abominable Snowmen,* and *The Moonbase*. So information about the first two Doctors was sketchy.

The upshot is that the *Five Faces* repeats ended up being foundational to fan impressions about the Doctors in question. The direct links are in many ways obscure, but when you remember that a generation of fandom knew Hartnell entirely by the story where he nearly bashes a guy's skull in, it's easy to see where the view of Hartnell as angry and unpleasant came from. While this is not untrue, especially in comparison with later Doctors, as an axiomatic statement of the Hartnell era it erases and ignores far more than it describes. And yet its prevalence was tremendous. Even watching the series in the early 90s, the sense that Hartnell was like that had permeated through fandom, making his era the one I was by far the least interested in seeing just by the reputation of his Doctor—a reputation formed almost entirely by reruns that had happened before I was even born.

Troughton poses a more interesting problem. Even today there are only two complete four-part Troughton stories, and in 1981 there was only one, hence *The Krotons*, a serviceable but largely anonymous Troughton effort. But in this regard Troughton is perhaps helped as much as Hartnell is hindered. The Troughton era has always been caught between two poles. One camp of fans—the ones who dominated 1980s fandom, specifically—valued the era for its great monsters and bases under siege. For them the highlight of the Troughton era, and indeed of the series, is *The Web of Fear*.

The second camp prefers the stranger and more... mercurial Troughton era. I unabashedly belong to this camp, preferring *The Mind Robber* and *The Enemy of the World* to any base under siege. (In this regard, the 2013 recovery of two stories could hardly have been better chosen, and the question, "Which did you prefer, *The Web of Fear* or *The Enemy of the World?*" turned out to be almost as effective as "What's the biggest problem with *The Talons of Weng-Chiang*, the giant rat or the racism?" in sorting out different camps of Doctor Who fans.) And by chance it was *The Krotons*, a story that is firmly in the stranger and more psychedelic tradition, that was the sole option to represent the Troughton era. One has little doubt that Nathan-Turner would have run *Tomb of the Cybermen* or *The Moonbase* if he could, but he was stuck with *The Krotons*. And as a result the more mercurial and psychedelic Troughton era—the one that had largely been forgotten by 1981—enjoyed a fortuitous resurgence.

The Pertwee era, on the other hand, has a more unusual fate. It gets, at least, both a UNIT and a space story, and a fairly good one of each. *Carnival of Monsters*, while in no way a standard Pertwee story, is rightly well-regarded—certainly I think it's the highlight of the Pertwee years. It's in many ways the best choice of Nathan-Turner's. There are nine four-episode Pertwee stories, and while not all of them existed in color at the end of 1981, Nathan-Turner was not low on options. He picked an odd Pertwee story that was both very good and very much not what Pertwee-era devotees would have looked for.

*The Three Doctors* is a stranger choice, however. The opportunity to squeeze out a bonus Hartnell and Troughton with *The Three Doctors* was an obvious plus, so that made sense in its own right, though it creates a bit of an oddity by contrasting the pop-science of 1973 immediately with Bidmead's pop science of 1981. Presumably Nathan-Turner wanted a UNIT story, but *Day of the Daleks* was in usable shape, so the choice here has to go down to wanting to double dip on Hartnell and Troughton. On the flip side, the Pertwee era ends up being disproportionately represented.

The effect of this was to allow Nathan-Turner a somewhat troubling bit of erasure. The rerun series jumps from 1973 to *Logopolis* in 1981, neatly sidestepping the entire six seasons of Tom Baker that Nathan-Turner didn't produce. That *Logopolis* had to be rerun is sensible enough—it's the only way to get a fifth face of Doctor Who in and it serves well as a lead-in to *Castrovalva*, which aired just a month later. But if you're going to double-represent an era, surely the seven years of Tom Baker are a better choice than running two stories not just from the Pertwee era but from the same season of the Pertwee era—indeed, two consecutive stories, albeit presented in reverse order.

The real issue, let's be blunt, is that Nathan-Turner knew better than to rerun something from the Whitehouse-hated and very technically adept Hinchcliffe era. So the real obvious choice of rerunning *The Brain of Morbius* or *Pyramids of Mars*—both quite old and nostalgic—got skipped. Given the ferocity with which Nathan-Turner would begin adamantly insisting that the memory cheated with regards to this era (despite the fact that the era was being released on VHS and it was becoming abundantly clear to everyone that, for instance, *Pyramids of Mars* and *The Robots of Death* really were a damn sight better than *Time-Flight*), it is difficult to read this omission as anything other than Nathan-Turner not wanting to deal with direct comparisons between his era and the Hinchcliffe era. Instead he claims the entire Tom Baker era with his own work. A highlight of his own work, but as bad a representation of the Tom Baker era as *An Unearthly Child* was for Hartnell.

Still, that Nathan-Turner managed to swing the repeat season at all was impressive, especially given that Doctor Who's ratings in Season 18 had been... problematic at best. Five weeks of BBC2's schedule were heavily occupied by Doctor Who. And so we return to the sort of light side/dark side of Nathan-Turner. His skills at self-promotion really were remarkable. And that was to the show's benefit on a number of occasions, this being one of them. Between this and *K-9 and Company* he managed an incredibly well-hyped lead-in to the debut of Peter Davison and heavily counteracted the "Oh, Tom Baker's gone, who cares" effect. He also effectively trained Doctor Who fans to watch Doctor Who on weekdays, which was going to be exactly what they'd have to do come Tuesday. Once again, his skill at reading the television landscape and using the paratextual elements of the medium becomes clear.

But more importantly, this marks another step in the transition of the show from an ephemeral model to an enduring one. The possibility of classic episodes being re-aired was starting to matter. This in and of itself marks a major change in the attitude of the BBC towards its classic material. And here is where the recovery of missing episodes really happened fast. Of the thirty-three episodes found since the first census of missing episodes, three had already been found as of December 1981. Another sixteen were unearthed in the three-year period following these reruns. That's half of the missing episodes in just three years. The twenty-six years from 1985-2011 yielded only fourteen more. I would not be so silly as to claim that there's a causal connection between the efforts to recover episodes and these reruns, but the sudden active effort to find missing episodes and the existence of the *Five Faces* series are , as we've discussed before, symptoms of the larger shift in what television was becoming. Indeed, the *Doctor Who Monthly Winter Special* in 1981 contained an interview with Sue Malden, the person responsible for ending the junking policy and making sure nothing else got destroyed. That came out in November, making this, in essence, the month where the missing episodes problem became public knowledge (and which provided a tacit explanation for the odd choice of *The Krotons*).

The result, taken with everything else, marks a subtle but crucial shift in what Doctor Who is. At last, the show has become something with an experienced history. Though there are obvious flaws and gaps in its memory, it can really be said that the majority of fandom can remember the series' past directly. And that will, as ever, only grow more true.

## Pop Between Realities, Home in Time for Tea:
### *Coronation Street*

The early Davison era is described, usually by its detractors, as a soap opera, generally on the basis that it had a four-person TARDIS crew, which hadn't happened since the early Troughton era. "Soap opera," it should be noted, is one of the great derogatory terms in science fiction fandom. There is nothing, including the *Star Wars Christmas Special*, quite as bad in the world as being a soap opera.

To anyone outside of science fiction or soap opera fandom this is completely insane since the two are self-evidently the exact same thing. To someone uninvolved in either there is no difference whatsoever in what die-hard sci-fi fans do and what die-hard soap fans do. Both are equally objects of mockery. One dresses up more, the other sends panicked letters in that don't quite seem to grasp that the characters are fictional. But other than that they're exactly the same thing.

Consider a recent example. In 2011 *Coronation Street* brought back the character of Dennis Tanner, who had not appeared in the show since 1968. The only thing that can possibly be reached for as an analogy would be something like bringing Sarah Jane Smith back to Doctor Who in 2006 when she hadn't appeared in it since 1983. Or bringing Leonard Nimoy back as Spock in the *Star Trek* film reboot.

More simply, consider this: virtually every long-form serialized text (as opposed to something like, say, *Garfield* that is serialized but consists of one-off strips instead of continuing storylines) that exists in either the US or UK is either a sci-fi/fantasy story or a soap opera.

And yet it's difficult to imagine two genres that are more diametrically disdainful of one another. Under the hood much of this comes down to the fact that although their basic narrative structures match almost exactly, their subject matter is wildly different. Soap operas are emotion-based character dramas; science fiction stories are usually action-adventure yarns. But understanding the fact that they're basically the same in terms of structure and audience interaction is key to understanding why, starting around the 1990s, sci-fi/fantasy shows began working hard to try to cater to soap watchers as well. It's just good business—if the two work similarly, you may as well try appealing to both audiences.

While it's true that the average soap fan and the average science fiction fan are very different, the perception that soap operas and science fiction are diametrically opposed is not quite fair. This is the logic behind the other event that would justify a *Coronation Street* essay, the scheduling of Doctor Who opposite *Coronation Street* in the Sylvester McCoy years on the grounds that, as Michael Grade put it, nobody in Britain watched both shows. But the logic behind this line was delightfully skewered years later in Russell T. Davies's *Queer as Folk* when Vince Tyler reminisces about how irritating it was to have both shows on at once. And, of course, Phil Collinson's leap from producer on Doctor Who to showrunner of *Coronation Street* has made the idea that the shows are in some way opposites almost farcical.

But here we're scrying events still a long way off in the future. Let's return to the dawning of the Davison era. Miles and Wood discuss the way in which the Saturday teatime slot that Doctor Who occupied from 1963-81 had, by the start of 1982, completely imploded. They give an almost entirely technologically determinist account of why this was, but it's a compelling one, so let's go with it. But first, some context.

The thing to realize is that the very existence of a Saturday teatime slot demonstrates a big difference between American and British television. The first draft of this essay was written on a Saturday afternoon in February 2012. That night, the major network lineups were as follows: CBS had repeats, ABC ran an old Charlie Brown Valentine special followed by repeats, NBC aired an encore performance of their current big music variety show, the CW was devoted entirely to local programming, and Fox showed *America's Most Wanted*, which is essentially free to produce.

In other words, nothing important happens on Saturday. The main prime-time lineups of US television networks run from Sunday-Thursday, with the big ones putting some stuff out on Friday—often sci-fi programming on the assumption that its cult audience isn't going out on a Friday. But nothing airs on Saturday because nobody is home. In contrast, BBC1 and ITV are showing new programming. Mostly reality programming, though BBC1 has a new episode of *Casualty* up. And, of course, Saturday is now Doctor Who's transmission day once more.

The nature of the Saturday lineup is and was, in other words, peculiarly British. Unlike American TV's multitude of channels, British TV consisted of ITV, which was fragmented into regional variations, and the BBC, a channel that was consistent across the country. So television in the UK was a unifying experience. The country sat down to watch. And Doctor Who was a part of one of the biggest lineups in the UK: the Saturday teatime one. For all that we've talked about Doctor Who fandom over eighteen seasons here we mustn't forget the fact that through these eighteen years Doctor Who simply was not a science fiction show in the sense that we usually use the term. It may have had science fiction fans, but it was unambiguously and completely mass entertainment for the entire country.

But at the start of 1982 the conditions that allowed that to be possible were changing. Miles and Wood track social conditions—the downfall of the very notion of community that Thatcherism heralded with its declaration that society didn't exist—but their more compelling reasoning is simply that televisions had gotten cheap enough that everyone in the family could have their own; they were remote controlled, which meant that changing the channel was trivial; and they heated up and started displaying images almost immediately, which meant that you didn't have to turn your television on in advance of what you wanted to watch. All of this cut against the always-on lineup-based model of television that Doctor Who had been a part of.

This posed a significant problem, and John Nathan-Turner knew it. Of course he did. For all that he's going to come under some real fire over the course of this book, John Nathan-Turner was not a stupid man. A tasteless one, perhaps, but not a stupid one. With the Saturday slot dying, he oversaw the program shifting timeslots to where it would air twice weekly on Mondays and Tuesdays. This was actually a big deal, making the front page of the *Sun* when it was announced. First, it changed the nature of what the show was. Doctor Who still made twenty-six episodes a year, but from Season Nineteen on it was only around for a quarter of the year. This is a massive change from the "always on" model of the first six seasons and the "around for half the year" model of the next twelve. Doctor Who was no longer a continual part of the fabric of television.

Second, Doctor Who was now a show that had to draw its own set of fans. On Saturdays, Doctor Who could draw from the whole country as long as it wasn't appreciably worse than whatever ITV was showing—and even then it would do OK if the rest of the Saturday lineup was strong. But on Mondays and Tuesdays, Doctor Who has to get people to turn on the television in the first place. This, in other words, was the real impetus for Nathan-Turner's switch to trying to appeal to Doctor Who fans first and foremost. Pitching the show towards a sci-fi cult audience is an obvious decision in the wake of losing access to the family audience that had defined it for eighteen years. For all that his continuity fetishism is knocked, one has to remember that there was a sensible motive behind it. Doctor Who had to change. Again.

But in the accusation that the Davison era is a soap, there's an interesting secondary narrative going on. The usual story is that Nathan-Turner changed to a model of continuity fetishism. And he did, yes. Absolutely. But the idea that he did this entirely to appeal to a cult science fiction audience is not quite fair. Had Doctor Who simply moved to a weekday slot and aired one episode a week it would look like any other cult science fiction show. But it didn't. It aired twice weekly. And that suggests something entirely different.

The twice-weekly timeslot was due to the BBC conducting early experiments for what would eventually become *EastEnders*—which, of course, we'll deal with in 1993. But the schedule picked for *EastEnders* was just the schedule used for ITV soaps like *Coronation Street* and *Emmerdale Farm* (then starring Frazer Hines as Joe Sugden). In other words, the "Davison soap" description of Doctor Who is apropos not just because of the bickering companions and larger main cast, but because it was actually airing in a soap opera timeslot. And the bickering crew wasn't the only soap-like element of it. For example, Nathan-Turner nicked the silent credits at the end of *Earthshock* from *Coronation Street*. Plus, it's worth remembering at this point that Doctor Who was, in fact, a broadly popular show and not just a show for adolescent male sci-fi fans. When you combine all of this, the hypothesis begins to look clear—Nathan-Turner was trying to cobble together a broad audience for Doctor Who by merging the obviously similar genres of soaps and science fiction. He attempted the transition that happened more broadly over the course of the late 90s and early 00s, but about fifteen years early. He failed spectacularly, of course, and yet it's hard to avoid the sense that this was what was supposed to be happening. (Even the casting of Davison, already appearing in *All Creatures Great and Small* and *Sink or Swim*, suggests an effort to go for a broadly appealing and fairly well-known television personality.)

And so, in order to better serve you, my readers, I watched a month's worth of period *Coronation Street*. Unfortunately, the accessibility of vintage *Coronation Street* is limited. The closest I could get to the time in question and get consecutive episodes (instead of a "best of" set that wouldn't capture the feel of watching the show) was December of 1979. And so I watched all nine episodes from December of 1979. For you. My readers. You bastards.

Actually, I shouldn't be that hard on the show. The appeal of it is relatively straightforward and isn't any more trashy than Daleks. By the end of the ninth episode I could more or less understand why someone would watch the show. Which is not a huge surprise given that I've followed my fair share of American primetime soaps in my day. Or that I'm a *Game of Thrones* fan, for that matter.

The way that a soap opera works is fairly straightforward. You build a large ensemble cast of characters up and then you serialize plotlines for small subsets of them over several episodes while avoiding ever starting or finishing more than one plot per episode. Contrary to the stereotype that soaps feature decades-simmering plotlines that are impossible to jump in on, this rapid churn of plots actually makes jumping on fairly easy. The first episode or two is rough, but after that there's usually a solid majority of any given episode that you can follow because it's either introducing a new plotline or continuing the things you've seen a lot of. By the end of one month's worth of viewing there were only a few characters I didn't have the gist of.

But equally important is the fact that long-time viewers are rewarded. This comes in two real forms. The first is relatively familiar to a sci-fi fan, and that's the continuity reference. Old characters make returns, or a long-ago plotline comes to the fore. For instance, in one of the episodes I watched, a character who had been absent for a month or so of episodes, Elsie Tanner, returns and has a fight with another character with whom she clearly shared a long-running plotline. The major purpose of this scene is obviously to tie up that long-running plotline. But what's interesting is that the scene pulls double duty. The nature of their relationship is reiterated in their dialogue, and the scene works equally well as a good introduction to Elsie's character, neatly serving the needs of new and long-time viewers at the same time.

This sort of back-referencing, at least if Wikipedia articles are to be believed, continues today—hardly a departed character on the show doesn't have some mention of an episode years after they left in which their final fate (usually death) is finally announced. And, of course, it's implicit in doing something like bringing a character back over forty years after their last appearance.

But there's a second type of reward for long-time viewers, and that comes in the form of character consistency. Long-running characters in soaps typically get plotlines or moments where what is significant is not a specific reference to their history but rather the fact that they act in a manner consistent with their character type. The most charming moment along these lines in the month I watched was when Annie Walker, the landlady at The Rovers Return (the requisite and iconic pub) chats up the obligatory punk rocker character and gets along with him well—a moment that is fun primarily because Annie Walker has been on the show since the first episode and it reconfirms her defining character traits of being gracious and discerning. What's significant about this is that even though it is not a moment that depends on any long-term knowledge of the show, it's still one that rewards it. It's significant primarily if you have a built-up appreciation of Annie Walker. A similar moment appears in the first episode of December, in which Hilda Ogden, a character defined in no small part by her ability to irritate everybody else in the show, is shut out of a wedding reception. Annie gives her an opportunity to pick up a shift working at the inn, giving her a tacit invitation—another small character moment that is endearing because of the existence of prior investment in the characters as opposed to because of its own intrinsic dramatic tension.

In this, then, we can already see the seeds of where Nathan-Turner's efforts to soapify Doctor Who fail. The ability to build these character moments is based on the long-term consistency of characters—on the fact that Annie and Hilda are behaving in line with over a decade of previous stories. But Nathan-Turner never really pays the sort of attention to long-term characterization that's needed to do things like this. For instance, in *Logopolis* the Master is responsible for the death of Tegan's aunt and Nyssa's entire planet, and is furthermore walking around wearing Nyssa's father as a skin-suit. In a soap opera, these sorts of things would be referenced and become fundamental aspects of the interrelationships among the three characters. On Nathan-Turner's Doctor Who, they're never mentioned again, even as both Tegan and Nyssa have numerous further encounters with the Master.

It's also worth discussing the biggest difference between Doctor Who and *Coronation Street*. It is, perhaps surprisingly, not the existence of aliens and time travel. Rather it is that Doctor Who is thoroughly middle class and *Coronation Street* is thoroughly working class. This is particularly clear when you look at the cast making up the ostensible Davison soap: a noblewoman, a boy computer genius, a cricketer, and an Australian stewardess. Tegan is the closest thing the series has to working class, and she's an Australian with a job defined by all the exotic locations it takes her to.

Compare to *Coronation Street*, where the show is almost entirely dominated by working class people who often struggle to make ends meet. It's a sharp difference, and it's one that Doctor Who suffers from. The last working class regular the show had was Sergeant Benton; the last working class character who filled the traditional companion role was Ben. And although it makes a stuttering effort at it with Ace in 1987 it's not really until Russell T. Davies goes with a Mancunian Doctor and working class companion in 2005 that this can really be said to be addressed at all substantially.

But then, the working class wasn't really the goal with Nathan-Turner's Doctor Who, and this can hardly be called an accident. The rise of the soap-style Doctor Who coincided with Nathan-Turner's increasing interest in fandom, with Nathan-Turner and the cast frequently nipping off to the United States for conventions in between weeks of filming, and with an ever-increasing amount of merchandise for the program, including things that he profited directly from, such as a pair of books he penned on the series and his partner Gary Downie's infamously horrible *Doctor Who Cookbook*.

This was, increasingly, part of the series' conception of itself and what it was for. And on some level, it made sense. Especially when one considers the shoestring the series was often made on, Doctor Who was enormously cost-effective for the BBC, and part of that was that it had middle class obsessive fans with disposable incomes. The switch to a soap opera transmission schedule tacitly tailored the show towards these sorts of fans. And, it's worth reiterating, financial exploitation of the show is a crucial part of its twenty-first century success. But in the 1980s, when Nathan-Turner was doing it, there was an obvious drawback: BBC politics largely forbade consideration of any of the series' merchandising potential or overseas fandom in determining its budget or renewal. And so while Nathan-Turner was savvily identifying the show's most profitable fans, he wasn't identifying a segment of the audience that would actually, in the long term, help the show very much.

## We've Materialized With Considerable Finesse (*Castrovalva*)

It's January 4th, 1982. The Human League are at number one with "Don't You Want Me," but are unseated by Bucks Fizz's "The Land of Make Believe," a song whose lyrics, by former King Crimson member Peter Sinfield, were supposedly a subtle attack on the Thatcher government. Very subtle, in fact. Also charting are ABBA, Adam and the Ants, Kool and the Gang, and, now in the top ten, Kraftwerk!

In real news, AT&T agrees to being broken up, the coldest temperature ever recorded in the UK is managed in Braemar, and, most importantly (at least from my perspective), the Commodore 64 is introduced. Although I'm still nine months out from my debut (I'm strictly gestational for Season 19), when I was about two years old my parents got themselves a Commodore 64 in the name of getting it for me, and my earliest memories are of playing it.

This serves, in part, as another transition point. The fact that my first Doctor Who story was *Planet of the Spiders* meant that I largely kept my personal reflections out of the Pertwee era. I have memories of the Hinchcliffe era, but those were the stories I watched in 6th grade; the Williams era I missed, but as I noted in passing when writing about *The Keeper of Traken*, the final episode of *Warriors' Gate* was the last episode of Doctor Who that I watched for the first time in order to write about it for *TARDIS Eruditorum*.

More than that, though, this is some of the first Doctor Who I ever watched. Davison and Pertwee, as I've said elsewhere, made up the overwhelming majority of my parents' VHS tapes. Since I was not fond of Pertwee, and in the absence of the Baker stories I desired, Davison was the first Doctor I watched with any avidity. I treated him at the time as my second favorite Doctor, behind Baker, but as I loved a theoretical ideal of Baker as opposed to someone I could actually watch, this was a lie. Until I discovered the existence of Sylvester McCoy (my parents' guidebooks all left off in the vicinity of Davison's regeneration—I knew Colin Baker existed and that my parents hated him, but I'd been a Doctor Who fan for a solid year before I learned that there was even a Seventh Doctor), Davison was my favorite Doctor. It's a little tricky to reconstruct because I found a couple of Davison stories on mislabeled tapes after I'd started getting commercial VHS releases, but the "core" of Davison stories I remember watching young are *Castrovalva, Four to Doomsday, Kinda, Time Flight, Arc of Infinity, Snakedance, Mawdryn Undead, The Five Doctors, Resurrection of the Daleks, Planet of Fire*, and *The Caves of Androzani*, though I remember getting *The Visitation, Black Orchid*, and *Earthshock* all relatively early as well.

So we are, in other words, now in one of three sections of Doctor Who that I experienced as a child while in the general vicinity of the show's targeted age range. But unlike the first such section, we're also in an era I was alive for part of, and even if I wasn't fully aware of the culture, or, really, of anything other than Big Milk Thing, there is something about the culture you were alive for that feels different from things that predate you. Even the things you're far too young to remember are somewhat more real for having come about in a world wherein you existed. But with Doctor Who the sense is heightened. My parents' Doctor Who books were mostly stuck in about 1983. Peter Haining's *Doctor Who: A Celebration* was the main reference I had. In a real sense, up until late 1993, Davison was for me the "present" of Doctor Who.

All of which said, *Castrovalva* is an odd start. Doctor Who has very few clear-cut transitions in its time. Few things do. That's why the terminology of the "long 1960s" and "long 1980s" exists. Because it's not as though everyone on the planet woke up on January 1st, 1980, set fire to their bell bottoms, and decided in unison that what they really wanted to be when they grew up was a hedge fund manager. But *Castrovalva* is oddly transitional even for Doctor Who. After the longest gap between episodes the series had ever seen, the basic act of picking up immediately from the previous story was an odd one. Yes, the story had just recently aired again in the *Five Faces* series, and there were some obvious issues to deal with immediately, but the degree to which this story follows up on *Logopolis* not just in terms of the Doctor and company having to escape the Pharos Project but in terms of theme and villain is genuinely strange. Put simply, it's not clear why the Master is here.

But there's more that's strange here. The extended time between Seasons Eighteen and Nineteen allowed Season Nineteen to be shot heavily out of order. The production order was *Four to Doomsday, The Visitation, Kinda, Castrovalva, Black Orchid, Earthshock,* and finally *Time-Flight. Castrovalva* was furthermore the fifth script commissioned, with Bidmead being hired back nearly six months after he finished work on *Logopolis* to fill in the gap between it and *Four to Doomsday.* Indeed, Bidmead got the commission only a month before *Four to Doomsday* started filming, and was asked to incorporate things like Nyssa's modified costume into the script. In other words, like *Meglos* (only even moreso) this was an example of Doctor Who going and filling in a gap left between stories that had already been shot.

The problem is that all of this got taken a bit too far. The desire to smooth the transition becomes, under Nathan-Turner's brief, four episodes of Davison's Doctor not showing up. If the point of delaying Davison's debut to his fourth story was to make it so that he had the part down in his debut then he must have found this story, in which he essentially doesn't get to play the character he'd developed over the previous three stories, a puzzling one.

Actually, let's just come out and say it: Post-regenerative trauma is a dumb invention. It extends out of an egregious misreading of *The Power of the Daleks*. Troughton's off-putting and strange nature in that story isn't an attempt to create some tradition where the Doctor is confused after regeneration, but a necessary aspect of the jarring nature of that first change in actors. Subsequent installments verge into the openly ill-advised: keeping Pertwee's Doctor functionally out of *Spearhead From Space* until late in the third episode was a strange decision that works only because there's a whole new premise to set up in the background before dropping the Doctor into it. Letts and Dicks, to their credit, practically do away with it in *Robot*, allowing the new Doctor half an episode of comedic larking before expecting him to get on with it. But for everyone from Davison through Paul McGann the insistence on this tiresome ritual is excruciating.

Even in the new series you can see producers struggling with it. It's notable that Davies simply keeps Tennant out of *The Christmas Invasion*, and yet still contrives to give him a big scene at the ten-minute mark to get the big reveal of what Tennant's Doctor is going to be like out of the way. Moffat uses it to build tension, letting Smith play the part basically as he'll go on to but using the post-regenerative trauma primarily to ratchet up tension and let Prisoner Zero become more of a threat. And for *Deep Breath*, post-regeneration trauma is basically used as an excuse to let Capaldi experiment for his first few scenes and to give Jenna Coleman some space to mildly reinvent Clara. And these solutions show what the problem with all of this actually is. The entire appeal of a new Doctor's debut is to see the new Doctor. So when you go through the first week of a story without remembering to show us what the new Doctor is going to be like you're fundamentally failing to deliver what your audience is there for.

And then there's the Master. With nobody having made any effort to come up with a motivation for him beyond hatred for the Doctor, at this point the program is facing an overt storytelling nightmare. The last time the Master made a hard drive towards overexposure, back in Season Eight, he at least had schemes of world domination. So when he was defeated at the end of one story he could pick up again with something new. On top of that, Season Eight didn't have the stories dovetailing into each other on a plot level. But this "trilogy" (and let's note that a sudden interest in making things into trilogies is a dead-on symptom of egregious pretension) consists of a single twelve-episode stretch where the Master harasses the Doctor with no interruptions whatsoever and little motivation other than defeating the Doctor for the sake of it. The result is that, by the end, the Master has ended up on something like fallback plan number eight, each one more frighteningly over-elaborate than the last.

The degree of ineptitude displayed here is somewhat astonishing. They bring the Master back to provide an epic menace for the Doctor and then, by the end, they're treating him like a pathetic joke. And Bidmead really is, in the end, left with no choice but to leave the Master as an obviously deluded lunatic at the end of *Castrovalva*. The scene of him trying desperately to break open the Zero Cabinet is overtly set up as a scene about a man who hasn't just gone completely around the bend, but has become blatantly pathetic. And while that's the best thing to do, dramatically, with what they've got in *Castrovalva*, it doesn't change the fact that it was a dumb idea to have the Master back in the first place.

Despite this, Bidmead copes admirably with the Nathan-Turner brief from hell—certainly better than anyone not named Robert Holmes ever did. (That he was coping is evident in the anecdote that he picked the name and setting of the story based on remembering a pair of Escher prints hanging in someone's office that Nathan-Turner hated. The reasons Nathan-Turner hated them, according to Miles and Wood, is that he believed that "art should exist to soothe, not distract." If I had to reduce my objection to Nathan-Turner to a single fact, incidentally, that would be it.) To his real credit he thinks through the twice-weekly structure and builds a story that is functionally a pair of two-parters on a common theme—something that isn't done nearly enough in the Davison era.

And despite giving him a bad set of directions, the basic idea here is sound. Bidmead was absolutely the right person to have do this story because the particulars of his style are so distinctive and so vividly animated the series over the six stories prior to this. Giving the new cast a chance to establish themselves in a Bidmead-style story provides a needed aesthetic and thematic continuity to the series. And as it descends further down the rabbit hole of embracing continuity in everything but tone and theme, this is sensible.

That said, there's not a huge amount to say regarding Bidmead's approach beyond what we already discussed in the last book. He creates a mathematical and logical game, he conceptualizes his ideas in terms of visual event, and he works out a quite nice introduction to the idea of recursion. He's got another technobabble concept that works out of pure linguistics—"recursive occlusion" belongs firmly in the pantheon of "chronic hysteresis" and "charged vacuum emboitment." He also ends up defining much of the modern lore of what the TARDIS is. Even though *The Invasion of Time* was the first big "run around the bowels of the TARDIS" story, there the sequences set inside the TARDIS were a desperate attempt to stretch out the story by an episode and get away with shooting everything on location. Here there's actually a unified aesthetic to the TARDIS that continues the sense from *Logopolis* of it actually being a scary place.

But the real credit and revelation here has to go to Peter Davison. Steven Moffat has suggested that Davison is the best actor to take the part during the classic series. I'm skeptical mostly because of Patrick Troughton (and indeed,

Moffat's claim that Davison is the only one with a successful post-Doctor Who career was also wrong: Troughton had an extremely busy post-Doctor Who career), but it's clear from his first appearance that Davison is a genuinely talented actor (as distinct from a "performer," which is how Tom Baker self-identifies). The most obvious moment is his mimicry of Troughton and Hartnell, which is not impersonation as such, but something altogether subtler. He at once clearly evokes the Doctor he's imitating and does so in such a way as to make it seem like an echo of them instead of a return. Even Pertwee—a gifted voice artist who probably could have done the mimicry—would be hard pressed to do it in such a way that would feel like Pertwee's Doctor imitating Hartnell, as opposed to a Hartnell impression.

But more impressive is just the range of emotion that Davison gets into the Doctor. Davison declines to take on the dashing hero role that the Doctor has been for over a decade now, but instead continually reacts to events. It sounds like an utterly basic thing, but this is actually the first time since Troughton that the tone which the Doctor responds to another character is actually dictated by what the other character says or does. Davison has the range to portray the Doctor as something other than an immovable force, and it's a revelation.

The key scene—and one of the best in the story—is where the Doctor shows the Castrovalvans how strange their world is by having them draw a map and then asking them to locate where things are on it. It's something that simply wouldn't have happened in the Baker or Pertwee eras—the overt decision to give the "figure it out" moment to another character instead of the Doctor. This is how it's going to be for the next three years—the Doctor is going to interact with the worlds of the stories instead of just imposing himself on them.

While it's the Doctor's absence from this story that allows Nyssa and Tegan to really take center stage, it's the fact that Davison is a much less domineering presence than his predecessors that allows them to stay there. Added to this is the fact that Sutton and Fielding have fairly solid chemistry and make a good double act. Though this has disastrous effects on Waterhouse, whose acting finally falls out of the "minimally acceptable" range around this point, Nyssa and Tegan form a sensible unit. Tegan still has her problems, but it's here that Nyssa starts becoming a functional Doctor surrogate. The Doctor may tag Tegan as the "coordinator" of the bunch, but it's obviously Nyssa who keeps everything going here, her own restrained style working well as a parallel for Davison's.

So while *Castrovalva* is a confused story with obvious narrative faults, it serves as a useful transition. It's recognizable both as the sort of story that follows from Season Eighteen and as the sort of story that will define the next three seasons. The second most difficult regeneration of the classic series has been successfully accomplished. On with the Davison era.

## Time Can Be Rewritten: *Cold Fusion*

As novels that I couldn't possibly avoid go, this one ranks pretty highly. I've noted several times that within the classic series, McCoy is "my Doctor," so to speak. As the only Doctor (after my first three episodes) I didn't originally know existed, he was the one I got to discover without episode guides. But even still, when I got into Doctor Who it had been off the air for three years. The McCoy years may have been the televised Doctor Who that I came to freshest, but until the dark days of 1996 the only Doctor Who that I got to follow as it came out were the Virgin books.

I'm going to cover much of the Virgin and BBC books lines over the next two volumes, but suffice it to say that my relationship with the Virgin line was... interesting. I was reading them roughly from the ages of 11-13, which is just a bit too young for them. But this is in some ways the perfect way to relate to the Virgin books. Their darkness, complexity, and occasional jaunts into overt sexuality are perfect for that age—especially as I think you can make a strong case that Doctor Who is always at its best when it's slightly too old for its audience, and at its worst when its audience is only slightly too old for it. The mixture of scandalous and salacious content with the fundamental safety of Doctor Who is as gentle a gradient to tackle emerging sexuality as they come— like having a copy of *Timeframe* with its Katy Manning/Dalek photo as your sole piece of pornography (which, for years, I did).

So as Doctor crossovers go, this one is, for me, as good as it gets. Not just because it's two of my favorite Doctors, but because there's such an intrinsic contrast between them. The relative gentleness of Davison's Doctor combined with the dangerous and manipulative nature of the Virgin Books version of McCoy's are an inspired pairing that offers no shortage of drama. All of which said, any multi-Doctor story is less about the particulars of a man meeting himself at a different point in his life and more about the comparison of two eras of the show. Doubly so in a book, where we do not get Davison's Doctor or McCoy's Doctor but rather their textual ghosts. The Doctors themselves are televisual performances—things created by actors, directors, and writers in a collaborative environment. These are purely literary characters, responding almost entirely to the whims of a singular creator. They are echoes. That does not diminish the validity of their stories, but this book belongs to neither the Davison nor the McCoy eras.

This gets at another issue with the Virgin books (and for that matter the BBC ones) that I've largely danced around. I poke at it a little bit in the Hartnell book essays on *The Man in the Velvet Mask* and *Empire of Glass*, and deal with it more extensively in the *Scales of Injustice* essay in the Pertwee book, but it's been a while and it's high time we tackled the issue of fanwank again. Because Lance Parkin is a master of it.

Back in the *Scales of Injustice* essay I distinguished between two types of fanwank. The first is what we might call explanatory fanwank—the sort of thing that tries to stitch together an extended explanation that resolves a host of alleged continuity problems over multiple stories—for instance, Gary Russell's writing of an entire novel to try to explain a single line of dialogue in *Warriors of the Deep*. The second is what we might call value-added fanwank—the sort of thing that happens when, for instance, the Minotaur at the end of *The God Complex* is referred to as being a relative of the

Nimon, a throwaway line that's charming for fans and invisible to anyone sensible enough to have never seen *The Horns of Nimon*. But this book introduces a third sort of fanwank—one that is not nearly subtle enough to be called value-added, but is not the sort of sprawlingly doctrinal mess that characterizes fanwank for the sake of explanations.

Take, for instance, the fact that the novel spends over a hundred words describing a bunch of people singing a drinking song that consists only of the line, "We're in a chronic hysteresis," repeated over and over again. It's a deft little joke for fans, yes, but at a hundred words it's considerably more substantial than the Nimon reference in *The God Complex* or even the use of the Macra as the primary monster in *Gridlock*. Similarly, the near exact replay of the Third Doctor's meeting with Sarah Jane in *The Five Doctors* as the dialogue between Roz and the Doctor after Roz mistakenly believes him to have regenerated into the Fifth Doctor is just a bit too large to be called offhanded.

But this gets at something important to realize about continuity, particularly before we take our careening nosedive into the televised fanwankathon that extends from *Earthshock* through *Warriors of the Deep*—a stretch of thirty-eight episodes (counting *The Five Doctors* as if it were a four-parter) in which every single story features a villain who has appeared before. A lot of the nature of fanwank is dependent on what assumptions can be made about the audience for a given story. Fanwank is a different problem in a television series expected to go out to a general audience than it is in a book series that is overtly catering to die-hard fans.

In truth this is one of the appeals of the books. There are things you can do when you have access to the full and mad breadth of Doctor Who continuity that you just can't do when writing for a general audience. Not things merely in the sense of a wealth of nods and winks, nor in the sense of broad explanations, but in the sense of genuinely clever and interesting commentary. *The League of Extraordinary Gentlemen* series, for instance, creates considerable sparks and depth out of literary history and that works only because of the extreme referentiality of the work. Doctor Who's history is, at this point, deep enough to permit similar (though to date nowhere near as good) explorations—stories that work in part because of the sheer depth of history that Doctor Who can call upon.

Lance Parkin is particularly good at this (and it's perhaps worth noting that Parkin has written two books on Alan Moore), and this is very much what *Cold Fusion* is about. Not in the references we've talked about so far—those are just cute little jokes that are the size they are because the book can safely expect an audience who will get them—but in the sections dealing with Patience.

Ah, yes. Patience. A character sufficiently massive in her implications that she largely overshadows the multi-doctor nature of this story. See, Patience is an ancient Gallifreyan—explicitly not a Time Lord—who is strongly implied to be the Doctor's wife. This may attract eyebrows from those who are not familiar with the Virgin era. Central to the Virgin era is the idea that along with Rassilon and Omega (who are, following from Alan Moore, contemporaries) there is a third major figure in Time Lord history: the Other. The nature of the Other is left mysterious for most of the run, but it is strongly hinted that it is, in fact, the Doctor. (I will not be the one to spoil the outcome of this, but we'll cover it when we get to the book *Lungbarrow*, and again when we get to Parkin's *The Infinity Doctors*.)

In a fundamental way, this makes sense. It's an inevitable consequence of the narrative structure of the series. The more that the series, over time, flits about the nature of the Time Lords while focusing on the Doctor as the main character, the more it becomes inevitable that the Doctor plays some central role in the history of the Time Lords. The fact that in the narrative world of Doctor Who the Doctor is always by far the most important of the Time Lords affects the nature of the Time Lords. No matter how much one loves the image of the Doctor as just a small little man who wanders the universe and does good things, the fact that he is narratively at the center of Doctor Who means that the universe of Doctor Who will always revolve around him. Anything that doesn't give the Doctor an implicit role in the nature of the Time Lords is simply fighting against the fundamental gravity of Doctor Who as a series. That's not to say that giving the Doctor a role in the origin of the Time Lords is a good idea. Just a historically inevitable one.

Different writers handle the shape and implications of this differently. Parkin, however, is always one of the ones that fights most thoroughly against the idea of a singular Doctor Who. It's Parkin in *The Gallifrey Chronicles* who most overtly sets up the "it's all true" theory of Doctor Who continuity, having the Doctor declare that "every word of every novel is real, every frame of every film, every panel of every comic strip," and then being uninterested when someone points out that this implies all sorts of contradictions. And it's Parkin, of course, who wrote *AHistory*, an attempt to create a fixed chronology of all events in the Doctor Who universe. (The correct term for this project is "hilarious.")

For Parkin, in other words, while it's inevitable that the Doctor is in some sense at the heart of Gallifreyan history, it's in no way necessary that this take any particular shape. (This culminates, for Parkin, with *The Infinity Doctors*, which is based on taking everything said about Gallifrey over the course of thirty-five years seriously while not bothering to try to come up with a way to reconcile it with the present state of Doctor Who at the time.) Hence the lengthy sequence in which the Doctor and Patience do a sort of mind meld and we get a bevy of accounts where we're explicitly told that the Doctor can't tell which ones are his memories and which ones are hers. (How Iris Wildthyme.)

What we get in this section is a mad smattering of references to past stories mixed in with allusions to a history that may or may not be the Doctor's. *The Brain of Morbius*, *An Unearthly Child*, *The Creature from the Pit*, *The War Games*, and *The Mind of Evil* are explicitly referenced, along with the existence of the missing episodes. It's wonderfully bizarre. And at one point, it's noted that "these accounts contradict one another," but this is immediately followed by the observation that "memories often do."

I have occasionally made half-joking reference to the fact that one of the basic premises of the blog is that Doctor Who is a quasi-sentient metafiction authored by an anarchic spirit within British culture. Some commenters have, very sensibly, suggested that I might want to explain this, a viewpoint that, while utterly reasonable, I have generally avoided catering to, largely for that exact reason. Still, having now inflicted the *Logopolis* essay (and book) upon the world, an essay that, like *Logopolis* itself, seems very much like it approaches some sort of limit point in that particular method of thinking about Doctor Who—and as we now make our step out of Bidmead's neo-Whitakerian take on Doctor Who and towards something altogether less magical—it is perhaps worth finally unpacking it.

The root idea is, for once, borrowed from Grant Morrison instead of Alan Moore. Morrison has several times suggested that the DC Universe line of superheroes is sentient and has an animating consciousness. My disagreement with Morrison is not on this point, but rather on the implications of it—Morrison seems rather to like this fact, whereas I think that the DC Universe is, while sentient, a dangerous sociopath (albeit one capable of moments of staggering beauty). But the underlying idea, obviously, appeals.

At the moment I don't want to go too far into the comparison of Morrison's *Final Crisis* with the nearly identical Series Four finale of Doctor Who that was airing at nearly the exact same time, but suffice it to say that the plot of that comic is a narrative collapse, in which the entire idea of storytelling in the DC Universe is threatened. And Morrison's suggestion is that the DC Universe is able to, by its own intrinsic nature, repair the damage caused by the narrative collapse. I make a similar argument about *The Chase*, and I'll repeat the phenomenon in *Trial of a Time Lord*, and then again in the Davies and Moffat eras where narrative collapse becomes the default mode of storytelling for season finales.

But the point remains. Doctor Who has an odd ability to tend to itself both in an internal narrative sense and in an external social one. Internally, Doctor Who is capable of endless adjustment to its premise that allows it to adapt to what, at this point, can be safely described as an infinite set of narrative circumstances. Doctor Who offers one of the handful of fictional characters that it appears genuinely impossible to exhaust the stories about. Bad writers can still write bad Doctor Who stories, but good writers seem capable of redrafting the character into any format. Or, put another way, any narrative collapse you attempt to impose on Doctor Who will have some resolution possible within the world of Doctor Who. There is no way to write yourself irredeemably into a corner. (As evidenced by Davies successfully writing the series out of the seemingly intractable corner of being not only cancelled but already the subject of a failed reboot.)

Externally, meanwhile, Doctor Who shows a genuine ability to adapt to changing social circumstances. Though it does not always find an immediate response to the social conditions around it, in time it always manages to reinvent itself to be relevant to its present. It always maintains some connection with the larger culture.

I use the term quasi-sentient to describe this tendency because it appears to manifest itself absent any author. No single animating presence has kept Doctor Who relevant to culture for nearly fifty years now. Certainly no one in 1963 designed a show to be able to narratively track the course of social history. And yet here it is. Much as the Time Lords appear to be keepers of a model of history that is based on a sort of historical gravity, Doctor Who appears to be created so that it organically shifts around to respond to history. It's possible to tell a continual narrative—as I have been for several books now—that treats Doctor Who as a continually evolving and linear thing even though it is pragmatically impossible for it to be so.

This is why there are Pop Between Realities essays—not only to firmly show the way in which Doctor Who fits into a historical narrative that is, of course, equally lacking in (or suffering from an excess of) authors, but in order to occasionally come up for air from the story of Doctor Who and show that, no, the same story is playing out across the real world. And likewise, this is why there are Time Can Be Rewritten essays. Because if Doctor Who is, in fact, a singular consciousness that is capable of responding to history as opposed to simply being an old thing that has tracked history just by virtue of being around for most of it, then it must be possible to track backwards. It must be possible for the series' future to intrude into its past in a way that is sensible. And so these essays are in many ways the checksums—the points where we see how the future interacts with the past, making sure that there is a coherent scope to this imaginary landmass we are mapping.

*Cold Fusion*, then, is a perfect instance—a book that is quite literally about the intrusion of the future onto the past. The whole Other theory of the Virgin books has nothing to do with the Davison era, which has its own rewriting of the Time Lords looming. And yet this book works. The Virgin Books version of the Seventh Doctor and a reasonably fair portrayal of early Davison interact. And the book is able to portray the Seventh Doctor as an extension of the Fifth, and it's full of lovely touches—the handling of Adric, and the hints at his tragic role in the Doctor's later psyche are deft, and further set up the impending death of Roz in the New Adventures line.

But what is most interesting is the fact that the two Doctors never quite clash. The Fifth is horrified by the Seventh's manipulativeness and willingness to destroy and punish his enemies, but is also made to tacitly accept that this is genuinely his future. He protests that other futures exist, but when the Feratu (the book's main villains) suggest otherwise he accepts it. The Feratu themselves, defined by the inversion of Clarke's law and the line between magic and science, are similarly the clear heirs of the play between the two concepts that has been going on in the just-concluded Bidmead era, and yet they are unmistakably the Seventh Doctor's antagonists in this story, not the Fifth's. After setting up a pair of Doctors that seem uniquely destined for a clash, Parkin manages to write a story that reminds the reader that these two apparently different characters are, in fact, the same man. And in doing so, this gestures at the darkness that lies ahead for the Fifth Doctor—not just in Adric's death, but in his own relationship with violence and destruction.

The future, in other words, fits functionally into the past. Time can be rewritten without having to rewrite one line of history. All of the contradictions and absurdities of Doctor Who's narrative fit into some larger, ephemeral whole.

Plus, it's the original source of Moffat's "we're both reversing the polarity" joke in *Day of the Doctor*.

## Because We Don't Quite Fully Understand (*Four to Doomsday*)

It's January 18, 1982. Bucks Fizz are at number one with "The Land of Make Believe," with Kraftwerk threatening to take it over. Unfortunately it is instead Shakin' Stevens with "Oh Julie" that inherits the number one. Elsewhere, The Human League have two separate songs in the top ten and are joined by Kool and the Gang, Foreigner, and Meat Loaf.

The trouble with these twice-weekly airings is that I get very little window to cover any non-musical history in. To wit, all I'm finding is that the post-war peak in unemployment happens in the UK, with over three million people out of work. Ah, the triumphs of Thatcherism. (Yes, she cut the unemployment rate later. But in the process she presided over a complete realignment of the economy that was... less than ideal.)

While on television, it's *Four to Doomsday*. With the exception of *The Highlanders*, which is, of course, missing, I am reasonably certain that this is the second appearance of a Doctor that the fewest people care about one way or another. The next two Doctors get two of the most reviled stories in the series' history for their second outings (only one of which is correctly reviled), while Hartnell, Pertwee, and Baker get all-time classics for their second go-rounds. Davison, on the other hand, gets this—a story nobody really likes, but that is hard to work up much passionate hatred about, either.

Frankly, one suspects that nobody much thinks about *Four to Doomsday* beyond "that one between Castrovalva and Kinda" with a side of "that was the first story Davison filmed." And, occasionally, "the one with that absurd cricket ball scene."

While I would not go so far as to call this story an overlooked gem (or an overrated disaster), it is a fair bit more interesting than its reputation. The first thing to realize about it is that it very much sets the tone for Season Nineteen. Of the seven stories in Season Nineteen, three are unabashedly attempts to redo things the series has done in the past in a new format. The first of these is, of course, *Castrovalva*, which we already noted was an effort to go back and build a transition out of the Bidmead era several stories after that era's conclusion. (The other two, for people keeping score, are *The Visitation* and *Black Orchid*.) Three more are conscious attempts to try new things that the series couldn't previously do. And then there is *Four to Doomsday*, a story that it is difficult to firmly describe as forward-looking or backward-looking. In a season that is equally committed to finding ways to rework the standards into the new approach for Doctor Who and to finding new things to do, *Four to Doomsday* is actually the one story that's splitting the difference between the two approaches.

On the one hand, as Miles and Wood point out, this is essentially built like a Hartnell story. From the start, this is clear: the story opens with the Doctor failing to get his companion back to Earth and the TARDIS crew trying to figure out what sort of world they're in. The exploratory mode hasn't been completely absent from Doctor Who, but its uses after *The Underwater Menace* have been few and far between. But it goes further than that. The particular flavor of moral dilemma on offer here is also peculiarly old-fashioned. It's been a long time since the central conflict of a story is a purely philosophical one. This story is about whether Monarch's autocratic rule is good. This isn't explored in terms of its effects on people, or even in terms of Monarch's psyche, but as a question of political theory. If one were to pick a past story that *Four to Doomsday* is most similar to it would be difficult to come up with a better choice than *The Savages*, of all things. So in that regard its status as more or less completely overlooked can be seen as a flawless mimicry of its source material.

But this shoots far, far past redoing the classics. The tendency introduced in Season Nineteen, of "Let's update the format of X," is never going to depart the show—to this day, the series does one or two such stories a season. But those stories usually riff on iconic classics that there's a relatively clear motivation to pilfer. The idea that anybody consciously said, "You know what the series should be more like in 1982? *The Savages*!" is difficult to take seriously.

The truth of things is visible under the hood. It's not really until *The Visitation* that Doctor Who starts having the remake be a conscious style decision. *Four to Doomsday* fits better into the tradition of things like *Full Circle* and *State of Decay*—stories that referenced a much earlier flavor of what Doctor Who was, but did so because of the idiosyncrasies of their writers, not out of a meta-philosophy of Doctor Who. The idiosyncrasies in question are almost polar opposites—*State of Decay* felt like a Hinchcliffe script because it basically was one, whereas *Full Circle* felt classic because its writer had grown up on classic Doctor Who. But the result was the same—stories that felt like old Doctor Who because they were by people who were steeped in old Doctor Who.

For the most part, this method of having the past influence Doctor Who's present because of its influence on the writers is vastly superior to the overt remake plan—a fact that's going to be one of several problems going forward. Unfortunately, *Four to Doomsday* is basically the end of the period we've been enjoying since *Full Circle* where the show's relationship with its past was based on influence instead of mimicry. This is one of Nathan-Turner's many wrong turns, but it's a real one. However, that's two stories from now. For now, we have Terence Dudley, who was an old hand at the BBC. Miles and Wood suggest, quite sensibly, that this explains the somewhat old-fashioned nature of this story—that Dudley's conception of the series is based on the Hartnell era because he was a working television professional for that era.

In many ways this gestures back at problems we were discussing around *Destiny of the Daleks* and *The Creature from the Pit*—the fact that it's a very, very unusual person who can maintain a 20-year writing or directing career in television. Certainly it explains the weaknesses of Terence Dudley's writing—and there are many. But while the datedness of his writing is a drawback, it's also worth noting that *Four to Doomsday* is in no way just a Hartnell remake. As much as its themes and structure are old-fashioned, this is also where the attempt to make the show more character-based and soapy really gets going. (Which is unsurprising, given that it's the first story made under the new brief.)

It's actually worth thinking a little more about *The Savages* in order to understand this. Back in the day we noted that one of the things that really stood out watching *The Savages* was how, in modern times, the story would have been done in such a way as to have the whole story be about Steven's journey from the Doctor criticizing him for being unable to make his own decisions at the start to being ready to take over and run things. And now, sixteen years later… well, we're still not quite to the point where the character-based storytelling is up and running, but we're getting closer. This story at least tries to do something with its characters, framing the major conflict as being between the extremes of Tegan's reaction to Monarch (we have to get back to Earth and warn everyone) and Adric's (ooh yay, fascism, maybe it will make the icky women go away).

This, of course, gets at the real problem here. It's trying to create soap-like character tension and drama here, and good for it, but it's doing so with appallingly broad strokes. Adric is sexist and embraces stupid ideas, Tegan is rash and doesn't think things through, and the Doctor mediates between them with Nyssa serving as the actual companion for the story. It's very, very superficial and doesn't actually work like character drama at all. I mean, it's got all the moving pieces—setting characters against each other for ideological reasons, having dramatic tension within the TARDIS crew, using the differences between characters as the engine to tell the story. It's all there. It's just not being put together very well.

Many of the problems here are rooted in the story's traditionalism. When the moral dilemma at the heart of the story can be summed up as, "Totalitarian dictatorship by a reptilian overlord named Monarch, yay or nay," you're really not setting yourself up for success in the compelling drama department. There's never any serious doubt that Adric is wrong and that Monarch is evil. Likewise, within the storytelling framework of Doctor Who, "Run and warn Earth" is never going to be the correct decision either, so Tegan hardly comes out as a sympathetic character in all of this.

Add to this the fact that both Adric and Tegan have their own problems. I do not want to pile on excessively to the vast body of criticism that already exists regarding Matthew Waterhouse's portrayal of Adric, but it is safe to say that Season Nineteen is not a good season for the character, and that all his faults are on display here. Tegan, meanwhile, is defined entirely by her desire to get home. It's been a long, long time since the Doctor had an unwilling companion, and with good reason. It worked in the very early days because we didn't know the Doctor very well yet. And even then, by the second season Ian and Barbara had essentially made their peace with the Doctor and were OK with travelling in space and time. When they talked about going home, it was couched as a wistful possibility rather than as a decided goal. Once the show reaches a point where the audience unambiguously is on the Doctor's side and wishes they could travel in the TARDIS, a companion who doesn't want to be there is actively working against audience sympathy. So whenever Tegan visibly hates being on the TARDIS, the audience finds itself siding with her altogether too much: we wish she'd sod off, too. (To her credit, Janet Fielding does as well as can be done with the character, and Tegan does develop much along the same lines as Ian and Barbara, eventually coming to travel with the Doctor by choice.)

But look, we're essentially bitching at this story for doing a poor job of a type of storytelling that Doctor Who has never really tried before. As I said, the parts are all there, just not in fully formed ways. And even the concept of this story has some intriguing stuff in it. The various performances of cultural rituals are, for example, an interesting update of the old Hartnell-era mandate towards education into the realm of the visual. And, when paralleled with the invocation of the Dreamtime (a core concept in Australian aboriginal mythology) on the part of Kurkutji, the referencing of the Fleshtime by the Urbankans seems to gesture at an interesting idea of human culture influencing the Urbankans. So there's genuinely compelling stuff here, even if the script doesn't quite know what to do with any of it.

But incremental change happens. The mere fact that this is a half-step forward is, strictly on its own terms, no more of a problem here than it was in *The Sontaran Experiment*, *The Underwater Menace*, or any other early story of a new Doctor. The problem is that the other half of the step was not really ever taken here. Instead, this is the start of a long period of meandering uncertainty. What it does right will be done better in subsequent stories. And, unfortunately, what it does wrong will be done worse. But as stumbling first efforts go, it's not all that bad.

## One Tiny Little Gap in the Universe Left, Just About to Close (*Kinda*)

It's February 1st, 1982. Kraftwerk! They're at number one! With "The Model/Computer Love!" It only lasts a week, but they're overtaken by The Jam, also a fabulous band, with "A Town Called Malice/Precious." The rest of the top ten isn't hugely interesting, although some mention needs to go to the rather fabulously named Orchestral Manoeuvres in the Dark, who chart with the equally fabulously named "Maid of Orleans (The Waltz of Joan of Arc)." Meat Loaf and Christopher Cross also chart, taking the positions on either side of OMD. Oh well.

In real news, Hafez al-Assad, father of current Syrian leader Bashar al-Assad, conducts a scorched earth campaign in Hama that kills between seventeen and forty thousand people, mostly civilians. Like father, like son, clearly. And British airline Laker Airlines abruptly goes out of business, stranding six thousand passengers when their flights are cancelled due to lack of airline, and in doing so puts the creative in "creative destruction."

And then on television, *Kinda*. As such things go, *Kinda* is one of the most overdetermined Doctor Who stories in existence. So we'll start with a book that I'm kind of largely going to avoid, namely *Doctor Who: The Unfolding Text*. There is, to be clear, nothing particularly wrong with this book. It's a fabulous example of early 1980s media studies.

Unfortunately, the 1980s were basically the earliest days of media studies. And so reading *The Unfolding Text* in 2012 one gets the sense of a clever book where the only bits that would be at all new to someone who is reading this are basically the bits where some mildly arcane bit of literary theory is being evoked. I mean, I don't think most of my readers are necessarily going to be solid on Greimasian oppositions and their relationship to *The Krotons*, but even there I think they'd do fine on the actual analysis. (And, I mean, don't knock Greimasian oppositions.)

But *The Unfolding Text* has a particularly detailed reading of *Kinda* due to the fact that the authors were allowed to hang around the set during filming, and so among we academic types *Kinda* has a bit of a reputation simply because its been analyzed in particular depth. All of which said, the reading is a bit flat—various codes of meaning overlap and partially cancel each other out and the end result reinforces established social codes based around a BBC image of "professionalism." It's a fair enough approach and hard to argue with, but it falls a bit too neatly into the general tendency of early cultural studies work to find oppressive cultural hegemony everywhere, a tendency that is not wrong so much as it is, in hindsight, stating the obvious. I, also somewhat obviously, prefer a different approach. Not to break out the theory excessively, but I tend to favor an approach where it's assumed that nothing is ever fully erased and that overlapping codes of meaning—which obviously happen in any collaboratively authored text, and, frankly, in most single-author ones—do just that: overlap, leaving each meaning intact as one of a number of routes through the text.

To put it in less heady terms, *The Unfolding Text* belongs to a school of thought where a lot of effort goes into showing how mass media is a tool of the established social order. Today hardly anyone needs to be told that anymore. It can safely be taken for granted, and I largely do here, finding myself instead interested in the odd contours of the world as depicted in a piece of mass media aimed at the general population that nevertheless consistently works as a rabbit hole to a world of strange concepts and avant-garde techniques and ideology. I'm interested in the way in which the strange survives in mass media, in other words, not in the rather banal fact that mass media is by default an apparatus of existing power. I understand why, in 1983, at the dawn of media studies, the observation of how mass media worked to reinforce structures of power was important, but the result is that *The Unfolding Text* is, as I said to start, a bit basic.

For instance, *The Unfolding Text* argues, basically, that *Kinda* is a Buddhist allegory that has been Christianized by the BBC (or, if we want to be more blunt, an exotic allegory that has been normalized—*The Unfolding Text* does precious little to work through the Buddhist nature of the story, focusing almost entirely on the way that it got mainstreamed into a Christian allegory instead of on what it might have said or done on its own). I am inclined to see a story in which the signifiers of both overlap in interesting and compelling ways. Or, at least, I would if this were particularly Buddhist. As Miles and Wood point out, the degree to which Bailey can actually be said to be particularly Buddhist is kind of minimal. The Buddhism of the story exists more on the level of character naming as a sort of crass symbolism than on the level of actual content (although this is mostly due to Saward's revisions to the script—Bailey's original was more overtly Buddhist, and the themes are certainly still visible). Had *Kinda* been a particularly Buddhist story then the Mara wouldn't simply be removed from Tegan's mind but accepted as a part of her own internal landscape—a representation of her own demons that she cannot simply erase. That's kind of pointedly not where the story actually goes, and that's on the level of scripting, not on the level of Christianizing that *The Unfolding Text* goes for, whereby a Buddhist script is recuperated by the BBC.

A more interesting issue of Christianization comes in the "serpent in paradise" aspects of the story—aspects that are very clearly drawn from the book of Genesis and not from a

Buddhist source. Were we interested in sloppy readings we'd go with some sort of Joseph Campbell monomyth bullshit, but I've expressed my utter disdain for Campbell already, so clearly that's not what we're going to pick. Instead let's embrace the postmodern and simply accept that the Christian imagery of the Garden of Eden and the more Buddhist concept of the Mara as Tegan's internal libidinous desires are being juxtaposed, with the Mara being couched in the more culturally familiar concept of original sin and primal evil. This isn't Christianity overwriting Buddhism, but an active hybrid concept that simultaneously evokes both.

But all of this is presupposing that a sort of symbolic deciphering of this story is the most interesting way to go about it. And it's not. The merging of the image of primal temptation with Tegan's obviously libidinal possession with the childlike logic of her dreamspace is the most symbolically rich part of this story, sure, but if we're being honest, it doesn't hold a candle to the symbolic rabbit holes of *Logopolis* or *The Deadly Assassin*. It's a potent little knot of symbols, yes, but it's thus worth taking seriously on precisely those grounds: it is both potent and compact. That is, it resonates strongly without being all that difficult to grasp. Without any mucking about with Buddhist terminology it's relatively clear what's going on with the Mara and temptation. It may feel a bit too grown up for a given viewer—the degree to which it's immediately familiar is, as Miles notes in *About Time*, kind of directly related to the degree to which the viewer has gone through puberty. But even for a "too young" viewer there's a familiar sense of the inaccessible here. The Mara feels like a part of the world you're not old enough for, and retains its primal power. Indeed, for an audience slightly too young to grasp the sexual overtones of the Mara, the creature is in many ways even more potent.

This gets us closer to what's really interesting about *Kinda*, which is not the density of its symbolism but the quality of its storytelling, and particularly its character work. In a season consciously modelled to be like a soap opera, it is ironically the story that had to sideline one of the four cast members that most pays off the implicit idea of character-based science fiction that a more soap opera sort of Doctor Who promises.

We've largely gotten at what Tegan's character does here. She is, of course, particularly well-suited to this—her rashness, impulsiveness, and anger all play right into this sort of libidinous transformation. Similarly, Adric's teenage rebelliousness make him the obvious person to put in the dome under Hindle's cruel and arbitrary authority—this is arguably the last story he can really be said to work in. And the young and fresh-faced Doctor is perfectly positioned to be the Idiot who, free of preconceptions, is able to piece together what the world is and respond to it.

But this commitment to character goes beyond just the TARDIS crew. Character traits also provide much of the sense of danger in this story, with Hindle being a sort of madman that we haven't seen before. For all the scenery chewing of the episode one cliffhanger, with Hindle screaming that he has "the power of life and death over all of you," there's something unnerving about it. Hindle isn't an insane villain in the Master sense of just being insanely evil, he's a villain whose madness makes him wholly unpredictable. For all the excess of Simon Rouse's performance it remains a deeply, deeply unsettling one in which the audience understands Hindle without ever being able to anticipate what he might do next—an ideal situation for an antagonist to be in. Equally deft is the way in which Bailey sketches out his other characters so that there appear to be character motivations for what they're doing as well. For instance, Karuna's actions in part are clearly rooted in her relationship with Aris, even though the details of this relationship are never quite spelled out.

The result is a world in which everybody appears to be acting as characters, but the interactions of those characters tell a larger story about the philosophical and imaginative concepts of the story. Which are not simply an allegory but are instead thematic. At the heart of this story is a series of stories about the destructive relationship between desire and power, with every given interaction being defined by that relationship. So Hindle is driven mad by his anxiety over power, Aris is tempted and destroys his people because of his desire for power to take revenge on the colonists, et cetera.

There are problems—given all of this, the resolution of just trapping the Mara in a bunch of mirrors because evil can't stand to gaze upon itself is, frankly, lame and underwhelming (although it likely worked better in the earlier, more overtly Buddhist drafts of the story). After building an entire complex network of character traits and thematic implications all the story can find to do with them is to blow them all up. Except that Bailey is working actively to avoid being so violent, going instead for a functional zero-death story, so instead we get a giant snake.

Ah yes, the snake. One of the legendary bad effects of Doctor Who—one so bad that they redid it in CGI for the DVD. This is silly in several regards. First, the anti-historical nature of it simply jars. Surely by 2011, when the DVD came out, we can simply be at peace with the fact that Doctor Who had some crap effects in its time. Beyond that, there's not that much benefit to fixing just one dumb thing in the story. I mean, let's CGI out Matthew Waterhouse while we're at it. The idea that Doctor Who's past is somehow fixable is ridiculous. For that matter, the idea that it's possible to make *Kinda* look less like it was made in early 1982 is ridiculous. *Kinda* is absolutely part and parcel of television in 1982, ill-advised giant pink snakes and all. (And if you don't believe me, flip ahead to the essay on *The Cleopatras*.)

Which gets at the second and rather more significant issue, which is that, as I said, it doesn't matter how well-done the snake is given that it's a fundamentally unsatisfying ending in terms of what comes before it. The visual quality of the snake isn't what's wrong with the ending. What's wrong with the ending is that it doesn't extend from any of its characters. It's not about Hindle, restored by the Box of Jhana, taking a sane decisive action to save everybody. It's not about Tegan facing down her demons. It's not about Adric facing his fear. It's marginally about Karuna's growing up and taking on the role of wise woman, but Karuna hardly had the most compelling character arc. It's mostly just about the Doctor finally getting around to having a clever idea in the fourth episode like he usually does.

But if we gave *Four to Doomsday* some leeway for being the first story to try soap opera style storytelling and getting the characters wrong we need to give *Kinda* some more leeway for attempting to try character-based storytelling that was wedded firmly to science-fiction concepts. This is an extremely mature story, technically speaking. And in the end, it's still 1982 and Doctor Who doesn't hit the point of doing this sort of thing elegantly for a while yet. All of which said, it's not like the new series hasn't flubbed the ending on a story here and there. *Victory of the Daleks* happened, and *Kinda*'s weak ending is no worse than that one. So forgiving the ending—essentially the story's only major lapse—is relatively easy.

There is, however, one rather ominous fact on the horizon. In hindsight, of course, everybody recognizes that *Kinda* is a classic piece of Doctor Who. And yet in the *Doctor Who Monthly* poll on Season Nineteen it ranked dead last—as the absolute worst story of the season. This is particularly notable because the season finale, *Time-Flight*, is one of the most reviled stories in all of Doctor Who—the fifth worst ever in the Mighty 200 poll. And yet in 1982, *Time-Flight* polled nicely in the middle of the pack. Given that the sorts of fans who voted in *Doctor Who Monthly* polls were, under Nathan-Turner, rapidly growing in influence, this starts to become a genuine problem. Because by most metrics, even in 1982, it would have been clear that there are really interesting and praiseworthy things going on here and that this is a model story for how to do Doctor Who. Instead, though, the whims of fandom had sway. In hindsight it's blatantly clear that this is the most sophisticated and aesthetically successful story Doctor Who has done yet. But it's not the model going forward at all, and it's not until five years from here that this begins to be what the program shoots for by default. Instead the program tries to cater overtly to the *Doctor Who Monthly* audience.

It's not as though there's an immediate downturn in the quality of the show after this. There's not, and the Davison era remains, on the whole, quite good. And heck, this story even gets a sequel. But on the other hand, if you want to point at the wrong turn that kills Doctor Who, I think it would be hard to find a better one than this. Because the ratings for Season Nineteen were generally fantastic—short of the ITV-strike bolstered Season Seventeen they're the best that Doctor Who has done since the Hinchcliffe era. And ratings-wise, it's all downhill from here. *Kinda* was, by a trivial margin, the lowest-rated story of Season Nineteen, and it still beats every single story from subsequent seasons. This season is the last season of Doctor Who that can validly claim to be massively popular. The directions it goes after this are, at least in the short and medium term, the wrong ones.

And if you want to identify a specific error, it's difficult to come up with a more compelling example than making it a matter of policy to actively listen to people who thought *Time-Flight* was a better story than this. Never mind the absurd stupidity of some fan comments, never mind the discussions of fanwank and continuity porn. Doctor Who made a point of taking seriously people who preferred *Time-Flight* to this.

No wonder it died.

## Nothing Ever Changes in London (*The Visitation*)

It's February 15th, 1982. The Jam remain at number one for the entirety of this story with Soft Cell, XTC, Depeche Mode, and Hall and Oates also charting, making this the only time that list of four bands has ever happened. Depeche Mode, it should be noted, debut here in their better known "sans Vince Clarke" lineup with "See You," their first single written by Martin Gore. Lower in the charts Journey appear with "Don't Stop Believin'," which will peak at 62 before vanishing, getting the reception it deserved until the damn thing reappeared repeatedly from 2007-2012, eventually becoming a top ten single.

In real news, a general election in the Republic of Ireland boosts the centrist Fianna Fáil party which, after a few weeks of jockeying, forms a government. The DeLorean factory in Belfast is put into receivership. And, two days after this story airs its last episode, the European Court of Human Rights determines that caning, belting, or tasing students without their parents' permission is a human rights violation, which is at once a stunningly obvious conclusion and a strangely inadequate one that suggests that tasing students with their parents' permission is somehow just fine.

While on television it's the debut of one of this volume's major characters, namely Eric Saward, who takes over as script editor shortly after this story, a position he maintains through the dying days of the Colin Baker era.

Unsurprisingly, given the history of that era, he is a controversial figure. Some of this is of his own making: he had a colossal falling out with Nathan-Turner at the end of his tenure, and, more to the point, dished freely about this in an interview after leaving the show. But he's also controversial for his writing, both on his own scripts and others. In terms of his own scripts, it has to be admitted, they're fairly well received. One, which we'll talk about soon, is largely considered an absolute classic. All four are in the top half of stories in the most recent *Doctor Who Magazine* ranking. But his scripts have prominent detractors in ways that other well-regarded writers don't, and he benefits more than slightly from the fact that several stories he's directly responsible for the failings of don't have his name on them. And, not to spoil the rest of the book, he's a writer I'll freely admit I have relatively little time for.

But for all of that, I find myself sympathetic to him, simply because his fundamental problem as both a writer and a script editor is at once obvious and painful. Simply put, Eric Saward has very, very good taste, but a chronic inability to live up to that taste in his own work. The best example of this comes in his relationship with Robert Holmes. The active relationship between Saward and Holmes doesn't begin until Season Twenty, but I'd make a strong case—in fact, I'm going to—that the writers need to be considered in tandem from the start of Saward's career. Miles and Wood suggest that this is the first attempt to do a "traditional" Doctor Who story, but this is a slightly dodgy claim. For one thing, the pseudo-historical isn't exactly a format with a long tradition. It was reasonably popular in the Hinchcliffe era, which had three of them, and then the Williams era started with one, but prior to that there were only three of them: *The Time Meddler, The Abominable Snowmen,* and *The Time Warrior*. Indeed, there's a case to be made that the style as we recognize it today, with its inevitable celebrity historical figure, was an invention of the Saward era.

So while it's true that "aliens mess with history" is one of the standard plots of Doctor Who now, that wasn't really the case in 1982. There'd only been seven of them in the first eighteen years of the program—but that number will more than double in the final eight years of the show. Furthermore, the seven that predate this could hardly be said to form a coherent genre. *The Horror of Fang Rock, The Talons of Weng-Chiang, The Masque of Mandragora, The Pyramids of Mars, The Time Warrior, The Abominable Snowmen,* and *The Time Meddler* have very, very little in common as a list beyond their historical setting. Some involve aliens meddling with concrete facts of history, others just use the historical setting as a set of tropes and conventions. Actually, about the only thing other than the historical setting that can be generalized about that list is that five of the seven involve Robert Holmes in some fashion. Which is amusing, given that he hated doing history in Doctor Who.

But this gets at what's really going on in *The Visitation*, which is not about redoing a Doctor Who standard in the 1980s so much as it's a flat-out 1980s remake of *The Time Warrior*. Saward, in his first outing, is trying to redo a Robert Holmes story. And to his credit, it's not the worst idea. I was a little rough on *The Time Warrior* when I covered it due to the fact that it's got some egregious sexism problems. But that's the sort of thing why I insist that *TARDIS Eruditorum* isn't about reviewing stories. Because considered as a piece of entertainment, *The Time Warrior* is a highlight of the Pertwee era, and indeed the series. When it comes to stories to go back to and try again, there are few better choices—it's a great story that, unlike something like *Warriors' Gate* or *Carnival of Monsters*, doesn't rely on a high concept one-off premise, but that can instead be repeated with subtle variations. So as source material to pinch goes, Saward is on firm ground here.

And let's also be clear, Saward is not a talentless hack by any stretch of the imagination. There are some real strengths to his writing. He has a sense of pace that's genuinely admirable. In all of his scripts there's a sense of mounting and pressing drama—a sense of tension and suspense that satisfyingly animates his stories. He's good at stringing together set pieces—a talent he shares with Holmes—and while he uses bickering among the TARDIS crew as a crutch to pad out episodes, the fact is that he writes those scenes quite well. It is, in other words, not hard to see why this was one of the most popular stories of the season—it was fast-paced, exciting, and had a lot going on. It's very much fun to watch.

The word "but" hangs over that paragraph like a Sword of Damocles, however, and so let's drop it. Saward is no Robert Holmes. And the real case in point is Richard Mace. On the one hand, Mace is a flagrant effort to create an archetypal Robert Holmes-type of character—the larger than life comedy rogue, specifically. It's not that Mace isn't funny—there are parts of the story where he's downright charming. But for some inexplicable reason Saward hangs the entire story on him—he's the only supporting character in the entire thing who can accurately be called a character. And it doesn't work at all. Mace just isn't a good enough character to support the entire plot. He's great fun, but that's all he is. Garron, another one of the comedy rogue characters in question, was one of the most fun parts of *The Ribos Operation*, but he was balanced out by a well-characterized villain and the Unstoffe/Binro storyline that provides the emotional heart of the story.

It is, in other words, as though Saward watched some Holmes scripts, noticed that comedy rogues were the best part, and so he wrote a script consisting of nothing but a comedy rogue and some action set pieces. It's maddening because it's so close to working. He's got the right model. He's correctly identified many of the best parts of the model. But he doesn't have a sense of the underlying mechanics of *The Time Warrior* to actually imitate it. *The Time Warrior*'s comedy rogue is Irongron, and he's a bad guy created to play endlessly off of the alien. Saward makes the comedy rogue the Doctor's sidekick and doesn't bother developing the world any further.

The real giveaway is the Tereleptil leader. Holmes, in creating the Sontarans, creates a specific character in Linx. Whereas the Tereleptil leader never gets a name—he's just the Tereleptil leader. Saward, in Part Four, goes for a moment of suspense where it suddenly turns out that there's three Tereleptils. The idea that it's suspenseful because the lone Tereleptil was a real threat all story and now there are three of them is unfortunately more along the lines of *The Horns of Nimon*. But with the lone Tereleptil already being little more than a featureless monster who gets some moustache-twirling lines the sudden reveal of more of them is little more than a reveal that the story's monster is... a monster. Yay.

All of which said, it's not that the story doesn't work. It does. It's just that it only works on transmission, and even then would only work at the heightened pace of the twice-weekly episodes. This story depends on the fact that the audience doesn't really have time to think about what's going on. And we're starting to exit the point where only working once is a sound choice, as it's becoming increasingly obvious that Doctor Who is going to be out on video someday. Even if, in 1982, the VCR was still a bit of an obscure object (only 10% of the households in the UK owned one) it was clearly a rising technology. And so while *The Visitation* can get something of a pass on the old "it was only meant to be watched once" defense, that defense is going to stop working very soon.

One final thing that has to be commented on: the destruction of the sonic screwdriver. The reasoning behind it, stated ad nauseum by John Nathan-Turner over the course of his career, is that the sonic was a cheat that made the Doctor too powerful and encouraged lazy scriptwriting. Somewhat astonishingly, this nonsense is still repeated within some corners of fandom, and while the idea that it might be put to bed for good is surely ludicrous, let's take a stab at it.

First of all, the thing that makes the Doctor too powerful is that the show is named after him. I've slaughtered this horse in past essays, but this is one of the most egregious outbreaks of this sort of twaddle, so let's be perfectly clear: Anyone who is watching Doctor Who in any spirit based on the idea that the Doctor might not save the day is simply being televisually illiterate. The drama of Doctor Who cannot reasonably be said to come from whether or not the Doctor is going to be OK. And so on those grounds Nathan-Turner's entire crusade to remove Romana, K-9, and the sonic screwdriver on the grounds of excessive power was simply silly.

The idea that the sonic screwdriver encourages lazy scriptwriting, on the other hand, may be even more bewildering. In that it seems to suggest, with alleged seriousness, that the purpose of Doctor Who is to watch the Doctor do clever things with locks. If anything, the sonic screwdriver discouraged lazy scriptwriting because it made it harder to justify putting the Doctor in an endless sequence of captures and escapes. It dramatically reduced the amount of stupid padding that could be shoved into a story, and it does so even more in its modern day version as a tool that can accomplish anything so long as it wouldn't be more interesting to do it another way. But as of *The Visitation* lazy scriptwriters can now stretch out episodes with lengthy scenes focused on manually fiddling with wires. There is no shortage of sequences over the next few years that excruciatingly demonstrate how bad an idea this was.

But this is fundamentally related to what's wrong with *The Visitation*. It's an imitation of a story about characters written by someone who doesn't really understand storytelling beyond the level of action sequences. And, even though it was Nathan-Turner's idea, the destruction of the sonic screwdriver is the removal of something that speeds through some of the dreck of action sequences. Whereas one of Russell T. Davies's fundamental innovations in 2005 is to bring back the sonic screwdriver, make it more powerful, and add the psychic paper to it so that he can speed through trivial setup and wire-fiddling and get on with the actual character drama.

And while I am usually disinclined to criticize the classic series for failing to live up to the standards of television from over twenty years later, this is genuinely troubling right after the ahead-of-its-time *Kinda*. Doctor Who is spending more time figuring out how to get more captures and escapes into its format than it is on character-based storytelling. This while simultaneously trying to act more like a soap and have character conflict. It's problematic to say the least. And while every individual story of the Davison era thus far has more or less worked fine and been at least somewhat entertaining, it's also clear that the show has ambitions on the level of story arcs beyond just single adventures. It's inviting the viewer to judge it on the grounds of how it handles its characters over multiple stories and on its ongoing development. And it's doing so actively, unlike in the Graham Williams era, where even as the series moved towards season-long arcs it subverted the possibility of the epic and actively declined to offer plot arcs. Nathan-Turner is actively offering a type of series where there should be plot arcs and character development. And then he's failing not just miserably but bizarrely at even delivering them.

## Just a Hint of Mint (*Black Orchid*)

It's March 1st, 1982. Tight Fit are at number one with "The Lion Sleeps Tonight," while Toni Basil's unforgivably awful "Mickey" is at number two. Soft Cell and Depeche Mode also feature in the top ten, while Iron Maiden pokes around just outside of it. While in real news... well, we've got here a story that only covers two days, so actually, based on the detailed historical research I do for these essays (aka "look the year up on Wikipedia") nothing whatsoever happens. Queen Elizabeth opens up the Barbican the day after this story finishes. The Barbican is an interesting little thing—a massive performing arts centre full of good intentions and muddy executions. But I did see a phenomenal RSC production of *A Midsummer Night's Dream* there in what a quick check of the Internet suggests was just about their final performance at the Barbican. So that was nice.

While on topic, *Black Orchid*. This one's an interesting beast. It doesn't work at all, first off, but the reasons why it doesn't work are almost completely separate from the larger problems that Doctor Who is having in this time period and have very little to do with the story as an idea. Because as an idea, this is the story that really demonstrates how Doctor Who's relationship with its past can and should work.

The first and most important thing to realize about this story is that it comes after *The Visitation*. While this is a stunningly obvious point, its implications may not be. *The Visitation* restored Earth's past as a place where the series goes, much as Tegan quietly restored Earth as something that was actually important to the series, as it had been almost entirely de-emphasized following *The Hand of Fear*. And it did so by introducing Earth's past as the sort of place it's been ever since *The Time Warrior*—a place that is visited to do muckabouts in history with cool aliens.

So when *Black Orchid* comes along and reintroduces the straight historical it's every bit as much a surprise as when *The Time Meddler* came along and broke the straight historical. In fact, this story can be read as the inversion of *The Time Meddler*. In that story we're led repeatedly to think that we're watching a straight historical only to discover that in reality we're watching something else. Here the production repeatedly gestures at the possibility that there is something uncanny in the story—like, that the Master might be involved, for instance—but instead we are repeatedly shown that it's actually just a 1920s mystery story.

By and large, this is a very, very smart thing to do at this point in the series. First and foremost, it shows a relationship with the show's past that goes beyond merely catering to obsessive fans. There was no loud clamoring for the return of the historical, which has always, within fandom, been viewed primarily as a discarded relic of the early days of the show and as something rightly phased out in favor of more monsters. This is, of course, rubbish. Although I do think that the pseudo-historical is largely a superset of the historical, the idea that the historical was a dead end for the series is simply nonsense. And so returning to it is a heartening sign that the increasing tendency towards mining the series' past is about finding wrongly discarded approaches and not about mere fetishism. Simply put, trying a historical out is a brave move.

Secondly, however, it's satisfyingly concerned with the small scale. Much like *Kinda*, *Black Orchid* focuses on characters. In *Black Orchid*'s case, however, this isn't a choice. It's a 1920s murder mystery—by definition a genre that requires a focus on characters. Given our premise that Season Nineteen is in part a failed attempt at making Doctor Who into a soap opera, this sort of story is a real help—a reminder that Doctor Who can be about the concerns of ordinary people instead of about giant psychic snakes, historical disasters, and universe-threatening dangers. The danger in this story concerns nothing more than a family and their internal politics. One struggles to remember the last time the stakes in a story were so low—even the character-based Williams era never went for anything quite so small scale. And it's a good thing—a helpful regrounding of the series.

It's particularly beneficial to Peter Davison, whose Doctor is very well-suited by this downsizing of scale. As I've said before, every Doctor is in part a reaction against his predecessor. And so Davison's Doctor is defined first and foremost by his comparative lack of a dominating presence. One is tempted to cite Raymond Chandler's description of the detective in "The Simple Art of Murder," specifically the bit about, "But down these mean streets a man must go who is not himself mean, who is neither tarnished nor afraid. The detective in this kind of story must be such a man. He is the hero, he is everything. He must be a complete man and a common man and yet an unusual man. He must be, to use a rather weathered phrase, a man of honor, by instinct, by inevitability, without thought of it, and certainly without saying it. He must be the best man in his world and a good enough man for any world."

That is very much where Davison's Doctor is pitched. He is not a world-saving hero so much as a good man in a not very good universe who nevertheless loves the universe and wants to explore it. And this is a very important story in developing that because it gives Davison the opportunity for a fantastic performance in a small scale. His protestations of innocence in the second episode and frustrated efforts to get out of the legal system and back to the plot are fantastic. One of the things Davison is phenomenal at is making sure every line he delivers is doing something. This is an important dramatic principle—that every line in a script should involve a character engaging in some active verb in order to attain what he or she wants. Davison, quite frankly, is far better at this than the scriptwriters, and he manages to make every line he delivers into a dramatic action. Pairing that with small stakes helpfully reinforces the character—it means that when we see him, next story, running frantically about a space freighter trying to warn people about Cybermen, that becomes a smaller and more intimate story as well.

Unfortunately, Davison is the only person whose character is helped here. Sarah Sutton does well enough, finally getting a story that's largely focused on her, and she does as credible a job with playing two parts as any actress has. But the quality of her two-character turn only reveals the paucity of characterization she's getting as Nyssa. Not for the first time, the story forgets to give its characters something to do. The prospect of Nyssa trying to talk George down herself would make for a phenomenal scene. Instead she gets to be kidnapped and flail about. There's even less to say about Tegan and Adric, who don't even seem to belong in this story.

And then there's the ending, in which the Doctor partially talks George down on the roof only to have him conveniently run off it and plunge to his death so as to wrap things up in time for the closing credits. It's appallingly rushed and fails to provide any actual dramatic payoff to any of the events preceding it. In this regard it's a typical failure of the sort that's been infesting the entire season—a character drama created by people who neither understand nor care about characters.

But there's a more fundamental problem under the hood here, which is the two-part structure. It's not, for what it's worth, that two twenty-five minute episodes is too short to tell a good Doctor Who story. For one thing, if that were true it would follow that the new series must be wretched, and it's clearly not. Rather, it's that the cliffhanger structure does these stories no favor. In this case we have a murder mystery that doesn't get the opportunity to get underway until the second of two episodes, because the murder is held back for the cliffhanger of the first episode.

The problem is that the structure that works well for longer stories, in which each episode is a distinct phase of the storytelling, is a mess for two-parters. By breaking the story into setup and resolution Dudley squashes his entire mystery into an episode too small to contain it while having a first episode that luxuriates in the space it's afforded to do party scenes and cricket matches. Both of which are lovely bits of texture, or, at least, would be in a four-parter where three episodes were turned over to the murder. Admittedly the murder as it stands can't possibly sustain that either, and two episodes is probably the right amount of time. The problem is that the murder needs to happen at about the 15-minute mark in Episode One and the cliffhanger needs to be a shoved-in pro forma piece of "we've put a major character in peril" instead of a turning point in the plot. This is that rare case where the episode structure is just getting in the way and a contrived cliffhanger would have been so much more preferable.

But, of course, that was never going to work in the twice-weekly format where each episode is made with the assumption that the audience might have missed all or most of the other one. The second episode has to be a self-contained unit unto itself because it can't assume that most of the audience was around the episode before like it could if the preceding episode had aired on the same day of the week. So we're stuck with a shape for the story that cannot possibly hold the story it's trying to tell. While it's difficult, given his other two efforts, to imagine that Dudley would have filled in the character beats this needed given a forty-five minute single episode, or that Saward or Nathan-Turner would ever have noticed this problem in the first place, let alone worked to fix it, the fact of the matter is that even if he'd wanted to, Dudley would have had a hard time making this story work in two episodes. And so while two-parters certainly can work, it's difficult to come up with a compelling case that they can work in this particular timeslot and format.

So what we have in *Black Orchid* is another flawed experiment. It's less dramatically satisfying than several less ambitious stories in its season, but one still wants to give it more credit than, say, *The Visitation* simply because it's putting some effort towards trying to be a better story and missing spectacularly, whereas *The Visitation* is aiming at high mediocrity and falls just short of its ambitions.

One final note needs to be dealt with, because this story is the most problematic example of a longstanding trope. Doctor Who, throughout its run, has an unfortunate relationship with physical disability, tending to equate it to monstrosity. This is, admittedly, a broad trope in action-adventure literature. But the parade of small-sized or facially disfigured people who are also homicidal and evil over the course of Doctor Who is genuinely problematic. And it's a particularly nasty piece of discrimination because there's actually a metaphor to it. It's one thing when the show just blithely reasserts classism by favoring the middle and upper class and not giving a crap about the working class. It's another when the pattern of behavior is an active commentary. The use of disability as a signifier of evil is based on the equation of physical disfigurement with mental disfigurement—that what is ugly on the outside must therefore be ugly on the inside. Which is uncomfortably close to something like using people with darker skin as symbols of evil because white is good and black is evil.

And this story goes one step further by linking in primitive cultures—including a South American with a plate in his lip to add that extra level of exoticism and deformity. And having the deformity take place in the dark jungle at the hands of savages and... yuck. It's just a pile of yuck. It's another example of Dudley writing for the Hartnell era, except this time he's gone back a few stories, from *The Savages* to *The Ark*.

And like the crass characterization, it's something that could easily be at least somewhat fixable. The story is fairly insistent that George retains value and worth, but then shoves him off a roof and kills him instead of dealing with the inconvenience of sorting out some resolution. Again, given Dudley's overall skills as a writer it's difficult to imagine that he'd have improved on this if given the time. Especially because it could have been dealt with in the time allotted— even a single line in which the Doctor suggests that his family's mistreatment of him is as much a cause of George's madness as his disfigurement would go miles towards making this a better story. Instead, the actions of the family are largely given a pass and George is treated as a great man brought low by circumstance, to be praised only for his life before being captured.

So we get casual cultural imperialism, scorn for the disabled, and yet another failure to actually tell stories about characters. For all that John Nathan-Turner distances himself from the Williams era he manages a remarkable imitation of its essential nature: all the right goals and nothing like the ability to pull them off.

## A Pathetic Bunch of Tin Soldiers (*Earthshock*)

It's March 8, 1982. Tight Fit are still sleeping with a lion, and continue to do so all story. Fun Boy Three and Bananarama, ABC, and Iron Maiden also chart. So that's all terribly exciting, isn't it. Let's try the news—the US starts its embargo against Libya. That will end well, I'm sure. Mary Whitehouse's attempt to prosecute the play *The Romans in Britain* for obscenity goes down in flames when it turns out that the witness who claims to have seen a penis on stage could not possibly have actually done so, proving a delightfully high-profile defeat for Whitehouse. Also, syzygy!

While on television we have *Earthshock*. This is a tricky story in some ways. It's absolutely beloved by certain sectors of fandom, and I can't honestly pretend there aren't sane reasons for this. But it's never been one I've liked as much as its reputation. It's also, in many ways, the most successful negotiation of the series' past, particularly the fifth season, i.e. the stretch of Patrick Troughton where he's stuck doing a base under siege almost every week.

The bulk of my writing on the base-under-siege structure focused on the way in which it went from being an invigorating new approach to a formulaic and boring one. But a second strand that crops up throughout these essays is a process of contextualizing the stories in the changing tastes of Doctor Who fandom. This is, admittedly, an issue through large swaths of *TARDIS Eruditorum*, and especially in terms of the base under siege, which spent the early days of organized fandom as the presumptive pinnacle of all Doctor Who.

Obviously, I disagree. But this is the chunk of fandom that John Nathan-Turner was actively courting at this point in the series' history. And this story, more than any other, was the one that absolutely thrilled them. In the *Doctor Who Monthly* poll that proclaimed *Kinda* the turkey of the season, *Earthshock* was at the top, and it's still enormously popular. And this gets straight at what's a bit tricky with *Earthshock*, which is that it's tailor-made for the crowd that thinks that bases under siege are the be-all and end-all of Doctor Who.

For the most part, it is an astonishingly straightforward story. Cybermen attack Earth. Twice. The pleasures it offers are straightforward pleasures. There are Cybermen. There are gun battles. Things explode. It's a story that operates under the complete and unfaltering confidence that having action sequences involving classic Doctor Who monsters is inherently worthwhile television.

Given that premise, *Earthshock* is, if nothing else, as good as Doctor Who ever got at this, at least in the classic series. Over the entire run of Doctor Who, including the classic "monster" era of Troughton and the "Action by Havoc" era of Pertwee, this is the best the series did at a straight action story. It moves at a brisk pace, has reasonably competent action sequences throughout, and has a pair of genuinely striking moments with the surprise appearance of the Cybermen and the death of Adric. It makes the clever decision to take the base under siege format—traditionally a six-episode structure—and break it down to two linked two-parters so that the action actually moves at a real clip. (And once again, there's that sly technique of having each week of a four-parter be a distinct approach and story.) If what you like about Doctor Who is its action sequences then this is rightly your favorite story. Even if that's not what you like about Doctor Who, there's admittedly a kind of infectious fun to this one. Its sheer glee at reenacting various iconic Cybermen moments is catchy. Lawrence Miles describes it in *About Time* as a guilty pleasure, and he's absolutely right. If you're a Doctor Who fan who is capable of being invested in the fact that the Cybermen are reappearing then this story is a real hoot.

The problem is that so much of fandom seems unaware of the "guilty" part of guilty pleasures. The stereotypical social awkwardness of the science fiction fan occasionally, in the case of Doctor Who, spills over into an odd aesthetic awkwardness. Put another way, people are inexplicably of the belief that the faults of this story are more excusable than those of *Kinda* when it comes to showing Doctor Who to a general audience. This is very strange. *Kinda* has two major problems, both of which center on its conclusion. The first is that the conclusion is emotionally vacant, the second is that the conclusion focuses on a terrible giant snake. But as problems go, this second one is an interesting one.

First of all, the superficially obvious problem that the snake is rubbish helpfully distracts from the scripting problem underneath it. But second, and this is particularly key, there's actually something fun about a dodgy giant snake. For all that people mock the bad effects of Doctor Who it's genuinely easy for fans or non-fans to get a kick out of them. Science fiction is established enough that poor effects are part of its charm. And this was true by 1982. The purpose of special effects is often their visibility—the question of "how did they do that." And thus a bad effect still fits into the basic grammar of special effects. It's just an effect in which the question of "how did they do that" is painfully answerable. And so a good story with terrible effects is not only something that the general public is more than capable of accepting, it's actually something they can generally be counted on to enjoy somewhat perversely. There's a camp glee to a bad effect. (I've often thought that a brilliant piece of science fiction television would be to take top notch scriptwriters and then produce their scripts on an appalling shoestring budget with good actors and competent directors who are just unabashedly directing men in rubber suits, glove puppets, and wire models. This thought is generally followed by a realization that I've just described Doctor Who.) Whereas *Earthshock* is frankly nearly impossible to love if you're not a Doctor Who fan.

Consider, for instance, the much vaunted Episode One cliffhanger. Remember that a key part of the appeal of this cliffhanger is that the return of the Cybermen was a genuine surprise and that nobody knew it was coming. Then look at how it's actually done. The Doctor refers to whoever is controlling the android, then we cut to the people controlling the android as one of them shouts "Destroy them! Destroy them at once!" And, of course, the people controlling them are Cybermen.

But this is never actually stated. I mean, it's not a huge botch—the Cybermen are well known villains that a fair portion of the audience legitimately would have recognized, even in their redesigned form. But the impact of that cliffhanger depends 100% on the fact that the audience is going to recognize the Cybermen from their handlebars and actually care that they're back. To anyone who is not at least a casual Doctor Who fan the cliffhanger looks like the people controlling the androids are, in fact, more androids. And yet people seriously believe this is somehow more appealing to people than a story where the only problem is a poorly done giant snake.

But there's a larger issue at play here—one that gets back to the sorts of comparisons we dealt with in the bemusing *Space: 1999/I Claudius* essay back in Volume Four. And that is that the BBC is not exactly great at doing space action-adventure. *Earthshock* is by far the most competent that the classic series ever got at imitating *Aliens* and *Star Wars*, but the best job the BBC did is still not really a pinnacle of the genre. The BBC just can't do this sort of thing all that well. *Earthshock* manages "not a disaster," which is a tremendous accomplishment for the BBC, but the fact of the matter is that if in 1982 you're pitching the major appeal of Doctor Who as space marines then it's pretty tough to account for why anybody would prefer Doctor Who to other things on the market—a point that would eventually be raised, not entirely senselessly, by Michael Grade.

The best account that presents itself is one of nostalgia—that this is Britain's great contribution to science fiction television and so is rightly beloved on those grounds. And so we bring the Cybermen back because they're the monsters that people remember from their childhoods. And we do space action because that's what science fiction is these days, and it's what Doctor Who did so well in the Troughton and Pertwee eras.

Ironically, of course, it's John Nathan-Turner's own maxim that dooms him here: the memory cheats. Not in the sense he used it—which was to suggest that old Doctor Who wasn't as good as people remembered it being—but in the sense that people don't remember why something was good years after they watched it. Yes, the scene of Cybermen bursting out of their tombs in *Tomb of the Cybermen* was absolutely fantastic, but it turns out to have been one of about three good moments in the entire story. It stuck in the memory, sure, but it wasn't the heart and soul of the series, it was just the bit that stayed with you a decade later.

This is the biggest problem with the "monsters" model of Doctor Who. The sad truth of the matter is that Doctor Who was never all that good at monster action. Over the course of its fifty-plus years it has had some gloriously brilliant monsters, but most of them were the product of a particularly good BBC design team or of particularly inventive writing. The Daleks are good because Raymond Cusick's design hit it out of the park. The Weeping Angels are good because they're a quintessentially British version of a J-Horror monster. But the fact of the matter is that the Ice Warriors didn't come back because green lizard-men from Mars are a good idea, they came back because the costumes were expensive and had to be justified by re-use. And when the costumes wore out the Ice Warriors were never seen again in the classic series, and with good reason: they were literally just green lizard-men from Mars.

This, more than anything, is responsible for the sort of sad and pathetic status of Doctor Who fans. It's not, as with most genre fans, that they liked something unpopular. Doctor Who has, even at its lowest moments, enjoyed a measure of genuine respect in Britain. It's telling that "Doctorin' the TARDIS," KLF's gloriously trashy Doctor Who-themed single, hit number one during the Cartmel years—at the absolute lowest ebb of the series' actual popularity. Even in the worst days of the 1980s the series enjoyed a sort of theoretical popularity. No, the sad thing about Doctor Who fans has always been that they think the best part about the series is its monsters and its thrills.

And at the end of the day this is where I have to just draw an aesthetic line. Because I'm on the other side of that debate. I couldn't care less about the series as an action serial, and the points where it becomes one are generally among the ones that interest me the least. For me Doctor Who is interesting because of its inventiveness, and while I can get a guilty thrill out of mimicry of other popular texts of the time I cannot invest myself in the idea that it's what Doctor Who is for. Doctor Who isn't a chameleon just so it can consistently fail to distinguish itself in any meaningful sense from anything else around it. In this regard the two Saward scripts in Season Nineteen are in many ways my least favorite of the set—and I even include *Time-Flight* in that assessment. It's not that *The Visitation* and *Earthshock* have no ambitions other than entertainment—that's something I'll never really fault Doctor Who for. It's that they have no ambitions other than serving as echoes of other people's creativity. Can I enjoy them? Yes. Absolutely. But I cannot bring myself to love either of them. They have next to none of the animating spark that I genuinely love about Doctor Who.

But in the case of *Earthshock* I'll push that critique one step further. *Earthshock* has the unfortunate distinction of airing two weeks before the Falklands War breaks out. I am not actually going to cover the Falklands War in massive depth, but it's a sobering problematic moment in British history. There's not really a way around the sense that the war was, if not wholly motivated by the fact that there would have to be an election soon, at least firmly conducted with one eye on the polls. The Argentinean side—a fading military dictatorship in desperate need of a propaganda coup—was certainly no better, but the sudden reversion to raw militaristic jingoism in the UK was genuinely chilling, doubly so because it worked so well in the 1983 general election. Similarly, those inclined to despise Rupert Murdoch and the *Sun* have little evidence substantially better than the paper's war coverage and reflexive support of the Thatcher government.

So to see Doctor Who, two weeks before the war broke out, running a story in which even the Doctor ends up as an action hero wrestling a Cyberman and rubbing gold into its chest plate before Nyssa guns it down and where the main supporting good guys are just space marines with big guns is... dismaying. In the worst days of the UNIT era there was at least a sense of tension between the Doctor and UNIT. Pertwee's sort of drag action man, the camp sensibility of UNIT, and the fact that Pertwee even at his worst had at least some visible antipathy towards authority figures all cut against the myriad of problems introduced. But here there's just a love of guns and shooting bad guys for the sake of it.

Because the fact of the matter is that the military is, by definition, a tool of establishment power that prioritizes brute force and is organized according to an authoritarian focus on conformity for its own sake. There's no way for the military to be anything else. This isn't a statement of pacifist belief or anything along those lines—it's simply an acknowledgment of how an organization like the military needs to function, and what a society needs and wants its military to be. And thus the Doctor—mercurial, anarchistic, and intellectual—is at the core of his concept at least mildly hostile to the military. That doesn't mean the Doctor is a pacifist, nor does it mean the Doctor must always oppose the military. But it does mean that using Doctor Who to blindly and uncritically valorize the military cuts against its very nature.

I don't want this observation to be read as a critique of Saward's politics. In his next scripts he displays considerably more skepticism towards the military, and one gets the sense that he grasped the problems of this story in hindsight. But the fact remains that on a fundamental, ethical level, someone who loves the bulk of Doctor Who ought to have some problems with this story. If you're the sort of person who likes Doctor Who then, quite frankly, you really should be the sort of person who likes subversive and mercurial play on and around a concept more than you like militaristic action.

There are two other things to talk about with this story. One I'll take up in the *Spare Parts* essay. The other is the death of Adric. This gets back to the sort of running theme of this essay, which is that fandom has a very warped sense of what works in television. The death of Adric is, for the sort of orthodox fandom that heralds the return of the Cybermen as inherently worthwhile, one of the great moments of drama in the series and a triumphant confirmation of how John Nathan-Turner has discarded the silliness of the Graham Williams era and become a serious program again.

It is difficult to take this even remotely seriously. Part of this is because Adric was, let's be honest, a mistake. But what's remarkable is how little effort was even expended on trying to make his death work dramatically. He doesn't die heroically in any way, shape, or form—his death does not save the day. He basically runs into a crashing spaceship to prove that he's clever, and ends up dying as a result. His last words, "Now I'll never know if I was right," are so outlandishly smug that it is impossible to even figure out what Saward thought he was doing with them. And on top of that Adric gets an extra heaping of annoying scenes in the first episode that set up a voluntary departure and, on the side, remind everyone of why they hate him.

This gets at a larger issue, which is that there's an overt cynicism to the entire thing. It's not just that killing a companion is obviously a bit of a stunt; it's that they consciously picked the companion that was going to be least missed. If you're going to have the Doctor fail and have a companion die, fine. It's probably something worth doing every couple of decades just to forcibly broaden the possible horizons of what Doctor Who can do. And while the tragic departures of Rose and Donna are in every sense better versions of killing a companion, the fact of the matter is that it remains an effective way of increasing dramatic tension. The Doctor will save the day, yes, but there's the possibility of an egregious price to be paid. And there has to be—it's the counterpart of the fact that the Doctor can't possibly be "too powerful." Since you can't make him less likely to win, you have to make the sorts of victories he achieves include pyrrhic ones.

But to do it with the companion who is going to have the least emotional impact is just cheap. If you want to go down that route, do it in a way that's going to matter to the audience. What we get here isn't drama. It's the hollow shell of drama—a major character death, a silent credit sequence, a few minutes of horrified and morose main characters at the tail end of this and the start of *Time-Flight*, and then everybody—the audience included—moves on. It's not one of the most dramatic sequences of the 1980s. It's a cheap sham designed to look like drama. (Though this problem is perhaps only really evident when it's juxtaposed with the next story.) It's a sequence designed to rile up controversy—the exact sort of death scene that would be created by an executive who believes that art should "soothe, not distract." It's there to make people watching the show feel like they're watching serious drama without making any effort at being serious drama. Just like the supposed emotional plot arcs all season have been the hollow shells of character drama instead of actual character drama.

So, fine. Thrill at the reasonably well-done action sequences. Enjoy the hell out of Davison's and Sutton's acting around Adric's death, which really is, in both cases, damn good. Even enjoy the ridiculous macho posturing of David Banks as Cyber Leader if you want. Take your guilty pleasure from it. Fine. But at the end of the day, this is Doctor Who for people who read *The Sun*, two weeks before it becomes horrifyingly clear what that really means.

## Our Mode of Conveyance is Irrelevant (*Time-Flight*)

It's March 22nd, 1982. The Goombay Dance Band are at number one with "Seven Tears," and stay there all story. Derek and the Dominos, ABC, and Bucks Fizz also chart. Lower in the charts are Flock of Seagulls with "I Ran" and U2 with "A Celebration." While in real news, the Vietnam Veterans Memorial has a groundbreaking ceremony. In less American news, the Canada Act passes the British Parliament, giving Canada the power to amend their own constitution instead of having to ask Britain to do it. In similarly partially-UK news, *Chariots of Fire* wins Best Picture at the Academy Awards, beating *Raiders of the Lost Ark*. *Time Bandits*, in hindsight the actual best film of 1981, was not nominated.

But for me it's about a decade later, and we're on scratchy VHS tapes from PBS again. Because *Time-Flight* was my first Peter Davison story, and one of the earliest Doctor Who stories I ever watched. Which sets up an interesting situation. *Time-Flight* is, after all, absolutely hated. Apparently the worst story of the Davison era by some margin, and the fifth worst of all time if the Mighty 200 poll is to be believed, which, of course, it shouldn't.

One of the nice things about watching Doctor Who as a child with only the Peter Haining book to go by is that you simply don't know things like that. I could identify broad eras of Doctor Who that I didn't care for as much as others, but even the Pertwee era, the one I actively liked least as a child, was fun. I was disappointed whenever a tape turned out to be Pertwee stories, but I still eagerly watched the whole thing. The idea that there were crappy Doctor Who stories besides *The Gunfighters* (which I hadn't seen, of course) isn't one that occurred to me until much later in life, specifically when I discovered that this story and the next were widely hated. So when I watched this as a child I didn't hate it. It didn't occur to me to hate it. It was Doctor Who. I liked Doctor Who. So I liked it.

To some extent, of course, there is an immature naiveté to this approach. Uncritical viewing is problematic. Of course, I wasn't wholly uncritical at age ten—I knew I liked Doctor Who and that I didn't like other things. But assuming that something is good just because it says "Doctor Who" at the beginning is still fundamentally uncritical. Equally, though, there's a difference between growing to dislike something like *The Celestial Toymaker* (which I had no idea wasn't the classic I'd been told until I watched it and realized which use of "celestial" was in play) because there's something fundamental about the story you didn't realize, and growing to dislike something like *Time-Flight* because you've stopped being able to enjoy something in the way that you used to.

(All of which said, there's a racial issue in *Time-Flight* that I should quickly deal with, having just compared it favorably to *The Celestial Toymaker*. Kalid is an appalling racial stereotype of a character. Yes, he's not actually a character but is instead a disguise for the Master, but given that the audience is meant to take pleasure in the Master's endless disguises, this hardly helps.)

I've talked very briefly in past essays about the idea of redemptive readings, and as we step closer and closer to the "bad part" of the classic series this becomes a more immediate concern. So let's use the example of the turkey of the Davison era to sort out a matter of aesthetic principle that's been quietly underlying this blog from day one: it is preferable, given the choice among reasonable arguments, to like a piece of art rather than to dislike it.

The underlying logic here is straightforward. Any argument for the worth of art is an affirmative argument, not a negative one. That is to say, on the whole we value art because of what good art does, not because of what bad art does. If you care about art, you care about good art. And thus, all things being equal, an argument that something is good is preferable to an argument that something is bad.

Now, of course, all things are not always equal. *The Celestial Toymaker* is overtly and destructively racist. There's no way around that. Arguing that *The Celestial Toymaker* is good art anyway means that you have to argue that its virtues are sufficient to justify its appalling racism, and that's an essentially impossible lift. In a lesser example, *The Invisible Enemy* really just doesn't give you much of anything to hang a "good art" argument on. I'd love to like *The Invisible Enemy*, but when there's absolutely nothing to base that argument on... well, I'd love to be able to psychically cure cancer too, but alas, reality intrudes.

But there is also a vast array of grey areas within aesthetics in which one is left with multiple sets of standards by which one can plausibly judge a work of art. *The Chase* is a good example. There are many, many sound arguments under which one can conclude that *The Chase* is rubbish. But there also turns out to be one under which *The Chase* is a remarkably compelling piece of postmodernism. Given that all of these arguments are plausible, it is my assertion that one ought pick the one that makes *The Chase* good.

This is what I call a redemptive reading—the active decision to try to like something. The risk here is that one becomes uncritical. And that's what a redemptive reading always has to fight against. A good redemptive reading should actively attempt to overcome every argument against the quality of a text. This isn't about blindly liking all art, but rather about carefully liking as much art as possible—about doggedly arguing on the side of aesthetic quality against all comers. Sometimes you're defeated; sometimes there's an argument against a text's quality that you just can't refute. But you should try, I think, and that's a central premise of how I approach Doctor Who.

All the same, we're entering a period of Doctor Who where that does become, in the general case, impossible. Material reality intrudes. The series fails in concrete and measurable ways. Getting cancelled is necessarily a failure case for television. And while the failure could viably be seen as existing anywhere along the production line—it doesn't have to be a failure on the part of the producer or script editor, for instance—it still means something went wrong, whether in the making of the show or in its paratextual elements.

So somewhere in the course of the next three seasons of essays we need to come up with an account of what went wrong. But we also ought try to minimize the damage, if you will. If we can manage it, we should favor an account of the 1980s in which we have to dislike as little of Doctor Who as possible. And so, against all consensus, I propose the following heresy: it's wiser to dislike *Earthshock* and appreciate *Time-Flight* than it is to like *Earthshock* and condemn *Time-Flight*. *Earthshock*'s flaws are indicative of an aesthetic approach to Doctor Who that is outright flawed—a belief that Doctor Who should be something that it is not only ill-suited to but that is on the face of it inferior to other possible models for what Doctor Who can be. *Time-Flight*'s flaws, on the other hand...

Well, let's tick them off. It looks cheap. Yes, indeed, it does. But again, as sins of science fiction go, cheap isn't the worst option on the table. Cheap is at least interpretable within the general realm of what science fiction television is. We might manage some sort of critique on the grounds that the story itself seems to avoid taking itself seriously, giving you an airline crew that rather campily disbelieves in the cheap-looking ancient world, insisting that they're still in London. But again, there's a frame of reference that works here. Almost everyone plays their part straight, and where there are problems it's that everyone is just a little too eager to take the cheap sets seriously. But the story is in on its own joke, and just as the Williams era was able to get away with this sort of double-layered meaning, so does this.

The difference is that where the Williams era all too often found itself hamming it up to compensate for a weak script, here the script is actually functional in its own right. Over the course of its hundred minutes *Time-Flight* manages to move among several ideas and reversals, most of them interesting. Disappearing airplanes works as a story. Evil sorcerers in the ancient past works as a story. The Master trying to take advantage of an ancient race of aliens works as a story. The final part—an extended sequence of TARDIS repairs—is the weakest link, but we've got a story here that moves confidently through a large number of ideas while maintaining a pleasant grin about the sillier aspects of it. It's got a whiff of Bob Baker and David Martin about it, but there's never the sense of ideas being abandoned before they're allowed to develop.

Even the Master isn't that problematic. Yes, his scheme is bonkers, but it's so recognizable as a villainous scheme that it doesn't have to make much sense. The fact that he has zero motivation whatsoever to dress up as an Arabian sorcerer just isn't that big a problem—dressing up in outlandish disguises is the sort of thing that black-hatted villains do. It's completely consistent with the narrative codes this story is operating under.

Which leaves the complaint that it follows *Earthshock*. Admittedly, for me at age ten, it didn't. It came out of nowhere on its own, and the bits about Adric made no real sense to me. Nevertheless, it is, I think, the most substantial of the many criticisms. Certainly in terms of the dramatic structure of the season, it was an incompetent decision, leaving the image of "cheap and silly" in the public's mind for the nine-month season break instead of leaving a flawed but nevertheless dramatic character death. These days, the idea that you'd end a season with your silly fluff story instead of your big crashing epic is inconceivable. And it should have been so in 1982. Still, that's a fault of the running order more than it's a fault of *Time-Flight* as such.

And amidst all the problems there are things to appreciate. This is the first Davison-era story to actually have room for all of its main characters in the plot. We have Sarah Sutton finding new ways to simultaneously convey strength and vulnerability with Nyssa, and Davison showing that he really can make anything look convincingly suspenseful. Even Janet Fielding is starting to show that she can work as a companion. All she really needs is to leave her dire "lost stewardess" concept behind and instead become someone who wanted to travel the world and only to find something far more wonderful to travel. And between this story and the next one, that gets accomplished too.

So we have a functioning TARDIS crew having an interesting and plausibly fun adventure. Now, there are things going direly wrong with Doctor Who in 1982, slowly but surely. And indeed, there are things in *Time-Flight* that directly contribute to this, most obviously the idiotic decision to make it the season finale. It is, admittedly, a deeply flawed story, albeit one with some cool ideas. But it's difficult to escape the sense that most of the stick this story gets is from the same people who want to pretend that *Earthshock* successfully recreates *Aliens* on a BBC budget, and as such their biggest problem with *Time-Flight* is that it's an unmistakable reminder that *Earthshock* is not actually what Doctor Who does. What Doctor Who does, and more to the point what *Time-Flight* does, is put together a series of interesting ideas that don't seem like they should go together on a screen in a way that has its an intelligible logic to it and a cast that's fun to watch. Does anyone seriously not want to know what the people who came up with "Arabian sorcerer kidnapping a Concorde into ancient history to harness the power of Jekyll and Hyde aliens" are going to come up with next?

Well, yes. But only people who already know what's next.

## Time Can Be Rewritten: *Spare Parts*

Although the books all have essays on Big Finish stories, this was the first one I covered on the blog itself, simply because I felt like I should start with a "proper" Big Finish audio from their most distinguished line. This, in other words, is not something I threw in as a bonus for book readers, but something I considered (and consider) to be an essential part of understanding the Davison era, even though it came out decades later. So it is, perhaps, worth starting by talking about what Big Finish is.

This is especially important in the context of the Nathan-Turner years, because Big Finish is in many respects the crowning achievement of the professional fan industry—a bunch of people so good at fan-made Doctor Who audios and audio adaptations of some of the Virgin books (with the Doctor taken out) that they managed to secure a license in 1999 to do original Doctor Who audios. This is important in several regards. First, it led to a considerably muddier sense of what current Doctor Who was in the half-decade before the return of the series. During the Virgin era there was one official continuation of Doctor Who: the New Adventures. You could love them or hate them, but they were the quasi-official Doctor Who. Their replacement with the BBC Books line was controversial enough in its own right, but the fact that the BBC Books line took a turn into the massively controversial a year after Big Finish started and that six months later Big Finish began its own line of 8th Doctor stories meant that for the bulk of the McGann years there were two barely compatible versions of "new Doctor Who" being made.

Second, like the Virgin books, Big Finish has had a visible and explicit impact on the new series. Two stories—Rob Shearman's *Jubilee* and this one—were consciously adapted into television stories, and the line is given explicit acknowledgment in the Paul McGann regeneration short, *Night of the Doctor*. Big Finish staff have also worked on the program (more about this in a moment), and, perhaps most impressively, Big Finish has managed to retain the rights to produce audios to this day, recently expanding their license to include *Torchwood* and the Kate Stewart version of UNIT. On top of that, there is a genuinely touching element of public service to their existence. Big Finish in effect provides a retirement home for former Doctor Who actors. Its creative merits aside—and there are, in fact, many creative merits—the fact that it gives a modest paycheck to a large number of people who have contributed substantially to Doctor Who, and that it does this by giving them creative work instead of putting them on exhibit in convention halls, is a genuinely good thing. The Big Finish line is genuinely important to the story of Doctor Who—you simply can't cover the beginnings of the new series without also stopping off and talking about things like *Jubilee* and, well, *Spare Parts*.

Right. Intro material sorted, onto the good stuff. The first and most striking thing, when listening to *Spare Parts*, is how maddeningly possible it is. Marc Platt wrote for Doctor Who just seven years after the period we're talking about. The media technology needed to make this story's basic concept—a true return of the original *Tenth Planet*-style Cybermen—sensible and coherent is just a few years off. The style of writing here is firmly in the tradition laid out by *Kinda*. It's not quite true that this story could have actually been made in 1982, but it's so very, very close to true as to actively hurt.

Because *Spare Parts* is a tour de force. It is a triumphantly good story that illustrates brutally what the move to a more continuity-aware vision of Doctor Who should have been. It uses the history of Doctor Who to tell a story that is only possible with a large amount of mythos feeding into it instead of one that treats the history of the show as intrinsically worth repeating. It's character-based, it has dramatic moments that put the supposed drama of *Earthshock* to shame, and it's one of the best Doctor Who stories covered in *TARDIS Eruditorum* so far.

It's impossible not to constantly compare *Spare Parts* to *Earthshock*, so let's just embrace it. First, let's notch one last complaint I had about *Earthshock* but left out of that essay because it was already getting long and I knew I had this one coming. The Cybermen in *Earthshock* suck. They are nothing but puissant robots who strut around and gloat. Nothing of the original horror in their concept is retained. They are the blandest and most interchangeable of monsters imaginable, treated in such a way as to fundamentally undermine the basic logic of bringing them back.

I bring this up because *Spare Parts* is the return of the Cybermen. The real Cybermen. The ones who killed the Doctor in 1966. The most striking aspect of this is the mind-wrenchingly bold decision to actually reproduce the Cybermen voices from *The Tenth Planet*. This, in turn, brings us to Nicholas Briggs, who makes fairly regular appearances across the Big Finish line doing various monster voices, and is good enough at it that he got brought on as the voice of several monsters in the new series. And this is one of his absolute triumphs.

What is extraordinary about Briggs's monster voices is that he is capable of taking the design of a monster voice and then making it do things well in excess of the distinctive scariness it was actually made for. His Daleks are extraordinary in this regard—one of the most astonishing moments in Doctor Who comes in Rob Shearman's *Dalek* when the Dalek screams in pain. The moment works not just because that's not something a Dalek is supposed to do conceptually, but because of the frisson of hearing the iconic Dalek voice doing something it was never made to do while still retaining all of its iconic power. And that uncanny fusion is all down to Nicholas Briggs.

Here he manages to take the sing-song voices of the original Cybermen and weaponize them. They were always compelling in part because they were a perverse parody of human speech, but Briggs spends the audio constantly finding new ways to push them. They remain ridiculous, but they rapidly become a genuinely scary sort of ridiculousness that leaves you laughing nervously at them.

This frees up the Cybermen to be what they were always supposed to be—twisted parodies of humanity instead of iconic monsters. Throughout *The Tenth Planet* the basic horror of the Cybermen is, "What the HELL is that thing?"—a threat that is lost in every subsequent appearance of them when they simply become, "Oh cool, Cybermen." But here it's back, with the Cybermen being made horrifying and shocking simply by going back to their original, rejected form.

Similarly, effort is constantly made to make the Cybermen a natural outcropping of Mondasian culture. For instance, Mr. Hartley has a chest-box despite still being human, establishing the Cybermen as the endpoint of a gradual cultural shift. Similarly, the name "Cyberman" is not here a monster name but a variant of the Mondasian pattern of job descriptions—the story also features Sistermen and Doctormen. Mondas is similarly played as a twisted reflection of Earth—we continually see a celebration that sounds identical to Christmas only to find out late in the story that all of the symbols of Christmas serve double duty as symbols about the long, dark journey of Mondas through the night. All of this works to restore the Cybermen as our qlippothic doubles. (The establishment that it's the formation of the moon that cast Mondas off into the darkness is, for those interested in the occult symbolism of the Cybermen, as great as their weakness to gold.)

There are two important things to note about this. The first is that it sets up a gleefully savage twist as it turns out that the Doctor is, in fact, the template for the design of the Cybermen. On the surface this sounds like a lame variant of the "the Doctor helped create the Time Lords" idea that is at once inevitable and depressing. But Platt (largely responsible for that twist as well) pitches it differently, making the Doctor's role in the creation of the Cybermen a tragic and inadvertent accident borne of being in the wrong place at the wrong time. But the result creates a compelling circularity with *The Tenth Planet*. The Doctor doesn't realize that the Cybermen are, in fact, his own dark mirror. Of course their energy destroys him. Hartnell's regeneration becomes literally reframed as him being killed by the future of the franchise.

Second and more important is the relationship this has with continuity in general. This is something I've poked at for several essays, but here we can firmly set it up as a narrative principle in contrast with *Earthshock*. Undoubtedly both *Spare Parts* and *Earthshock* rely on references to past Doctor Who stories. But there's a very, very big difference and the role of the Cybermen in them illustrates it. *Earthshock* is based on the premise that seeing the Cybermen again is inherently worthwhile. That is to say, the references to the past are an end in themselves. *Spare Parts* references the past, but goes further by having something to say about the past. It doesn't just treat playing with old Doctor Who concepts as intrinsically entertaining, but as a springboard to look at the nature of the concepts and as a source of dramatic tension (by having the implicit possibility that stopping the Cybermen from existing would save Adric). The former is masturbatory and doomed. The latter, on the other hand, is a type of storytelling that is only possible when dealing with mythic characters with a lot of history. The fact that you can do a story like *Spare Parts* in Doctor Who is a reason why Doctor Who itself is valuable instead of the basic premise of an anthology time travel show with a new setting every story. Because you can't do *Spare Parts* with Inspector Space-Time.

This sense of drama gets at the second reason why *Spare Parts* is miles better than *Earthshock*. *Earthshock*'s big dramatic moment—the death of Adric—is an ersatz simulacrum of drama. It acts like drama without actually risking being compelling. Compare it, then, to the scene in which Yvonne, partially processed as a Cyberman, returns home to show off her uniform to her family. Apart from being the best use of the Cybermen voices in the entire story (and I'm not actually sure if Cyber-Yvonne is voiced by the same actress who voices her regularly or by Briggs) it's a moment that is just horrendously upsetting. I was at that point in the audio while I was first writing this essay when I happened to take a ride with my wife in the car, and she ended up hearing it. She's a new series fan, so familiar with the Cybermen, but had heard none of the audio leading up to that point. But without any context whatsoever beyond about two sentences of "here's what's going on" she was still floored and horrified by the sequence. It packs more dramatic punch with a character who has only appeared for two episodes—with a character you don't even have to have met at all—than two seasons of buildup prior to the death of Adric could ever have.

The sense of character extends beyond this. Nyssa's plotline fundamentally depends on her kindness and desire to help others, the Doctor repeatedly makes poor decisions because of his own internal conflicts over what he should or shouldn't do to stop the Cybermen, and the secondary characters have motivations and personalities that inform what they do, most obviously within the Hartley family. And Platt is willing to push characters to genuine emotional extremes—Doctorman Allen angrily drinking herself to oblivion is a deliciously extreme emotional high that serves as an effective reminder that intensity in drama matters.

This also gets at the third thing that *Spare Parts* and *Earthshock* both do, one brilliantly and the other ineptly. *Earthshock*, largely by accident, involves itself visibly in the politics of its time by presenting an image of the military. I say largely by accident because the early Nathan-Turner era is fairly deliberately apolitical, but on the other hand, there is no such thing as apolitical fiction. When you represent real-world institutions, whether directly or allegorically, you make political comments. (This is a point driven home repeatedly by *The Unfolding Text*, to its credit—they absolutely eviscerate Terrance Dicks for trying to claim that the Peladon stories were apolitical.) *Earthshock* does this without thinking about it, and as a result ends up lending moral support to principles that rapidly showed themselves to be genuinely horrific.

*Spare Parts*, on the other hand, is written by one of Andrew Cartmel's merry band of anti-Thatcherite radicals and it shows. Platt is writing about a society in crisis and about the terrible things that people use crises to justify doing. He is writing about the ways in which government secrecy and keeping things from the people allows things to be done in the name of the people that would never be done if the people could weigh in and see each incremental step. *Spare Parts* is not an overt political screed about the time it's written in or the time it's set in. But there's a materialism to it—a commitment to the ideas of social realism that have animated Doctor Who at its best—that is direly lacking in *Earthshock* and that is why *Earthshock* is almost sociopathic in its approach to the world.

So what we have here is a story with something to say about our world that says it through genuine character and drama and that could only be told within the structure of Doctor Who. If this isn't what Doctor Who is fundamentally for—the reason why we still have it fifty years later—I honestly don't know what is. *Spare Parts* is straightforwardly an example of why the show exists.

Unfortunately, one of the stories—not the only story, but one of them—that goes on over the next four seasons of Doctor Who is the story of a series that tries desperately to get from where it is to what this audio is doing and finally makes it only to find out that it was too late to save itself. How fitting that this is basically the plot of *Spare Parts* as well.

## Pop Between Realities, Home in Time for Tea: *The Cleopatras*

Defense of *Time-Flight* aside (and the looming complete lack of defense of *Arc of Infinity* aside as well), watching Doctor Who in the John Nathan-Turner era often involves a fair amount of staring incredulously at the screen and bewilderedly asking, "What the hell were you people thinking?" This is somewhat odd. *Time-Flight* is not, in point of fact, worse made than *The Power of Kroll*, to pick one of five or six examples from the Graham Williams era that people are far more willing to defend. Nothing *Arc of Infinity* does to Gallifrey is prima facie stupider than *The Invasion of Time*. The Black Guardian is no more of a ham sandwich in *Mawdryn Undead* than would be expected given his servant in *The Armageddon Factor*. And yet what is defensible, if not necessary forgivable, under Graham Williams is a source of incredulity under Nathan-Turner.

There are reasons for this. We've just wrapped 1982 in the series. Defending it because it compares reasonably well to Doctor Who five years before increasingly doesn't wash. On top of that there is a question of overall aesthetic. The Graham Williams era was cheap and silly, yes, but it was cheap and silly within an aesthetic that could at least tolerate cheap and silly. John Nathan-Turner eviscerated the Williams era, denounced cheap silliness, and touted his ability to deliver serious-mindedness and increased production values.

You can't do that and *Time-Flight*. Even if *Time-Flight* is argued to work, it surely doesn't work according to the principles and aesthetics that John Nathan-Turner espoused, does it?

And then one watches *The Cleopatras*. Airing on the same nights as the Tuesday episodes of *Snakedance*, *Mawdryn Undead*, *Terminus*, and *Enlightenment*, *The Cleopatras* manages the previously almost unimaginable task of making the John Nathan-Turner era look, if not immediately sensible, at least wholly consistent with the overall approach television was taking. But to get at *The Cleopatras* one has to start with *The Borgias*. *The Borgias* was a 1981 attempt at historical costume drama in the vein of *I Claudius*. It was also an unmitigated disaster that essentially killed the genre. Fast forward two years and you have *The Cleopatras*, the BBC's effort to revamp the genre as... well, it's not entirely clear they got that far.

It's key to remember, when watching *The Cleopatras*, that it is not a joke. Indeed, all the elements of seriousness are here. The writer, Philip Mackie, was an acclaimed writer with a history of successful costume dramas, most obviously ITV's 1968 *The Caesars*. The cast is impeccable—though somewhat oddly most of the highlights seem to have associations with either Doctor Who or Harry Potter. On the Doctor Who side of the ledger you've got John Bennett (Chang in *Talons of Weng-Chiang*), Christopher Neame (Skagra in *Shada*), Graham Crowden (Soldeed in *The Horns of Nimon*), and Ian McNiece (eventual Winston Churchill) in fairly substantial rolls, plus Patrick Troughton in a maddeningly small cameo. Whereas on the Harry Potter side you've got Richard Griffiths and Robert Hardy, or Vernon Dursley and Cornelius Fudge if you prefer. Everything about the people making this, their track records, and their stated objectives, points towards this being a completely serious effort at legitimate drama. The trouble is that when you watch it you basically get River Song's impersonation of Cleopatra in *The Pandorica Opens* extended over eight fifty-minute episodes.

Like Doctor Who in the same period, its reception was decidedly mixed. But the basic existence of the show means that we have to approach the John Nathan-Turner era differently than we might have expected. After all, so much of *The Cleopatras* is familiar to someone who follows the John Nathan-Turner era. Both attempt drama via a focus on artifice and spectacle, both have a sort of tawdry love of the lurid, and both have something of a fondness for taking really good actors and putting them in mildly questionable roles. Even if both are also, in hindsight, not entirely successful, the fact that both happened means that we cannot treat the frailties of the Nathan-Turner era as merely being indicative of the flaws of Nathan-Turner himself.

So what the heck is this apparent aesthetic?

That's not an entirely easy question. An initial clue can be gleaned from looking at the musical charts during these eight weeks. Obviously we'll do that over the course of the four essays coinciding with *The Cleopatras*, but the short form is that we're at the pinnacle of the Second British Invasion in music. Bands like Kajagoogoo are hitting number one around here. This is a moment in music history that requires far more than a passing mention, but one important thing to observe is that the music of the time marks the complete mainstreaming of the synthesizer as a major instrument in pop music. Synthesizers were absolutely everywhere in early 1983.

The implications of this are fairly straightforward. Synthesizers were, by this point, no longer tangibly strange— they'd been around for years. But that doesn't mean they'd lost their overt artificiality. That is, in fact, the point here— the popular music of early 1983 demonstrated the degree to which the overtly artificial had become completely normal. This ties in with the rise of the music video in the US prompted by the launching of MTV. Music was now packaged in artificiality and visual spectacle. What had previously been the province of specific subcultures—glam, punk, and so on—had become a general phenomenon. Everybody and everything looked willfully strange in the world of pop, and not willfully strange in a more or less defined look. The world had rediscovered performativity in a big way.

The shift involved here did not apply exclusively to music. The personal computer was increasingly recognized as the next big thing even before anyone really had a very firm idea what the heck it did. Nor did this shift restrain itself to the self-consciously new. A year earlier *Chariots of Fire* had won Best Picture by combining a 1920s period piece with a (desperately cloying in hindsight) synthesizer soundtrack—a more significant antecedent of *The Cleopatras* than is normally appreciated. And the release of Quantel Paintbox in 1981 suddenly meant that manipulating video images in a variety of ways was wildly easy, meaning that anything could look like *Tron* if it wanted to.

*Tron*, actually, is a good touchstone here, because it illustrates one other key thing to realize about all of this. Or, more accurately, it's just about the only counter-example to something that's key to realize about all of this. In 1980 John Nathan-Turner reinvented Doctor Who in part by becoming more overtly cinematic. But by 1983 television and cinema were in a period of divergence instead of convergence. The culprit here is largely Quantel Paintbox, actually. As video effects became increasingly easy to do in television they began, unsurprisingly, to look increasingly common. What this meant was that television was starting to acquire a distinct visual look unto itself.

This look was not "cinematic realism," though to be fair, the "realism" part of that phrase was always a bit of a misnomer. The idea that the video effect looks "cheaper" than cinema is really just a variation on the already strained film/video distinction. Video effects are associated with looking cheap and superficial because they were television effects, not film effects—not because of any actual inherent visual difference.

But that doesn't mean that the "cheap" tag didn't stick. This moment of divergence was, in the end, fighting against the inevitable gravity of television and film collapsing into a single medium that the growing home video market heralded. This flair-up of bizarre video effects in the early 80s is, in many ways, the last gasp of television having an identity other than "little film." (Though arguably we're currently at a point where film is struggling desperately to manage an identity other than "big television.") The visual characteristics and logic of *The Cleopatras* and Doctor Who in this era make complete sense, though, when you take them as an active attempt to think about what television could do in the artificial and visibly superficial aesthetics of the 1980s. It didn't take, though. It couldn't possibly, as I said. The idea of television as something that aspired to be film was too firmly embedded.

But this is, for several reasons, a real pity. First of all, television trying to be film is what produces *Earthshock*. But second of all, television trying to be television in 1983 produces *The Cleopatras*. Which is, in fact, terribly good. Philip Mackie has talked about the "horror-comic" tone he went for, and it's a good description of what's going on here. *The Cleopatras* is as chock-full of poisonings and murders as *I Claudius*, but what's interesting about *The Cleopatras* is that when people are casually hacked to pieces it usually happens in a delightfully tiny little sequence. The norm is that a visual effect creates a screen-within-a-screen, we see a brief and hazy clip of the murder, and then we go back to people talking to each other.

This sort of aggressive underselling of the drama is typical of the series. A strong contender for my favorite moment of the series comes when Fluter, one of the later kings, casually orders the execution of his daughter and, when someone expresses shock, he dryly notes that he has other daughters, apparently seeing the number of backups available as the only significant impediment. Though frankly almost anything involving Richard Griffiths's Potbelly, aka Ptolemy VIII, is a strong contender. Griffiths plays the character with delightful over-the-top sadism, loving every minute of casually having large swaths of the population executed. (A second contender for favorite—and the one that convinced me that I was going to have to watch all eight episodes instead of my usual practice of taking a sampler for one of these essays—is the one in which Potbelly orders the execution of all of the Jews. Notably, he instructs a pair of Jews to carry it out, and when they hesitate he notes that they can just have themselves killed once they get it all set up.)

The lurid superficiality of it all serves to highlight the way in which the viewer actually enjoys these historical dramas. The entire selling point is the fact that powerful people are going to do terrible, terrible things to other people and alternately get away with it or get spectacular comeuppances. Or, more accurately, it's the juxtaposition of lurid events with serious acting and BBC production values. So the usual means of showing someone's murder—having serious character actors doing a scene, only to have a little sub-screen pop up in which something lurid happens—is absolutely delightful. It's a case of giving the audience exactly what they want so blatantly as to expose the absurdity of it in the first place.

The question is whether there's more to be done in this aesthetic. I mean, although overt superficiality and aggressive performativity can and does work, it's not entirely clear that it has a long shelf-life. Or, actually, let's be more accurate. It has an enormously long shelf life that continues to this day, but only when merged more with the structures of traditional Aristotelian drama. To be fair, *The Cleopatras* largely accomplishes this, merging its willful luridness with a set of serious actors who manage to ground it in what is recognizable as serious drama.

And this is where Nathan-Turner's approach does let him down. Beryl Reid, whose turn in *Earthshock* I didn't talk about, is indicative. She's a good actress. But the role he shoves her into is a bizarre choice. The result is deeply entertaining, and from a certain perspective the best thing about the story, but one gets the sense that the program is not having the same fun its viewers are. Elsewhere, in his defense, he manages it. Casting Richard Todd in *Kinda* was a stroke of genius, for instance. But by and large his larger problem is that he fails to figure out how to wed the willfully superficial production style he favors to actual storytelling, not that the overall style he's pursuing in 1983 is wrong at the time. Yes, he's going to hold to the style for far, far too long. And yes, his deficiencies in drama are always going to be a problem for him. But the fact remains—the overall whole of what Doctor Who is trying to be in 1983 is not, on the face of it, wrong.

## You Ask Me To Appreciate It (*Arc of Infinity*)

It's January 3rd, 1983. Renée and Renato are at number one with "Save Your Love," which is... a song. Phil Collins removes it from number one in the second week of this story with "You Can't Hurry Love." Culture Club, Men at Work, Madness, Malcolm McLaren and the World's Famous Supreme Team, and David Bowie and Bing Crosby also chart.

In real news, ooh, we get to do a big wrap-up since last time, don't we? OK. So there's the Falklands, obviously. Canada fully patriates its constitution and achieves full political independence from the UK. Ronald Reagan addresses a joint session of the British Parliament. There's a World Cup. England does well in its first group stage, then manages a series of two 0-0 draws in its second group stage, knocking it out of the tournament. The Equal Rights Amendment fails, to the delight of Phyllis Schlafly, who is basically the American version of Mary Whitehouse. (Like all American adaptations of British source texts, she is bigger, louder, and stupider.) The queen's bodyguard, Michael Trestrail, resigns over excessive use of male prostitutes. The first lethal injection is carried out in Texas, the first emoticons are posted, and *Time Magazine*'s Man of the Year is the computer.

Also, at this particular moment in time I am exactly one hundred and sixteen days old, and this is the first episode of

Doctor Who to air in a world in which I exist. So I guess this is all my fault. Really, really sorry.

I talked, the last time we did a television story, about the way in which it is at times helpful to watch Doctor Who without remembering actively that there is such a thing as a bad story. And that's true to an extent. But another aspect of childhood watching of Doctor Who—or of any television series, really—is that rubbish episodes pass you by forgettably. *Time-Flight*, for all its flaws, was oddly memorable. *Arc of Infinity*, on the other hand? Here are my childhood memories of *Arc of Infinity*: it had Time Lords, it brought Omega back, and it had Colin Baker being as horribly unpleasant as I assumed his eventual Doctor would be. I remembered virtually nothing else about it. This, as it happens, is a very bad sign. While not every story that fails to make an impression as a kid is, in fact, wretched, it is striking just how often a failure to remember a story at all on my part coincides with it being a truly and epically awful one.

To be fair, of the things I did remember, I was not quite right about any of them. My initial dislike of Colin Baker was motivated purely by my parents badmouthing him on the grounds of his strangling Peri in *The Twin Dilemma*. In truth the character improved and was not as wretched as Commander Maxil, and it is by now clear that the problem with the character was not, in fact, Baker himself. On the other hand, good lord, Maxil is a wretched character. As for the Time Lords and Omega, well, we'll get there.

But other than that, this story left very little impression on me on first watching. Which means that whereas I could attempt a redemptive reading on *Time-Fight*, which I'd had a vague sense of it having been interesting, and spent much of the time watching it going, "Oh, yes, I remember this bit," in a vaguely satisfied way despite its glaring flaws, here I found myself with very few options. *Arc of Infinity* isn't even bad for interesting reasons. It's just bad. I said one ought do a redemptive reading if one can. But I can't. I just can't.

It is, at least, and this is about the extent of the defense I can muster, not awful in the way that *Earthshock* is awful. (Mind you, it's also not watchable in the ways that *Earthshock* is watchable.) It's not a betrayal of moral principles underpinning Doctor Who or anything like that. It's just thoroughly misconceived and badly done in a way that makes it difficult to even take seriously.

There was an interview with Gareth Roberts a while back in *Doctor Who Magazine* in which he suggested that there are no stories in the classic series that couldn't be saved by a good rewrite, using this as his limit case scenario—he suggested that even this story could have been saved by a Russell T. Davies rewrite and that the audience would be crying for Omega at the end. (Roberts tends to single out this story for particular criticism.) Which gets at about the one interesting thing I can think of to focus on with *Arc of Infinity*, so let's do it. Simply put, is there anything that is even remotely a good idea here? Not being one for suspense, I'll suggest that the answer is, "Yes, but barely."

Much like *Time-Flight* before it, we have a case of the program constructing what is, if nothing else, a unique set of genre tropes. The Amsterdam sections through the first three episodes are firmly in an exploitation horror genre about the terrible things that happen to tourists abroad—I think *Hostel* is roughly the most recent movie of significance to mine this territory, though horror isn't really my bag, genre-wise, so I may be missing something obvious. The Gallifrey sections are palace intrigue. And then there's a big cosmic event gloss on the whole thing that's all very mythic sci-fi. These three things do not go together. And yet here they are, all piled on top of one another.

The thing is, this is what Doctor Who does. This is the very definition of what the program is for, at least on the surface. But this raises a question—why put those particular three things together? What is the point of that juxtaposition? Or, more broadly, what's the point of using juxtaposition in the first place in Doctor Who? Because this story seems to demonstrate that it's not simply to put things together for the sake of it. In 1983 it can't be anymore—everything, as we saw last time, is doing that. The mere spectacle of juxtaposition doesn't cut it. So what does Doctor Who bring to juxtaposition?

The easiest way to answer that, of course, is to turn to the past. Which is exactly what *Arc of Infinity* does. To kick off the big 20th Anniversary celebration it goes and begins mining the series' past. Which, again, isn't the wrong decision. The 20th Anniversary is a perfect occasion to do the "here is what the program was and here is why that is still relevant today" moment. The problem is that *Arc of Infinity* gets it appallingly wrong. It thinks that the thing Doctor Who brings to the work of juxtaposing genres is Doctor Who itself. That the value of Doctor Who is that it's an effective frame for genre juxtaposition, so that's its point. So to bring three totally disparate genres together all you have to do is slather on a big, fat layer of Doctor Who.

Whereas the position of this blog, of course, is that the thing Doctor Who brings to genre juxtaposition is alchemy. And in *Arc of Infinity*, that, above all else, is exactly what's required. Specifically the principle of "As above, so below." The reason you peg together a mundane horror genre like "terrible things happen to tourists in Amsterdam" with the absurd pretension of a phrase like "arc of infinity" is to show a fundamental equivalence between them. You do the vast shifts of universes and ancient Gallifreyan history alongside tourist horror in order to show that the stories, at every level of the structure, are identical. You're going for *The Ribos Operation* here.

So what the story needs, more than anything in the world, is a dramatic hook that allows its three narrative levels to function in parallel. There needs to be something that operates similarly within the tourist horror, the political intrigue, and the basic cosmic arc of the universe. You can take your pick on what. It barely matters, just so long as there's something. The one that springs to mind for me as an obvious choice, at least, is the callousness of deflected responsibility. Because that's at least a theme that's just about there at every point in the story already. At the bottom of the totem pole you have the lack of interest or concern in Colin's fate on the part of authorities who see him as just another careless tourist. On Gallifrey you have the callous willingness to let the Doctor die simply because it's more convenient than the other options. And on the grand scale you have the basic failure of the Time Lords to ever take responsibility for the sacrifices involved in their own creation vis-à-vis the abandoned Omega. And the way you end it is by having the people at the bottom of the chain finally take some responsibility for the situation at the top. You have the characters at the Amsterdam end of the story stepping up and doing what nobody else in the universe has been willing to do. Or, if you want, you have it come from the top, making the story a redemptive arc for Omega—which it comes close to, actually, with its big Amsterdam runaround. Either would work. Hell, there's another dozen options you could come up with. You have loads of options.

But "anchor every piece of the story on nostalgia for its own sake" isn't one of them. Actually, no, let's be fair. The Amsterdam section isn't based on nostalgia. Its entire emotional hook is based on Tegan asserting that some dude who gets a grand total of twenty-one lines before being possessed is her favorite cousin. So that one is more emotional hook by fiat. The other two plotlines? The Gallifreyan politics matter purely because they're Gallifreyan politics, and the overall cosmic scheme of things matters entirely because it's Omega behind it.

Let's be clear here. I'm not saying these things matter for the same reasons that Gallifrey and Omega mattered in the past. I'm saying they matter purely because they are Gallifrey and Omega, which are both, apparently, magic words that instantly summon audience engagement. Or, at least, that's apparently the hope. And that in many ways is the most obnoxious problem with this story. I'm not going to bitch about dense continuity. I love references to past stories. The problem here is that there's not any actual references. I mean, just look at the scene where Omega's backstory is explained so that viewers know who he is and why they care.

Oh, right. There isn't one. There's one line from Chancellor Hedin about him, and that's it. It's difficult to stress just how idiotic this is. This is a character who has appeared once before in the series, a full decade prior to this story. Yes, the story re-aired a little over a year ago on BBC2, but that is not sufficient to just drop him in and expect that anyone in the audience is going to care. The show spends more time doing exposition dumps to help people that might have missed the Monday episode get up to speed with the Tuesday episode than it does catching up viewers who might have missed the episode that aired a decade ago. And the fact that it's Omega is the only thing that holds this part of the story together. One of the major throughlines of the story is, "Who is this mysterious figure trying to use the Doctor to break into our universe?" The answer isn't just underwhelming, it's pointless.

And the problem isn't that the answer is Omega. A story bringing Omega back makes, if not perfect sense, at least some sense. But they didn't bring Omega back. Omega was the original sin of the god-like Time Lords—the cast out inversion of all that the Doctor and his people were. Omega was an unthinkable menace that negated the very fabric of Doctor Who. This is just a pub quiz answer—"Who was the masked villain in *The Three Doctors*?"

The same problem applies to the Time Lords, brought back here only in their most abstract sketch of a form. Sure, they wear the right robes, have the right names and positions, talk about the right things like the Matrix. But these are not the Time Lords of *The Deadly Assassin*. They're not even the Time Lords of *The Invasion of Time*. What is the Matrix in this story? What is a biodata extract? They're nothing more than MacGuffins with familiar sounding names. The show is trusting absolutely that setting a story on what they call

Gallifrey will lend it dramatic weight, but nobody involved in this has even begun to think about what that means. Much like the death of Adric, this isn't drama, it's the desiccated corpse of drama. The vaguest shell made to look like drama but with no actual thought as to what is going on or what reasons there might be to care about it. There's no concept to Gallifrey. It's just a set of funny robes assumed to matter intrinsically. And it doesn't. It can't. Not like that.

There's a line of critique against Monty Python's musical *Spamalot*—really just Eric Idle's musical—that amounts to the accusation that a troupe whose comedy was once about transgression and surprise now amounts to nothing more than delivering lines that the entire audience has memorized and calling it comedy. Here we have Doctor Who doing the same thing, celebrating the abstract form of the past with no attention to what the past actually was.

Or more basically, this is the problem with the faux-drama of *Earthshock* extrapolated out to the entirety of the series. In *Earthshock*, at least, there was an attempt to provide the abstract shell of other things. Doctor Who was providing ersatz drama and ersatz action. But here we have that approach taken to its logical and horrific end: Doctor Who is now providing ersatz Doctor Who. It's no longer a show that's valuable for what it can do. It's not even valuable for what it once did. It's value, apparently, amounts to nothing more than its ability to quote itself without remembering what it was it meant.

Happy anniversary.

## The Void Beyond the Mind (*Snakedance*)

It's January 18, 1983. You can't hurry Phil Collins off the number one spot, but given time Men at Work dispatch him, replacing him with "Down Under." The lower portions of the charts are somewhat more optimistic, with Madness's "Our House" and Kajagoogoo's "Too Shy" both appearing. OK, optimistic might be selling that one a little too strong. But both are, at least, wholly valid guilty pleasures.

In real news, Klaus Barbie, who represents what is possibly the biggest disparity between quality of name and quality of human being in history, is arrested in Bolivia. Between the end of *Arc of Infinity* and this story the police manage to shoot a perfectly innocent man named Stephen Waldorf, seriously injuring him. The police officers involved are eventually cleared of attempted murder, despite shooting Waldorf five times (out of the thirteen tries), holding a gun to his head and calling him a cocksucker, and finally pistol-whipping him a bunch after finding out that they were out of ammo. Oops. In cheerier news, *Breakfast Time* debuts on the BBC, their first attempt at a morning program. The first broadcast passes without anybody being shot, pistol whipped, or called a cocksucker.

Elsewhere on television... *Snakedance*, I can vouch first hand, is one of those bits of Doctor Who that properly gets into your head and unnerves you. I'll admit to a longstanding distaste for mind-control plots, simply because I tend to just not like stories in which people are out of character—I tend to have a similar lack of enthusiasm for body-swap plots and the like. But as mind control plots go, Tegan's possession in this story is particularly creepy and memorable. And though the rubber snakes in it are still not great, the image of snake tattoos that crawl off of your flesh are downright fabulous.

It is in such a regard that I, as an adult, recognize it as a perfect piece of childhood Doctor Who—a story that is remembered vividly without being loved (and, of course, without being hated, either). Though it's by no means universally the case that these are the stories that then grow into beloved classics in adulthood, they're certainly prime candidates for it. And *Snakedance* is certainly an example of this. As a child, it gets in your head. As an adult, you see why it got in your head in ways that make it even more compelling.

Much of *Snakedance* involves taking conventions of Doctor Who and looking at them from slightly oblique angles. (A suitable hat tip here to Lawrence Miles, whose analysis of the story in *About Time* underpins much of this.) The story essentially takes what *The Daemons* tried and almost but not quite succeeded at, and inverts it. The point of *The Daemons* was, ostensibly at least, that the Doctor was acting against type—that the character who we would usually expect to be haranguing superstitious people was instead running around talking about how they can't open the crypt on Beltane. What Letts was trying to go for there was to make the Doctor seem at least partially unreliable or suspicious. It doesn't quite work, simply because using Jon Pertwee's Doctor as an unreliable character can't possibly work, but the idea is sensible and a variation on what the show frequently does, namely have the Doctor run around trying to convince everyone of terrible danger while nobody listens to him.

On the surface, at least, *Snakedance* appears to be a fairly standard execution of the trope that *The Daemons* is trying to play with—the Doctor runs around trying to convince everyone that there's terrible danger and nobody believes him. But under the hood there are some subtle changes. First of all, Manussa is, as Miles and Wood point out, unusually well developed as far as alien planets go. The script goes out of its way to give it little bits of character and color, and to make it feel like it has a real history. Second of all, everyone's performance is tuned in particular ways. Davison plays the part just a little more frantically so that we can see better than usual why people think he's crazy, whereas the Mannusans get outfitted with the set of tricks that smart people in science fiction get—they're far advanced beyond believing in the superstitious mythology of the ancient past. So a bunch of rationalists who act the way smart people in science fiction are supposed to act are taking on the Doctor, who is acting just a little crazier than usual.

The third change, and this, as Miles points out, is the kicker, is that the monster isn't a familiar part of mythology that turns out to have a Doctor Who explanation, it's a known Doctor Who monster that turns out to be a mythological figure. The combination means that we have a sort of double vision with regards to the plot. On the one hand we can see better than usual why the Doctor is mistrusted on the planet. On the other hand, our knowledge and the Doctor's knowledge coincide very well for this story. We know the Doctor is right, and we know a fair amount about the Mara. But we don't quite understand Manussan culture; we learn about it at the same speed the Doctor does. And so we're left seeing the Doctor's arrogance and naiveté while simultaneously knowing that he's right.

Much is made of the way in which Season Twenty has a recurring villain in every story—though to be fair, as I noted, it's actually every story from *Earthshock* through *Warriors of the Deep* that does this, not just Season Twenty, and it was an accident (albeit a telling one) that it happened in Season Twenty. But if Season Twenty is read as an active effort to engage with the series' past, this, at least, is an example of how to do it right: a story where the past history of Doctor Who is used to do a story that couldn't be told without it. It's the fact that we as viewers are already familiar with the Mara that provides the counterweight to the way in which the Doctor is made to seem hysterical and crazed. The viewers don't just have to trust that he's not, a la *The Daemons*. The fact that this is a known Doctor Who monster means that the viewers know the Doctor is right, which frees the story up to be almost completely unrepentant in making him look wrong. (Though the one real moment it gives him counter to that, where he figures out the Six Faces of Delusion mask, is absolutely delightful.)

This allows *Snakedance* to be something no previous story has ever really managed to be: a character piece for the Doctor. Not a thematic commentary on the Doctor (those are a dime a dozen) but a story in which the Doctor's character—who he is and how he acts—is central to the resolution of the story. Not surprisingly, given that they share an overt Buddhist inclination, it's the Pertwee era that works best to compare this to, most obviously with *Planet of the Spiders*. Not because of the obvious points of similarity like magic blue crystals, but because both stories work on a structure whereby the Doctor's attempts to defeat the villain throughout the story are fundamentally wrongheaded even though they're unquestionably right.

But again, where *Planet of Spiders* did this in a superficial way, eventually inventing a rather glib explanation about "greed for knowledge" to explain why the Doctor was doing it wrong, *Snakedance* manages to build it into the character. Davison's Doctor is intensely sympathetic, but is also typically written with a sort of exasperated impatience. By removing Tom Baker's overt bluster and scene-stealing from the role, Davison, in an odd way, makes the Doctor even more arrogant by opening up a larger gap between what he does and how he acts. Combined with Saward's addiction to "I'll explain later" as a line of dialogue, this makes Davison a Doctor with something approaching a real flaw.

And, of course, the crowning element here is the backdrop of Adric's death, coming as it did in part out of the

Doctor's ineffectual standing up to the Cybermen (followed by his resorting to brute force). The sort of ineffective bluster that the Doctor spends the majority of this story conducting is, in other words, recognizable to the audience a genuine failing on his part. But, crucially, and this is what makes Davison's Doctor such a good character, it's also still part and parcel of why we love the Doctor. Which is the heart of what's played on in *Snakedance*. We're on the Doctor's side. We want everyone to listen to him. But the nature of the story is that what he's doing just isn't going to work.

All of this means that Bailey is able to do what he couldn't in *Kinda*, which is to make the Buddhist aspect of the story sensible. However much the Mara parallels the devil— and as we talked about in the essay for *Kinda*, it was inevitable that it would—here the Doctor beats it the way he should have back in *Kinda*: by meditating and acknowledging but refusing to yield to it. Thus the Doctor wins not through bluster but by perseverance. It's exactly how a story like this is supposed to work—a much stronger execution of the approach than *Kinda*, and, more to the point, done with more ambition: making Tegan into the vehicle of a character arc was, frankly, somewhat easier than what *Snakedance* does with the Doctor, particularly less than two years after Tom Baker left the part.

That's not to say that the story is flawless. It illustrates better than any story to date why ditching the sonic screwdriver was a mistake with a third episode in which the Doctor is locked up for its entirety. Yes, he still manages to find things to do by solving mysteries and putting together pieces of plot, but it amounts to a flagrant effort to keep the Doctor from getting too close to actually resolving the plot before the big climax. This is the sort of laziness that the removal of the sonic screwdriver overtly encourages.

And Nyssa continues her staggering run as the best companion that nobody knows what to do with. To date, in her eleven stories as a companion, she's been stuck in the TARDIS virtually all story three times, introduced over halfway through another time, and possessed once. This time she gets to do things, but it's mostly straightforward "follow the Doctor around" duty of the most banal sort.

This gets at another problem that the Nathan-Turner era is increasingly running into, which is an overt aversion to competence. It's telling that of the three companions who came into Season Nineteen the first two that Nathan-Turner gets rid of are the two who are capable of doing more than getting in trouble and complaining loudly. This is not a knock against Tegan, who I largely like as a character, nor is it praise for Adric, but the degree to which the show is having to actively keep its characters from being too competent is troubling. In many ways *Snakedance* is not the real offender here—I should have railed against this with *Arc of Infinity*, which has an entire plot thread that depends on the Time Lords themselves being complete idiots.

But the real problem is how entrenched it's becoming in the Nathan-Turner era and how much trouble it has with characters who are actually competent. Nyssa is the last gasp of the idea that companions might be in some way competent or useful in their own right. Instead Nathan-Turner decides that he prefers companions who are "feisty." And so near to the end of her tenure it's just painful to see her underused like this, particularly in a story where her role has apparently been bolstered on her request. This is all the worse when one considers what's next: in her next story she takes stupid pills in a desperate attempt to draw out the Mawdryn plot. Then she gets to be a whimpering leper in a story that is ostensibly about her. Then she's gone. Pathetic, but in no way the fault of Sarah Sutton, who deserved so much better.

But on the whole it's the good side of the John Nathan-Turner era that shows up over these two weeks. A story that befits the occasion of the anniversary. *Arc of Infinity* was an ominous harbinger of how things are going to go terribly, terribly wrong. *Snakedance*, at least, is proof that they haven't actually yet.

## Time Can Be Rewritten: *Goth Opera*

The July 1994 launch of the Virgin Missing Adventures line was a strange moment in Doctor Who history. It's not as though it was the beginning of adding in extra adventures for past Doctors—that was in 1973. But there was an odd dissonance to the basic idea of it. The Virgin books were not exclusively experimental works that tried to push the limits of what Doctor Who could do, but they were certainly well enough known for it. And so the turn towards the Missing Adventures was, for the most part, a bit strange and uncertain. This level of actively rewriting the past had never really been tried before, and to have it done by a company with as much of a reputation for the avant-garde as Virgin seemed pregnant with possibilities, both good and bad.

In practice it rapidly became clear that the Missing Adventures, at least to start, were Virgin's attempt to better appeal to the so-called "trad" audience who were left cold by their more adventurous New Adventures line. (Or, as Paul Cornell put it in an interview from his "hilariously bitchy" days, to write for the line "you had to abandon any thoughts of originality.") But the launch of the line was interesting in this regard. July of 1994 had two releases—the debut Missing Adventure *Goth Opera* by Paul Cornell and a New Adventure called *Blood Harvest* by Terrence Dicks, with *Goth Opera* serving as a sequel to *Blood Harvest*. (Here, of course, we go in the other order, with *Blood Harvest* showing up next book.)

What's interesting about this is that Terrence Dicks is, for obvious reasons, the very definition of the "traditional" Doctor Who writer, whereas Paul Cornell was one of the leading lights of the New Adventures range. And, of course, they were flipped. Terrence Dicks, who had actually written the Fifth Doctor on television, wrote for the ostensibly weirder line while Cornell, at the time arguably the single most influential writer on the Seventh Doctor, wrote for the ostensibly traditional line.

Superficially, at least, the result of this was that both books were fairly traditional, with the Terrence Dicks aesthetic winning out over the weirder one. Certainly *Goth Opera* has its share of traditional moments, including a chapter that serves mostly to do some of the connective work between the two books, a beautifully fast-moving bit involving Romana that manages to, in rapid succession, heavily reference *The Five Doctors* and *Carnival of Monsters* prior to inserting a cameo from Sabalom Glitz. It so perfectly nails Dicks's style that I actually momentarily found myself composing a bit of this essay in my head before having to abandon the line of argument I was imagining once I remembered it was actually Cornell who'd written this book.

But this is unfair to what Cornell does here. Cornell's reputation in 1994 may have been for formal experimentation and "difficult" books, but this reputation was, if not misleading, at least only part of the picture. Cornell was, we can safely say at this point, one of the best writers to make their debut in the Virgin line. And more to the point, he was the earliest of them. His first novel was the fourth book in the line, he was the first writer to do a second book, and then he made it to three before any other writers had made it to two solo books.

But the formal experimentation isn't what set him apart from the other writers around him. Not really. It was there, and he used it well, but in hindsight, looking at his work beyond the New Adventures, it's relatively clear that his real talent lay in his character work. It's just that that wasn't nearly as flashy as his more experimental aspects. And it meant he was better suited to an assignment like this than he looked at first glance.

It's also the case that the assignment wasn't quite as straightforward as it appears. The idea that this could "fit seamlessly" between *Snakedance* and *Mawdryn Undead* is nonsensical in practice. First of all, it's set in 1993 and relies on the culture of the time: there are references to Morrissey, for instance, yet in early 1983 (the time of this story's pseudo-transmission) The Smiths had yet to release an album, let alone a single. More broadly, the entire book depends on the existence of goth subculture. It's a mashup of Doctor Who and Anne Rice, and though *Interview with a Vampire* had been published by 1983, it wasn't the big deal it would later be. By 1994, the film version was on its way and Anne Rice was nearing the height of her popularity.

In other words, the book is unmistakably a product of its time. As, of course, all the Missing Adventures are. Similarly, proleptic references to *The Five Doctors*, Sabalom Glitz, and, of course, *Blood Harvest* make it inevitable that this couldn't "really" be a 1983 story. But it's the content that is most significant, and it's here that it's worth thinking a bit about what the point actually is of such "missing adventures." I talked about this a little in the *Cold Fusion* essay, but that was more about why I care about missing adventures and why I do the Time Can Be Rewritten essays. From an artistic standpoint, what's the point of a missing adventure?

The answer, to some extent, has to be reparative. Gareth Roberts— probably the best writer to spend a lot of time on the task of missing adventures—is a useful illustration here. His pseudo-Graham Williams novels are overtly reparative: they're attempts to show how the Graham Williams era could have been done. Similarly, his Hartnell-era novel *The Plotters* is, in part, a deliberate queering of the Hartnell era—a historical that does the things that, thematically speaking, Hartnell-era historicals were perfectly suited to but that, for cultural and personal reasons, could never have been done at the time.

It's important to be clear about what this does and doesn't mean. Yes, missing adventures are inevitably about "fixing" past eras of Doctor Who. But this is a critique of the past, not a rejection of it. You don't write a novel queering the Hartnell-era historical on its own terms out of anything other than a genuine love for those terms. And indeed, in the same interview in which he snarked about the lack of originality in the Missing Adventures he also noted that the Davison and McCoy eras were the only two that he could really write for because those were the eras he loved.

Another way to look at the Missing Adventures, then, is that they're attempts to complete the eras they ostensibly belong to. As attempts, in other words, to take what the eras do and go further with it, capturing the sense of an era that can only be clear in hindsight. In this regard the claim that they fit "seamlessly" into the gaps of their eras is almost exactly the wrong phrase to use. They fit into the era precisely because the past of Doctor Who isn't seamless to begin with. Any era of Doctor Who that progresses from *Arc of Infinity* to *Snakedance* necessarily forgoes seamlessness. Adding these anachronistic texts that understand the era better than it can understand itself does not, obviously, remove the seaminess of the era. But it fits. At its best, a Missing Adventure is faithful to the era it's set in precisely by betraying those parts of the era that were already betraying itself.

And so the Davison era, in its high soap days, is the perfect place for Paul Cornell, eventual writer of *Casualty*, to be plying his craft. Here we have a writer who actually knows how to do soaps inserting a story into a soap era. We have a writer who gets that drama is defined by intensity, not by mimicry of the superficial form of drama, and who puts Nyssa through a properly epic emotional wringer. The idea of having Nyssa turned into a vampire is absolutely phenomenal. Nyssa lends herself to this sort of thing, which is an odd thing for me to say in some ways since I'm usually not the type to go, "Rah rah, let's put female characters through excessive torture so we can watch them suffer."

But in Nyssa's case it makes sense. Her first storyline was about a man wearing her father like a skin-suit and exterminating her entire race, and her reaction was the single biggest keeping-of-a-stiff-upper-lip in Doctor Who history. Yes, as I've said, there really should have been some sort of acknowledgment of this in a subsequent Master story, but Nyssa's character arc is, basically, that absolutely terrible things happen to her and she nobly endures them and then kicks ass. Nyssa is Doctor Who's version of Chuck Norris. In a velvet dress.

So the idea of making Nyssa into a vampire is perfect. It's exactly the sort of plotline the character deserves. She spends virtually the entire book simultaneously as an active character who does things and who has absolutely terrible things happen to her. Other than a somewhat unfortunate bit in which she apparently loses her cognitive abilities and decides trusting vampiric lords is a good idea because they're noble so they must be good (I'd ask if she was asleep during *Arc of Infinity*, except frankly, who could blame her for that), she's absolutely on fire in this book largely because the book is willing to actually push her character instead of blandly pretending to push it.

The Doctor does similarly well. The main antagonist in the story, Ruath, is a perfect sort of villain for Davison's Doctor—someone he left behind who, in their own view at least, has suffered for it. In the aftermath of Adric this cuts nicely, and it sets up a solid ending in which the Doctor's desire to try to let everyone save themselves and give everyone a chance is undercut by Nyssa ejecting Ruath out an airlock into deep space and the Doctor grimly admitting she was right. As for Tegan... well, if nothing else, the image of Tegan having true faith in the words of Primo Levi is very possibly the most unintentionally hilarious thing I've read in some time.

But all of this works in no small part because it's wholly consistent (well, aside from the Primo Levi bit) with how the Davison era is anyway. This was an era that tried to create soap-opera-like storylines for characters and built a TARDIS cast that was suited to emotional storytelling. Davison serves as the flawed patriarch, Tegan is Doctor Who's attempt at Hilda Ogden (this being Doctor Who, a middle-class Hilda Ogden), and Nyssa is a phenomenal soap character, as discussed. The era really does set the pieces out for the sort of thing that Paul Cornell does well. It just has an unsettling tendency to abandon them in favor of faffing about with Omega or something equally dumb.

There's a second aspect to *Goth Opera* that needs to be commented on, which is that Cornell goes to some length to work in an overt attack on the issue of satanic ritual abuse. This is an upsettingly dark period in the history of moral panics and psychology. In the mid-80s there was a fervor about the possibility that satanic cults were sexually abusing children as part of their rituals. They weren't, in no small part because satanic cults barely exist as a phenomenon in the first place, but this didn't stop the ensuing moral panic.

This is also not something that could have been commented on in 1983, in no small part because 1983 was roughly ground zero on the issue. Whereas by 1993 the tide of public opinion had mostly shifted and the consensus, not universally held, was that satanic ritual abuse didn't happen. But in this case the shift is subtler. Whereas doing a story steeped in goth culture set in 1983 is winkingly proleptic—goth culture existed in 1983 but was largely invisible to the mainstream—doing one about ritual satanic abuse is a different sort of commentary.

The reason is that even if the ritual satanic abuse scandal had been shifted a decade in the past so that by 1983 it was widely known to be a hoax, the John Nathan-Turner of 1983 would never have touched it. It's not fair to say that John Nathan-Turner was opposed to political Doctor Who—he did, after all, oversee Saward's fumbling efforts at it in Season

Twenty-Two and of course the Cartmel era. But it's equally true that in his first three and really four seasons in charge, Doctor Who was maddeningly apolitical. And as I've said before, to be apolitical is ultimately to be in support of the status quo, which, in the heyday of Thatcher's Britain, is frankly inexcusable.

Cornell, on the other hand, is firmly a post-Cartmel Doctor Who writer who is thoroughly invested in the overtly political work that characterizes the classic series' last and greatest days. And so to write a Davison story that is ahead of its time on a Davison-era political issue is, in this regard, a particularly pointed reparation of the era.

With *Spare Parts* we talked about the way in which it seemed to suggest an era that almost happened. (Indeed, I can find at least some references to a script co-authored by Platt and Jeremy Bentham rejected for Season Twenty, showing just how narrow the gap between *Spare Parts* and reality actually was.) Here, however, we have a slightly different issue. *Goth Opera* could never have worked in 1983. It doesn't even pretend to. Instead, it demonstrates the way in which even in this period in which Doctor Who is ostensibly in a terminal decline that it won't pull out of in time, things are being done that are unmistakably progress for the future.

For all its faults, the Davison era lays crucial groundwork for what Doctor Who eventually becomes. It is difficult to imagine this book working in any era of Doctor Who prior to 1983. That, in and of itself, is an important statement of faith in the Davison era. Whatever its faults—and let's be honest, even the much-vaunted Hinchcliffe era had tangible faults and face-palmingly bad stories—it is manifestly the case that it developed the show in ways that were crucial to its survival. Yes, we all know what goes wrong at the end of Season Twenty-One. And we're all capable of seeing the antecedents of that all the way back into Season Eighteen. But none of this means that the Davison era didn't, on the whole, work. It made Paul Cornell's work possible within the context of Doctor Who. That, by any reasonable measure, is working.

## And He's Just Wiped Them Out (*Mawdryn Undead*)

It's February 1st, 1983. Men at Work are at number one with "Down Under," remaining there all story. Kajagoogoo, U2, and Echo and the Bunnymen also chart, which starts to look like one of the best charts we've seen until you look at the second week when it's Joe Cocker, Wham, and Fleetwood Mac. Bauhaus, however, are in the lower reaches of the chart, and a post-breakup re-release series means that The Jam occupy fifteen spots of the top hundred. So that's nice. In real news, unemployment in the UK reaches its record peak. The Australian parliament is dissolved in preparation for elections. Klaus Barbie is actually charged with war crimes. And that's about it, I'm afraid.

On to television, then. *Mawdryn Undead* is another one of those stories that I was unaware was controversial and not widely liked until well after I'd seen it, and thus I'm unable to quite dislodge the way in which I was initially taken by it. I loved this story on the VHS tape that started with *Time-Flight*, thinking it easily the strongest of the four, and was gutted that the back two parts of the Black Guardian arc had been taped over with a track and field meet by my parents, leaving me unable to watch them for a good two years or so after becoming a Doctor Who fan. Rewatching it now, as with most classic Doctor Who, its flaws are evident, but like much of the Davison era its virtues are evident as well, with the embryonic forms of what Doctor Who could and would become on plain display throughout the story.

Let me first say that I am mostly going to set Turlough aside until *Enlightenment*. I have a lot to say about the character, but I don't think it's going to be well-served by splitting it up among three essays or by treating the early scenes of his character without reference to the later ones.

Second, let me deal very efficiently with the Brigadier. He's obviously not the right character for this story, but in this story's defense, he's also the third-choice character. The correct character is, obviously, Ian. They wanted to do the story for Ian. But William Russell wasn't available, nor was their second choice, Ian Marter as Harry, and so they ended up using the Brigadier. Nicholas Courtney is, of course, wonderful, but the fact of the matter is that very little about the story is meaningfully about the Brigadier. He is serving here as a stand-in for "generic past companion" and I'm mostly going to treat him that way, especially since there actually is a story in the future that deals with the Brigadier as the Brigadier and that, furthermore, is just as much a work of flawed genius as this one. (As for UNIT dating, I don't really have anything to add to what I said on the subject in Volume Two.)

All that set aside, then, let's start with Peter Grimwade, a strong contender for the most underrated writer in Doctor Who's history. There are reasons for this—he only has three stories, none of which are exceptionally strong and one of which is *Time-Flight*. But his CV is deceptive here. All three of the stories he wrote were nightmare briefs in which Nathan-Turner saddled him with a metric ton of things to shoehorn in ("The Master, Tegan's departure, and a Concorde," "the Brigadier, introducing Turlough, and the Black Guardian," and "the death of the Master, writing out Kamelion, writing out Turlough, introducing Peri, Lanzarote, and explaining Turlough's origin," respectively). Any scriptwriter is going to suffer from this. Just look at how Johnny Byrne was snowed under two stories earlier. Byrne is not a great writer, and it turns out that his best story, *The Keeper of Traken*, was heavily rewritten by Bidmead, but he's still a better writer than *Arc of Infinity* made him look. Even Robert Holmes finds himself staggering under the weight of *The Two Doctors*. The sorts of grotesquely overstuffed stories that Nathan-Turner tended to ask writers for were a real problem, and none of them are fair barometers of their writers' skill.

Given that, it's surprising just how well Grimwade's work survives the seeming onslaught of requirements. I mean, we'll never really know what "pure" Grimwade would have looked like. But given the evidence we have, he was a reasonably decent writer. First of all, let's point out that he's surprisingly deft at characterization. That's on particular display in this story, where he manages the non-trivial feat of having the two versions of the Brigadier feel like tangibly different characters. (And a hat-tip to Tat Wood for pointing out some of the subtler ways I'd have missed, such as the 1983 Brigadier using post-Falklands slang.) But it's true even in *Time-Flight*, where characters with similar jobs and stations and life sounded and acted visibly different, despite several painfully disappointing performances by the actors.

The other thing he doesn't get nearly enough credit for is the fact that he, better than any other writer in the Davison era, gets the soap opera structure. Miles compares the structure of this story to how Spider-Man comics typically work, and he's spot-on. The biggest weakness *Mawdryn Undead* has, as is the case with much of Doctor Who, is being sold as a TV movie in four parts instead of as four parts of the ongoing serial of Season Twenty. Grimwade is remarkably deft at a structure whereby every episode introduces a new complication and moves the characters to a slightly new situation. In many ways, this is a return to the style of the Hartnell era—something that would have made more sense had each episode gone out under its own title instead of acting as though it were a discrete unit separate from *Snakedance* and *Terminus*.

This is how the Davison era should always have been working: as a series of definable encounters that move characters from one point to another and that work meaningfully as serials within each encounter as well. This is consistently sandbagged by two problems. First, seemingly nobody but Grimwade gets how to write these sorts of stories. Second, the writers are largely incapable of communicating among each other. A scene about the Mara gets tacked onto the start of this to provide continuity, just as a scene about Adric got tacked onto the start of *Time-Flight*. But in both cases it's clear that in the midst of telling Grimwade to incorporate a Concorde or a man with a bird on his head nobody thought to mention, "Oh, and could you maybe create some sort of continuity in characterization from story to story?" Any lingering plot threads from the previous stories are gone by the five minute mark. All the same, it's clear that Grimwade understands how to do this sort of thing because everything within the story points to a writer who gets that sort of structure.

But this gets at a line of criticism against this story, and correspondingly a line of praise for this story, both of which are alarmingly wrong-headed. There's a debate about this story in which critics complain that it is small and boring and not enough happens, while defenders argue that it's based on a theme of lost innocence and retro-nostalgia where the point is the collapse of the big exciting UNIT days into the petty and soul-deadening mundanity of the domestic.

The two sides of this debate share a problem, which is the assumption that the small scale is in some sense troublesome for Doctor Who. Back in the *Black Orchid* essay we talked about how, for the most part, Davison's Doctor works very well on the small scale, and this is no exception. Particularly adroit is the choice of villains: a bunch of guys who just want to die. The Doctor's life is never in danger as such—only his ability to regenerate. This means that the conflict is taken to the personal level, with Davison getting to play with the limits of the Doctor's kindness, where his refusal to help (being, in this case, an unwillingness to sacrifice his life for mere "fools who tried to become Time Lords") is in conflict with his willingness to do so for Nyssa and Tegan. The smallness of the scale lets Davison actually have a story in which the Doctor has decisions to make and an opportunity for priorities, as opposed to one in which huge swaths of lives are at stake and the choices in front of him are straightforward.

But more troubling is the idea implicit in both ends of the discussion that the Brigadier's life of domestic teaching is in some sense a lessening of the character. Setting aside my immediate antipathy for the idea that teaching is in some way a lesser profession than shooting things, and remembering that as originally conceived this was not a falling off of the Brigadier but a return to first principles for Ian, let's get at the real issue here. There's a shockingly cavalier judgment here about the inherent superiority of having adventures over having a normal life. One that, if we take the Brigadier's role as "generic companion" here, treats everyone who has ever chosen to leave the Doctor as wrong or weak for doing so.

This is, admittedly, an issue that really does run through Doctor Who, and one that Russell T Davies eventually plays with overtly via both Rose and Donna. But by any standards, this is a particularly nasty flare-up of it. And it is at this point that we finally have to acknowledge another major presence over the arc of this book, Ian Levine, a wealthy and obsessive fan who served as an unofficial and unpaid "continuity adviser" for the Davison/Baker era, and who was part of the creative vision behind all these returning concepts from past stories. We'll look at Levine in depth in later essays, but it's worth establishing the outright pathological nature of the fandom he represents. To pick just one example from Levine's long and colourful association with Doctor Who, back around the 2010 general election Levine explicitly discussed basing his vote entirely on the question of what party would be best for the BBC's continued funding of Doctor Who. I bring this up because I think it's worth drawing a direct line from that moment to the treatment of the series' past in 1983 and the reading of that past. Because the logic that says "exciting science fiction adventure is inherently superior to the domestic sphere" and the logic that says "having more money for Doctor Who is more important than the future of the NHS" are, in essence, identical.

And this is my rather stark problem with the usual defense of *Mawdryn Undead* as a story about fading glory. If it is in part an act of mourning for the program's past in which the adventuring days of UNIT are preferred to the soul-crushing domesticity of a public school (American readers—please be aware that this term does not mean what you think it means) then in essence the past is being mourned because of its anesthetic qualities. The UNIT era is, in this reading, valorized for its rejection of worldly concerns. A cursory rereading of my essays from the late Troughton era and the Pertwee era will reveal how shocking a misreading I find this to be. This is exactly counter to what I view the fundamental purpose of Doctor Who as being—the claim that material social progress is the solution to alchemy—and so, to my mind, rejecting the domestic sphere borders on overt sociopathy. Certainly it's a stark rejection of the actual UNIT era, where the notion of a past "golden age" of Britain was explicitly condemned, most obviously in *Invasion of the Dinosaurs*, but in no way exclusively. To reject the material world as fallen and unworthy, especially in 1983, in the run-up to Thatcher's re-election, is monstrous.

But crucially, I don't actually think that's what's going on in *Mawdryn Undead* at all. I think it's almost a complete 180 from the correct reading of the Brigadier's emotional arc here, which is not about his fall from grace but rather about his recovery from the Doctor. Because everything about his amnesia is, at first, played as post-traumatic stress disorder. The implication isn't some "you've grown up and can't go to Neverland anymore" bit of fairy-tale. It's that the Brigadier has blocked out the terrible and traumatic things that happened to him when the Doctor was around, and now the Doctor traipsed back into his life and upended it again. (In this regard it's a return to the actual original version of the Brigadier—the Colonel who was left shell-shocked when his attack on the Yeti went disastrously wrong and he lost his entire squad.)

Unlike the appalling "faded glory" interpretation, this interpretation has the benefit of integrating the various parts of the story. The Doctor finds himself facing down a narrative collapse that is averted by the Brigadier's acceptance and reintegration of the past he'd rejected. The central antagonists have turned away from wanting to be Time Lords and now want only death as a result of how traumatic trying to be Time Lords ended up being. The possibility of an endless life of adventure is treated with considerable anxiety throughout the story.

Taken in this light, the story clearly isn't about the faded glory of the Brigadier, it's about the need to integrate the mythic realms of science fiction with the mundane and about the fact that they're not antagonists at all. Back in the *Logopolis* essay I suggested that a flight into the esoteric was the only reasonable response to the brutal horrors of the early Thatcher era. But correspondingly, there has to be a return to earth. Magic without materialism is a banal masturbation.

But this also gets at the thing I will concede is a problem with the story, which is the same thing that's a problem with most of the drama in the Davison era—it's not there. The story desperately needs a real confrontation between the Brigadier and the Doctor instead of a simulacrum of one about the Brigadier's mental health. It needs the Brigadier to accuse the Doctor of being a danger to everyone around him so that the Doctor can successfully answer the charge and get the Brigadier to accept the moral validity of the Doctor. But these sorts of scenes in which the drama is actually pushed to a breaking point just don't happen in 1983.

There's a school of thought, of course, that says that this is a good thing and that contemporary drama likes to hammer home its moral point so as to shred any ambiguity. I'm not wild about this line of reasoning, mostly because I think that the "there's so much depth to what's implied" defense really amounts to "but if we imply it we don't actually have to deal with the consequences of saying it out loud and confronting it." But if you're going to give a story a pass on grounds along those lines it's tough to find a better candidate than *Mawdryn Undead*. Here we have a story where there's meaningful emotional subtlety up and down the story—where even the villains aren't straightforward moustache twirlers and where Mawdryn gets a sympathetic and tragic final line. In an environment like that, at least, there's room for implication like this. It's worth contrasting that to Tat Wood's attempted praise of the Brigadier's salute to the Doctor in *The Three Doctors*, in which he tries to suggest that it's more powerful because it's understated. Which is nonsense. I adore *The Three Doctors*, but nothing about a Baker and Martin script gestures towards understated and subtle emotional resonances.

But here at least there's room for it. The story is so densely populated with concepts (an actual benefit of Grimwade getting the nightmare brief) that the idea that things are pushed into the subtext doesn't jar. Especially because it's a story that treats the audience with such genuine respect (some of the Black Guardian's lines aside). This is a story playing with timey-wimey plotting a quarter century before Steven Moffat got around to it, and doing so almost casually and incidentally. It's a story that has absolute faith that its audience is going to stick with it and wait to see how the disparate strands eventually entwine, and one that actually pays it all off as well. The degree to which it assumes that the audience will be primed to accept Turlough simply because he's clearly an announced event and will thus be read straightforwardly as "the new and untrustworthy companion" from his first scene is a triumph of narrative efficiency—a fantastic example of how to use familiar structures as shorthand to tell stories.

Yes, it would be better if it actually did something with its returning companion premise and foregrounded the emotion. But when the series is actually treating its audience with respect and assuming maturity in them it can at least get away with sublimating some of the emotional commentary, if not benefit from it. Indeed, the last time the series was regularly assuming an intelligent audience—the Williams era—was also the last time in which it managed to build tremendous sexual chemistry between its two leads without putting a single moment of actual romance on the screen. *Mawdryn Undead* marks a return to that, and is one of the most overlooked gems of the classic series.

## The Original Viking Settlers (*Terminus*)

It's February 15th, 1983. Kajagoogoo are finally at the top of the charts, prancing about for both weeks of this story with one of the great pieces of 80s trash. Michael Jackson and Tears for Fears also chart, making this perhaps the single most 80s chart we've dealt with yet. Fitting, that. The news is relatively quiet. Some particularly bad fires in Victoria and South Australia, a multiple homicide in the robbery of the Wah Mee gambling club in Seattle, and the Environmental Protection Agency announces plans to completely and permanently evacuate Times Beach in Missouri due to an excessive amount of deadly poison in the soil.

While on television, *Terminus*. There was, in the drawer of VHS tapes that constituted the initial guiding principles of my Doctor Who fandom, a tape on which the words "Terminus" and "Enlightenment" were written and crossed out. The tape now contained a track meet. This is one of several standing grievances between my parents and me, along with my not being allowed to trick or treat when I was a child and their failure to buy a life-size Dalek when they had the opportunity. Some day I will put them in homes and laugh at them.

The result of this is that when I finally got my hands on a copy of *Terminus* I was positively chomping at the bit to watch it. The fact that I remembered virtually nothing about it going into rewatching it for the blog, then, was a bit unnerving. As I've noted, there are few worse omens when talking about a Doctor Who story than to say that it was forgettable as a child.

Of course, this meshes with the story's reputation. And, let's be honest, with its quality. There are a lot of things that are very, very wrong with *Terminus*. It represents a particular sort of show-on-autopilot that grows increasingly common in the Nathan-Turner era, where everyone just throws up their hands and says, "Right, we're doing a naff runaround on a generic space station and we really don't care," while Nathan-Turner himself never moves out of the first stage of grief, just grinning maniacally as he insists that the story worked and was good and the memory cheats and please, please love me. This is one of the worst offenders—a poorly made piece of television in almost every sense from writing on. But other than the script, production design, direction and acting, this is pretty good stuff.

What makes this really weird, though, is that for most of the Nathan-Turner era this process is almost but not quite entirely unrelated to the quality of the script. The Nathan-Turner era will periodically go to the mattresses trying to make a classic out of a story with a script that is never going to be one and, equally, will occasionally just decline to lift a finger to help a brilliant script. Which brings us to *Terminus*, which is tedious, shoddily constructed, clearly as boring to everybody in it as it is to anybody watching it, and nominally by one of the best writers to work on the classic series. Perhaps the most shocking thing, when watching *Terminus*, is trying to figure out how this could come from the pen of the man who'd written *Warriors' Gate*, and who is one of a handful of classic series Doctor Who writers to have a writing career that spans functionally into the present day. The answer, of course, is that it didn't—it came from the pen of Eric Saward, who did considerable damage to it. And then, on top of that, it was flaccidly directed and encumbered with severe design problems because the costumes, while visually impressive so long as nobody moved, were not designed with sound recording in mind, meaning that everything screams, "I was shot on a BBC soundstage!" All of which is a perverse fit with Gallagher's script.

Lawrence Miles, defender of the Davison era that he is in *About Time*, gives the start of an explanation, which is that this is meant to be Wagnerian space opera. This is not, in and of itself, a winning concept, but it's intriguing. Miles goes on to suggest that the story should have been played entirely in sweeping, epic gestures, with everything overplayed and shouted thunderously, preferably with a cast consisting of an endless sequence of Brian Blessed clones. While this is an interesting suggestion, it is also very clearly not what the actual finished product is.

But for all of this, there remain occasional flashes of that sort of epic glory. The skull image that appears within the TARDIS to provide Nyssa her way off the ship is one of the most chilling images in the series, and the crowd of Lazars clawing and milling around everybody is one of the best efforts at straight scares since the Hinchcliffe era, although let's be fair, that is a relatively small pool to be swimming in, a pool that has Mandrels in it.

Equally, it's true that the things that fall short of the epic tend to fall short with an unfortunate vigor. The degree to which the Vanir are bored middle-aged men arguing with each other is deeply unfortunate, as is the failure to choreograph any of the fight scenes with even a modicum of quality (a problem closely related to the poor costume design). And it's tough to muster any love for the casting of the space raiders, who are so 1980s that it causes physical pain even if you're enormously fond of the decade, as I am. It's also frustrating that Nyssa is left to simper and be abused through so much of the story, one that was ostensibly meant to focus on her and that serves as her departure. Tegan and Turlough spend the majority of it crawling around in ducts, but for all that she actually does in the story Nyssa might as well have been there too. Her actual final scene is handled with pleasant dignity, but as usual Sutton mostly demonstrates how frustratingly wasted she was on the part, and thank god for Big Finish so that we have an idea of just how much that's true. All three companions seem to shrink in the face of *Terminus* just as much as the story's supporting cast does. But Miles's account isn't the full account of it either.

Still, let's start with what Miles does say and is right about, and build off of that. At the heart of this story is a sense of cyclical cosmology built on the idea of ancient orders of things that have survived in partial forms. Miles makes much out of a concept that is elided in the televised version, which is that the space ship is a relic from a previous universe whose destruction brought about the creation of our universe. In this reading, the end solution of the Garm managing to hold back the lever and reverse the explosion is not, as it initially appears, just about a superstrong wolfman. It's about the idea that only something from the old universe can properly interact with the ship. It's not supposed to just be a question of strength, but of a sort of narrative teleology—the fact that the old universe has its own rules separate from our universe. We're in territory much more like *The Impossible Planet/The Satan Pit* than we are in the "stuck fast-return switch."

It is worth reflecting, then, on the Doctor's role in this. Unlike *Warriors' Gate*, it is not true that his role is one of strategic inaction. But it's also true that the Doctor does relatively little here. This is, of course, not that unusual for Doctor Who, where the plot often consists of the Doctor figuring things out so that other people can do stuff. But it's still worth making the exact format of this within *Terminus* explicit. The Doctor is a wandering outsider who gains knowledge about the fundamental workings of the universe and uses it to preserve the order of things. Within the Norse context of the story at large, the correct term for this person is "Odin."

I mention this because there's a train of thought that really peaks in the late McCoy era and into the New Adventures (particularly those written by Paul Cornell) in which the Doctor becomes an overtly Odinic figure. It is an interesting role to cast the Doctor in. Certainly Odin is a mercurial figure—indeed, he's rather unique as gods go in that he is at once a martial, patriarchal figure and, for the most part, a trickster archetype. He is still defined first and foremost by cleverness and an ability to outfox people. And he is in many ways a natural fit with the idea of the Time Lords, particularly those of *The Deadly Assassin*. His ravens, after all, are named Thought and Memory.

There is an important transformation that happens here—a sort of steady refocusing of the lens of the series made necessary by time. Early on the Doctor is most visibly allied with some form of Hermes. But as he becomes increasingly entrenched in culture this changes. (Indeed, one theory, admittedly based largely on Tacitus making shit up, casts Odin as being derived from Mercury. But even this fraudulent theory carries some potency—a sense of the Roman pantheon slitting its own throat in a desperate bid to evolve into something weirder and stronger.) Even as the actors playing him and his superficial tropes become progressively younger, he gets played as an older and older figure. Hartnell may be the most "old man" Doctor, but he plays the Doctor as a sort of giddily mercurial patrician. Davison, on the other hand, plays him as a weary young adventurer.

But more to the point, when the program is facing its twentieth anniversary there is an extent to which the Doctor cannot help but be a figure of the establishment. Once you're the longest-running science fiction show in the world you are, in a necessary sense, an institution and a part of the establishment. That doesn't mean that the Doctor has to abandon his sense of the anarchic. But it does require a change. To some extent this has been lurking since the Pertwee era, as the Doctor has become increasingly sage. It's not until the 1970s that it becomes the norm for the Doctor to know a lot about a given situation before he arrives and to be able to rattle off extensive facts about the location off the top of his head. Indeed, one of the interesting things about Davison's Doctor is that this sort of extensive foreknowledge is temporarily and partially stripped away again (particularly in the two Bailey stories, which overtly hinge on the Doctor's lack of knowledge in a way that would never have happened in the Baker era).

But Davison's Doctor, equally, is not a return to the Hartnell/Troughton mould. He may be without extensive knowledge, but he's also world-weary in a way that Troughton never was and Hartnell rarely was. And if one extends the scope out from Davison, treating him as the model for future Doctors (and it's fair, I think, to say that his approach defines how at least five of his six successors play the part), he rapidly starts to look like a reconceptualization of the Doctor as an Odinic figure instead of a Hermetic one. In Davison he is overtly a "young" Odin—the wandering figure gathering wisdom and knowledge. But this merely prefigures the more explicitly Odinic natures of McCoy and all of the new series Doctors. And *Terminus*, spiritually, marks that transition point.

But *Terminus*, as written, has depths beyond what Miles points at. Yes, it's Norse space opera, but that's just a cool style. Oddly prescient in its casting of the Doctor, yes, but on its own it's not entirely functional without a slathering of "sentient metafiction" more liberal than even I'm eager to lay down. It's enough, perhaps, to elevate it to *Time Monster* territory—brilliant ideas that just go terribly, terribly wrong. But there's a second layer to *Terminus* that Miles doesn't pick up on.

The clue actually comes in something Tat Wood points out when he snarks about Saward's tin ear for dialogue, complaining about how the line, "Do they think we're stupid or something?" got changed to, "They must think us fools!" It's a poor rewrite, to be sure, but the most striking thing about it is that it does actually completely meet Miles's assertion that everything is supposed to be overplayed as if by Brian Blessed. What's more telling, though, is what it replaces—a line of frustration that is framed and played as working class employees grousing angrily, and pointedly not as Blessedesque bombast.

This is something Gallagher has played with before. *Warriors' Gate* also featured a spaceship crew that was visibly coded as working class. But that was under Bidmead, and now we're under Saward, who scuppered a script by Pat Mills in part because Mills wanted to do the story with a visibly working-class captain whereas Saward wanted to portray only classless futures. (The story was later adapted by Big Finish as *Song of Megaptera*, and is covered later in the book.) All of the class issues that Gallagher put into the script are systematically removed. The Vanir were, in the original conception, working-class gods, on the one hand given names of Norse myth and made to stride around in armor and on the other hand tired, worn out, and screwed-over wage slaves. This cuts right to the core of them as designed. They're literally living paycheck to paycheck—actual wage slaves dependent on the Terminus Corporation's shipments of Hydromel to survive. They have no choice but to work, and the need for them to do their work obliges them to be completely blind to the needs of the sick people in their care.

Likewise, the Garm turns out to be a wage slave from a previous universe, bound into servitude and finally set free from his wage slavery when he saves the universe by waking up and doing something for the sake of it instead of because he's ordered to. Or, to put it in blunter political terms, the Garm attains class consciousness and is freed by it, thus facilitating the subsequent freeing of the Vanir. The cyclical structure of mythic history is explicitly wedded, in other words, to a sort of Marxist dialectic of history. Only Saward, in his infinite wisdom, preferred a depiction of a classless future and took it all out in favor of epic bombast that he should have known full well they couldn't deliver. He took an intelligent script and tried to make it *Earthshock*, and got what he deserved, unlike the licence payers.

So we're left with two *Termini*. One is a Marxist Norse space opera that clearly flags the transition of the Doctor from a Hermetic figure to an Odinic one while maintaining an explicit connection to the idea of alchemy as material social progress. The other is a poorly paced story about a bunch of middle-aged men grousing around a shoddy space station in silly costumes. Unfortunately, of course, it's the latter one that actually aired. And unlike something like *The Creature from the Pit*, where the fault can be fairly and concretely pinned on one person's head, here it's a systemic failure: a case of nobody bothering to give Gallagher—whose previous effort had been good in part because of the striking visuals—the sort of production attention he needed. But through the horrid pallor of neglect and tedium the last remnants of *Terminus*'s old universe still rage gloriously. The result is one of the odder critical endpoints I've found myself resting on—a story I absolutely despise for the way in which it serves as an effaced memorial to one of my favorite Doctor Who stories ever.

## He's Gay and She's an Alien (*Enlightenment*)

It's March 1st, 1983. Michael Jackson is at number one insisting that Billie Jean is not his lover. Lower in the charts are the Eurythmics (with "Sweet Dreams (Are Made of This)" of course), Bananarama, Toto, and Tears for Fears. But for the purposes of this essay perhaps the most significant fact about the charts is Bonnie Tyler hitting number one in the second week of this story with "Total Eclipse of the Heart," which is notable for several reasons, one of which is that it's one of the gayest songs ever written, so, you know. Thematically apropos, that. In real news, there's not a lot. The compact disc goes on sale in England sometime in March, so let's give that to this story. The final episode of *M\*A\*S\*H* aired between *Terminus* and this. Bob Hawke becomes Prime Minister of Australia, and the IBM PC/XT is released.

So on television we have *Enlightenment*. Which is a fantastic little story with one of the most wonderfully captivating central images in Doctor Who. Barbara Clegg is, of course, not the first person to put tallships in space, but it's such a reliably wonderful image that she really ought to get proper amounts of praise for it. On top of that you have a story that effortlessly moves from historical texture to science fantasy in a way that offers one of the most thorough blurring of genres in Doctor Who, has a bunch of clever ideas and good characters, and is all around one of the gems of the

Davison era. None of which I want to talk about in this essay, because there's loads of very accurate reviews about the virtues of *Enlightenment* that I think cover most of what there is to say. So I want to talk about Turlough.

The first thing we should establish is that Turlough is the first companion who is overwhelmingly easier to read as homosexual than not. There have been homoerotic undertones to companions before, most obviously Mike Yates, but there's never before been a companion who is so consistently and from the top down conceptualized in gay tropes. It's not, in the case of Turlough, a subtext. Turlough is gay. Through and through, Turlough is gay.

There's no point in pretending that this statement does not intersect with the creative personnel involved. Simply put, there were a lot of gay people involved in Doctor Who in 1983. Peter Grimwade, writer of *Mawdryn Undead* and *Time-Flight*, and director of *Earthshock* and *Kinda*, was gay. So was unofficial fan adviser Ian Levine. And perhaps most obviously, so was John Nathan-Turner. Indeed, Nathan-Turner was openly gay, a fact that unquestionably cost him at the BBC, and accordingly had a direct impact on the material future of the program. More than that, Nathan-Turner was invested in an aesthetic that extended out of gay male culture. He produced Doctor Who willingly and, at first, eagerly, but his goal was always to move on to soap operas or, better yet, his true love: light entertainment. He adored and embraced camp in all its forms. And so it is impossible to ignore when a character like Turlough shows up and starts ticking off boxes of stereotypes about gay culture. Simply put, when that happens, there's no way it's not something everyone involved knows is happening.

For the sake of completion, let's enumerate the various ways in which Turlough is coded as gay. He is overtly "cowardly," deliberately played as an unmasculine character. He's repeatedly shown to be delicate and fragile. He's introduced in the context of an all-boys school, and seen leading another boy to temptation and ruin. And that's before you get to moments like his first scene with Captain Wrack in Episode Three of *Enlightenment*. He's thrown to the ground by strapping young men and told to "crawl." He slowly makes his way across the floor to come to the leather boots of an unseen figure. And who, exactly, is this figure that Turlough looks up at in sheer and unbridled terror? A female pirate queen who, in staggeringly camp fashion, declares him "just what I've been waiting for" before swinging a sword around cavalierly. Not until *Terror of the Vervoids* will the *vagina dentata* be quite so blatantly literalized in Doctor Who.

(It's worth pointing out that Captain Wrack is as consciously designed as a gay icon as any female character in Doctor Who who isn't the Rani—the overpowering maneating woman who visibly wears the pants and is more masculine than any of the lumbering pieces of manflesh who follow her is archetypal. Think of her as a drag queen who happens to be played by a woman. Not for nothing was the woman in question, Lynda Baron, brought back in *Closing Time* to riff on the notion that the Doctor and Craig are lovers.)

But it's worth remarking on exactly what sort of homosexual Turlough is presented as being, because it's a slightly historicized one, grounded in the *fin di siècle* figure of the aesthete. Certainly the tropes are all there. Turlough is exceedingly cosmopolitan in his tastes, in particular in *Mawdryn Undead* where his knowledge of alien technology is constantly played off of the "provincial" nature of contemporary Earth. But more striking is his first appearance, admiring a classic car. This sort of appreciation of the beauty of mundane objects is textbook aestheticism (which was, in a particularly famous *Punch* cartoon, parodied as worshipping teapots). Add to that the aforementioned seducing of another young boy to ruin and a textbook aesthetic plot, and you have the general shape of the character fairly well pegged. (The aesthetic movement, to be clear, is intimately connected with homosexuality, with same-sex attractions both spoken and loudly unspoken permeating the movement. Its most prominent member was Oscar Wilde.)

But what's particularly interesting about the aesthetic structure is a focus on the lengthy exploration of a moral choice in which the negative choice is explored at length. Which is exactly what we get for the twelve episodes of the so-called Black Guardian Trilogy (though he's an exceedingly minor character in the trilogy—the Turlough Trilogy would be wholly more apropos). Or, at least, what we get for eight episodes, with four episodes of him crawling around some ductwork shoved in the middle. Turlough is given a moral choice—betray and kill the Doctor or not—and spends the whole of the trilogy dithering over it, generally committing to the idea that he will kill the Doctor but not actually ever doing much of anything to accomplish it.

All of this could basically be written off as peculiarities of *Mawdryn Undead* if it weren't for the fact that the story arc is book-ended on the other side by *Enlightenment*, which is about a bunch of bored decadents who like dressing up in the trappings of various exotic cultures and having yacht races. Which is to say, more aesthetes. At this point the series is practically begging for it.

But if we take this as the setup for Turlough, what do we make of the endpoint of this story arc? After all, the point of dallying with the negative choice in aestheticism is, ultimately, the idea that there is beauty in what is forbidden and profane. In which case, Turlough's wholesale rejection of the Black Guardian at the end of this story seems to be in part a repudiation of his coding as homosexual. This is an unfortunate endpoint, to say the least.

Several alternative ways to argue through this do seem to present themselves, and it's worth exploring them. First and foremost is the fact that the usual hullabaloo about the ambiguously oppositional relationship between the Black and White Guardians is on display here, cutting against the idea that the Black Guardian is evil. The problem is that this means taking one scene at the end of *Enlightenment* as more central to the understanding of the Guardians than all the moments where the Black Guardian shows up shouting things like, "In the name of all that is evil, the Black Guardian orders you to destroy him now!" and cackling like he's played by Valentine Dyall or something. The Guardians have been impossible to take seriously as a concept since their debut, where they came pre-skewered by Robert Holmes.

A second, somewhat cheekier approach would be to suggest that Turlough is only trading one model of queerness for another. Certainly, as I've already argued, Davison's Doctor is a strong contender for the most slashable Doctor in the classic series. So Turlough breaks up with his abusive boyfriend and goes with the Doctor. But if we're being honest there's a circularity to this. Davison is slashable as much because he's surrounded by at least one of Adric, the Master, or Turlough in all but three stories of his run. And one of those is *Snakedance*. He has, in other words, the incidental combination of being young, played by a television star known for acting in more feminine television series (i.e. *All Creatures Great and Small*), and being the only classic series Doctor since Pertwee to have a male companion in a majority of his stories (Smith also ended up at twenty-seven out of forty-one). I'll readily grant that the show is overtly coding Turlough as gay. Davison's Doctor, not so much.

A third defense, which is at least slightly more satisfying, comes by just trying to deconstruct the ending. The declaration that "enlightenment was the choice" is obviously supposed to indicate that for Turlough enlightenment was the act of escaping the Black Guardian's control. But if we take the long view of the choice, treating it as the entire twelve-episode arc, then enlightenment is the same extended dalliance with corruption that is partially responsible for coding Turlough as gay in the first place. But while this works, it just feels smugly clever.

No, let's go with a fourth defense, which is that the deferral of and stepping back from same-sex desire is part and parcel of what aestheticism does. Aesthetic novels are awash with points at which potentially scandalous details are visibly elided, the most famous of which is probably the moment in *The Picture of Dorian Gray* in which Dorian is told, "Your name was implicated in the most terrible confession I ever read," but no information about the content of the confession is actually forthcoming. In other words, aestheticism constantly performed this precise double gesture of alluding to some scandalous content—generally implied, if not outright said, to be homosexual—and visibly obscuring it.

This is, of course, a subset of the larger category of the closet, with which gay culture at large has an ambiguous relationship with to this day. But in 1983 it was still a fairly straightforward one. Homosexuality may have been decriminalized, but it was nowhere close to being destigmatized, especially in the face of the dawning AIDS crisis that would decimate the gay male community. Section 28 looms over 1983 as surely as the hiatus looms over Season Twenty. The consequence of this is something we talked about the last time the series was getting fabulously gay, which is that gay culture became defined in part by the ways in which it hid itself. This has been tacitly clear through the whole of this post, where I've been using words like "coded" to describe how we know Turlough is gay. Because coding was, in 1983, still a huge part of how gay culture self-identified and how people in the gay community successfully identified each other. It's misleading to talk about Turlough's homosexuality as subtext in this regard. Yes, it's never explicitly stated. But that doesn't mean it's not completely explicit—homosexuality, in the culture of the time, always existed in code and subtext.

(The nature of the closet in the present day is tremendously conflicted, I should note. On the one hand, major battles have been won in terms of acceptance of homosexuality that obviate the need for the closet. On the other hand, gay culture has existed for decades with the closet as a major force, making its removal the occasion for some real ambivalence and anxiety due to it threatening the makeup of the culture. The debates within the gay community over gay marriage, with a small but significant section of the community arguing that gay marriage serves to functionally "straighten" their relationships, are one of many, many examples.)

So if we treat Turlough's storyline as a mirroring of the classic aesthetic structure then the fact that it ends with a phoned-in attempt to defuse it and take Turlough out of his decadent gay lifestyle is hardly a big deal. It's exactly the sort of closeting move that defines aesthetic literature and the gay community more generally. The fact that there's an overt turn away from some of the tropes that code Turlough as gay really can't be fairly taken as a rejection of homosexuality in a meaningful sense. Anyone who was aware of the coding up to that point would also have seen it as an inevitable and necessary part of grappling with the subject on a BBC1 family program in 1983. It doesn't change the basic fact that the series, at this point, was visibly gay-friendly.

So the ambiguities of the ending need not be taken as undermining the point at all. A somewhat tortured relationship with the tropes of homosexuality is itself a useful commentary on them. The extended meditation on a negative moral choice that the Black Guardian represents is part of Turlough's gay coding. So, of course, are many of his more villainous traits. But does anyone seriously look at post-Enlightenment Turlough and stop seeing the gay coding? Of course not. He's gay all the way through *Planet of Fire*. His rejection of the Black Guardian, as such, is not a rejection of homosexuality, but of a particular subset of stereotypes about homosexuality. Taken this way, "enlightenment was the choice" takes on another meaning, given that this scene also marks where he "comes out" to Tegan and the Doctor as having been an agent of the Black Guardian. (And the implication, of course, is that the Doctor knew all along. As did Tegan, who long suspected that there was "something funny" about Turlough, so to speak.) By rejecting the Black Guardian and making an affirmative claim to his identity,

Turlough comes out instead of just being outed. The choice thus consists of him having his cake and eating it too—he remains situated in a long tradition of gay culture while at the same time vocally rejecting those aspects of the culture that are negative stereotypes. Turlough's arc, in this reading, is about a broader question of what gay culture is. And its very existence on BBC1 demonstrates the relevance of this—gay culture clearly was emerging into the mainstream, and its emergence raises the exact questions this reading situates the story as answering.

As I've noted, the prominence of various sorts of homosexual coding in the John Nathan-Turner era in no way begins with *Mawdryn Undead*, and we're still not up to either of the two most overt engagements with a gay audience in the classic series (both of which are in the next book). But the Turlough arc marks what is probably the most extended treatment of the issue in the classic series. And, of course, all of this is worth discussing in part because Doctor Who's engagement with the gay community is a fundamental part of its revival. This may not be the era of Doctor Who that Russell T. Davies grew up with, but there's no mistaking the fact that there's a coherent line of influence from the homosexual coding that takes place under Nathan-Turner's watch to the nature, if not the very fact, of its return in 2005.

## *Enlightenment* Redux

Oh, all right, we can talk about other bits of *Enlightenment* besides Turlough. It is, after all, one of the best stories of the classic series. Much of this is down to its sense of the visual. Simply put, tallships in space is brilliant. It's been brilliant every time someone has come up with it. It will always be brilliant. That's not to say that every story featuring the idea will automatically be brilliant, as any *Dungeons & Dragons* fan with an old copy of *Spelljammer* will tragically confirm, but as a basic, iconic visual it works wonders.

The reasons for this are not terribly complex. Space-exploration sci-fi has always been an exercise in extending the narrative of European colonialism into the realm of the fantastic, hence the tendency to prefer alien races that are just humans with different cultures (generally, as Ted Sturgeon notes, Meiji Japan) as opposed to alien races that stem from the weird fiction tradition of the radically unknowable. So putting one of the most aesthetically pleasing images of colonialism—the tallship—in space is a powerful juxtaposition because it materially equates what had previously only been symbolically linked. The void of space and the open expanse of the sea are visually similar enough to avoid too stark a sense of disunity, meaning that the image at once feels like a logical extension of its underlying components and like something uncanny and weird. So it's just a great, memorable start that is, broadly speaking, within BBC capabilities.

It also has a great alien race in the form of the Eternals, whose sociopathic detachment and fascination with humanity is presented at once as a logical consequence of their status as immortal beings and as a perverse extension of their status as imperialist figures. As with tallships in space, malevolently indifferent gods are one of those sci-fi ideas that are pretty much never a bad one. Boredom really is one of the great character motivations, and the bored god is marvellous as an existential threat.

And for the most part, this is what works about *Enlightenment*. It's got two solid ideas that go together well (the linking thread of imperialism doing much for the story), and it explores them with conviction. It's this latter point that really marks it as different from much of the era at large as well. The key plot point is the Eternals hiding the TARDIS inside the Doctor's mind, which is at once an arresting idea and one that doesn't make an excess of sense within the larger logic of the TARDIS and Doctor Who. It's the sort of thing that cuts against the increasing continuity fetishism of the show, a welcome case of just making the mythology up on the fly based on the rules of a given story. Within *Enlightenment*, hiding the TARDIS inside the Doctor's mind makes total sense, and so who cares how the Eternals and the Time Lords measure up and are or aren't related to each other?

Which does come somewhat close to suggesting that this story would be improved if it didn't have to deal with all this silly Guardian business. The Guardians were always a bit of an odd choice for Nathan-Turner to bring back; they hail, after all, from the otherwise largely effaced Williams era, and come from a period where the program very much didn't care about the particulars of consistent continuity. They're a relatively incongruous idea for Doctor Who, in other words—interesting within the context of a story, dodgy if made a recurring part of the show's cosmology.

And it's true, one does kind of wonder what Clegg might have come up with if left entirely to her own devices. (Big Finish provides several answers to this, as is their way.) But equally, *Enlightenment* basically works as far as the Guardians are concerned. Again, this due to some peculiarities of the story's influences and DNA. The Eternals owe an obvious debt to Michael Moorcock's *Dancers at the End of Time* series, which features similarly hedonistic immortals sampling the delights of the past. And the Guardians are similarly Moorcockian, embodying the order/chaos dualism and the idea that this recurs on various levels throughout the universe, a central concept to Moorcock's larger mythology of the multiverse. And so unlike *Mawdryn Undead* and *Terminus* the Guardians end up fitting into the overall iconography of this story pretty well, and thus avoid being an inconvenient imposition on the plot.

And that's the crux of why this works so much better than much of what's around it, which is in many ways the secret to all the good stories of the often disappointing Davison era. It's a story where all the ideas have a clear relationship to one another, which means that all aspects of the production are actually working in the same direction and trying for the same general effect.

## A Space Helmet for a Cow (*The King's Demons*)

It's March 15th, 1983. Bonnie Tyler remains at number one with "Total Eclipse of the Heart," with The Eurythmics' "Sweet Dreams (Are Made of This)" nipping at its heels, and the rest of the charts being a similar burst of pure and unadulterated 1980s of the sort that you really probably need to cut with some do-wop or something lest you risk an overdose. Also in music news is the debut of Michael Jackson's moonwalk dance two days prior to this story's transmission. In real news, Thatcher's government passes massive tax cuts. That's about all we've got.

Speaking of not having much, it is difficult to say anything about *The King's Demons*, which stands as one of the most strikingly unambitious scripts of the Davison era. It was, admittedly, not supposed to be the season finale, so we can at least give it a break on those grounds and acknowledge that this is not another case of the foolishness that led to things like *Time-Flight* and *The Twin Dilemma* being used as finales. (The finale was supposed to be the story that became *Resurrection of the Daleks*.) But it does represent the degree to which the two-episode stories that every season of the Davison era is saddled with are generally unfortunate beasts.

One gets the acute sense that this story is a dumping ground. Terence Dudley, with whom Saward did not get on, is brought back and given the short script. Anthony Ainley's Master, who here becomes nearly impossible to take seriously, gets abandoned in it. And so too is the introduction of Kamelion. To be fair, not all of this is intentional. The degree to which Kamelion was going to prove not at all workable wasn't really clear until the story filmed, and the decision to keep bringing Ainley back demonstrates that he wasn't being snubbed with this assignment. But intentionality counts for less than one might hope in these things. Tacked on at the end of the season, after the Black Guardian trilogy, and only a two-parter to boot, this story gives nothing so much as a sense of all the steam going out of Doctor Who.

For the most part the "something old returns in every story" idea of this season has not been the disaster it could have been. Everything, at least, had a fresh take on its returning concepts, even if, in the case of *Arc of Infinity*, that fresh take was to abandon all notion of the concepts themselves in favor of soul-crushing tedium. But here we're back to the awkwardness of *The Visitation*'s redoing of *The Time Warrior*—an ugly case of everything in this story having been taken from other stories and just redone with an "it worked before so it must work again" attitude.

This contributes to something I've been accusing Doctor Who of for a while now, which is the use of simulacra in place of actual content—whether it be *Earthshock*'s hollow aping of the form of a dramatic death, *Arc of Infinity*'s empty recitations of past concepts, or, really, several other bits over the past two years. Here, though, we get at something that starts to tie in with the 1980s at large, and harkens back to what we talked about back in the essay on *The Cleopatras*, which is that this is part and parcel of what the 1980s were doing. The focus on artificiality that underlaid so much of 1980s popular culture is inexorably connected with the collapse of things into hollow recitations.

This pulled in multiple directions. On the left you had a growing critical discourse that was capable of articulating the ways in which the establishment used the contentless forms of ideology to advance their causes. A perfectly textbook example is the way in which the Thatcher government objected to the BBC's declining to cover the Falklands War with naked jingoism, and further how effectively *The Sun* was able to use a sense of patriotism for nakedly propagandistic ends. There was, in the 1980s, an increasingly mainstream awareness of the idea that there is something inherently unreal about the corporate. To use just one example from Doctor Who, in 1970 the Autons were scary because they were plastic people. But in 1980, when Alan Moore did an Auton story, the idea was that Autons were the perfect image of business in general. They weren't just the product gone mad, they were the entire teleology of the economy gone mad.

This was contrasted with the open fascination with the artificial discussed in *The Cleopatras* essay. Or, rather, it laid right alongside it. The result was a very, very fine line between postmodern subversion and a garish and ill-advised travesty. Which goes a long way towards explaining how Doctor Who finds itself lurching back and forth between stories like *Arc of Infinity* and *Snakedance*, or, for that matter, *Enlightenment* and this. (Or, to fess up and admit where this line of argument eventually lands us in a few essays' time, between *The Caves of Androzani* and *The Twin Dilemma*.)

I don't want to follow the argument of Miles and Wood too closely here, but it is worth remarking specifically on the way in which this story relates to history. Miles and Wood make much of the fact that this story comes from the history books, rather than from actual history. It presupposes in a way that was terribly untrendy in 1983 that disrupting this history of Britain is coextensive with disrupting the history of the world. This was, admittedly, the point behind *The Time Meddler* as well, but there's a difference. In 1965, when the national myth (like any national myth, based largely on truth) of Britain standing alone against the Germans and holding them back long enough for the rest of the world to get its act together was still relatively recent, it was one thing to position the idea of undermining Britain as being the same as undermining the planet. Nearly twenty years later, in a world where a great military victory for the UK was beating up

Argentina over some raggedy islands, there's just not the same punch. It's a bad sign when even the Doctor has to admit that the Master's scheme is naff this time around.

So instead we have the program setting something in what Miles and Wood slyly describe as "Heritage Themepark Britain." This story represents Britain for the export market: a stitched-together checklist of period details, at times assembled with essentially no care for piddling little questions like whether all the details are from the same period. It's a story composed entirely of willful quaintness—the sort of British-esque stuff that sold well abroad, particularly in the United States (where, of course, the program was becoming increasingly popular). The problem, of course, is that Doctor Who may function for the export market, but it's still first and foremost a BBC program sent out in a rather nice timeslot on BBC1. And this sort of "Look at us, we're being terribly British history here!" approach is just... dull in that context. (It's notable that in the Hartnell era the only two historicals to draw primarily from tourist-friendly British history were *The Crusade*, which cut it heavily with its Middle Eastern material, and *The Time Meddler*, which subverted its entire genre.)

It's a sign of just how uninspired this approach is that Dudley is able to get away with just reversing the trick he used in *Black Orchid*. There, the first episode is spent making everything look like it's going to be a standard Doctor Who story only for it turn out to be a historical. Here is the inversion: everything in the first episode save for the mystery of who's impersonating the king gives the appearance of being a historical, and then the bottom is pulled out at the end as everything turns out to have a sci-fi explanation. That this reversal is even possible when Doctor Who has done only one "pure" historical story in recent memory shows just how crushingly flaccid all of this is. The fact that the show can play off of these conventions when it hasn't done any work establishing them as Doctor Who conventions suggests that they are beyond commonplace. We're in a version of history here that's so utterly and vapidly familiar that it doesn't even need to put effort into itself.

Unfortunately, any hope that this one feeble twist might be pulled off is extinguished by the unfortunate decision to have "James Stoker," who plays Sir Gilles Estram, self-evidently be Anthony Ainley. Whatever one might say of the idiotic Kalid revelation in *Time-Flight*, at least the makeup Ainley was wearing that time around successfully obscured his identity. This time you have someone who is obviously Anthony Ainley gone ginger doing an appalling French accent. Never mind the theme of returning villains in this season. Between this, Michael Gough, and Mawdryn's rather spectacularly poor Doctor impression, the theme of the season is at this point utterly rubbish revelations of the secret villain.

Of course, it doesn't help that it's the Master who has over his last three appearances been systematically undermined as a character. The Delgado version of the character was the Doctor's equal and opposite number—a charmingly perverted parody of Pertwee's Doctor. But Ainley, while perhaps a plausible choice for an inversion of Tom Baker, isn't close to a viable inversion of Peter Davison's comparatively staid Doctor. But on top of that, the Delgado version only became a tacky plot extender in the dying embers of his eight-story run. The Ainley Master, on the other hand, basically started that way after a compellingly menacing turn in *Logopolis*.

Much of this comes down to the irritating practice of disguising the Master. Miles and Wood observe the way in which this speaks volumes as to the difference between Ainley and Delgado as actors, remarking on the degree to which "hiding" Delgado in a story would have been impossible. This is slightly unfair—the elaborate makeup job in *Time-Flight*, for instance, would have hidden just about anybody. But it does get at the degree to which there's a real lack of confidence in the ability of the Master to actually hold down a scene or justify himself on his own terms.

Put this way, it becomes possible to see the real problem with the Master over these last three stories, which is that he's only being used to stretch out other stories. When *Castrovalva* runs out of things to do with its actual concept of eccentric geography, it wheels the Master back out to extend things. *Time-Flight* gets in an extra two episodes after defeating Kalid. And here the Master gets trotted out dutifully at the halfway point in order to spice up a historical gone flat. In none of these stories do we get a situation where the plot is actually about the Master in any meaningful sense. The Master is nothing more than a device to salvage a plot gone wrong. Here he nearly gets upstaged by a robot.

This is unfortunate, especially as Ainley does eventually show—even if it arguably takes until *Survival*—that he can do the part. Just as, actually, he showed he could back in *Logopolis*. But the damage done by the series' supreme lack of confidence in the character over his first three Davison-era appearances is difficult to shake off. This is, admittedly, where the idiotic "disguise and anagram" era of the Master ends, at least until Russell T. Davies does his little homage to it with Mister Saxon/Master No. Six. But that homage works because it's not about trying to hide the Master—it's an Easter Egg for the bulk of fandom that figured out that Season Three was going to end with the Master somewhere around *Rise of the Cybermen*. But as with much of the Cartmel-era renaissance, it's too late. The character has already been revealed as one that even the series isn't taking seriously anymore, and for at least the next three times he shows up there's going to be a sickening sense of "Goddammit, it's him again" that takes hold before he even does anything. It's a terribly unfortunate circumstance for the character to be in. And while Ainley's performance does the character no favors at times, he is capable of doing worthwhile things when he's actually given some material.

But he's not, nor is anyone else. Instead we get an EPCOT Center version of British history and a sense that this is two episodes mostly as a mercy. And with that our anniversary season comes to a premature end, with the closing Dalek story felled by a union dispute. There is, of course, still the small matter of the actual anniversary story, which we'll come to shortly. But on the whole, there's an awful sense that this has been something of a drab affair. It's not that the season has been bad—three of the stories are quite good, two are utter train wrecks, and one is *Terminus*. But there is the sense that the series doesn't know what its strengths are—that it seriously thinks that bringing back Omega, the Master, and the Black Guardian were the high points of the season and not the fragmented dream-myths of *Snakedance*, the Teutonic grandeur of the *Terminus* that might have been, or the combination of the epic and familiar in *Enlightenment*. It's not that it's difficult to love Season Twenty. It's really not.

It's just that the show doesn't seem to be among those loving it.

## You Were Expecting Someone Else: Longleat and *Doctor Who Monthly*

Longleat, even by the standards of *TARDIS Eruditorum*, is an archaeology project. Certainly I have nothing that could accurately be called a memory of it, having been one year old and in the wrong country for it. But grasping about for points of comparison proves oddly unsatisfying. It was a major convention in 1983, yes. In this regard, it was a known quantity. But analogy is terribly unhelpful here. To compare it to the 2012 "official convention" in Cardiff, for instance, or the authorized 50$^{th}$ Anniversary is pointless. These modern day events are slickly professional affairs and, more to the point, are executed by a BBC that has full mastery of the concept of fandom and its relationship with Doctor Who. Their slickness covers for the real key fact, which is that they are official conventions in every sense of the word—active promotions of an official narrative of what the series is and how it is to be properly loved.

Longleat, by and large, was the opposite. If anything it marked the point where it became possible to talk about alternatives to the official narrative in a meaningful sense. But to understand this we need to move over and look at *Doctor Who Magazine*, which was called *Doctor Who Monthly* through early 1984. We talked a bit about the rise of the fan industrial complex towards the end of the previous book, but by late 1983 it was in full effect. Starting with Season Nineteen the magazine offered a thoroughly familiar and reliable structure. First it would leak scattered tidbits of information about an upcoming story in its Gallifrey Guardian column, which offered a smattering of Doctor Who news items. Then, in the last issue that would hit the stands prior to a story's transmission, a one-page preview spelling out much of the premise would be released. Finally, usually about two issues later, the magazine would run a review of the story, typically positive and never strongly negative. Some months thereafter would come things like the end-of-season poll and the periodic John Nathan-Turner interview that would further cement the official "end consensus" on a story.

What's important to stress about this structure, though, is that the information was carefully tuned to regulate and shape how the stories were watched and remembered. This is most obvious with a story like *Earthshock*, where, of course, Nathan-Turner's insistence on keeping the return of the Cybermen a secret required that the story be previewed in a manner almost but not entirely unrelated to what the story was actually about.

In other words, *Doctor Who Monthly* had become a major part of formulating a paratext of Doctor Who that resulted in a highly complex structure for interaction with the series. This contextualizing of the current series was reinforced by an active effort to historicize the show's past, with features not only covering the plots of long-lost Hartnell and Troughton stories but also including interviews with writers and directors of past serials that served to educate the reader about the material reality of television production.

(This was, of course, something of a transition from the magazine's original form as, essentially, a weekly comics anthology with a Doctor Who theme, although the main comic continued, with artist Dave Gibbons staying on for the first three stories to feature Davison's Doctor, and Steve Parkhouse writing the entire Fifth Doctor run. Parkhouse's version of Davison's Doctor is essentially indistinguishable from his version of Baker's: the only new character trait he adds is an obsession with cricket. Beyond that he just continues plotlines from his last Tom Baker strip, "The Neutron Knights."

His first three Davison stories form a somewhat directionless arc that is long on compelling images and short on any sort of structure to hold them together. Parkhouse gestures continually at an alternate conception of Gallifrey, very much in tune with the one that Moore sets up in his "Time War" triptych. But he never develops it and leaves vast tracks of plot unresolved. Despite this, there are moments of real quality here worth pointing out. Parkhouse is very good at writing a dark fantasy tone, with stretches here and there feeling like they came out of an infinitely budgeted *Warriors' Gate*.

But in general, the increase of the magazine's focus on the series as a whole and serving as a paratext came with an increasing de-emphasis of the comic strip. In the *Doctor Who Weekly* days, the rest of the magazine was just filler for a Doctor Who comic book, whereas in the Davison era the comic becomes almost extraneous to the publication.

What is important to note about this is that the legitimacy of this paratext was necessarily based entirely on an argument of authority. Which is to say, the point of view of *Doctor Who Monthly* was legitimate primarily because it was the officially sanctioned magazine, not because of the merits of what it said. This doesn't mean what it said was rubbish—it was often, if not quite a good magazine, at least a far better magazine than it needed to be. But there's something tangibly strange about this authoritative version of fandom. The easiest place to see where it falls down is in the magazine's efforts to resolve continuity issues—and not just in cases like its reasonably well-documented aborted effort to treat the Hartnell-Troughton transition as something other than a regeneration. No, I'm talking about moments like its attempt to adjudicate the *Brain of Morbius* faces dispute by saying that all of the other faces are what Hartnell's Doctor looked like, or to set *The Five Doctors* in the 19th century in order to explain that the Cybermen were actually encountering Gallifrey for the first time, all to explain the Planet Fourteen line in *The Invasion*, an exemplary case of swallowing the spider to catch the fly.

These particular efforts all failed spectacularly—tellingly, none of them are even remotely part of any current discussion over their respective continuity points. There are two reasons for this. First, obviously, is that all of them are stupid. The idea that a group of eight middle-aged men, none of whom even look like each other, were all younger versions of William Hartnell, who, as it happens none of them look like either, is on the face of it ridiculous. Similarly, the sheer and massive weight of the implications raised by the claim that Gallifrey's "present" is equivalent to 19th century Earth is in staggering excess of a throwaway line from the late 60s.

But secondly, and in many ways more significantly, fandom on the whole never wanted definitive explanations of these things. Yes, of course they complained constantly about the errors, but it fundamentally misunderstands the desires of fandom to assume that just because they're complaining about something they want it fixed. In fact, the reason for pointing out something like "What are those faces in *The Brain of Morbius*?" or "What's with that Planet 14 reference in *The Invasion*?" is the fun of debating and proposing answers for the questions. The last thing anyone kvetching about Planet 14 wants is for some blowhard with a magazine column to offer some half-cocked "definitive answer," doubly so if the "definitive answer" is rubbish anyway. Fans don't want answers. They want things to argue about.

And so the authoritative paratext offered by *Doctor Who Monthly* was never going to be sufficient. That doesn't mean that it's useless, of course. The paratextual approach to television is a necessary part of managing a show with fans successfully. It's telling that Nathan-Turner's dance with fandom and selective doling out of information to keep them engaged and excited about the show is, these days, the playbook for every single creative force engaged in revamping an existing property with an extensive base of fans. Nathan-Turner's eventual fate of having the fans turn against him has been the death knell of more than one big Hollywood property, and while everybody grasps that you can't have a hit catering exclusively to hardcore fans, they equally grasp that when hardcore fans reject something they do so loudly; likewise, if they like it, they serve as enormously useful free advertising.

But more importantly, the paratextual approach can work tremendously well on a creative level. The most obvious example in the Davison era is *The Caves of Androzani*, Davison's regeneration story, which gained an entire second level of buildup and suspense from the early announcement in *Doctor Who Monthly* that it would be written by Robert Holmes, a writer whose reputation the magazine had bolstered in its overviews of past stories. It helped, of course, that the story was phenomenally good and that the build-up to it was actually paid off by what was transmitted, but on the other hand, part of the impact the story had on fandom was undoubtedly the fact that it was built to in the way it was.

Even from a fandom perspective, there's something satisfying about having a canonical paratext, so to speak. Yes, modern taste often differs sharply from the authorized accounts of the show, but it's still invaluable to have the authorized first draft of history around so as to understand how the conversation developed. Fandom history necessarily assumes a paratext to the show, and having at least some common ground in that paratext makes all of this much simpler.

So if *Doctor Who Monthly* is to be faulted it is not for creating a unified and authoritative paratext for Doctor Who, but in the particular ways in which it went about it. The most odious of these, of course, is the increasingly obvious way in which Nathan-Turner situates himself as a celebrity in his own right, developing catch-phrases (most obviously at this stage "stay tuned"). Nathan-Turner has an unfortunate tendency to conflate self-promotion with promotion of the show, making him impossible to extricate from the larger hagiography of the paratext.

Longleat, of course, was not the singular remedy to this. It couldn't be. But it marked a significant turn in this regard. And the heart of this turn comes out of a key fact about Doctor Who fandom, which is that there's a surprisingly long period during which it didn't really exist, which in turn means that once it started existing it didn't really act like a normal fandom. To some extent this is just cultural difference. *Doctor Who Monthly* covered with bemused distance the goings-on of American versus British fandoms fairly often in these days, reporting on conventions in other countries and the fans who did weird things like dress up in costumes. But the tone of the coverage makes it clear that these were the odd things that happened in America, where Doctor Who was a cult show.

In the UK, at least, Doctor Who never was a cult show, or, at least, it wasn't supposed to be. Its traditional Saturday evening slot was, as we've discussed before, a family slot such that Doctor Who was something the whole country watched. And even if it had been, the cosplay and fanfic aspects of fandom that define it in most people's minds were American inventions that hadn't migrated to the UK yet. The UK's Doctor Who fandom was, for a long time, an altogether different beast, and the fandom that leads to the quasi-official or outright official positions of involvement in the series remains so.

And in at least one argument, advanced particularly by Tat Wood both in *About Time* (I'm assuming the Longleat essay was by Wood, who was there, and not Miles, who was 11 at the time) and in his piece "Full Metal Frock Coat" reprinted in the second volume of *Time Unincorporated*, Longleat forms something of an origin point for this.

It may be helpful, some two thousand words into this piece, to explain what Longleat was. For years there were two permanent exhibitions of Doctor Who props and memorabilia, one in Blackpool and one at Longleat. In 1983, to celebrate the twentieth anniversary, the Longleat exhibition was, for Easter weekend, expanded to a full-blown convention with visiting actors, a screening room showing various stories, a huge number of props on display, and other such goodies. The BBC was famously overwhelmed by the number of people who showed up, with more people showing up on the first day than they had estimated for the entire weekend. (The number I'm seeing was 100,000 total. The Cardiff convention, meanwhile, was 3,000.)

This misestimate, it should be stressed, was not down to the BBC not understanding how many people were Doctor Who fans in the first place. Rather it was down to them misunderstanding the range of what Doctor Who fans were. They assumed, not unreasonably given the available data, that Doctor Who fans were just British *Star Trek* Fans. They weren't. *Star Trek* had always been a cult show. But Doctor Who fandom was a motley of people who didn't fit smoothly into any existing fan category—who, as Tat Wood put it, always assumed they were normal right up until their liking of Doctor Who was used to mark them as culturally "other."

And there's an incredibly narrow window in which that happens. In 1983 there's Longleat. Not two years later, there's the hiatus. This, in many ways, reflects one of Nathan-Turner's most fundamental misunderstandings. Because he, as much as anyone, assumed Doctor Who worked like a cult show and that teasing the audience endlessly with the return of various past glories was the way to build it up. The same failings that led the BBC to badly misjudge how many people would show up for Longleat also led them, in other words, to misjudge what "showing up" meant in the first place and to double down on a "for the fans" approach that left the series exceedingly vulnerable when Michael Grade came along. (More on that later.)

In reality the Doctor Who fandom of the early 80s was far better served some twenty-five years later by *Love and Monsters* than they ever were by anything Nathan-Turner put on the air. And Longleat was, for a substantial number of people, the moment they realized that another sort of fandom was sustainable. The sort that was less interested in the displays of trivia needed to lash together outlandish theories of Cybermen history, and certainly less interested in a final answer to the question, than they were in going to the pub and arguing about it for a few hours, preferably with digressions about whether or not you're going to foreground the Cybermen as instances of body horror, Soviet infiltrators, or clanking steel super-soldiers, and how these varying interpretations affect how you structure their history.

This would take years to blossom fully, but as a practical matter, at least, it remains key. In essence, this is where the fandom that would eventually bring the show back came from. And it's a very different sort of fandom—one that is more willing to slay sacred cows, one where mockery of the program is a form of love for it, and one where the show was consistently taken in a larger social context instead of as an end in itself.

It's tempting, of course, to contextualize this in terms of the show's inexorable march towards the myriad of blunders that resulted in its cancellation. But it can't be. Yes, the way in which the BBC attempted to interact with fans was a key part of how Doctor Who imploded—as was the nature of the more visible minority of fans who were closer to what the BBC expected. But on the other hand, it's difficult to imagine this strange sort of fandom evolving any faster than it did, or to imagine it riding to Doctor Who's salvation in the mid-80s. It's more accurate to say that even as the collapse approached and you began to be able to see it as inevitable, there were developments underway that were fundamental to the future of the series.

So with the future attended, then, let's turn to the past.

## In the Great Days of Rassilon, Five Great Principles Were Laid Down (*The Five Doctors*)

### Introduction to the Guidebook

It's November 23rd, 1983. Lionel Richie is at number one with "All Night Long (All Night)." For one of only two times in *TARDIS Eruditorum* we are forced to use the American charts, as this story actually aired two days earlier in the US than it did in the UK. This fact reflects the way in which Doctor Who, in the 1980s, was increasingly turning into a global export—a massive brand that raked in money for the BBC. This, of course, is not what you expect. In any other context global success would matter tremendously and would justify the show's continued existence. But the BBC is beholden to different rules, as is appropriate given the nature of its funding. The license payers deserve not to be ignored in favor of Americans. And so far from being a reason to keep the show on the air, Nathan-Turner's mad quest to chase American cult television fans at the expense of the license payers is, increasingly, a major problem.

Not, however, here—a story that is rightfully and properly delightful when it airs on November 25th, 1983. Billy Joel is at number one with "Uptown Girl," with Paul McCartney and Michael Jackson below him with "Say Say Say." The Cure are also in the top ten with "The Love Cats."

In real news, since March, sci-fi and the real world have merged uncomfortably with Ronald Reagan announcing the space-based and comically unfeasible Strategic Defense Initiative, derisively nicknamed "Star Wars." Samantha Smith manages the impressive feat of being used as a cheap propaganda tool by both the USSR and the US. Her resulting celebrity is the only reason she is on the plane whose crash kills her at the age of thirteen two years later.

Margaret Thatcher wins reelection in June in a landslide whereby an outright majority of voters opted for more left-wing parties, resulting in Thatcher having a 61% majority in the House of Commons. This massive vote of confidence emboldens Thatcher's government, and the Thatcherism we all know and loathe really begins here. Pioneer 10 flees the solar system four days later.

The Famicom, known in the US as the Nintendo Entertainment System, launches in Japan. The Global Positioning System is opened for civilian use. The GNU project is publicly announced. 38 IRA prisoners escape from Maze Prison. And US cruise missiles arrive at Greenham Common.

While, of course, on television we have a big one. *The Five Doctors*.

The problem with occasionally doing what I think of as the gonzo essays is that there is occasionally the sense that I'm expected, for a given "big" story, to provide one. In practice it's a bit more idiosyncratic than that. What makes a classic story and what makes a story that lends itself to an over-the-top gonzo essay do not, in fact, completely coincide. What enables a gonzo essay is a story in which there is some excess—in which the story messily signifies more than it quite means to, gesturing, often against its will, at a greater, more mythic order of things.

In this regard it is easiest to compare *The Five Doctors* with its obvious antecedent, *The Three Doctors*. *The Three Doctors* bristled with mythic possibility precisely because what it offered was so troubling within the context of Doctor Who.

The story broke rule after rule, at once connecting with a history of the program that the Pertwee era had at least briefly gestured at erasing, and breaking decisively with that past to open onto an altogether grander vista. So *The Three Doctors* invoked the past, but it was an unfamiliar and uncertain past that pointed towards a strange and unpredictable future. Blakean visions ensued. *The Five Doctors*, on the other hand, does little to facilitate such an essay. And this, more than anything, speaks volumes about the fallen state of the program.

It is not, of course, that it is bad. *The Five Doctors* is pure, unbridled fun. It does all that is required of it, and to ask more of it is churlish. What is telling, though, is that in ten years (or, really, closer to eleven) the nature of what is required of a multi-Doctor anniversary story has changed dramatically. In 1973 the history of the program was, oddly, both completely obscured due to the unavailability of documentation and thoroughly present—Hartnell had only been off the air for seven years, and Troughton just over three. By 1983, however, the history of the program had almost completely inverted. It was thoroughly well-documented, with *Doctor Who Monthly*, the Target line, the Haining book, and a wealth of other sources making information about the program more and more available. However, it had been almost a decade since Pertwee was on screen, and well over that for Troughton and Hartnell. The massive and monolithic wall of the Baker years stood between the present and the early history. In 1973 we didn't think we knew what the program had been, but in fact we remembered the spirit of it well. By 1983 we thought we knew exactly what the program had been, but couldn't be more wrong.

As a result, revisiting the past is not, in 1983, a sort of quasi-mystical and ritualistic act of self-definition to gather the whole of what the show was. It's a trip to the Doctor Who museum—Longleat for all. A butterfly gallery of once-magical creatures chloroformed, catalogued, brought out to flutter weakly for the license-paying audience. Far from gonzo, we have little more than an exhibit catalogue.

Program notes for the special exhibit, an eight quid extra ticket on top of your free museum admission:

## Exhibit 1.1: William Hartnell (Reconstruction)

The First Doctor, of course, never existed. Hartnell played only the Doctor, a unique character, replaceable only in hindsight. In *The Three Doctors* Hartnell returned, but too ill to summon the character, his appearance more a painful farewell, a last visit to the bedside of an ailing loved one. There are flashes of the animating fire that crackle beneath the surface, but merely flashes, the body serving as a living memorial to the spirit it once housed.

But what we have here is, in some ways, less ghoulish than that, at least. With only the already fading memory of *An Unearthly Child* from the *Five Faces* series to actually base a memory of the character on, Hurndall's imitation of the character is at least less painful than an obviously ailing Hartnell peering at his cue cards. It is not Hartnell's Doctor—not even close—but it is a credible First Doctor, the encyclopedia entry set of character traits that defined the first iteration of the character: a cranky old man, all "hmm"s and "dear boy"s. The physical resemblance is reasonably impressive—no worse than the obvious shifts in Davros and the Master that took place over the Baker era.

Still, it is telling that both Dicks and the story's original writer, Robert Holmes, instinctively wanted to sideline the character. In Holmes's script the First Doctor was to be an impostor diegetically as well as extra-diegetically, whereas in Dicks's original the Doctors' roles were to be recalibrated to include Tom Baker. Baker was to have the Gallifrey portion of the plot, with Davison taking the portion that went to Hurndall, and Hurndall being stuck in the TARDIS in the non-role given to Turlough and Susan. While perhaps a better handling of Hartnell's decline and death than was managed in

1973 while he was still alive, there is something terribly inadequate about it, a degree to which it proves the moment when the claim that *The Five Doctors* engages in an authentic history of the show becomes unsustainable.

## Exhibit 1.2: William Hartnell (Archive Footage)

An odd claim, advanced by some, is that the choice to include the brief clip of Hartnell before the credits undermines Hurndall's performance. This, of course, assumes that Hurndall was meant to fool anybody—an odd claim given that his appearance was milked as a trivia question from day one, or that Hartnell's death was an obscure mystery.

Hurndall's performance was always presented as a memorial to Hartnell. To say that it is imperfect—to illustrate that Hurndall is not a seamless replacement for Hartnell—is hardly an insult to either. Nobody would be so dismissive as to say that Hartnell was interchangeable with any other actor. The inclusion of a clip of Hartnell himself serves to underline this, to position Hurndall as what he is—a man paying homage to someone else's character and someone else's performance. To say that seeing Hartnell spoils the illusion suggests that the illusion could ever be maintained, or that even John Nathan-Turner would be crass enough to try. Of course Hurndall was talked up as being able to duplicate Hartnell. That's the polite thing to say in this situation. Nobody was meant to be fooled, and nobody was.

## Exhibit 1.3: Susan Foreman

Oddly haunting the proceedings, as she must, it is fitting that she is the only companion that we don't see summoned to the Death Zone; she simply shows up in the middle of a hallway. There's tacit acknowledgment that she's a Time Lord, at least—she recognizes Gallifrey and Gallifreyan history.

But this, in turn, only exacerbates the larger problems of the character. The Problem of Susan has been, hazily defined, a recurring theme of this project. It is, on the one hand, a placeholder for the more general problem of the companions and the Doctor's relationship with them. In Susan's case we first phrased this as the tension between the possibility of her growing up and taking some action on her own behalf, and of her subservience to the Doctor—a problem, in essence, of budding teenage sexuality.

Since then we have discovered the problem to exist in a more general sense. The transience of all companions when compared with the permanence of the Doctor means that the Doctor/companion relationship is always asymmetrical. No companion can ever be unique and irreplaceable to the Doctor because the structure of the story dictates that they all must be replaced. Nobody gets to travel in the TARDIS forever. Not even Romana—the one companion who in theory could have stayed forever. And so the companions are all interchangeable, simply because they must be interchanged. On the other hand, drama requires that they be essential and not extraneous to proceedings.

The result is that no companion quite makes sense outside of the limited context in which they exist on the show. They are optical illusions, tricks relying on forced perspective. Move the lens an inch onto their lives before or after the TARDIS and the illusion is shattered as we are forced to try to grapple with lives designed for the TARDIS outside that context. This, more than a fascination with mawkish and depressing sentimentality, is why all companion-return stories in the professional fanfiction are so bleak. Because these characters cannot and have never been able to sustain anything beyond the window of their lives that we see.

Susan, of course, is the first case of this—a character who only makes sense when she is travelling with her grandfather because of the weight of expectations involved in his departure—the endlessly deferred return that we know can never happen. But more than that, she is a character who only makes sense prior to the development of the series' mythology. It is telling that nobody on Gallifrey ever asks of their other prodigal, their other great renegade. Even when she appears on Gallifrey, in the Death Zone, she is ignored, treated as just another pointless human. The Problem of Susan is, in the end, that nobody who knew how the series would go would ever have written her in. She's a stranded artifact, at once central to the series mythology and unrevisitable because she no longer makes any sense. (The Virgin books entire Other mythology can, in one sense, be interpreted as a desperate attempt to shoehorn her into the otherwise seemingly family-free structure of Gallifrey. And while the Eighth Doctor's return to her in a few Big Finish audios—particularly *An Earthly Child*—are fairly well done, just the fact this can only happen in the show's ancillary materials rather demonstrates the point.)

And so Susan haunts the narrative, necessary and yet impossible to integrate. Ironically, by ignoring her, treating her with no characterization other than a tendency to hurt herself, and then shoving her in the TARDIS with no plot, she becomes the one piece of the series' history to be treated with complete authenticity and honesty.

**Exhibit 1.4: Dalek**

Obligatory, which says more about its involvement than anything else. Dicks has said that his strategy in writing *The Five Doctors* was to just put everything in and trust that nobody was going to look too hard at the glue. This is, again, essentially correct. The story proceeds not according to narrative logic but according to a paratextual logic. It is driven by a need to shove in every signifier of Doctor Who it can find, and more to the point, its audience knows it. It works not according to plot logic but according to the logic of nostalgia.

The Dalek is the point where this is most blatantly signposted. It appears, gets one scene, and is abandoned, having served its purpose. The audience, upon seeing this, knows exactly what sort of story this is.

But for those who approach *The Five Doctors* hoping for a significant story in its own right—a story that is about doing something instead of a live-action version of the Peter Haining book—this marks the point where it's obvious we will be disappointed. As, let's be fair, would anyone who might have been excited by the prospect of the Doctor fighting the Daleks once more, given that they'd not appeared in four years. (Again, though, they were supposed to have been in the previous story.)

## Exhibit 2.1: Patrick Troughton

The hardest presence to confine to a museum, of course. Mercury and pigeonholing were never going to be comfortable bedfellows. But the matter of encapsulating Troughton in a reunion story is more complex than just that. All of the Doctors suffer from a reunion story simply because they are forced to go from being lead actors to being part of an ensemble—something only Hartnell had previously had to deal with, and even then only in his earliest stories.

But Troughton is in some ways uniquely suited to this reversal simply because his character always controlled scenes from the margins. Relegated to the supporting cast, he is in his element. (Indeed, in one of the most subtle touches in *The Five Doctors*, Troughton even gets to peer out of a television monitor at the Fifth Doctor.) While quicksilver cannot be pigeonholed, its method of resistance is to be so free-flowing and amorphous that it can adopt any form, and so Troughton's Doctor in the reunion stories is the one who is most distant from his original characterization. Yet Troughton's ever-shifting nature in the role means this distance is, in many regards, just another manifestation of the mercury.

This leads, in these stories, to an odd effect. Troughton is, in all three of his returns to the series, the most compelling and likable thing on offer. The underlying mischievous twinkle that animated his Doctor still exists in what Tat Wood memorably describes as his "potty professor" guise. All of his charm is intact. And so watching him, in any of the three stories, they serve as effective first encounters. The three reunion stories were my first three Troughton stories. But they worked marvelously as gateways to his era proper, in which all of these pleasures of the character survive along with the other myriad depths Troughton was able to lend to the role.

## Exhibit 2.2: Brigadier Lethbridge-Stewart

It is impossible not to notice the fact that the companion pairings in *The Five Doctors* are completely wrong. It is, of course, a logistical problem, as ever, centering on Tom Baker's late departure and Frazer Hines's being unavailable due to commitments on *Emmerdale Farm*. But the result is unfortunate—Troughton is paired with the Brigadier, a character he'd only previously met in three stories (one of them a reunion) and has no particular attachment to.

Courtney, of course, is pure class and makes it work, pitching his performance with Troughton into a sort of retired buddy cop movie—two old warhorses dragged out of retirement for one last adventure. *Unforgiven* with Yeti. As it is impossible to train a camera on Nicholas Courtney and Patrick Troughton without something satisfying happening, this works.

But there's an obvious flaw in the plan. The decision to delay the big meet-up of the Doctors until the very end means that there is no time for a key scene, namely the one in which Courtney and Pertwee reunite. And so one of the most iconic and memorable pairings of characters in the series' history ends up being the simple exchange of two sentences before Pertwee blows off the Brigadier to go translate an inscription. Again, the checkbox nature of this story becomes altogether too clear—the fact that this story is about nothing more than the most abstract form of the past.

## Exhibit 2.3: Yeti

It is, of course, inexplicable what this is doing here. Apparently the Great Intelligence is casually animating Yeti on Gallifrey for no reason other than the desire to bring back some classic Second Doctor monster. But the sheer brevity of its nonsensical appearance only highlights the degree to which the zeal to add bits of everything into this story was ill-advised. One of the things that increasingly comes up in Doctor Who as it speeds towards cancellation is its low budget, but when one hits something like this, what, exactly, is one expected to do? They wasted money building a Yeti costume for a two-minute sequence instead of giving us more than two lines of dialogue between Pertwee and Courtney? Seriously?

## Exhibit 2.4: Jamie and Zoe

Ah, the big continuity error. And it was an accident. It was supposed to be Victoria Watling returning, not Wendy Padbury, and the Doctor was supposed to figure out that they were illusions when Victoria misidentified the Brigadier's rank, as he'd only been a Colonel when they met in *The Web of Fear*. Instead, of course, we have Troughton aware of the circumstances of his own regeneration, sparking the whole Season 6B thing (covered in Volume Two).

But what's really striking is the cruelty of this scene. Here, for one scene, we get a proper reunion—the core cast of the best-preserved season of Troughton—the one that people had gotten to see recently in *The Krotons*. And it's just illusions and phantasms—a trick from the mind of Rassilon. The touch of having the phantasms scream as they disappear is particularly bleak.

## Exhibit 2.5: *The War Games*

Curiously, nobody ever points out the extent to which Dicks is self-plagiarising here. The entire idea of the Death Zone and the Time Scoop is, after all, just *The War Games* applied to Doctor Who history instead of Earth history. But in positioning a game like this in the ancient and lost history of Gallifrey, especially around the time of Rassilon (who both put an end to the games and was entombed in the Death Zone) Dicks complicates the basic conception of the Time Lords. Or, rather, he brings them back to what they were when he first created them, when they were implicitly linked with the War Lords. That the Time Lords were, in the past, guilty of the exact same crime for which the War Lords are punished speaks volumes. The most obvious suggestion is that the War Lords were in fact rogue Gallifreyans, but the possibilities are vast and intriguing; another lost alternate history of Doctor Who.

## Exhibit 3.1: Jon Pertwee

The Doctor who ought be most suited to this style of reunion is, puzzlingly, the one least served by the script. The Pertwee era, more than any other era, lends itself to this museum approach, given that at times it seems to want to be nothing more than a collection of memes waiting for the Internet. And yet there is no Pertwee death pose, no Venusian aikido, no UNIT. He's even denied his proper costume, unlike Troughton, who gets to shed his overcoat once he's in the studio. (Here I must also cite my choice for the funniest moment in Volume Five of *About Time*, the observation that no theory of continuity can possibly account for Jon Pertwee's hair.) The brief interplay with the Master, the appearance of Bessie, and a quick polarity reversal are the extent to which the Pertwee era is plundered for references.

Pertwee is left to play an inchoate mass of paternalism, and he acquits himself well. But this transition from the action hero of memory to a doting old man who is kidnapped on his Sunday drive captures an interesting aspect of how the two Doctors who are actually brought back return. Both Pertwee and Troughton play their parts as though their characters have retired—as old men coming back for one last adventure. Indeed, the entire past of the program is shown implicitly as "past its prime."

This, of course, captures the fundamental anxiety at the heart of these proceedings, and, in many ways, at the whole of the program since *Earthshock*. On the one hand, Nathan-Turner is obsessed with strip-mining the program's history. On the other, Nathan-Turner remains obsessed with distinguishing himself and glorifying his tenure as producer. And so the program is increasingly obsessed with referencing its past for the sole purpose of trying to show how much better it is than the very past that it sees itself as primarily existing to reference.

The tightrope of ambivalence that I've been walking in this essay amounts, in most regards, to an ambivalence of execution and conception. The story does exactly what it has to and is charming. Nothing more was required than this cheery museum catalogue, and in many ways nothing more was wanted. But one cannot embrace this without also embracing the reduction of Doctor Who to a set of trivia answers that has happened over the season. Had this not been the capstone of a museum project that had been running for eighteen months and would continue interminably into the next story, it would be one thing. Instead it stands out as the one defensible moment in a sea of misguided self-indulgence, like an unpleasant drunk's one genuinely funny bit at a party.

## Exhibit 3.2: Sarah-Jane Smith

There is no scene that exemplifies the job of playing the companion quite like Lis Sladen gamely throwing herself down a small embankment and screaming in terror. All of which said, seeing her go from prospective leading woman in *K-9 and Company* back to interchangeable peril monkey is physically painful.

## Exhibit 3.3: Bessie

As strange as it is to see the era of the program's past that can most easily be reduced to a bunch of signifiers largely unmined, it is difficult to argue seriously that, in bringing back Bessie, they picked the most necessary of them. There is perhaps no symbol of the Pertwee era's wonderful and ludicrous excess as the action hero in a yellow roadster.

I never liked the Third Doctor era that much, and by the time I got my license was largely out of love with Doctor Who as well. Nonetheless, I still named my first car, a rusting sky blue Chevy S-10 pickup truck, "Bessie."

## Exhibit 3.4: Liz Shaw and Mike Yates

Ironically, Richard Franklin turns out to be terribly good at playing a character who is unsettlingly malevolent for reasons you cannot quite put your finger on. But again the shoehorn approach lets the story down, not least because this sequence comes prior to the corresponding sequence with Troughton. With two "phantasm" sections, the appearance of Jamie and Zoe is completely drained of all tension. As grim and cruel as that sequence is, it at least has real impact, or would have if we hadn't just seen Pertwee solve the exact same mystery a few minutes before. Was anyone so clamoring for the return of Liz Shaw and Mike Yates that this seemed like a good idea?

## Exhibit 3.5: Cybermen

There are, in the whole of this story, exactly two interesting ideas of what to do with the past Doctors. One we'll talk about later, and the other is pitting Pertwee against the Cybermen. This latter one is interesting because, of course, Pertwee is the only classic series Doctor to not have a Cybermen story in his era.

By most standards this is a trivia answer. But here it gets treated as a serious lack—as if Doctor Who had some real flaw in its past because one particular incarnation of the Doctor had never faced one particular monster. Aside from turning a given era of the program into a bucket list (Nicholas Courtney—check, Daleks—check, Cybermen—check; OK, on to the next old fuck with an Equity card) it serves as evidence of that strange breed of thought that thinks that monsters are the most important part of Doctor Who. This strain of thought is unfortunate, having produced exactly one good idea, ever. (Paul Cornell's idea of the Doctor being what monsters have nightmares about, natch.) And its increasing prevalence in this era is part and parcel of why *The Five Doctors* had no expectations resting on it beyond checking boxes. The Cybermen, in this vision, are treated as an abstract idea, valued because they appeared on Doctor Who. Why would the series do more than check boxes for its anniversary when a substantial portion of its audience actually gives a damn whether this particular set of tin soldiers faced off with this particular actor?

I'd say that the onscreen results of this obligatory confrontation (again, picked over having Jon Pertwee actually meaningfully interact with his own supporting cast) should be forcibly shown on repeat to anyone who thinks that Doctor Who is mostly about monsters until they repent, but the fact of the matter is that most of them wouldn't understand the problem in the first place. To quote, or at least paraphrase Gareth Roberts, those people got what they wanted: *Attack of the Cybermen*.

## Exhibit 3.6: Terrance Dicks

For all my bitterness surrounding this story—a bitterness that focuses mainly on the fact that it's now impossible to do another reunion story with Patrick Troughton and Jon Pertwee and so I'm forced to look at this as the missed opportunity for the sort of epic and totemic reunion story that I genuinely believe could have been done, and, indeed, that was done in 1973—I ought stress for the umpteenth time that it is utterly delightful and fun. It must, of course, have been far more so at the time, when the home video releases didn't exist and all of these returns were thrilling and new and, for many, the first time they'd gotten to see Troughton or Pertwee. Now that this has fallen into nostalgia as well, it's indistinguishable from all the other Pertwee or Troughton stories on one's DVD shelf save for the fact that it's dodgier. At the time there was real magic to it.

So much of the credit for that magic goes to Terrance Dicks, whose strengths as a writer are utterly played to here. His ability to stitch a ludicrous set of elements together with nothing more than the ability to sketch a high concept idea out efficiently and his knack for plucky adventure yarns is the thing that saves this story from being *Arc of Infinity 2: Biodata Boogaloo*. It takes a very, very good writer with a very, very good understanding of how audiences work to grasp that the script doesn't have to make plot sense if it makes thematic sense. Realizing that he didn't have to figure out how to make it all sensible, but just get it all on screen, was a stroke of genius.

## Exhibit 3.7: Robert Holmes (currently on loan to another museum)

Seemingly everybody agreed that the writer of this story would finally break Nathan-Turner's "no writers from before my time" rule that he clearly develops after Season Eighteen. Initially it was to be Robert Holmes, a decision spearheaded by Eric Saward, who, not unreasonably, felt him the best of his predecessors. Holmes took poorly to the "everything and the kitchen sink" approach, having famously not given a shit about continuity, and was politely eased out in favor of Dicks, who had been sounded out as a backup plan early on. Saward and Holmes remained on good terms, however.

## Exhibit 4.1: Tom Baker and Lalla Ward (Archive Footage)

Several times in the comments of the blog, there's a bit of a debate over how long the shadow of Tom Baker really hangs over the program. The answer is at least "until *Rose*" if not "until David Tennant finally beats him in a most popular Doctor poll." Here we see it at, perhaps, its sharpest and longest.

Baker had, of course, only been out of the role for two years when the story filmed. It is wholly understandable why he did not want to return at this point. It's harder to credit in the context of his later reluctance to engage with the program, admittedly, but that's neither here nor there. And if we're being honest it would have been a challenge to integrate him. In this story Davison's alleged "blandness"—a trait that really means his tendency not to recklessly steal scenes from everyone around him—is largely a benefit, simply because it means everyone can be on about the same footing in the big shared scene at the end. Whereas, let's face it, the scene would have been harmed by inserting a Tom Baker-sized ego into it.

Still, his absence here is palpable. I remember being crushed when I put the tape in for the first time, thinking I'd finally get my third Tom Baker story, then being doubly thrilled to see that I was going to get my first Romana story, then finding out that they weren't really in it and it was just old footage from *Shada*. Delightful footage, of course, but still, only a fragment.

Again, as with the *Five Faces*, the real effect of this is the erasure of a significant period of Doctor Who. The way in which the six seasons between Pertwee and Nathan-Turner are so barely referenced in anything that comes after creates an odd effect. For a program so obsessed with its own past, the blatant ignoring of the most popular segment of the past is telling, if only inadvertently. Given the lack of respect Nathan-Turner shows to the past he plunders, his failure to ever engage with the most popular period looks like cowardice, regardless of whether or not it was.

## Exhibit 4.2: Tom Baker (Reconstruction)

Hypothesis: If the moment in which Lis Sladen hurls herself down a small hill in the name of peril monkeying is the moment of Doctor Who that most perfectly embodies the companion, the decision to have a wax dummy of Tom Baker stand in for a photoshoot is the moment that most perfectly embodies John Nathan-Turner.

## Exhibit 4.3: Leela (currently on loan to another museum)

While researching this piece, the fact that most staggered me was that Louise Jameson had offered to return for the story and was turned down because they couldn't find a way to put her in. Let that sink in for a bit, as it serves as one of the more damning pieces of evidence that Nathan-Turner deliberately sidelined the Baker years.

Yes, Jameson lacked a Doctor to be paired with. But the task of integrating her into the story would have been trivial given that she was already on Gallifrey. You know, where the story is set. Indeed, adding her would have done little more than give Davison someone to play off of in the Gallifrey scenes and, perhaps more importantly, would have represented the Baker era in more than just passing. Indeed, Leela is in many ways the perfect companion for this, given that she's the companion that spanned the two main producers of the Baker era—the one who has something resembling a legitimate claim to represent the whole of it.

And so her absence stings the most. Because her omission, when she was available and wanted to appear, constitutes a real failure to represent the Baker era in a story that is otherwise preposterously obsessive about shoehorning everything in. And no, Sarah Jane doesn't cut it. Yes, she's primarily a Baker-era companion, but she's explicitly used here as a Pertwee companion. This only heightens the sense that the Baker era is getting actively ignored.

No way to write her in. Feh.

**Exhibit 4.4: K-9**

Well, and then there's K-9. Whose cameo status is, at least, wholly understandable—with the bulk of the story being filmed on location in Wales (standing in as the dark secret at the heart of Gallifrey, lol) he was never going to work well, and Dicks specifically asked to be spared dealing with him, which is, given that he was stepping in at the last minute because Robert Holmes couldn't get the scripts to work, more than fair.

K-9 is, in many ways, the last throw of the dice for the Baker era, and reiterating his new pairing with Sarah Jane makes this the one non-Shada scene to evoke the Baker years. But, of course, they only appeared together on Nathan-Turner's watch. That irritating egoism and tendency of Nathan-Turner to just cut out the bits of Tom Baker he didn't do persists even here. And so a scene that does encompass virtually the whole of the Tom Baker years—he only appeared in seven stories that didn't feature one of Sarah Jane or K-9—is somehow prevented from actually serving to honor his tenure.

**Exhibit 5.1: Peter Davison**

If ever there was a Doctor one might worry about getting upstaged in this, it would have to be Davison. At Longleat he was voted the worst Doctor because, apparently, he was bland—a classic case of why you can't always trust the audience to tell you what they want. Davison's Doctor may have his flaws—although I frankly don't really see them, viewing him as one of the finest actors to have played the part—but blandness isn't one of them. Bad writing often is, but even in his worst scripts Davison manages to sell the part, making his Doctor a flurry of activity. "We don't like Davison because he's bland," is in reality little more than an inarticulate way of saying, "We still miss Tom Baker." In practice, Davison is magnificent here, and even if he doesn't get to be paired with Tom Baker, he more than shows that he belongs in the company of his predecessors.

It was Troughton, of course, who encouraged Davison to leave after three years. And in the rehearsals for *Castrovalva*, apparently, Troughton dropped by to say hello and stood in for Davison in setting up a scene. Troughton, in other words, was always a bit of a mentoring presence for Davison, and that carries over here to how he plays the role. It's worth watching his scenes with Hurndall, in which he manages at once to defer to Hurndall, recognizing that in this story he's not the real main attraction, while simultaneously putting his stamp on things. Troughton-like, he flits on the edges of the scene, managing to provide a commentary on his earlier selves without upstaging them.

He is, of course, helped tremendously by Baker's deciding not to do the special and, accordingly, getting the Gallifrey plot instead of being one of the "to the tower" Doctors. This makes him the odd Doctor out—the one who gets a plot that's unlike the others. Yes, it also means he's the one who gets cheaply mind controlled, but nobody's perfect.

**Exhibit 5.2: The Master**

Amusingly, he works here, if only because the story has no illusions that he works anywhere else. He is unapologetically played as a bit of a buffoon. His scene storming into the Tower at the end and whining angrily that the Doctors were all terribly mean to him is not only deft characterization, it's wonderfully spot-on. I'd say that it's the perfect end for the character's somewhat superfluous role in proceedings here, but it's not. The Brigadier decking him is the perfect end, and just about makes up for the appalling three-line scene with Pertwee.

Note also that Dicks quietly fixes Robert Holmes's (in hindsight) poor decision to set a definite endpoint for the series, by establishing that giving a Time Lord a new cycle of regenerations is not only possible but the sort of thing that gets handed out as casual payment.

**Exhibit 5.3: Tegan**

The other interesting idea that the story has is pairing Tegan with the First Doctor. Unfortunately, almost nothing about the idea actually works. It's based on the misapprehension that the First Doctor's character is defined merely by his crankiness, first of all, and that there's something strange about pairing him with a loudmouthed or strong-willed person. In practice, of course, Hartnell got paired with strong-willed characters all the time. Tegan has nothing on Barbara. Nothing. (To say nothing of the episodes where Hartnell is paired with Nicholas Courtney's Brett Vyon.)

But on top of that, nothing gets done with it. There isn't any hilarious banter between Tegan and the First Doctor. They don't share quips. Tegan doesn't get to put the Doctor in his place. It turns out that what happens when you pair Tegan with the First Doctor is that Tegan looks sullen and grouchy and doesn't do anything, an outcome that comes perilously close to suggesting that all Tegan really needs is a disciplinarian who will shut her mouth.

## Exhibit 5.4: Turlough

Turlough is also in this story, as it happens, though you'd hardly know watching it. Still, at least he gets to appear in all the other stories around this, so, you know, it's less depressing watching him get pointlessly shoved in the TARDIS than it is to watch Carole Ann Ford get hired only to be wasted in the TARDIS with Turlough.

## Exhibit 5.5: Gallifrey

Ah, yes. Gallifrey. This is the last of the four Gallifrey stories, though *Trial of a Time Lord* flirts with the iconography. Everyone points out that Cardinal Borusa is played by four different actors in the course of four stories, but what's pointed out less is that there are unmistakably multiple Gallifreys. In *The Deadly Assassin* the Doctor needs to be told who Rassilon is. Here everybody knows rhymes and stories about Rassilon and his tomb, and Gallifrey manages to find another dark secret in the heart of it all.

Given this it's actually surprising just how well Rassilon's appearance works. The moment when the faces on his tomb come to life and begin looking around frantically is one of the great moments of a horrific concept overcoming its technical limitations and managing to be really creepy anyway.

But on the whole Gallifrey suffers the worst from the museum approach, and it's here that the gulf between 1973 and 1983 becomes most apparent. In *The Three Doctors*, Gallifrey was still treated as a mysterious place of powerful beings we knew little about, with secrets that would be revealed. Here, Gallifrey is treated as something we all know everything about, with the Death Zone being just one previously unmentioned detail. The lushness of *The Deadly Assassin* has given way to excessive glitter and "space" doors that, as is hilariously pointed out by David Tennant in the

25th Anniversary commentary track for this story, are just doors with two handles screwed on.

And then there's the mind probe.

All of which said, we here reach the limit of my critical capacity, and that limit is Chancellor Flavia. Nothing about Dinah Sheridan's performance or the role as written begins to account for her status within fandom. And yet I, without having any real knowledge of that status, similarly took to Chancellor Flavia as being a terribly important character. Part of this was that she was, apparently, the new Lord President of Gallifrey and thus would presumably be important. But this seems insufficient to explain the level of fascination she holds (for instance, Davies and Collinson nicknaming the "Time Lordy" music of the Davies/Tennant era as "Chancellor Flavia's Theme"). Nor is her potential as a camp icon quite enough. She transcends all reason.

**Exhibit 5.6: Theme Music**

While I am not among those who hate the Peter Howell arrangement of the theme music, the moment in the closing credits when the Delia Derbyshire theme gives way to the Howell theme is horrible, and not just because of the rough change in key.

**Exhibit 5.7: How it All Started**

The story goes out of its way to have its ending supposedly mirror "how it all started," with Tegan getting in a painfully awkward line about the Doctor "deliberately choosing to go on the run from your own people in a rackety old TARDIS" at the end. But, of course, that's not how it all started. It started with two people falling out of the world into a strange and mysterious space that didn't make sense. It didn't start with Time Lords at all. And it certainly didn't start following a ninety-minute museum tour of the series' past.

This is, in many ways, a microcosm of my ambivalence over this story. By returning to an imaginary past and then making an ending that amounts to shouting, "Twenty more years, just like this!" the series is, in effect, completely abandoning all possibility of what it once was—a show about the strange and the unsettling. Doctor Who has, at long last, given up all prospect of being anything other than comfort food for a particular sort of nostalgia fetishist. This story isn't what does it. The Nathan-Turner era has been careening towards it since Bidmead left, and it has more brutal collisions with it to come. It's implicit, in many ways, in the shift from being a science fiction show at Saturday teatime to a sci-fi soap opera.

And it's in many ways implicit in the general cultural turn towards franchise/property-based science fiction. Doctor Who is first and foremost a brand, and when brands have anniversaries this is the sort of anniversary they have. All of this is just the consequences of 1983 playing out over poor Doctor Who. But it's very hard to be anything short of dismayed by it. As wonderful as the program can be through the Davison era, and even though it hits wonderful far more often than it is given credit for, it's impossible not to be more than faintly disappointed by what the program is here, compared to what it once was.

## Exhibit 5.8: The British Broadcasting Corporation

*The Five Doctors* gave the classic series its last *Radio Times* cover, as well as its first since *The Three Doctors*. Many people have tremendously fond memories of it, myself included, and I didn't even see it on transmission. It was a moment of absolute love for Doctor Who, fuelled, crucially, by the existence of absolute love for Doctor Who.

But ultimately the BBC did not see it that way. The program, in its halls, was a joke—a lingering contractual obligation to dump lesser talent on. In the eyes of many, this was why John Nathan-Turner had the job in the first place.

The budget for a ninety-minute special was allocated because of the special occasion, and the fact that it was a populist moment that had importance under an ideological vision of what the BBC was that still endured, even if it was now a much smaller aspect of the BBC's self-image than it had been when Sydney Newman suggested science fiction as the new family entertainment. But for all of it, in a grim application of alchemical principles, the situation outside the production team mirrored that within: "Let's celebrate our anniversary by lying back and thinking of England."

## Pop Between Realities, Home in Time for Tea: *The Adventure Game*

I am not entirely convinced that I have, in the course of writing *TARDIS Eruditorum*, actually watched anything weirder than *The Adventure Game*. It is the sort of thing that, as one watches, one has the increasingly clear realization that nobody who has never seen this would ever believe me about what it's like. *The Adventure Game* is really the first 1980s example of what we saw back with *Children of the Stones*—one of those pieces of television that sticks in the brain, deeply embedded, to later come out in a triumphantly cathartic conversation to the effect of, "Yes, yes, I remember that!" It's just that where *Children of the Stones* was a work of supremely effective horror, *The Adventure Game* is just sort of the living embodiment of the 1980s.

The easiest way to describe *The Adventure Game* is that it's what everybody who foolishly wants the Celestial Toymaker to make a return appearance should watch instead. It is, in effect, that story done right and as an ongoing series. In each episode a trio of celebrities from the B-list or below (possibly far below—I'm not actually sure everybody who appears on the show is actually a celebrity) are stuck on a fictitious alien planet called Arg and left to escape by playing odd real-life board games and solving puzzles. And, you know. Talking to angry plants that they have to address with the proper terms of respect or risk evaporation.

What is most important to *The Adventure Game* is not its almost completely incoherent world-building, but its sense of tone. All of the elements are familiar in the abstract as parts of a *Captain Kangaroo*-esque children's television show. But instead of being presented straightforwardly as a world that the viewing children are invited to understand, *The Adventure Game* presents its world as a puzzle to be continually figured out.

A prime example is Rongad, a character in the third and fourth series of the show, who speaks backwards. That is, he reverses the letter order of every word he says as well as his sentence structure. In a normal piece of children's television, this would be presented as, essentially, an in-joke for savvy viewers. His appearances would serve to reintroduce the central concept, and the pleasure would be in the ability of the audience to make sense of the apparent randomness.

But *The Adventure Game* doesn't give them the chance. Even if you know the trick to Rongad it's impossible to make sense of what he's saying simply because auditory parsing of backwards English at conversational speeds is not actually possible. So we get a world in which there are rules, but knowing the rules is not entirely useful. The show is not a comforting piece about learning by repetition, but one about living under the capricious exercise of power.

This, of course, corresponds with what the show is actually about. The content of the show is based on watching the guest stars try to figure out puzzles and maneuver their way through Arg. So, for instance, in the episode of most interest to Doctor Who fans, where Janet Fielding appears, there's a puzzle based on floating an egg up from the bottom of a glass to acquire a piece of string tied around it, where solving the puzzle hinges on a sort of pragmatic scientific knowledge of the fact that the egg will float in salt water. Elsewhere the players are confronted by strange logic games and expected to figure out some account of what's going on. All of it is structured so that the audience, particularly if they're familiar with the show, is just ahead of the players, but only just. The show isn't about watching people try to figure out a set of rules the audience already has down, but about watching them make sense of a not-quite-scrutable world at a slightly slower speed than the audience.

But to anyone who's been reading *TARDIS Eruditorum* from the start, all of this should be terribly familiar. Using schoolboy science to solve mysteries on an alien planet with defined rules that the audience figures out slightly faster than the characters? That's no 80s piece of children's television, that's the Hartnell era. But there's a key difference between *The Adventure Game* and the Hartnell era: in the Hartnell era, the whole point was the juxtaposition of the ordinary people (represented by Ian and Barbara) and the bizarre and hard-to-figure-out world. But in *The Adventure Game* the point is the lack of juxtaposition. *The Adventure Game* hinges on the fact that B-list celebrities can and do habitually drop in on strange alien worlds to engage in some puzzle solving. Put another way, the Hartnell era hinged on the fact that it was unusual that Ian and Barbara were in these situations, whereas *The Adventure Game* is utterly unconcerned with this question, and indeed takes it off the table by making it perfectly ordinary that these sorts of people might be confronting Rongad.

I'd engage in a rhetorical flourish here of holding off on explaining why for a few paragraphs, but anyone who has seen even fragments of *The Adventure Game* would get the answer immediately, so there's really no point. The entire visual iconography of *The Adventure Game* is based around computer games. And not just in a vague "cheap 80s computer graphics" way. No, *The Adventure Game* goes out of its way to invoke specific games, including bits of what are obviously *Pac-Man*, *Asteroids*, *Space Invaders*, and *Frogger* in its credit sequence, among others.

Lest anyone think this is just a show about video games, however, the montage of video game footage is paired, in the beautifully dissonant opening credits sequence, with a lovely bit of chamber music. The result is striking, and communicates the strange tone of the show perfectly. It's about video games, yes, but it's not about the culture of video games. Rather, it's about the intellectual aspects of video games. This phrase sounds a bit odd to 2015 ears, when video games have become mass entertainment, often of the crudest sort. But from the perspective of 1980, when the series debuted, it makes perfect sense. Video games—or, more accurately, computer games—were part of the rapidly emerging technology of the personal computer, which was still a technology dominated by the computer nerd. Those were the days when hackers really were bright kids in their bedrooms messing around and not associates of Eastern European organized crime rings.

I talked a bit about this back in the *Logopolis* essay, and a bit again back in the Hitchhiker's Guide essay (and it's worth slipping in a comment that Douglas Adams was invited to write *The Adventure Game* but declined) but here it becomes necessary to dial it in a bit more. Simply put, the early and mid-80s were the heyday of fascination with logic games, puzzle solving, and, oh yes, let's not forget, *Dungeons & Dragons*. Which I mention in part because *The Adventure Game* was explicitly modeled on *Dungeons & Dragons*.

To the modern roleplaying ear this may sound ludicrous, but go look at the supplements to some proper old-school *Dungeons & Dragons*. *Tomb of Horrors* is always a good choice. Far from being an adventure about killing monsters, the *Tomb of Horrors* module spends considerable effort telling potential Dungeon Masters that this is not an adventure about killing monsters; indeed, it goes so far as to suggest that they're bad people if their games are mostly about that. From there the module proceeds into what is the most infamously absurd set of roleplaying puzzles ever, including opportunities to die horribly trying to find the entrance to the dungeon. From there you get rooms with levers on the wall that will kill you if set them improperly, holes you can climb through that permanently destroy your character, secret doors leading to death traps, and other works of pure sadism. There is even a hallway that will change your gender if you traverse it. If you attempt to go back through it to reverse the effect, your character is teleported out of the dungeon. Naked. Not that anybody was working through some issues here or anything.

I go into this tangent to communicate something that may not be apparent to people whose knowledge of *Dungeons & Dragons* comes primarily from more recent gaming, which is that in its original conception *Dungeons & Dragons* is basically about the repeated and extended torture of its would-be players for sport. But perhaps stranger than this is the fact that people actually thought it was fun. *Tomb of Horrors* is not some hated adventure widely loathed for its unfairness and lack of entertainment. It's one of the all-time classic *D&D* adventures. And this is the thing that people who are not familiar with the roleplaying games of the period don't quite get—that classic roleplaying games are about solving willfully sadistic logic puzzles—a spirit that *The Adventure Game* captures perfectly.

Equally important is the connection between this and computer games. The ones shown in *The Adventure Game*'s credits are not, however, the really relevant ones. No, the relevant ones are things like *Zork* or Richard Garriott's *Ultima*. And the thing that becomes immediately clear if you play one of these games, particularly if you play them with, say, *The Space Museum* on in the background, is that in a very real sense these games are the true and proper heir of Hartnell-era Doctor Who and the old "hard SF" tradition that got displaced by *Star Wars*.

Indeed, in many ways these games are better at this sort of thing than the media that used to contain them. The influence of *Dungeons & Dragons* on *The Five Doctors* is blatant, but the really strange thing is that there's no particular reason to think it was deliberate—Terrance Dicks is not exactly the sort of guy you expect to know what THAC0 is. Rather it's that the basic dynamic of "and then everyone goes on a quest to the scary tower" has, in 1983, been so subsumed by gaming that everyone goes to *Dungeons & Dragons* instead of "Childe Roland to the Dark Tower Came." Without anyone meaning to, *The Five Doctors* becomes Doctor Who as roleplaying campaign. Patrick Troughton even gets to cast magic missile at the darkness. Sorry. "Galactic Glitter."

So by just doing what he and Doctor Who had been doing for twenty years, Terrance Dicks found himself writing a *D&D* game with Time Lords. Except this is also where the wheels come off. By any reasonable measure the most cringeworthy sequence of *The Five Doctors* is the lethal chessboard that's as "easy as pi," an attempt to shoehorn in a good old-fashioned maths lesson into a Doctor Who plot. But by 1983 this sort of schoolboy know-how/technobabble blend just didn't work anymore. Anyone watching could see immediately that there was no actual relationship between pi and how you crossed the floor. And in 1983, that wasn't going to cut it. In a culture where sci-fi fans were accustomed not only to problems like this but to actually figuring them out themselves, you can't just hand-wave it. Nor can you explain it terribly well, because lecturing about pi and mapping it to a chessboard somehow makes for terrible television.

Well, usually. Somehow, of course, *The Adventure Game* manages it. But, of course, its trick is fairly obvious—the people playing *The Adventure Game* are actually solving the puzzles in real time. They're not delivering dialogue, but muttering and poking at things trying to figure them out. Indeed, in an interview the producers of *The Adventure Game* noted that one of the hardest parts of getting the show to work was figuring out how to edit the puzzle-solving into watchable television, since it couldn't be made to sound like TV dialogue no matter how they cut it.

All of this marks, then, the final and sputtering death of the original conception of what the series was for. The idea of Doctor Who as a show about seeing the Doctor solve puzzles is now over. It hasn't been the main focus of the series for a while, but now we're at a point where it really can't be the focus at all. It's simply not satisfying to watch someone figure out logic puzzles when you can figure out better ones yourself. I said that *The Adventure Game* was what *The Celestial Toymaker* was trying to be, and given that, it's telling that *The Adventure Game* has as its marquee logic puzzle a kind of cool and reasonably complex maze-based board game whereas *The Celestial Toymaker* has the Towers of Hanoi.

I'm rarely one for the argument that video games let you "be" the character in the story and that this is preferable, but when it comes to puzzle-solving, it largely is. It is, in fact, more satisfying to solve the logic puzzles in *Zork* yourself than it is to watch William Hartnell play Towers of Hanoi, or to watch Richard Hurndall make some vague comments about pi before walking across the room the same way he would have for any other explanation. The reason, of course, is sensible—because puzzles were something for self-solving first. The idea of showing other people solving puzzles in books or on television was a temporary invention of the golden age of science fiction. Once computers came along they reverted back to type, becoming what they always were: games.

But because Doctor Who started in that milieu there remains a sizable chunk of people who think that the series is about a practical handyman who solves puzzles. In practice, that approach to storytelling was a blip in the narrative tradition. And *The Adventure Game* is a fascinating artifact of the period where that function moved back to media more suited to such a task.

## Three Hundred Million Years Out of Your Comfort Zone (*Warriors of the Deep*)

It's January 5th, 1984. The Flying Pickets are at number one with "Only You," with Paul McCartney's "Pipes of Peace" knocking them off a week later as they manage one of the most impressive drops I've ever seen from a number one single, plunging down to ten. Billy Joel, Kenny Rogers and Dolly Parton, Culture Club, and Frankie Goes to Hollywood all also chart, the latter with "Relax." (Frankie Goes to Hollywood, it should be noted for Americans, were not a one hit wonder in the UK at all.)

In the month and change since *The Five Doctors* aired, Lynda Mann was murdered, though the newsy part of that came many years later when the murderer, Colin Pitchfork, became the first person in Britain to be convicted based on DNA evidence. An IRA car bomb exploded outside Harrods in the Christmas shopping center. Pope John Paul II visited the man who attempted to assassinate him to forgive him. And during this story a hurricane-force storm kills six in Britain.

While on television. It has been pointed out, back when these essays were just blog posts, that my views on the Davison era are considerably closer to the standard critical consensus than my views on most other eras of the show. This is a fair point, and this book, or at least the first section of it, is somewhat more focused on explaining why the era is looked at the way that it is than in coming up with new readings. There is, on one level, a very simple reason for this: I think the overall consensus on this part of the Nathan-Turner era is solid, which, in turn, is because it's just about the most analyzed portion of Doctor Who around save, perhaps, for the new series, which is so deliciously oversignified that the existing critical consensus can't be grasped at all.

All of which said, I think the era as a whole gets an unfairly rough ride. There are systemic problems, which I've pointed out at length and will continue to do so, but there are also moments of real quality, including in oft-overlooked stories. And then there is *Warriors of the Deep*, about which I sadly, if not unexpectedly, find myself with virtually nothing good to say. This is a universally hated story. It is rightly hated. All of which said, the reason it's hated is so limited: its poor effects. Yes, this story has lamentable effects, ranging from a badly overlit set to a giant lizard monster called the Myrka that is flagrantly just a pantomime horse. But I've kept a decent policy of not criticizing Doctor Who for poor effects and I'm not going to break it here. To suggest that the Myrka, or any of the shoddiness of the production, really, is the actual problem with the story is ridiculous. They're symptoms of the problem. The story wouldn't be significantly improved by better effects. It just wouldn't have quite as obvious a punching bag.

Michael Grade, responsible for pulling the trigger on the 1985 hiatus, has apparently cited this story as the one that persuaded him that Doctor Who was crap, a claim that Eric Saward took issue with, pointing out that Grade was in a position to give the program more money. But on the flip side of this, what possible reason would Michael Grade have for giving more money to a program that's blowing what it has on a pantomime horse? I mean, it's tough to point at this and call it a compelling case for giving the program more money.

This is not a defense of Michael Grade as such, as he's guilty of the same basic mistake. Neither Grade nor Saward, apparently, can conceive of Doctor Who as anything more than the BBC version of *Star Wars*. Which, of course, it cannot possibly be on any budget that the BBC could possibly provide. I mean, that's just not what the BBC is good at. It never has been.

To some extent the confusion understandable. Everybody loved *Earthshock*, and like any era of Doctor Who, the Saward era proceeded to try to get lightning to strike twice. And this is blatantly a remake of *Earthshock*, right down to the returning monster and the bleak ending. This is completely understandable, as was redoing *The Silurians* two years later in the form of *The Sea Devils*, or *The Tenth Planet* four months later as *The Moonbase*. The problem was that *Earthshock* was largely unrepeatable, having been the biggest case of getting away with it in the classic series. *Earthshock* worked by changing directions sharply in the second episode, having a genuinely unexpected ending, and featuring the shock return of the series' second-best-known monsters (even if their unexplained appearance at the end of Episode One was probably stretching it for some viewers).

*Warriors of the Deep*, on the other hand, is exactly what it looks like it will be after its first episode: the massively hyped return of twelve-year-old monsters and no shock in its ending at all. With none of that gut-punching impact, we get what *Earthshock* was all along—a mediocre action serial that was remarkable for its chutzpah, not its execution. So when that execution dips, as it had to here when the 1983 general election led to Doctor Who losing studio time, the fragile soap bubble of quality that *Earthshock* represented bursts traumatically.

But the conclusion everybody draws from this—that all *Warriors of the Deep* needed was money—is ludicrous. First, what *Warriors of the Deep* needed was to be made by people who weren't trying to do things they self-evidently could never do well. It needed to be a story that wasn't going to have all of its hopes rest on the ability of the BBC to get the Myrka to come off, simply because there's never been a point, in the twenty-year history of the program, where it ever looked like the BBC could do something like the Myrka. The list of successful "giant X" monsters in the pre-CGI era of Doctor Who is simply nonexistent. So why the hell was it trying to do an action movie based around a giant monster? To blame the Myrka's execution for letting the story down is like blaming gravity when a man jumps off a building. A pantomime horse is exactly what anyone pitching the Myrka should have expected for Doctor Who, and the only people really implicated in its failure are the ones who decided to do it anyway. Which, in the case of this story, includes John Nathan-Turner, who demanded the Myrka be included even after director Pennant Roberts, realizing it was going to be a disaster, begged to scrap it.

Second, and more importantly, *Warriors of the Deep* really needed people who understood the underlying premise of the original source material. The rip-off of Malcolm Hulke's work here is painfully ironic, given that Hulke was the writer who showed the most anxiety about the last time Doctor Who mistook itself for a militaristic action show. (Though admittedly, ill-advised attempts at giant lizards are a staple of Malcolm Hulke's scripts; the only script of his to lack one had a giant testicle instead.) *The Silurians* was, at its heart, about Hulke's own dislike for the idea that the Doctor was going to be an employee of the military-industrial complex. The entire concept of the Silurians was that they weren't monsters but another race with as legitimate a set of views as the humans. The point of the end of the story was that there was another way, it was just precluded by assuming that the series was going to be military action where the Doctor's primary support was coming from people who were good at shooting stuff. Even in *The Sea Devils*, when this aspect of the plot is systematically marginalized, the point is that the humans make a wrong decision at a key moment that prevents the possibility of peace. Even if this is taken away, at the very least the point of *The Silurians* is that the "monsters" actually have distinct personalities and are not a blank monoculture to be blown up.

Whereas in *Warriors of the Deep* the Silurians are interchangeable, the Sea Devils are a mostly mute warrior race, and both of them have inexplicably adopted the human names for them (which is bewildering, given that by any standard "Sea Devil" is a pejorative in its original context). They spend the entire story acting like generic monsters, with the Doctor being the only person who gives any sort of argument that they might be different. When the Doctor finally meets up with their leader, he's told, "Oh, no, we've gone generic monster." It would be difficult to approach this story in a way that more systematically undermines the point of these specific monsters. Every possible effort is made to take monsters whose entire *raison d'être* was to not be generic monsters and make them into generic monsters.

Given this, the Doctor's "There should have been another way" ending has to go down as one of the most gobsmackingly po-faced and moronic moments of the series. I'm not among those who is hugely bothered by the level of violence in some of the Peter Davison stories, nor even, generally speaking, by the sequences where the Doctor gets a bit physical. But the sequence in Episode One in which the Doctor decides to handle the possibility that they'll be caught by overloading the base's reactor to distract them, then proceeds to beat up the guards who are not thrilled with the prospect of him overloading their reactor, is just appalling. There should have been another way, Doctor? Sure. And we might have called it, "Don't introduce yourself by needlessly sabotaging the base and beating people up." Similarly, to suggest the value of "another way" when the script has been bending over backwards to ensure that all of the other ways didn't exist is just cheap. This conclusion might be forgivable if we were actually using generic monsters—if the Tereleptils were the ones besieging the base or something. But these are Malcolm Hulke's potentially peace-loving Silurians. They come with another way built into the script, only Johnny Byrne takes the thing out for no discernible reason.

So what we have instead is a story about the horrors of nuclear war in which no alternative is actually presented. Far from being a story about the importance of peace, this is a story in which massive slaughter of the other is necessary, if regrettable. Even the Doctor's last line undermines any actual point about the merits of not slaughtering everybody. There should have been another way. Not that there was one. Or that there must have been one that the Doctor missed. There should have. But there wasn't. Everyone, apparently, deserved to die. And here we get to the heart of my objection to supposedly apolitical writing. Because this is shooting for that. Yes, it's about nuclear war and the Cold War, but given that nobody was actually overtly in favor of nuclear war, this is a straw man. By being unwilling to commit to any viewpoint beyond, "Gee, it sure would suck if we completely annihilated the species," the story ends up tacitly endorsing it.

And again, this sucks even more given it's Hulke they're ripping off, as Hulke was the writer least afraid to take off the gloves and do consciously political Doctor Who. But this is part of the lengthy and torturous period where Doctor Who avoids politics at all costs. And here we see why that was such a terrible idea—because the series isn't about anything anymore. There's no content here. Saying you're going to be apolitical just means that you've given up on being about the real world at all. Which is fine right up until you remember that reality is inescapable and that flights of fancy come back to Earth eventually. Here's our crash landing. But to have the crash happen in a Malcolm Hulke homage is just taunting. There should have been another way? There was. You had it in the script you were ripping off. Fundamentally, things never would have gotten this way on Hulke's watch.

Making matters even more frustrating is Byrne missing the one idea he had that didn't amount to cannibalizing Malcolm Hulke's work and taking all of the actual thought out. *Warriors of the Deep* has, as an incidental detail, a world in which human-computer synthesis is a common and everyday part of life and where people have backup personality discs that can be used to control them. This, however, is used only to sustain a plotline in which saboteurs make things worse for the base. Maddox is by far the most interesting idea in the story, and he's nothing more than a plot hammer.

And as with Byrne's previous turkey, *Arc of Infinity*, there's a good story shuffling about in these ideas. Worse than *Arc of Infinity*, however, this time the good story is so blindingly obvious that one is left with no sense of how the hell the production team missed it. You've got enough money to do some fairly impressive monster costumes, but not much else. You spend them on the monster from the series' history that lets you do a story that's not about special effects and fighting but about negotiation and debate. You are, in other words, setting everything up for a story that Doctor Who can actually do and do well—one about conversation and acting. Maybe you do monster costumes that let you see the actors mouths and eyes—redo the Silurians to look more like the Draconians did. That way you can really have them act and have a proper, tense thriller.

But instead we do a pantomime horse. And I'm left in a terribly unfortunate position, because I pretty much have to say that, on the evidence of this story, Michael Grade was right to cancel the show. I mean, not in his actual reasons, but in the basic decision. Because this, in all seriousness, is what they think a good season opener is? They think the way to open their season is to give twelve-year-old monsters a makeover in a frighteningly generic story? I mean, even if we excuse all of the decisions that went into filming it, how is it that nobody saw it needed to be swapped with *The Awakening* or *Frontios* in the running order? Both, after all, have self-contained openings. At worst it would have required redoing a handful of TARDIS scenes. They surely could have looked at the Myrka shots on rushes and seen that they needed to change the order of things.

But no. Because Nathan-Turner isn't making the program for the general public, who would have, on the whole, much preferred to see something that had an interesting idea beyond, "Wow! Silurians! And Sea Devils!" He's making it for Doctor Who fans, and then as much the ones in the US and Australia as the ones in the UK. If you're not the sort of person who's excited because a Pertwee-era monster is coming back, you're no longer the sort of person the program is for. All the program has to say is, "Look at me, I'm Doctor Who."

I said back in *The Five Doctors* essay that there was an inherent problem with the program being done "for the Americans," and there is. This is a moral point, and it's a real one. The BBC is funded by what is essentially a tax, and the people paying that tax have a right to be catered to by the resulting channel. That's where the Reithian idea that the BBC has to have something for everybody comes from. So when the program so cavalierly discards the idea of doing interesting or relevant drama in favor of doing things that get cheered at American conventions, frankly, there's a real problem with it. To present this as the season premiere—as though this is the way to get things started, right after the high-profile and beloved *Five Doctors*, is just insulting. To say this should be taken off the air and replaced with something that actually takes the viewing public seriously is not, quite frankly, a controversial proposition to anybody who isn't a blinkered Doctor Who fan. But this is, after all, an era where the program was literally and consciously being made to the tastes of one of the most staggeringly blinkered Doctor Who fans ever born. And that's what really separates *Warriors of the Deep* from the many other bad stories in Doctor Who history: it was all but designed to be this awful.

## Tea from an Urn (*The Awakening*)

It's January 19th, 1984. Paul McCartney is still at number one with "Pipes of Peace," with Frankie Goes to Hollywood now up to number two. The lower reaches of the charts are basically as described last time, so let's go even lower and see if there's anything interesting. The Police have "King of Pain" near its peak, which isn't nearly as high as you'd expect for that song. The Smiths are in with "This Charming Man." There. That's worth noting. Ooh, and on the album charts the first volume of *Now That's What I Call Music!* is at number one. So there's a symbol of the death of culture and hope. In real news, though it's between this story and the next, we may as well give this one credit for the Apple Macintosh being introduced, just because otherwise I'd have absolutely nothing to talk about before I moved on to Doctor Who.

So here is something that I didn't realize how much I'd missed writing about until I sat down for this essay: a thoroughly underrated gem. Not one I have to provide some rescue operation on like *Terminus*, but a story that's just quite marvelous and largely overlooked. I think the last one of these was, what, *The Stones of Blood*? Regardless, *The Awakening* is absolutely marvelous.

Perhaps the most striking thing about it, at least to a modern eye, is that it figures out how to do the two-part story. Or, at least, rediscovers it—David Whitaker had the gist of it back in the mid-60s. (Then again, to some extent the entire history of Doctor Who after 1968 is just people figuring out what David Whitaker understood all along.) But as *The Awakening* is the only forty-five minute story between *The Rescue* and *Rose* to actually work, it bears some analysis on those grounds alone.

To some extent its central innovation is just blindingly obvious: it gets the cliffhanger right. Consider, briefly, the cliffhangers of the classic series' two-parters post-*Rescue*. *The Sontaran Experiment* ends with revealing the villain of the piece. *Black Orchid* ends with the incident that kicks off the murder mystery. *The King's Demon*s ends with the revelation of the Master. All three of these are cliffhangers in the game-changing mould—they promise a shift in the nature of the story. And this is how the first episodes of Doctor Who stories usually work, to be fair.

But compare those to Whitaker's two cliffhangers on his two-parters. *The Rescue* has the Doctor stumbling upon a spike trap, and *The Edge of Destruction* has a particularly vivid moment of the crew betraying each other. These are not cliffhangers that change the shape of the story; they're sudden intrusions of danger that we know will be squared away within a minute or two of the start of the next episode so we can get back to the plot. They're the sorts of cliffhangers that tend to get used in the later episodes of a longer serial.

In most circumstances it is the game-changing cliffhangers that are most interesting within Doctor Who. Indeed, the ones that set up a week of trying to figure out what this means about the story are, by and large, the best cliffhangers in the series. But these cliffhangers already suffer in the Davison era, when half the time the cliffhangers are resolved only twenty-four hours later instead of in week-long waits. This is, in some ways, the worst part of the *Earthshock* reveal. The series went to great lengths to hide its "the Cybermen are back" shock cliffhanger, including turning down a *Radio Times* cover, and then it only got twenty-four hours of shock for its trouble. In a Davison-era two-parter, there's no time for the story to breathe at all, and so the idea of inserting the extended period of uncertainty and questioning that a game-changing cliffhanger involves is already a bit silly.

But on top of that, the game-changing cliffhanger creates a very wonky sense of structure, as we discussed back in *Black Orchid*. The structure that works is the one Whitaker used, in which the cliffhanger is just a pro forma event to end the episode and instead we have a forty-five minute piece of storytelling that works according to its own logic and tells the story at its own pace. Which, in the compressed and tight confines of the two-parter, is necessary.

But *The Awakening* manages to have the best of both worlds. Superficially its cliffhanger is the archetypal example of a game-changing cliffhanger—a monster reveal. But in practice it's not actually an interruption of the story's plot. It's obvious from fairly early on that there is some sort of malign alien presence involved. The revelation that it's a face with glowing green eyes is an impressive visual moment, and thus makes a good cliffhanger, but it changes very little about how the story is progressing. It doesn't actually require that the Doctor do anything differently. So *The Awakening* ends up having its cake and eating it too. It has a cliffhanger that is in a real sense a big moment, but doesn't require an alteration to the structure of its overall plot.

Its overall plot, of course, is a completely standard-issue assortment of Doctor Who clichés: shady dealings in rural villages, power-mad authority figures, sympathetic skeptics, and malign ancient presences. But far from being a set of clichés, *The Awakening* uses the standards with a real and definable purpose. This is something that is increasingly important in forty-five minute stories—the ability to use recognizable elements as a shorthand to sketch out the rules of a story efficiently.

What this allows is for the series to cut down on the sleuthing moments—the sorts of things that were, as the essay on *The Adventure Game* showed, on the wane in this period anyway. Instead of having a story primarily about watching the Doctor figure out the nature of things, we get one about people reacting to the nature of things. (This too is just rediscovering Whitaker, who used this structure to massive effect in *The Enemy of The World*, where the cliffhangers were largely based on characters finding out things the audience already knew, making the question "What will he do about X?" instead of "What is X?")

But what *The Awakening* does that's deliciously clever is that it proceeds to comment on the nature of this shorthand. The central plot of the story focuses on the village's love of pageantry and war games. In other words, on the sort of "heritage theme-park" version of history that was the animating spirit of *The King's Demons*. The problem with this version of history, of course, is that it removes any sense of progress or change. History stops being a series of material events that lead to the present day and starts being a set of fun things to "experience"—an excuse, in other words, for dressing up and acting silly.

It is in some ways difficult to think of an approach more fundamentally morally opposed to that of Doctor Who than the pure "heritage theme-park" one. Animating Doctor Who at its best, after all, has been the idea that the mercurial spark underlying the Doctor and the phenomenon of material social progress are two sides of the same coin. In other words, Doctor Who is almost completely uninterested in history except inasmuch as it is a form of progress. Heritage theme-park history and Doctor Who don't get along at all, except as it allows the sketching of a genre, which is a different kettle of fish.

Central to *The Awakening*, however, is the idea that there is, underneath the heritage theme-park version of the English Civil War, a Lovecraftian evil. And it's telling that it is a blatantly Lovecraftian sort of evil—one of those great lurking malevolent presences. Because the Lovecraftian view of the universe, with irreducible and unavoidable Others lurking in the forgotten and erased, is the perfect commentary on this sort of whitewashing. The central horror of Lovecraft is that underneath all the science and rationality of the world is an unspeakable and incomprehensible terror that is barely and temporarily repressed. And here, underneath the sanitized and easily encapsulated version of history is an unspeakable evil that is specifically manifested by the materiality of history—by the violent viscerality that is consciously erased by turning history into "games."

And as soon as the series starts poking at that, of course, its more alchemical inclinations rear up to conjure some inadvertent supplemental horror. At this point in the series, after all, the viewership has been actively primed to interpret everything in light of the series' past. This is the first story since 1981 to feature no returning concepts. It's been nearly two years since the series offered a story that was meant to be read on its own merits and terms instead of as a set of allusions to history. Which means, of course, that approaching this story with the expectation that it is a commentary on the series' past is wholly understandable. Indeed, the series has actively invited us to. It's even gone and given us a clear door with which to do it, what with its overt nicking of the end of *The Daemons* and its repetition of the phrase "*War Games.*" I mean, it's practically begging for it.

If we do read *The Awakening* in the explicit light of these two stories we get two major tools to add to our reading. The first is the idea that Doctor Who occupies a gap between the materialist empiricism of science and the alchemical storytelling of magic. The second is its evolving conception of time and history, focused particularly on the Time Lords.

It is not a particularly novel observation to note that the Time Lords steadily fell from being interesting to being painfully dull. And we have just exited the fourteen-year period of the show in which Gallifrey was ever visited, *The Five Doctors* being the last time the Doctor actually visits the planet until 2013. So we have, in a sense, completed that fall from grace. And as has been a continual theme of *TARDIS Eruditorum*, that fall from grace was a movement from being embodiments of the material dialectic of history to being men in funny hats—to being, in other words, pageantry. So when *The Awakening* attacks the notion of heritage theme-park history while invoking the story name in which the Time Lords first appear after two years of unrelenting continuity references...

What's funny, of course, is that it's the later repurposing of the Time Lords as envisioned by Holmes and Dicks into men in funny hats that is the most blatantly magical. Under Holmes and Dicks, the Time Lords were at least material, if not empiricist. They were fantastic, but they were always bound by a worldly connection to material history. It's not until *The Invasion of Time, Arc of Infinity,* and *The Five Doctors* that they became a purely symbolic narrative function with no relationship to actual things.

(Since we are having ourselves a brief stopover in the realm of the overtly occult, I should note that, historically, we're now in the early rise of chaos magick, a school of magical thought based on the idea of discarding the idea of an overall metaphysic and instead focusing on the pure material act of magic—the statement of intent and the use of will to effect change on the universe. *The Awakening* marks the point where Doctor Who starts to play it that way too. The idea that master narratives—a central feature of Thatcher's occultism—are inherently opposed to effective magic is a matter of pure delight to the animating ideology of Doctor Who.)

The irony of this is that *The Awakening* restores Doctor Who's alchemical power by pushing away from the purely magical and back towards materialism and reality. The lurking Lovecraftian horror is materialism, not symbolic horror. But this has always been at the heart of Doctor Who's power. Just as it's never really been about a purely empiricist and rationalist viewpoint, it's also never just been a masturbatory engagement with the symbolic. It's been about the alchemical tempering of symbol and object. And here we see that taken to one of its most delightfully odd consequences—a case in which material reality serves as a lurking horror underpinning the play of the symbolic. In which the material is the uncanny Other of fantasy.

It goes without saying, of course, that the heritage theme-park version of history is the natural ally of Thatcher. The one where Britain can be reduced to feel-good moments and pageantry instead of material progress, where the past can be erased at will and replaced with empty rhetoric. Heritage theme-park history is the ultimate triumph of there being no such thing as society.

This marks the point, then, where, following a painfully long slumber, Doctor Who wakes up and remembers that there is such a thing as the real world. Unfortunately, of course, it's a little late. Those inclined to intertwine Doctor Who with the cultural movements of Britain cannot help but notice that Doctor Who essentially slumped over and fell asleep on the subject of material reality not long after Thatcher's first election and only woke up again when the left had been roundly humiliated by her second. Just in time, then, to watch the next miners' strike.

And just in time to suffer an equally brutal humiliation of its own.

## The Ground's Attacking Us (*Frontios*)

It's January 26th, 1984. Frankie Goes to Hollywood finally get around to being at number one, and stays there all story. By the end of it, Cyndi Lauper's "Girls Just Want To Have Fun" makes it to right below them, with The Eurythmics, Queen, and Echo & The Bunnymen also charting, the latter with the sublimely good "The Killing Moon." So the pop charts have gone and restored order, which is often a good sign for what's on television.

The news, on the other hand, is wholly mediocre. The big one is that the Winter Olympics kick off the day after this story airs its final installment, but that has relevance for the next story, not really this one. Nissan announces plans to open a plant in Great Britain, which will be the first time that non-British cars will be built in the UK. The first embryo transfer resulting in a live birth is announced? An untethered space walk? It's not thrilling news.

It is, however, thrilling television, as we've got *Frontios* on tap, and as it happens, *Frontios* is quite good. Perhaps the easiest thing to say about it is that it's not at all the script you would expect from Christopher H. Bidmead. While Frontios is very much unlike *Logopolis* and *Castrovalva*, based on the entirety of Season Eighteen one does not expect to see Bidmead going for body horror and grimy militarism. Nevertheless, this is unmistakably a Bidmead script. His stocks in trade—lost knowledge of the ancients, eccentric spaces—are all here. It's just that they're serving a story about slugs using human corpses for labor instead of some fugue on Escher or computers.

There is an almost ritual element to the progression of Season Twenty-One. After so long mining every part of Doctor Who's history save for its alchemical spark, the series unexpectedly brings back two of its last three alchemists in Bidmead and, later, Holmes. On top of that, there is an odd focus on the buried. Story after story in this season focuses on imagery of caves, tunnels, or the deep. With the miners' strike looming, there is in hindsight something slightly uncanny about this. It is not quite a thematic link—the issues of the strike are not well reflected across Season Twenty-One, although there are moments that come close. But it remains (forgive me, dear reader) striking, as Doctor Who finally stirs even if temporarily from its torpor of museum pieces with a resurgence of alchemy, obliquely reflecting the looming politics of the day.

And yet there is something troubling and unsettling about the alchemy in these stories, of which *Frontios* is a prime example. Bidmead has always had a love of eccentric spaces, but here the unfathomable depths of the planet Frontios and the outer reaches of time do not hide a sense of wonder but instead a sense of raw horror. And not just any horror, but good old-fashioned body horror. The planet literally consumes people and uses them as meat. On top of that there's Turlough's race memory of the Tractators, which is played compellingly by Mark Strickson, who decides to convey "terrified" by simply gobbling up the scenery. It's a sharper choice than it sounds, as it's such an unusual position to have a companion put in that we really do get a strong sense of how fundamentally wrong and scary the Tractators must be.

There's a chilling callousness to this conception of the world—one where the earth itself is hostile to us. But it seems, in a real sense, like the appropriate midpoint between Bidmead's conception of Doctor Who and Saward's.

Bidmead's conception of Doctor Who is something we understand fairly well at this point, but Saward's is a trickier matter. His four scripts demonstrate a tendency towards action-based stories and the militaristic, but equally, and this is too often ignored, Saward is not straightforwardly pro-military. *Earthshock* can be accused of that, certainly, but come the next story Saward is far more ambivalent about the military and violence. Still, brutality is a major theme, both of his work and of the scripts in his tenure he takes the most pride in. (Also notable is that, at this point at least, Saward's love of black humor is largely invisible.)

So here we get Bidmead reinterpreting Saward's fascination with the brutal through his own love of eccentric spaces. And it's worth noting, *Frontios* is not merely eccentric because of its interior geometries but because of its position as the absolute edge of where the TARDIS can travel. Notably, *Frontios* is not set at the end of the universe. There is no sense of looming heat death or the destruction of all things. Instead, it seems, there is simply a point in history beyond which the Time Lords simply cannot go. (And given that *Frontios* is positioned as one of the last dying outposts of humanity, it seems that the scope of Time Lord society is coextensive with human society. This is not uncommon—it is oddly difficult to construct any explanations of Time Lords that do not require the centrality of humanity, a point that will become supremely relevant when we get to *Trial of a Time Lord* later in the book.) And so the lurking horror of the Tractators is positioned as the horror at the end of civilization—the literal end of history.

But equally, then, it's telling that we get one of the most straightforward "leave everybody to rebuild civilization" endings that we've seen in years. For all the meditations on the possibility of this brutal, visceral horror as the natural endpoint of history, we can't ignore the fact that the Doctor wins, civilization is restored, and everybody gets to go on. Equally, though, it's reiterated over and over again that the Doctor has to hide this from the Time Lords.

It is nearly impossible to wind a way through this set of ideas without returning to our old conception of the Time Lords as guardians of the arc of history. More even than *The Curse of Peladon*, the story that caused us to first formulate this idea, this is a story that just fails to make sense without that idea well in place. It is only when you have a concrete idea of the endpoint of history that the liminality of *Frontios* begins to make sense.

Given this, we oughtn't just make hay about the Tractators and the body horror. We should also look at the type of society that is the natural endpoint of civilization before it crumbles to dirt and meat. Miles and Wood make much of the fact that this, unlike most Bidmead worlds, is one in which the people defending scientific inquiry are thinly described, whereas considerable amounts of time are spent on the authoritarians. But what they don't comment on is the underlying issue of why. What has to be stressed isn't that the authoritarians are unusually well-entrenched here, it's that their entrenchment is tacitly positioned as the natural order of the universe—the inevitable end. This is a society where the barbarians aren't just at the gate, the people inside the gate are giving up and joining the barbarians. This is the endpoint of humanity—what the whole of human history is leading inexorably towards. And, of course, it's a very Sawardian society as well—full of dour military men.

The scale of this, of course, can't be sold purely by having the Doctor telling us that he shouldn't be meddling here. Indeed, the TARDIS itself is ripped apart. The script is not entirely clear on why, but nothing about Gravis and the Tractators suggests that they're A-list enough to be able to engage in that sort of narrative collapse. Thematically, if not literally, the culprit is unambiguously the nature of *Frontios* itself as somewhere the TARDIS shouldn't be in the first place.

But if this is the case then the Doctor's meddling here has to be taken as one of the most significant acts he's ever taken—one on par with his rendering of the Daleks as subject to history at their origin point. We don't really notice it here because such overt mythicism as we get with the Daleks is absent, but thematically, this is huge. The Doctor has changed what it is that the arc of history bends towards. He's not just altered history, he's, in a very real sense, altered the very nature of time itself.

There is a longstanding and not particularly interesting debate over what the killing blow for the classic series was. I say it is uninteresting because it is, quite frankly, supremely easy to answer: *Warriors of the Deep* ends up being so bad that not even the fans could defend it (it's telling that *Doctor Who Magazine* didn't even bother running a review of the story), giving open ammunition to Michael Grade. *The Twin Dilemma* cripples the incoming Doctor so that he is essentially never, ever going to be able to win over the public. And then *Trial of a Time Lord* botches the last throw of the dice, failing to bring a restored show that anybody can be excited about, let alone tout as the triumphant relaunch of Doctor Who. As a narrative of historical causes, this is pretty simple.

No, the difficult and interesting question is not what killed Doctor Who, but what saved it. It's not difficult to imagine that the show would have come back eventually—television production is far too remake-happy to let a property like Doctor Who sit abandoned forever. But what is unusual is that Doctor Who returned as a continuation of itself—and more than that, as a continuation that embraced large swaths of spin-off material. That's essentially unheard of. Even though *Star Trek* maintained a unified continuity over five series, over and over again it wildly altered the premise and lead characters. But with Doctor Who we have over fifty years with a single character; Peter Capaldi is playing the exact same person that Ian and Barbara met in Totters Lane. That's kind of weird. There's no real way to cut it so that it wouldn't have just been easier, in both 1996 and 2005, to reboot the series from scratch.

So what about the series enabled that? This is a surprisingly tricky question, because much of what we are looking for is slightly buried (how apropos). The bulk of the series during the Saward era is visibly making catastrophic decisions that lead to cancellation. But every once in a while there is a gem. Not just a good story—an *Enlightenment* or a *Snakedance*—but one that lays a bit of framework that provides a vision of the show that can be picked up on. Because that, in the end, is at the heart of the question of how the series survived: what you can find within the dying embers that constitutes a way forward.

And here one of the great alchemists of the series slips it in. He writes a story that is on the one hand unmistakably a part of the concerns of this era, but that on the other hand features the Doctor shamelessly cheating and altering the nature of time itself. And again, this is surprisingly topical. The Saward era, if only in hindsight, is almost overtly an attempt to figure out what Doctor Who should be like in the wake of the Falklands and Thatcher. It gets it dreadfully wrong much of the time, however. In part this is because it concedes the point and tries to be Doctor Who in a Thatcherite world. Whereas here Bidmead just won't have it. He starts in a world of militaristic institutions holding back the tide of chaos, then has the Doctor just kick the premise to the curb and change the world into one in which good old-fashioned "tear down the structures of society and leave smart, good people behind to rebuild it" is the order of the universe once again.

It's a small thing, isolated on the trailing end of an era of unfulfilled potential. But it's significant—a spiritual escape act. Instead of bending towards Thatcherite hell, the universe now takes a last minute swerve into rebirth.

As above, so below.

## Time Can Be Rewritten: *Time Crash*

One of my favorite continuity problems in Doctor Who is the placement of the handful of stories featuring Davison's Doctor and none of his companions, given that he has no visible periods in which he might travel alone. Convention is to place these sorts of things in the midst of the end of *Frontios* while the Doctor is depositing the Gravis, a convention seemingly begun by Paul Magrs's *Excelis Dawns* audio story for Big Finish. Magrs in typical fashion introduces far more continuity problems than he solves doing this, given that Tegan is on the TARDIS for that trip. Still, it's as good a place as any.

This also, of course, marks the first time I have to deal overtly with the new series instead of in passing reference. Every meaningful division of eras in Doctor Who involves factions of fandom who hate one side or the other of the divide. Still, the classic/new series one is by some margin the most entrenched of these splits, although that is perhaps more because it's an easy one to troll with than because it's a real one. All the same, it seems worth making clear: anyone expecting me to turn sour upon reaching the new series is going to be sorely disappointed. Even when I agree with those who criticize it—and I'll grant that the new series is not without its deep flaws in parts—the fact remains that making redemptive readings of the new series is not even remotely difficult. Disliking it frankly requires more effort than liking it, and I just can't be bothered. If you can, well, I win, because I get more television to enjoy than you do. So there.

But on top of that, there are a few more substantive issues I have with critics of the new series, and *Time Crash* makes a nice bit of a ground zero for dealing with them. There's an objection to *Time Crash* that serves as a perfect moment to repel a general critique of the new series, namely that there's something wrong with the sequence at the end in which Tennant's Doctor proclaims Davison's Doctor to be "his" Doctor. In fact, I'm going to have my Ian Levine moment here and simply declare this objection to be evil.

To be fair, the problem with it is not quite that it doesn't make sense on its own terms. If you are invested in the idea that the Doctor has a coherent "life" and that he is always the same character, then indeed the idea of him picking favorites among his past selves is absurd and jarring. I can and will readily grant that. What I not only won't grant but will remain openly hostile to, however, is the idea that it constitutes a problem just because there's a context in which that exchange doesn't make sense. And this encapsulates a great number of complaints about the new series, as a strange alliance of people who adore what they think the classic series was and people who just hate Doctor Who in general insist that there are things that don't make sense or don't parse, as though their inability to understand something makes them intellectually superior to the overwhelming majority of the audience who have no problem comprehending things.

Because to an overwhelming majority of the audience, what happens at the end of *Time Crash* is perfectly clear. The fourth wall becomes momentarily porous (permissible within the context of *Children in Need*) and we get a sequence in which David Tennant and Steven Moffat are both simultaneously addressing Peter Davison and the Fifth Doctor. Nobody who was watching the *Children in Need* telecast for any reasons that extended beyond catching the Doctor Who bit had any difficulty with this, nor, for that matter, did almost anybody who was just tuning in for *Time

*Crash*. This sort of breach of the fourth wall to wink at the audience is, after all, par for the course for a charity telecast.

But more to the point, this is a basic comprehension skill for contemporary television. Frames of reference switch rapidly. The traces of postmodernism that we noted in the early days of the Hinchcliffe era is by 2007 the default mode of how television works. If you can't seamlessly and without having to think about it go, "Oh, this bit is really the show talking about itself and not an attempt to provide a naturalistic depiction of how a quasi-immortal time traveler lives his life," when the show wants you to, well, you're just out to sea on the new series, and indeed on almost any contemporary drama.

No, what we have here is an exquisitely crafted eight-minute sketch that works well both for people who remember the Davison era and for people who don't give a crap about Doctor Who and who are watching *Children in Need*—a portion of the audience that, during *Children in Need*, one can safely assume is substantial. Everything in it is profoundly influenced and shaped by the past of the series and Peter Davison's time as the Doctor (right down to the wonderful happenstance of Graeme Harper being the director), and, equally, is perfectly suited to its task.

The first half of the piece, for instance, which consists mostly of an extended comedic misunderstanding as Davison's Doctor fails to grasp what's going on while Tennant's Doctor (and the audience) are well aware of what's happening, is gorgeous. Particularly worth noting is Davison's acting, which is on the one hand spot on for his portrayal of the Doctor (it helps, of course, that he'd been reprising the role for eight years thanks to Big Finish), and on the other hand allows him to show off his comedic skills. These skills are worth highlighting specifically, since one of the enduring puzzles of the Davison era is that they hired an actor known for his sitcom roles and then gave him three years of scripts with hardly any comedic material at all.

This gets at one of the things I've been meaning to deal with in one of these essays, which is, roughly, why people who think Davison's Doctor was rubbish are wrong. The usual criticism of him has shifted over the years. During his era the complaint was that he was "bland," but over time the complaint has turned to the idea that he's "weak" and "ineffectual," or, occasionally, "too fallible." And to some extent *Time Crash* would seem to nail that, spending half of its runtime with him failing to get the plot. But, of course, the end point of *Time Crash* is Tennant's effusive praise for Davison and his "dashing about" and ability to "save the universe with a kettle and string."

This captures an important divide about Davison—one we've already seen in the dismaying failure to give him any decent comedic scripts in his tenure (with *Black Orchid* being about the nearest attempt). Davison's Doctor and the writing he got were two different matters. Yes, the writing in the Davison era is too often disappointing, and often strays into grotesquely cynical pieces like *Earthshock* or *Warriors of the Deep*. But Davison's conception of the character isn't responsible for that. Davison manages a character who is mercurial, tempestuous, and breathtakingly quick-witted. As his ability to squarely hit the characterization of a role that's over twenty years old when put in a comedic context that the original role was never put in demonstrates. He's the only actor other than Troughton in the classic series who has a version of the Doctor that is this flexible. And like Troughton, he had writers who had little to no interest in using that flexibility. The difference is merely that Davison's era post-dates organized fandom and all of his episodes are not only surviving but were widely disseminated on videocassette not long after they aired (even if not in official versions), whereas Season Five's reputation is protected by the burning desire we all have to see it.

The big advantage of Davison's approach to the role is that it marked the first time since the 1960s that Doctor Who has actually been a show that, conceptually, could do anything. Given that Doctor Who has long been about injecting the TARDIS into an existing narrative structure, this is important. Davison has enough presence to deform and transform whatever narrative he's dropped into, but he's capable of doing it in a way that amounts to more than just running around mocking it. (In this regard he largely exceeds the ability of his co-star here.)

And *Time Crash* gives him the opportunity to do this to the future version of his own show. It's worth noting that through the comedic first half, while Tennant goes around making all of the obvious jokes at Davison's expense ("decorative vegetable"), Davison takes only one real shot at Tennant, but it's a pleasantly scathing one—pointing out that Tennant's patter really just amounts to describing everything in front of him. Obviously the story isn't anti-Tennant by any measure, but it's telling, I think, that it does give an actual critique of Tennant's portrayal. Even when playing the comedic fool—at his most seemingly ineffectual and fallible—Davison's Doctor quietly centers the narrative on himself.

Which, of course, sets up the finale, in which Tennant effusively praises Davison's portrayal. Obviously this moment is meant to work primarily on registers other than as an account of the Doctor's own psyche. It is an instance in which the Doctor becomes an authorial/actor mouthpiece. But this is still remarkable in that they are serving as mouthpieces for commentary on the classic series—something the new series has done very, very rarely. And what we get is historically interesting, in that it cuts against the received wisdom of fandom without being a flagrant erasure of history. Tennant and Moffat are real and documented fans of the series, but the opinion they give is miles away from the documented consensus of fandom.

Of course, the documented consensus of fandom is, for most of fandom's history, the consensus of a fandom that played a significant if inadvertent role in the series' cancellation. The fact is that much of what can and should be concluded about the John Nathan-Turner era changes dramatically when it is the lead-in to a lengthy break in the series instead of to the end of the series. Its teleology shifts from the well-worn "death of the program" to the much more interesting "survival of the program" we talked about in the *Frontios* essay.

And in this regard, Davison's portrayal of the Doctor is, in fact, absolutely crucial. Because Davison, as Tennant observes, inaugurated the idea of a young Doctor. Previously the role had derived a non-trivial portion of its otherness from the fact that he's been played as an older male who is slightly atypical for a leading man and who derives most of his immediate connotative effect from being "the wise old man," even if he subsequently subverts that to varying extents. But Davison throws away all of that and gets by on actually being mercurial and clever instead of on the fact that he's self-evidently the elder statesman in almost any circumstance he can find himself in.

The result is, in some criticisms, a more human Doctor who is too relatable, but I think this misses the point somewhat. First of all, making the Doctor more relatable introduces an interesting alternate mode of engagement with the series. The idea of the companion as "audience identification figure" is deeply entrenched in the series' logic. It's been flawed for some time, though it remains the case that the companion is largely there to ask the questions the viewer wants answered. But with a relatively relatable Doctor (and it's telling, I think, that Davison still excels at moments of being alien and eccentric—he's majestic at the start of *Frontios* when Bidmead is writing him as being a bit of a madman) there opens the possibility of the audience relating primarily to the Doctor. This seems to me wonderful. The show is, to my mind, wildly more interesting when it suggests being an anarchist alchemist instead of admiring one.

But secondly, I have trouble with the notion that the existence of relatable moments for the Doctor invalidates his alien moments. Indeed, I think the fact that the Doctor can seem relatable one moment and utterly alien the next makes him, on aggregate, more unfamiliar than a character who is predictably alien. The Doctor's otherness comes not from the fact that he's consistently inscrutable but from the fact that he flits between a known type of character and a cipher. And swapping the known type of character from a straightforward archetype (grumpy old man, dashing action hero, witty bohemian) to a complex character with relatable traits makes the moments when the Doctor is starkly inhuman far more off-putting.

But much of that is an argument for the future. For our purposes at the moment the fact remains that Davison's Doctor, in hindsight, proved to be as much of a template for the future as Troughton's did, and that, like Troughton, this is due to his capacity as an actor. The Nathan-Turner years are among the most critically well-worn sections of the program. *Time Crash* is a compelling argument that this consensus has become secondary in importance to a new reading. Regardless of what one thinks of the future, the Davison era ought be understood more in relation to the future we have now than the one we had in the 1990s.

## Little Green Blobs in Bonded Polycarbite Armor
### (*Resurrection of the Daleks*)

It's February 8th, 1984. Frankie continues to relax in Hollywood, with Queen lurking just below. Duran Duran and The Eurythmics also chart, and The Smiths have one of their biggest hits during their actual career with "What Difference Does it Make" just barely missing the top ten and peaking at #12. But perhaps most significant is Madonna making her chart debut with "Holiday," which peaks at #6.

The Winter Olympics run through this story, necessitating the merging of episodes into two 45-minute parts, an experiment that becomes the norm in the next season. Konstantin Chernenko becomes the head of the Soviet Union.

While on television (or, I suppose, elsewhere on television), Davison gets his obligatory Dalek story. There is no such thing as a great era of Doctor Who that has ended without a great Dalek story. The Pertwee era's inability to quite stick the landing on any of its Dalek stories is emblematic of the nagging doubts plaguing that era. The fact that the Williams era went to pieces on its Dalek story is almost a perfect metaphor for its failings. And on the other extreme, however good—and indeed better—stories like *The Brain of Morbius* are, it will always be *Genesis of the Daleks* that is the defining moment of the Hinchcliffe era; all the various weak spots of the Troughton era can be forgiven in a heartbeat in the face of his two Dalek stories. But perhaps no stories exemplify the way in which Dalek stories serve as the defining metaphors of their eras as the two penned by Eric Saward.

For all the stick I've given him, John Nathan-Turner was not untalented. The quality of work at the beginning and end of his tenure makes it very clear that he was capable of producing some phenomenally good television. But it is equally telling that he is by miles the least writerly Doctor Who producer. He is the only post-Innes Lloyd producer of the series to have no significant writing credits to his name. Bryant and Sherwin both served as script editors, Letts wrote several scripts, Hinchcliffe started as a writer, wrote three novelizations, and submitted scripts after his departure, and Williams stepped in on scripts in his era and was set to write one for Season Twenty-Three. Nathan-Turner, however, was not a writer.

This is not an insult, I should stress. The producer's job is not first and foremost a writing job, and writing is only one path to the chair. Nathan-Turner has a strong sense of publicity, is savvy about stretching the budget, and is attentive to the visuals even if his aesthetic is at times more invested in light entertainment than is entirely suitable for Doctor Who. But it does explain a fairly basic truth about Nathan-Turner's tenure, which is that he is more dependent on the quality of his script editor than almost anyone else. (Of course, with a nine-season tenure and three script editors, there's considerably more data available for Nathan-Turner.) When he's paired with a writer who has a strong creative vision for the show he's able to get that vision to execute successfully and compellingly week in and week out.

Unfortunately, for the better part of five seasons Nathan-Turner was paired instead with Eric Saward. Saward, as we discussed with regards to *The Visitation*, is a writer with a profound gap between his ability and his taste. And in *Resurrection of the Daleks* we get a very pure Saward script—one that has a lot to say, is profoundly concerned with the series history, and is constructed as an ambitious, exciting script, yet doesn't quite come off.

Let's start with what *Resurrection of the Daleks* isn't: an indiscriminate festival of violence. It is violent, yes, but to read the violence as the point of the exercise requires almost completely ignoring the fact that the story ends with Tegan appalled at the level of violence and leaving the Doctor with the declaration that it's not fun any more. Given that Tegan has fairly reliably been used as a moral mouthpiece in the series, and given that the Doctor is shown to be very much shaken by her departure, it's clear that we have to take this seriously as part of the story's point.

Given this, the structure that Saward is going for is clearly one of a sucker punch. After a lengthy stretch in which it appears that the story is about the pleasure of fast-paced action and space adventure, the rug is suddenly pulled out and the story critiques what we've been ostensibly enjoying for the past eighty minutes or so.

Not only is this a perfectly valid approach, it's a damn good one that's considerably savvier and more interesting, structurally, than Doctor Who has been in years. On top of that, there's also a savvy and interesting engagement with the past. The story is drenched in Dalek continuity, gratuitously picking up from the Movellan war exactly as absolutely nobody wanted, but its iconography is a loyal execution of the Terry Nation style. By situating itself as the extension of Nation's style of storytelling and then pulling the rug out, it ends up giving us what all of these engagements with the past should have been from the start—an actual commentary on the past that's interested in it as something more than cheap nostalgia.

It also marks a maturing in Saward's use of action set pieces. *Earthshock* was easy to criticize, not because of its violence but because of the complete lack of any engagement with it and its clear belief that having men in uniforms shooting things was just plain cool. And *Warriors of the Deep* repeated the error, treating massive casualties as an unfortunate but unavoidable consequence of the need to have cool men in uniforms who shoot things. But here we get something that actually holds its action heroes up to some inquiry. And not just in the ending: the whole of *Resurrection of the Daleks* plays an ongoing game with its mercenaries and soldiers, making them just a bit too ruthless and psychopathic to enjoy. The main example, of course, is Lytton, who plays a clear villain role, but who the story is visibly fascinated with.

Lest we assume, because of the more problematic aspects of his tenure, that Saward was not a savvy enough writer to attempt something like this, let's not forget that the writers Saward was most visibly fond of while working on Doctor Who were Philip Martin and Robert Holmes. That Saward had tremendous respect for social satire and structural complexity is evident. The idea that he would attempt it himself is surely uncontroversial. It seems to me difficult to argue seriously that this isn't what *Resurrection of the Daleks* is trying for.

And many aspects of it are quite solid. The direction is quite strong (no surprise that Matthew Robinson was tapped to launch *EastEnders*), and the action sequences come off better than they ever have before in the series. The acting is solid, and there's several moments where the violence really does successfully tick over to troubling—the sequences with the face-melting gas are particularly disturbing. All of the brutality is pitched exactly where it needs to be so that it's just troubling enough that we should be able to buy the sucker punch at the end.

So why doesn't it work? Part of it is, ironically, that this is the one bit of the series' past that you can't take this approach with. If you'd just swapped the monsters of *Earthshock* and *Resurrection of the Daleks*, both would have been dramatically improved. But the return of the Daleks after four and a half years is one of the few bits of continuity that carried enough inherent weight that it was difficult to undermine. Even if the final sequence hadn't looked for all the world like Davros and the Daleks ejaculating themselves to death, the idea of Tegan being horrified by a bunch of Daleks exploding just doesn't quite wash. There's just too much history of enjoying Daleks slaughtering everybody to use them as the basis of this critique. No matter how solid the critique is—and I think Saward does, in fact, effectively skewer the flaws with Terry Nation-style plotting—actually using the Daleks for that critique is just a bridge too far, simply because they've long been more than just Terry Nation villains.

Lawrence Miles speaks admiringly of the way in which this story was the last time that Doctor Who felt like an event, and he's surely right. But that's the problem—this is one of two times in the Davison era when the show is right and the weight of the returning continuity is genuine and big. There's a lot of room to play within that—as *Remembrance of the Daleks* will eventually show, you can do a lot, even within the classic series, with the Daleks. But the sucker punch isn't one of the things you can get to work here.

There are also some sloppy and unforced errors here indicative of the larger problem with Saward's work, which is that he's just not good enough to do the ambitious scripts he's shooting for. The decision to kill Laird in the third episode, for instance, is indefensible. As the one character Tegan is actually close to in the story, her death is an obvious opportunity to actually provide a motivation for Tegan's departure. She should have survived through to the end and died in the final battle so that Tegan actually had a proximate cause for her departure. Instead she gets killed almost as an afterthought, with the big dramatic supporting character death being Stein. Who is a well-acted character, but the struggle of a pleasantly cowardly man to overcome Dalek conditioning is not the best opportunity for dramatic impact.

Indeed, this scene gets at the crux of the problem that Saward has. Stein goes down with a snarky one-liner about the Daleks being just in time for the fun before he commits suicide to destroy them all. Miles and Wood describe it as "adolescent," but that's not the real problem. The problem is that it's macho action movie posturing of the most stereotypical kind. In other words, it's exactly the sort of thing the story is supposedly critiquing. And yet in this scene it's played as a big, cathartic moment. Never mind that the catharsis is unearned and that Stein is completely the wrong character to be using here given that his only settings in the story are "wet" and "traitor," it's just the wrong catharsis for the story—especially for a story that should be leading up to the dramatic departure of the Davison era's most iconic companion

Which starts to get at the big problem with Saward and his scripts. He wants to write a critique of violent storytelling, with all the resplendent alchemy that would ensue from such materially pragmatic goals. But he can't stop himself from giggling like a schoolboy at the very violence he's critiquing. The dead giveaway is the opening, with its "evil cops" routine that's a blatant homage to the *Terror of the Autons* scene with the Auton police officers that proved controversial. He's got a critique of violence going here, but he can't help but indulge in exactly what he's trying to critique.

Still, it's easy to like this story—considerably easier than people would have you believe, in fact. In context it's far from, as Miles would have it, cheap and lightweight. It's an attempt at a great story, and while it doesn't quite reach the brass ring, the attempt is worth something. In fact, in an era where the program has had trouble when striving for mediocrity at times, it's worth a great deal.

But this is by the script editor, and that points to more systemic problems. Especially when you have a producer whose blind spot is writing, if the head writer can't quite deliver the goods then you have a big problem. Saward is almost, but not quite, up to the task of greatness. And to work, Nathan-Turner's production requires actual greatness. As ever, Dalek stories have an uncanny knack for summing up their eras. What better, for Davison's, than an attempt at brilliance that falls slightly but agonizingly short?

# Tegan!

*A commissioned essay for Nightsky.*

Like most aspects of the Davison era, Tegan Jovanka is divisive. To people who like being wrong, she's annoying and her constant desire to get off the TARDIS and get back home is tiresome. To everyone else, she's one of the freshest, most vibrant, and interesting aspects of the era, an all-time classic companion. But even this phrase is misleading, suggesting, as it does, that Tegan is largely in the same mould as other era-defining companions like Jo Grant for Pertwee and Sarah Jane for Baker. True, she is in most regards the definitive Davison companion, if only by virtue of appearing in all but two of his stories, but there are key ways in which she's unlike any other companion.

Some of this is the peculiarity of her era. There's a stretch of time, starting with Leela, in which the program tried very hard to avoid the standard Doctor Who companion. Actually, this is a bit misleading. We act as though the single contemporary human female companion is the default mode of Doctor Who, but there are actually only five of them in the whole of the classic series—Jo, Sarah Jane, Peri, Mel, and Ace. It's really just that the new series has normalized this mode, having done as many of them in seven seasons as the classic series did in twenty-six. So the interruption that began with Leela is, in many ways, the last flourishing of the model of companions where something other than the single earth female was in place.

What's interesting about Tegan, then, is that she sits almost exactly on the halfway point between those. Not only is she one of the last companions to go before "single human female" reasserted itself, she's also a human female companion herself—just one who never got a solo adventure with the Doctor.

And this is the key thing about Tegan: because she is a human female companion, we tend to think of her as being in the "standard" mode. But she's not. Instead, she fills a niche we haven't really seen since the earliest days of the series— she's basically the only companion to fill Barbara's shoes. And many of the supposed "annoying" things about her are simply throwbacks to Barbara, most obviously the fact that she's a reluctant traveller on the TARDIS (at least for her first season), though also the fact that she's often in mild opposition to the Doctor. Her job is to give voice to a position that isn't quite the reverse of the Doctor's, but that is nevertheless unambiguously informed by a completely different set of values and judgments.

This leads, in some accounts, to Tegan being a bit thick. The show, after all, is fairly steadfastly aligned to the moral perspective of the Doctor. So Tegan, as a character who is actively set on a different perspective, is rather consistently proven wrong by the series. But this also lends a dignity to Tegan. She's one of only two female companions in the classic series to never really drift from her initial interesting "strong female character" conception into a bland peril monkey. She still gets captured with irritating regularity, but there's basically nothing that really ever cows her.

Some of this comes down to the specific tension that exists between Tegan and Davison's Doctor. Just as Davison's Doctor is often condemned as "bland" and "ineffectual," Tegan is often criticized for being overbearing. In this regard, then, the dynamic is very different from the Doctor/Barbara dynamic, "bland" being just about the last word you'd pick for Hartnell's Doctor. More broadly, Barbara's overt resistance to the Doctor came from a point in the program when the Doctor wasn't the moral center of the narrative yet, whereas Tegan's comes in an era where the Doctor is overtly the hero.

This ends up having considerable storytelling potential, however. It's a cliché, albeit one with some strength to it, to note that drama emerges from conflict. And, simply put, Tegan's propensity to bark up what is, at least in Doctor Who terms, the slightly wrong tree generates conflict aplenty. Not just in *Kinda* and *Snakedance*, although it's true that her portrayals of the old "possessed companion" chestnut in those two stories are significant parts of why they're highlights, but throughout the era, Tegan is particularly adept at getting the plot going, as it were. She's hardly the only companion in the Davison era this can be said of, however. Turlough, after all, was designed to be an expressly untrustworthy companion. Perhaps more to the point, Adric is just as adept as Tegan at getting things wrong, and yet doesn't work nearly as well as Tegan, which suggests that there's something more to this.

Part of it, I think, is that Adric offered the frustrating mix of being highly intelligent and frequently wrong. This means that when he gets it wrong within the story, it tends to be an actual moral failing. Adric is wrong because he's unduly selfish or arrogant. Tegan, on the other hand, is just as much the moral center of the program as the Doctor is; not for nothing is the catchphrase most associated with her "brave heart." She's just not nearly as intelligent. She generally gets it wrong by virtue of actually being wrong about things.

This is a key aspect of Tegan's character, and one that Janet Fielding has commented on, saying that she enjoyed the opportunity to play a female character who was strong without being intelligent. And within Doctor Who there's an importance to this—Tegan is in some ways the last moment of resistance against the current rhetoric that has the Doctor only taking "the best" on as companions. Without wanting to be in the least bit cheeky about the Davison-era cast, it's a real challenge to the idea of a meritocracy in the TARDIS crew.

Central to this working, then, is Janet Fielding herself. There are surely few people in Doctor Who's history that it is easier to like than Fielding, a tireless and unrelenting advocate for feminism within and without the series. Actually, that's demonstrably untrue: there's a clear band of people eager to tear Fielding down for her lack of respect for the program, whether taking umbrage at her delightful snark on commentary tracks, blaming her for the years Paul McGann declined to reprise the role of the Eighth Doctor for Big Finish (during which she was his agent), or generally acting as though her observation that the program had a sexism problem was a personal inconvenience to them.

A more reasonable view would note that Fielding carried the torch for feminist critique of Doctor Who through some eras where it was in short supply, and that you don't spend thirty years holding a show accountable without some love for it. But perhaps the more important thing to note is the way in which Tegan, as a character, comments on this. The entire point of Tegan, at least under Fielding's uncompromising portrayal of her, is that she is given a sense of dignity and strength that's independent of any notion of her as being "right" or "skilled." There's a profound feminist argument here: the acknowledgment that a woman doesn't have to prove herself the equal of the men in order to be treated with dignity and respect. (In this regard, of course, it helps that Tegan is initially set up alongside Nyssa, who is the equal of the men, thus insulating the show from any critique that Tegan's lack of intelligence is in some way a critique of her status as a woman.)

Which is to say that even if the gossip that says that Janet Fielding personally ensured that Paul McGann didn't work for Big Finish for several years out of sheer malice towards the show is true (and I am skeptical that it was out of animosity towards the show and not out of the, let's face it, entirely reasonable belief that an actor of McGann's stature has better things to do than direct-to-CD radio drama), it doesn't matter. Doctor Who, by necessity, must be big enough for dissidents. A fiercely independent voice that holds key aspects of the series accountable is invaluable, and far more important than any number of fannish cheerleaders who want to pretend that Doctor Who's treatment of the companions has generally been progressive for its time, or that accepting a job in the series is a life sentence requiring one to work for cheap reprising a role forevermore. Doctor Who without Janet Fielding is as unimaginable as the Davison era without Tegan Jovanka. Thank the Goddess we have both.

## Burn With Me (*Planet of Fire*)

It's February 23rd, 1984. Frankie Goes to Hollywood is still at number one, but they're finally unseated by Nena's "99 Red Balloons." Lower in the charts is equally satisfying—Rockwell's beautiful bit of paranoia "Somebody's Watching Me" and Slade's "Run Runaway" chart, though to be fair, the latter is far better when Great Big Sea does it as an overly fast-paced fiddle orgy. Also, The Smiths have their first full-length album out, and it debuts at #2. In real news, the U.S. pulls out of Beirut, Pierre Trudeau retires as Prime Minister of Canada, and, four days after this story wraps, the miners' strike to end all miners' strikes begins.

While on television, *Planet of Fire*. Peter Grimwade is nobody's favorite writer of the Davison era, and *Planet of Fire* is nobody's favorite story of the era. Neither of these judgments is necessarily unfair—I think you'd have a hard time arguing Grimwade as superior to any of Holmes, Bidmead, or Bailey, and arguing *Planet of Fire* as a classic of the era crosses the line from redemptive readings to outright psychosis. But in an era with Eric Saward, Terence Dudley, and Johnny Byrne submitting multiple scripts, treating Grimwade as one of the era's lowlights seems equally strained.

There's always some complexity to flying in the face of critical consensus. Here this gets at one of the fundamental tricky bits of understanding audience responses, which is that audiences are very good at identifying whether they like or dislike something, and very bad at explaining why. When it comes to making art, giving people what they say they want is almost always a disaster, particularly when those people are a self-selecting group of hardcore fans who are volunteering their opinions. This is not to say that populism is a bad thing, but there's a difference between giving people what they like and giving them what they say they want. In one you attempt to reproduce what has been successful. In another you base your aesthetic and goals off of what people say they like. For example, I would argue fairly readily that the complaint that Davison's Doctor was "bland" at Longleat and the resultant attempt to correct it via Colin Baker's portrayal was a case of the audience blaming Davison for the fact that he was being underutilized by the writers, not an actual criticism of his performance.

So we're faced with a bit of a puzzle. Grimwade's scripts are clearly jarring in some sense, but the degree of judgment against him seems in excess of the observable flaws in his scripts. What's the actual flaw here?

I dealt with this a bit in the *Mawdryn Undead* essay, where I observed that Grimwade is the one writer who's actually capable of working in the soap opera style that the Davison era half-heartedly aspired to. And *Planet of Fire* is a prime example of this. It's a four-parter in which several plot threads at various levels of development coincide. There's the short and self-contained plot arc of the planet Sarn, the end of the plot arc of Turlough, the end of the plot arc (such as it is) of Kamelion, another step in the Master's plot arc, and the start of a plot arc involving Peri. These are sufficiently interwoven to make sense. This is unusual for Doctor Who in that the series is approaching the structure of a show with A, B, and C plots in a given episode. Which is to say, this is how soaps work. It's how you have to structure plots to manage long-term storytelling with a cast of larger than about three. And here, with the Master in a sizeable role, there's basically a cast of five.

But this is not how Doctor Who usually works, which is why the long-term arcs of Nyssa and Tegan never really materialized. Despite setting itself up to be a show that could work as a sci-fi soap, every writer other than Grimwade has stuck to the traditional Doctor Who model of having a single storyline in any given story. Which means that when Grimwade shows up and does an incremental advancement of a bunch of different plotlines, it doesn't quite work in the context of everything that goes on around it, even though it's how the show should be working.

Given all that, Grimwade's juggling act here is solidly impressive. He manages to relegate to pure refrigerator logic the fact that the side trip to Lanzarote to pick up Peri makes no sense, and while the chain of coincidence that has the Master trapped on a planet that also happens to house Turlough's brother is relatively ludicrous, the fact that the two plotlines rarely affect each other keeps this from feeling excessive.

Nor should we ignore the extent to which Grimwade is set up to fail here. Faced with the need to do a triple replacement of Turlough, Tegan, and the Doctor along with the introduction of a new companion and a new Doctor, plus the need to tie off Kamelion and provide a potentially permanent end for the Master, Nathan-Turner elected to stagger the departures. The word "stagger" is a bit of a massive misnomer, though, for what is in practice a sixteen-episode run of continual upheaval in which these four episodes bear the weight of four of the seven changes. This is a ridiculous structure and someone should have pointed out that it might be a good idea to deal with the Master or Kamelion in one of the first three stories of the season instead of embarking on a massive and concentrated block of changes. (Or to give the show another story to breathe and not throw in Colin Baker's introduction on top of an already overstuffed season.)

The irony is that Grimwade's approach here, had it been followed by the rest of the show, would also have worked, and indeed, having been given the lion's share of Nathan-Turner's massive miscalculation to clean up, he actually does it the only way that possibly could have worked. But when everyone else is pulling against this and insisting on being relentlessly high concept, Grimwade's approach runs aground because suddenly his is the one story of the season that you can't summarize in a one-sentence pitch and so it looks like the boring one.

But as we said, so much of what Grimwade is doing is exactly what Davison's Doctor needed all along. The argument I made back in *Time Crash* about how making the Doctor at times relatable doesn't undermine his otherness as long as there are clear-cut times in which he is starkly alien plays in perfectly here, and the death of Kamelion, with the Doctor at once utterly ruthless and unhesitating in ensuring it while still clearly hurt by it, is a prime example. Similarly, the Doctor standing icily by as the Master burns, or his rebuke to Turlough that if Turlough is keeping a secret that the Doctor needs to know then their friendship is at an end, are fantastic moments that give Davison an opportunity to move between the warm, kind version of the Doctor and one that is a disturbing force to be reckoned with.

The problem is that those moments are building off relationships that were never established. As easy as it is to slash Ainley's Master and Davison's Doctor, one has to pour on the extra-diegetic readings to get that pairing to work. So we get a teasing "Won't you show mercy to your own—" as he burns, but nothing that it connects to. Nobody has been trying to write stories that lead up to an eventual denouement, and so there's no drama, just (as with *Earthshock*) a vague and lukewarm imitation of drama. What really needed to exist somewhere in the Davison era is the Doctor trying to save the Master from Castrovalva or the Xeraphin and being betrayed so that his standing by as the Master burns is a moment of him being once bitten, twice shy. But the Doctor has never looked at the Master as anything other than a villain to defeat, so there's no impact when the Master implies that maybe he's his brother or something.

Likewise, Kamelion has had, over his two stories, all of seven lines of dialogue in which he's not being actively used as part of one of the Master's schemes. The Doctor having to kill a companion is a moment of drama, but Kamelion never got the chance to be one. Yes, there were technical problems with him, but he's a shape-changing robot. Have him take a human form, choose to stick with it, actually build the character. Grimwade is right that a scene in which the Doctor is pained to have to sacrifice his friend (but willing to do it anyway in this case) is a fantastic one. But nobody has bothered to help Grimwade set that scene up, and so there's only so much it can achieve.

And, of course, there's Turlough. The exchange I noted in which the Doctor rebukes Turlough for still keeping secrets is a fantastic one. But of course it is, because Grimwade is the one who actually understood Turlough as originally conceived—a companion you can never quite trust. Everyone else just went with a generic "ruthless coward" characterization, whereas Grimwade is, in having the Doctor make the active but wary choice to let Turlough have his secrets, actually thinking about the relationship. And as it turns out, Mark Strickson can act and would have benefitted nicely from, you know, actual material.

Similarly, Ainley suddenly reveals himself as being quite good at his job here, finally getting a script in which the Master gets to do Mastery things and play the Doctor role in reverse instead of just getting to be unmasked halfway through with a dramatic synth stab. It's mostly too little too late for his version of the Master (and the revelation that the real Master is a tiny little man flailing about in a box is a depressingly apropos metaphor), but again, with Grimwade actually giving him decent material, Ainley shines.

In this regard Grimwade goes on the list, along with Strickson, Ainley, Fielding, Sutton, and, most damningly, Davison as creative figures who were frustratingly wasted on this era. Grimwade's vision of Doctor Who would have worked beautifully over a twenty-six episode season. But as four episodes of a twenty-six episode season where the other twenty-two had no interest in contributing to the same goals (despite those goals ostensibly being the goals of the production staff) they don't work.

Which is not to completely exempt Grimwade from the blame. Grimwade writes as though his plotlines have the support of the episodes around them when they don't. Yes, there's not enough buildup to make the plots with Kamelion or the Master or Turlough work. But the way to respond to that isn't to pretend that the rest of the show was behaving like it was supposed to if your brief was ever going to work. It's to crank up the volume and go all-out with the emotional storytelling. Instead we get a bunch of good ideas—Turlough following the course the Doctor did in *The War Games* (his beginning having been as an unearthly child), Kamelion having to be sacrificed, the Master begging the Doctor to save him—that are all underplayed as if they've been built to.

Even the Sarn storyline is flaccid. Grimwade's break from the high concept obsession of the rest of the season is in some sense refreshing, but this goes a bit too far in its lack of idea. A critique on religious dogma is all well and good, but why the heck is he blatantly targeting Islam with it? For all the world it looks like the main idea this story has is to go and pick a fight with another culture's supposed extremism. Sure, the pick of Islam isn't incidental—the 1980s were a classic era for depicting Muslims as dangerous extremists. (Oh how times have changed.) But the fact that such xenophobia existed isn't a justification in and of itself. Particularly because Grimwade had a more domestic target available; indeed, Miles and Wood suggest he had one in mind.

The suggestion seems to me largely credible. This is 1984. The AIDS crisis is decimating the gay community and nobody is paying attention because it primarily effects gays and drug users. Instead they were at best ignored, and at worst accused of things like, as James Anderton, Chief

Constable of Manchester's police, would put it, "swirling in a cesspit of their own making." And Grimwade was well aware of the way in which this moral judgment, based primarily on appeals to traditional and religious values, was killing people: the people dying were his friends, after all. But instead of pointing his critique at the domestic level he goes with the xenophobic attack on other people's fanaticism and blindness instead of using the exact same themes to make a commentary with some teeth. It's at best a missed opportunity, and at worse just crass, and it's no wonder Saward toned it down.

Which actually serves as an epitaph for the Davison era in many ways. Throughout, the possibility of what it could do and of how great it could be is present, crackling under the surface. At moments it breaks through. Or, as the joke goes, parts of it are excellent. Rewatching it was an extended process of wondering where the spark and wonder I knew I'd seen as a child was. And in the end, I realized that as a child I just didn't see the mess the spark was fighting to get through quite so clearly. But the ability to see the flaws doesn't mean that the brilliance of the era didn't exist. Just that it wasn't always the case that anybody knew what to do with it.

## Time Can Be Rewritten: *Warmonger*

Given that none of the BBC Books novels featuring Davison's Doctor are particularly beloved, the pick of a novel was always going to be one of the two golden turkeys—this or Gary Russell's *Divided Loyalties*. I picked this for two reasons. First, *Divided Loyalties* was a Season Nineteen book, and as I definitely planned to do *Cold Fusion*, and I wanted to spread the books around a little. But the second reason is that *Divided Loyalties* received mostly scathing and truly outraged reviews on the Doctor Who Ratings Guide, whereas nearly every review of *Warmonger* consisted of several paragraphs of admitting that the novel was unfathomably awful before the reviewer sheepishly confessed to loving it.

For those who have never heard of this... interesting book, allow me to provide a basic plot summary. Peri inadvertently gets her arm ripped off by a pterodactyl, so the Doctor rushes her to a pre-*Brain of Morbius* Karn in the hopes that Dr. Solon will reattach it. He does, but unfortunately the Doctor and Peri get caught up in galactic politics and the rise of Morbius such that Peri is stranded on an alien world as a fierce guerrilla warrior against Morbius's galactic army and the Doctor is rechristened the Supremo to lead an army of Draconians, Sontarans, Cybermen, Ogrons, and Ice Warriors against Morbius in what is, we are repeatedly assured, a terribly dire, ugly war. Eventually he rescues Peri and she makes a drunken pass at him, then they defeat Morbius, the end.

If this sounds like a hot mess, you are underestimating things. But let's pause for a moment and note two things. First, Terrance Dicks's gloriously readable prose continues to rescue him. As preposterous as this book is, Dicks is able to make each fresh absurdity another step in a standard plucky adventure, marching cheerily through the action with a horribly compelling glee. Second, Terrance Dicks is surely way too smart a writer to pen a book this bad by accident. In fact, it is my firm conviction that this book consists of Terrance Dicks, elder statesmen of the Doctor Who world, in his thirty-fourth year of working professionally with Doctor Who, just unrepentantly screwing with the audience.

Let us boil this question down to its barest essentials. There is a moment, fairly early in the book, in which guerrilla warrior Peri, the Scourge of Sylvana, is captured along with some other guerrillas. One begins to shudder as their captor, Lieutenant Hakon, ogles her. The following bit of prose then happens:

> Puzzled and repelled, Hakon released her. "What's the matter with her?"
> "She can't stand to be touched," said Peri.
> "Why not?"
> "She was gang-raped by some of your troops when the first wave landed."
> "Some girls have all the luck," said Hakon.

At this point we are forced into one of two possibilities. The first is that Terrance Dicks, Uncle Terrance himself, writer of the Target novelizations we adored as children, has, in fact, just written a character who jokes about how he likes to gang rape people. The second is that the dedication to Robert Holmes was serious.

If we're being honest, this does seem probable. Terrence Dicks commissioned Holmes's first script, script-edited four more after, novelized all but three of Holmes's stories, and wrote three scripts under Holmes. When Dicks says, as he does in the dedication, that Holmes was the best Doctor Who writer, he's not saying that from a position that doesn't understand exactly what Robert Holmes was good at. And one thing that Robert Holmes was very, very good at was bitter and cynical satires. My contention, then, is that *Warmonger* is Terrance Dicks offering a bitter and cynical satire of Eric Saward.

Doing this in the name of Robert Holmes is, of course, a complex proposition, doubly so when you set the book immediately prior to Robert Holmes's debut in the Saward era. But Holmes, as we'll see, tried to make the Saward era's approach work, at least in his first story. (Subsequently, things got more complex.) So Dicks steps in and writes the other thing Holmes could have written for the Saward era—something in the tradition of *The Space Pirates* or *The Power of Kroll*, in which the writer obviously decides, "Fuck it, I'm going to give the people what they want until they stop wanting it."

This explains one of the things that people bring up when talking about this book, which is that it's far easier to imagine the book working with Colin Baker than it does with Peter Davison. And of course that's the point. What Dicks is doing, in effect, is taking the Saward approach to its most horrific conclusions while remaining totally faithful to the basics of the approach. So since Saward covered both Davison and Baker, Dicks picks Davison, since that's by far the more extreme and absurd angle.

And then he goes to town. Saward likes militaristic sci-fi? Fine, Dicks gives him the most militaristic book imaginable—one where the Doctor doesn't just work with a bunch of space marines, but where he's the leader of an entire galactic army. Saward favors continuity fetishism? Fine, we'll make a needless sequel to a story that makes a complete hash out of dozens of other stories in the name of referencing them. And since Peri gets ogled by the camera repeatedly in both *Planet of Fire* and *Caves of Androzani*, Dicks takes every opportunity to have characters ogle and leer at her.

It's sublime in its willful wrongness, and not just in the scene I've already quoted. Thrill as the Doctor rescues Peri from the pterodactyl: "Leaning forwards, the Doctor fastened his teeth into the creature's neck, jaw muscles bulging as he clamped down hard." Laugh uproariously as Peri attempts to explain the Gaztaks (that would be the space mercenaries from *Meglos*, by the way) as having the look "you see in American cities—in the dangerous parts. Places where everyone who looks at you seems to be thinking, 'Do I mug this one or that one?'" (Clearly some American conventions have not been taking Mr. Dicks to the right parts of town.) Or go with my personal favorite moment, in which the Doctor, after getting his uniform as the Supremo, is sadly informed that his jackboots aren't quite ready yet.

All of these moments are not merely utterly wrong, they're almost meticulously crafted to be wrong. It would be difficult to actively shape bits of prose that feel more wrong in a Doctor Who book. And yet every reason these moments feel wrong is a description that's routinely laid at the feet of the Saward era. There's an impeccable sort of precision here—a sense that the book is too perfectly wrong to be anything short of deliberately so.

And, of course, this willful wrongness is paired with Terrance Dicks's usual sense of straightforward action-adventure. Which is to say that it's consistently good fun and moves along. There are no obvious structural or storytelling flaws here. So in this regard Dicks is outdoing the Saward era on two fronts—he's taking the era's tendencies to their logical extremes and then telling a better-crafted story than most of the era's actual writers could ever manage. That it feels so wrong and yet so fun is, in many ways, exactly what *Resurrection of the Daleks* tried for and missed.

I mean, this is the thing that nobody reviewing the book really admits. No, this could never be made in Season Twenty-One, but the reasons aren't the perversity of the Doctor as a military leader or that it's fanwanky. The problems are that it would explode the budget, that it's not a four-parter, perhaps even that there's a bit too much sex and that the nonlinear storytelling wouldn't wash. But anybody who says that the violence of the Doctor or the absurd continuity are a problem while saying this novel doesn't fit between *Planet of Fire* and *Caves of Androzani* is ignoring the reality of the era. In an era that brought us *Earthshock, Warriors of the Deep, Resurrection of the Daleks*, and the Doctor's killing of Kamelion, the idea that the content of this book would have posed a problem is dubious at best. This is exactly what the Saward era on an unlimited budget would be. It fits its era perfectly. That's the cruel joke of it. It fits its era too perfectly. For all that this isn't Davison as we like to think of him, it's alarmingly close to the sorts of things that routinely made it on screen in Season Twenty-One.

The problem, though, is that Terrance Dicks is just too nice for this. He's the sort of person who genuinely believes that war is a noble tragedy, and whose main view of war and the military remains the Napoleonic Wars with a side of Hitler. And so he spends heartfelt chapters on the brutal tragedy of the war and the "Butcher's Bill." One gets the sense that they're sincere—that they really are Dicks setting aside the jokes and trying to deliver sobering messages about how serious all of this really has been, but it doesn't work at all. The earnest nobility of it—a tone Dicks is actually quite good at—just cuts awkwardly against the perverse horror that precedes it.

The second point where Dicks really just seems too nice for his own book comes with Peri's drunken pass at the Doctor. The Doctor turns her down, comparing it to incest. The problem, frankly, is that this is just kind of an oddly prudish line for Dicks to draw in the sand—and it very much comes off as the one thing that he's just not willing to do. I mean, I'm not arguing for the Doctor to be shagging companions in the general case by any measure, but if you're writing a story that's deliberately kicking sand in the faces of taboos, raising the issue of Doctor/Companion sex just to have that be the thing you shoot down as beyond the pale is a bit much. Just go for it and make sure you piss everyone off, really.

Still, the book is terribly clever, and shows a vicious sort of humor that many would have thought beyond Terrance Dicks. And if it is a golden turkey, well, it accomplished exactly what it set out to do.

## The Grinding Engines of the Universe (*The Caves of Androzani*)

It's March 8th, 1984. "99 Red Balloons" continues to float along atop the charts, and will play out Peter Davison. Also in the top ten are Van Halen with "Jump" and Billy Joel with "An Innocent Man," while lower in the charts are King Crimson and the *Fraggle Rock* theme, a trivia fact I included just to use the phrase "King Crimson and the *Fraggle Rock* theme." Top albums are *Into The Gap* by The Thompson Twins and *Human's Lib* by Howard Jones.

In the news, Gerry Adams and three other Sinn Féin members are injured in an attack by the Ulster Volunteer Force, and the other William F. Buckley is kidnapped in Beirut. But the real news and, in many ways, most crucial backdrop for this story comes with the start of the miners' strike.

It is difficult to come up with a better illustration of the idea of a "clusterfuck" than the 1984-85 miners' strike. As a pragmatic issue, the strike consisted of Thatcher's government running rings around the National Union of Miners so as to humiliate them and break the back of what had previously been the most powerful union in the country. Thatcher's government stockpiled coal prior to announcing the pit closures that sparked the strike, thus blunting the immediate impact of the strike and preventing the calamity of the Three Day Week. Meanwhile, Arthur Scargill, head of the

NUM, made an egregious political miscalculation. Faced with an accelerated schedule for closing the pits and afraid that he'd lose the vote, Scargill declined to submit the strike to a national vote. This allowed Thatcher to delegitimize the strike, which she wasted no time doing, comparing striking miners to Argentina's invasion of the Falklands.

The resulting PR coup was, quite literally, bloody and brutal. Thatcher unleashed a police force that was spectacularly violent and corrupt, with *The Sun* and the other redtops cheering her on the whole way. Indeed, the extent of the depravity is still coming out: the South Yorkshire police, who arrested 95 people at the so-called Battle of Orgreave before having to drop prosecution on all of them due to having fabricated the evidence, would five years later be largely responsible for the Hillsborough disaster and the appalling attempt to blame the incident on Liverpool supporters. In both cases, of course, the police and government were aided and abetted by Murdoch and *The Sun*. The propaganda war, combined with Scargill's inept politicking, kept the strike from gaining broad support with the public, and it ended in failure a year later, leaving the mining industry and union but shadows of their former selves.

In more fundamental terms, the strike is a classic example of the false opposition. Of course closure of collieries had to happen. The coal industry was increasingly unprofitable, and even in 1984 it was clear that in the medium to long term a transition away from coal mining and towards other forms of energy was necessary. Equally, however, closing the pits devastated local economies and communities, and Thatcher had no intention of doing anything but leaving those communities and the people within them to die. The unexamined assumption here, however, is that economic progress and development has to carry a human price. Thatcher's government was never going to seriously consider coupling the pit closures with efforts to provide new economic stimulus to the affected regions, and Scargill opted to defend the moribund coal industry in the general case. In the end, every side was mercenary, aiming primarily to protect their own wealth.

The Caves of Androzani was written before any of this happened. Indeed, it was transmitted before most of it happened. And yet it is almost the perfect Doctor Who story for this—a bitter tale of profiteering rivals savagely cutting each other's throats to everyone's harm. In this regard it's Robert Holmes at his most gloriously cynical, portraying a world where every system is rotten and degenerate, run by psychopaths with eyes only for their own interests. Even comparatively noble characters are ruthless and callous, like General Chellak, who calmly sentences the Doctor and Peri to death despite believing their innocence.

Many sensible people have, of course, declared this the greatest Doctor Who story of all time. And deservedly so. It's gorgeously tense, better directed than anything else in the classic series, well-acted, and has a razor-sharp script. Combined with the natural tendency to favor "event" episodes, the idea that Caves of Androzani represents a high point for the series should be thoroughly uncontroversial.

But there's something just a little bit odd about its reception. For all that it is hailed as the greatest Peter Davison story and one of the greatest ever, almost nobody suggests using it as a representative story to introduce people to the Davison era. The consensus seems to be that its greatness is only properly appreciated when you've seen the rest of the Davison era, seemingly on the grounds that in order to appreciate how Davison's Doctor is put through the wringer here you have to see him in more normal circumstances.

On the other hand, it appears that Holmes, largely unfamiliar with Davison's portrayal, just wrote the script with Tom Baker in mind. Lawrence Miles suggests that this fact means that the resulting episodes are darker than what Holmes envisioned, but I think this is slightly off. Yes, almost all of the banter that Davison engages in and his mockery of his guards and captors is Baker-esque. But on the other hand, everything about the story is set up as an inevitable march towards destruction. The Doctor gets himself killed in Episode One by getting into the Spectrox nest to save Peri. This is a delightfully bitter piece of Doctor Who irony—what kills the Doctor, at the end of the day, is the fact that his companion trips and falls down a hole. Everything after that is just unspooling the consequences of the Doctor's landing on Androzani Minor.

So the entire piece is, from a writing perspective, set up to be doom-laden. The Doctor is throwing his witticisms in the face of events so brutal that they're going to kill him. Indeed, in the first draft the Doctor was just going to die from the sheer brutality of it all, just from the sum total of all the punishment and injuries he'd sustained. It's not that it's difficult to imagine Tom Baker in a story where his number is up from the start; that's *Logopolis*, after all. But it is difficult to imagine such a story with an imperious, wisecracking Tom Baker spouting Holmes's dialogue doing it. The idea of Robert Holmes trying to write *Logopolis* is jarring in the extreme.

I'd suggest that while Holmes is writing for Baker here, he's writing for Baker with the knowledge that it's going to be Davison delivering the lines, and thus that there's not going to be the imperious confidence of Tom Baker shining through every line. The script depends on the fact that Davison is taking a risk with every wisecrack—that he's provoking dangerous psychopaths and that this could all blow up in his face. The Episode Three cliffhanger seals it. The Doctor's mocking responses to Stotz are pure Tom Baker—"Sorry, seems to be locked," for instance, and the bit about not having much experience with the controls. But the overall content of the scene—the Doctor with nothing to lose crashing a spaceship into the planet because he no longer cares if he lives or dies—is completely beyond anything Tom Baker ever did or that one can imagine him doing. Holmes is giving Davison lines written for Baker, yes, but he visibly knows enough of Davison's portrayal to know that the lines are going to turn into quips borne of a desperate mania. Whereas when Holmes wrote Baker as desperate and on edge the result was the almost humorless *Pyramids of Mars*. Baker's Doctor played desperation as fear because manic joking was the normal order of things. Holmes's script relies entirely on the fact that he knows Davison's normal order of things isn't this.

But that's not quite right. It's not that this isn't the normal order of things for Davison. It's that this isn't how Davison's Doctor acts when he's comfortable with the situation. And this gets at why the idea that *Caves of Androzani* ought not be watched as one's first Davison story is a little weird. Because what the script requires isn't that Davison's behavior be different from other episodes, it's that Davison's behavior displays discomfort. But that's a function of Davison's acting, not of comparison of this story with previous ones. The fact that the Doctor is hurling wisecracks at people who really might shoot him in the head and be done with him isn't something you need to have watched *Arc of Infinity* to understand.

On the other hand, as we talked about with *Planet of Fire*, people are better at identifying what they like than they are at explaining why. Which is to say that just because the explanation of why this is better if you've watched other Davison stories doesn't quite wash doesn't mean that it isn't improved by the context of other Davison stories. Of course, as Miles points out, it's even more improved when you don't know that Peri is the companion for nearly the whole of the Colin Baker era. Then, given the brutal dispatching of Kamelion and the death of Adric, you can get something very rare indeed in Doctor Who—a moment where it's genuinely uncertain whether everyone is going to make it out alive.

But even without that, something about this episode shines a little brighter when put in context with the era. To some extent this is just the standard structure of a regeneration story. Given that every Doctor is in part a reaction against his predecessor, and given that a regeneration story is by definition a narrative collapse, it's very easy to read regeneration stories as rebukes of their eras. We did so with both *The War Games* and *Planet of the Spiders*, and it's worth remembering that even if he didn't write either, Holmes was around for both.

And it's easy to read *The Caves of Androzani* this way. Davison's portrayal doesn't gain much in contrast with past stories, but the apocalyptic tone of the story still resonates in contrast with past stories. The story sticks out vividly in part because Davison's Doctor hasn't ever been pushed like this before. He's way past talking about the pleasures of a well-cooked meal here, and he's more likely to be in the pile of bodies than standing above it tutting about other ways.

Put another way, Davison's Doctor has generally been used as a moral contrast instead of as an agent in the story. He doesn't have to actively overthrow the fanatical regime of Sarn, he just has to point out that they're intellectually bankrupt. He doesn't have to stop the Daleks, he just has to inspire Stein to blow himself up. Even in the hands of quite good writers like Gallagher and Clegg the Doctor serves to point out the situation to other people so that they will do the right thing. He's been used to pass judgment on genres instead of to destabilize and subvert them. There have been exceptions, most recently *Frontio*s, but the bulk of the time the Doctor has been restricted to inspiring other people to act. This isn't always a problem—as we pointed out back in *Castrovalva*, putting the Doctor at the margins and letting him nudge other characters is a refreshing change from Baker's bombast. Nevertheless, it's a thing to react against, just as Pertwee's imperiousness was in *Planet of the Spiders*. And so Holmes throws the Doctor into a situation with real teeth in which he's forced to act.

The heart of this change, of course, gets back to where we started—the fact that this is an exquisitely political story. But note that it's clearly not political in an allegorical sense. This isn't the crass "Arthur Scargill as angry badger person" politics of *The Monster of Peladon*. No, this is political for the simple reason that it's material, and that's what makes the situation so fraught with danger for the Doctor. It's not some facile fable that exists primarily to illustrate an abstracted moral point. This is a situation that is designed to look like real situations with the volume turned up to melodrama. And that is what makes this story spark so gloriously—the fact that for the first time since taking on the part Davison is shoved into a situation that acts like a world.

The secret to alchemy is material social progress, and the fact of the matter is that the show has been very, very far away from the material. For all its violence, the viscera of history have been dangerously absent. Despite this there have been flashes of quality—we've known since Davison's first few stories that his Doctor could be at the heart of a truly great story. But now we see the secret—now we see how well he could do when put into a situation that required more than symbolizing a moral point.

In essays past, this would be where I transition to the glorious conclusion—a carefully cadenced bit about the Doctor facing an inevitable destruction. Themes of narrative collapse would intertwine with proleptic allusions that start to form the basis of the next act of the narrative. The act of recognizing this era's failings would be read as exorcism, the pathos of the Doctor dying in the dirt used as a lead-in to a glorious rebirth, a gesture towards the endless possibility of the series. But I can't. Not here. Because the truth is that we all know what's coming next.

Past that, it would be one thing if *The Caves of Androzani* was an earned conclusion to the entire run of the Davison era. But it's not. Everything here could have been done before. Yes, Davison's Doctor benefitted from being put a little more to the margins than Baker's, but it didn't have to be the standard approach. The fact that the Doctor dies at the end of this story doesn't mean that a high-tension story where the Doctor has his back against the wall could only be a regeneration story. And who seriously thinks it could be? Are we just pretending *Pyramids of Mars* and *The Seeds of Doom* don't exist now?

The problem this time isn't a failing in the conception of the Doctor. It's not the logical endpoint of a phase of the series history where we see that something has to change. Yes, the story looks great in contrast with everything around it, but that's not because it pays off any buildup from them. It's because they were often a complete mess, and this story isn't. Yes, this story looks like an absolute giant compared to the rest of the Davison era, but that's as much because of the latter's flaws as the former's merits.

The fact of the matter is that they couldn't get the Davison era to work until his last story. They drove the best actor they'd had since Troughton away with the crap scripts of Season Twenty, and by the time they gave him a truly brilliant script he'd already decided to leave. And they only finally got the era to work by turning back the clock and hiring Robert Holmes to do it. Yes, he outdid himself, and yes, the production work here is phenomenal, but the fact of the matter is that this was made by the de facto director of swaths of *Warriors' Gate* and a writer who's been on the show since 1968.

This isn't some earned capstone to an era. No, this could have been done in 1981. It took the production team three years to get the show to work despite having a phenomenal lead actor. This is what the era should have been all along. The fact that they finally got it right after three years shouldn't have inspired any high hopes that they'd get it right out of the gate with the next version.

## Now My Doctor: Peter Davison

It's a strange thing, this essay, because in a very real sense, as I said, Peter Davison was my Doctor. In the period where my Doctor Who collection consisted of Pertwee and Davison stories my parents had taped, there was no real contest as to what I preferred. And yet with the hindsight of adult life, there's no more than half a dozen Davison stories I'd be eager to sit down with and watch for fun. And while that's about the same hit rate as the Williams era, the list has a very different feeling to it. With the Williams era I noted that I'd much rather sit down with *The Androids of Tara* than *Earthshock* if I was in the mood to watch something for entertainment value, and that really does stand.

There is, in other words, precious little of the Davison era that is particularly fun. The most obvious pick, *Earthshock*, is a story I'm simply not terribly fond of. *Caves of Androzani* is indisputably brilliant and one of the greatest Doctor Who stories of all time, but it's also a grim-faced thriller. *Kinda* and *Snakedance* are intricate and thoughtful pieces of televisual theatre. But there's not a lot of moments of charm and wit in any of them. It's all surprisingly serious.

That's not entirely fair, of course. There are stories that are overtly light-hearted like *Black Orchid*, *The King's Demons*, and *The Five Doctors*. But they generally feel a bit slapdash, as do no shortage of the supposedly serious ones, to be fair. The result is an era that has some real gems, but is very hard to feel good about.

All the same, I love Peter Davison's Doctor. And the reason for this is straightforward: he's a fantastic actor. Of the classic series Doctors, he and Patrick Troughton are the only two in their league. It's not that the other five actors are bad; they're manifestly not. But Davison and Troughton are of a different class, as evinced by the fact that both of them had significant careers in which playing the Doctor was merely the capstone, as opposed to careers largely defined by that role. They are the only two who would still be major television actors of their era even if they'd never gotten the role.

That said, it's a desperately inconsistent era, and Davison's Doctor is a victim of that. Notably, in two of his best stories, *Kinda* and *Snakedance*, he's conceived of in terms of his ignorance and youth, a characterization that doesn't really apply elsewhere. And in *Kinda*, as with *Caves of Androzani*, large swaths of the story were written with his predecessor in mind, further muddying the water. This puts Davison's Doctor in the odd position of having to be defined by the performance more than by the writing, and by someone who's capable of a subtle and nuanced performance that resists easy summing up.

Much like Troughton's Doctor, Davison's Doctor seems to wriggle out of any attempt to define him. He's ostensibly the nice, gentle Doctor, and yet it's easy to find instances of him being brutally violent and wielding a gun. He's the young, dashing one, according to *Time Crash*, but the historical development that story suggests doesn't really hold up to scrutiny—neither Troughton nor Baker played the Doctor as an old man, after all. He's accused of being bland, and yet has as many moments of charm as any other Doctor. And the complaint of "ineffectual" stands, but is mostly a factor of Saward's writing and one that applies just as well to Colin Baker, not that anyone ever uses it to describe his Doctor.

Also like Troughton, Davison is inclined to react and to skirt around the edges of scenes. But Troughton was routinely given significant sequences in which he got the spotlight and was allowed to just be enjoyable to watch. Davison, on the other hand, remains the victim of the "de-emphasize the Doctor" agenda, and is rarely actually given room to be the star of his own show.

And yet for all of this, he has very few actually bad moments. (And ironically, what is for me the most cringeworthy, the "well-prepared meal" scene in *Earthshock*, is one of the few things that attempts to give the Doctor a sort of normative hero moment.) Davison's Doctor is basically always a pleasure to watch. Even in a mediocre scene—and he has plenty of them—he remains compelling, always buzzing with activity and decision-making no matter how lame his dialogue.

At the heart of his performance, however, is something that hadn't really been a part of any previous effort, which is a clear decision to start from the question of, "What sort of person spends their entire life wandering aimlessly through time and space?" In particular, Davison visibly starts from that as opposed to from any notion of the Doctor as a hero. Davison's Doctor is a man who wanders the universe and behaves admirably when he gets into trouble. After three consecutive iterations that played variations on "the eccentric hero," this is a bracing and compelling take.

Central to its pleasures is, I think, an ability to convey the depth of the Doctor's outrage at evil. When the Doctor is more straightforwardly a hero, evil becomes something he almost expects to find. But Davison's Doctor feels as though he always has a real hope that he might walk out of the TARDIS and find a perfectly nice place to relax, only to instead discover nefarious schemes that he feels obliged to stop. He seems frustrated, angry, and saddened by brutality; he's far less likely to laugh at the villains.

This works well with a tendency throughout the Davison era to work on a smaller scale. For all that they're flawed stories, *Mawdryn Undead* and *Black Orchid* are simply not things that would work with earlier Doctors. In particular, the lack of an actual villain in *Mawdryn Undead* would have been a real problem for a grandstanding leading man like Tom Baker or Jon Pertwee. But for Davison the prospect of an antagonist who only wants to die is fascinating largely because his Doctor has more range to respond to villains than any previous one. Similarly, for all that *Warriors of the Deep* is a godforsaken trainwreck that does nothing to earn its final line, Davison hits the stunned horror of "There should have been another way" like no one before him could have.

It leaves one imagining the Davison era that never was. The most obvious gap is, of course, the reaction to the death of Adric, which is smothered in *Time-Flight* and a seemingly large gap between Seasons Nineteen and Twenty, colluding so we never actually see the Doctor mourn Adric, despite having, for the first time, a Doctor who would probably be compelling doing so. Davison's frustration at the departure of Nyssa is similarly easy to understand. One of the things that is most depressing about the failure to ever give Nyssa a plot responding to what the Master did is that we never really get to see her and Davison tackle meaty material. (Imagine the alternate version of *Time-Flight* where Nyssa and Tegan, reeling from the death of Adric, decide to kill the Master for what he did to both of them, and the Doctor has to try to stop them.)

And unfortunately, unlike Colin Baker, Davison is not especially well-served by Big Finish, partially because his subdued performance loses a lot when translated to audio, and partially because, let's be honest, Davison is less inclined to throw himself into the job than Baker is. The result is, I think, in some ways one of the biggest disappointments in the history of the series: an incredibly compelling take on the Doctor that is only given a handful of moments where it's actually allowed to work.

But in the end, that doesn't matter. I still love Davison's Doctor. Part of it is simply childhood nostalgia; the fact that for a time he was, in a very real sense, "my" Doctor. But more to the point, the character is a separate thing from his era. (I love Nyssa too, but I'd be terribly hard-pressed to say that she'd ever gotten a good story.) I love the cheery traveller whose luck inevitably turns bad. I love the frustration and desperation he can convey. I love the smile when he actually gets to be charming. Whatever problems I have with the era, and I've literally written a book about it, the fact remains: Davison's Doctor is a fantastic performance, and, more fundamentally, a fantastic character.

## Does It Offend You? (*The Twin Dilemma*)

It's March 22nd, 1984. Lionel Richie is at number one with "Hello," and remains so for the whole of this story. Sade, Culture Club, Bananarama, and Depeche Mode also chart, along with, at number two for the second week of this story, the Weather Girls with "It's Raining Men." Hallelujah. In real news, the heyday of the Satanic ritual abuse panic begins in sync with the Colin Baker era as teachers at the McMartin Preschool are falsely accused of it. (Meanwhile, numerous actual pedophiles remain safely protected by the vast amount of institutional power they wield.) Also, Andrew Lloyd Weber's *Starlight Express* opens in London.

While on television, we go from a supposed best Doctor Who story ever to the supposed worst. The articles there are deliberate; *The Caves of Androzani* won one of the last three *Doctor Who Magazine* polls to rank all of the stories ever. *The Twin Dilemma*, on the other hand, came in dead last all three times, generally by a non-trivial margin. On basic quality, this might not be quite fair. It's very bad, but as a matter of competent production and provision of a modicum of entertainment it's not demonstrably worse than many others. If you were to show someone unaware of fan politics a selection of *Warriors of the Deep*, *The Celestial Toymaker*, *The Horns of Nimon*, *Time of the Rani*, and *The Monster of Peladon* along with this and ask them to pick the worst, I don't think you'd see this one picked in particular excess to the others.

There are actually moments of it that border on the compelling. I mean, this is praising with faint damnation, but it's still worth noting that, taken on its own and out of context, and judged purely on its storytelling merits, this is merely among the worst stories ever made, as opposed to clearly being the worst thing ever.

But, of course, when have we ever taken things out of context in *TARDIS Eruditorum*? Yes, the biggest problem with this story is its context in Doctor Who, but the thing aired on television in a context everyone involved knew about, so really, that criticism sticks pretty well. Because what this story does is doom Colin Baker's tenure as the Doctor and, in doing so, ensure the show's cancellation. In this regard it is the single most destructive story to Doctor Who. Never mind Michael Foot. At one hundred minutes, this is the longest suicide note in history.

There are, of course, self-inflicted wounds prior to this. If the past two seasons hadn't started with pieces of utter crap like *Warriors of the Deep* and *Arc of Infinity*, if the Peter Davison era hadn't been a monument to wasted potential, et cetera, et cetera. *The Twin Dilemma*'s spectacular faceplant and sabotaging of the series didn't happen in isolation. On the other hand, it's also not the straw that broke the camel's back. It's the entire bale of hay fired at high velocity towards the camel's back. Doctor Who was vulnerable coming into this story, yes, but even if the Davison era had been a consistent triumph it would have been, at the very least, in serious trouble coming out of this story.

The core of the problem was the decision to put so many eggs in one basket in the first place. Nobody has ever really offered a clear explanation for why Nathan-Turner decided that Colin Baker's debut should be moved up to the end of Season Twenty-One instead of the start of Season Twenty-Two. It's a strange idea, particularly in contrast to how Davison was introduced. With Davison they went out of their way to give him three stories to practice before his debut so that he'd know where he was going with the character. Now, with Colin Baker, who, while not the crap actor he's belittled as by some, is by no means as skilled an actor as Peter Davison, they dump him in the role with less prep time and expect his first time out of the gate to set the tone of the character for nine months.

There's really no explanation for this. It's a dumb idea on the face of it. If at the start of a season the new Doctor is wobbly coming out of the gate, it's not a huge problem simply because there's a level of momentum carrying you from story to story. It's easy to tune in next week after a rough story. But this asks people to tune in nine months from now and in a different timeslot. There's much less margin for error in case of a rough start. If *Castrovalva* had proven to be a turkey, they had the opportunity to turn things around next week, as they did back in 1975 when Tom Baker's debut was, let's face it, not exactly inspiring but the next story was legendarily good. This is common sense—putting the debut of a new character at the start of the season gives you more than one chance to win the audience over. Putting the debut of a new character at the end of a season means that if you give a bad first impression that impression has lots of time to settle in.

But not only does the production team set themselves up for trouble, they seem completely oblivious to the idea that this may require a delicate hand. Even a moment's thought would indicate that if you have one story that's going to be the sole impression people have of your new Doctor for nearly a year then you want to throw away the old "regenerative trauma" structure and have the Doctor start with his feet on the ground. I mean, this really isn't some advanced and subtle trick of craft: you have one story that has to carry the entire load of establishing the new Doctor. You're going to want it to actually show what that Doctor is going to be like. You can't spend episodes mucking around with post-regenerative trauma when you're trying to cement your new lead in the audience's mind such that they're excited to come back next season. In this regard, at least, *The Twin*

*Dilemma* deserves some credit, in that Baker settles into his default mode reasonably quickly. But any points it gains are more than undone by the fact that they not only decide to introduce the Doctor in regenerative crisis, they go further with regenerative crisis than had ever been done before by having him try to strangle Peri. In the best of circumstances this would be an unwise way to introduce a new lead character, given how intensely unlikable it makes him. In these circumstances it is difficult to understand how the idea even got approved.

More broadly, if giving yourself one shot to introduce your new Doctor is unwise, to do so when your concept for the new Doctor is that he's an unlikable character who the audience slowly grows to trust and appreciate is simply farcical. The two ideas are completely incompatible. Even if we grant that one of them is good—and I don't really think "make your lead character unlikable" was ever going to be a winning strategy—"make your character unlikable and then put yourself in a situation where the first impression matters more than ever to the success of your show" is an idea that almost weaponizes stupidity.

Of course, the Colin Baker era is also shot through with dodgy post facto justifications. For instance, the new party line is that Colin Baker's Doctor was supposed to have a shameful secret that would eventually be revealed so as to explain his hostile demeanor and make him palatable to the audience. I don't doubt that this idea came up in conversation at some point, but there's a fairly easy way to check if this was actually a plan that people had or just something that was mentioned as an idea once that later got seized on to explain what they were really doing: What was the secret? Anybody? Have any of the people who allegedly crafted this idea of a multi-season "peeling back the layers of the onion" arc for Colin Baker's Doctor ever actually indicated what the big secret at the heart of his character was?

Of course not. Because there wasn't any. This was never an actual storyline that was being written into the series. And who would seriously think it might be? This was a production team that couldn't remember to have Tegan and Nyssa be upset with the Master over things that actually did get onto screen, and we're seriously expected to believe that they had some idea for deep motivations for the Doctor that never made it to screen? When nobody has even come up with a suggestion for what it might be? Or, for that matter, how it might work? I mean, how exactly does Colin Baker's Doctor suddenly acquire a dark secret that hadn't affected any of his predecessors?

No, the far more likely explanation is the one that occurred to everybody at the time—that every Doctor is a reaction against the previous one, and that they decided to follow "nice" and "bland" with "nasty" and "loud." Then decided to give audiences a single look at this deliberately hard-to-like Doctor and see if they'd tune in nine months later. Given this, it's a wonder that so many people were even around to be driven away by the first episode of *Attack of the Cybermen* instead.

But fine, let's accept that, against all logic, we're going to attempt this piece of madness. In that case we should, at the very least, make sure we have a solid writer. Not just someone with television experience, but someone who's got a proven track record of working with Doctor Who. Robert Holmes might be good. So might Peter Grimwade, who capably handled a complex list of requirements in *Mawdryn Undead*. Giving the story to Eric Saward would make sense, given its importance. Similarly, Christopher Bidmead, who did well with *Castrovalva*. But instead of any of the writers of the previous four stories, they pick Anthony Steven, someone who, although he had extensive television experience, has never done Doctor Who before, and who turns out to be dangerously slow and prone to claiming that his typewriter has exploded, and sure enough, his script needs a complete overhaul.

Again, one wonders why they even put themselves in this position. In the past, new Doctors were debuted by old hands—Bidmead, Dicks, Whitaker, even Holmes had ten episodes under his belt prior to *Spearhead From Space*. And yet instead of asking Bailey, Clegg, Gallagher, or even one of the writers they mistakenly have been putting so much faith in like Byrne or Dudley, they take a risk on an untested writer. Heck, have this be the story where Eric Saward writes it under his ex-girlfriend's name so that at least it's from the start overseen by someone who knows how this is supposed to work. Any of these ideas would have been smarter than letting the new Doctor debut under an untested writer.

To continue to check off obvious things the production team should have done, if this is the story you want to make a big impression, you want to put some time or money into it. As Tat Wood points out, when you have three stories—a regeneration, a debut, and a bit of transitional loose-end tying that shuffles the companions, you don't blow the budget on an expensive location shoot in Lanzarote for the transitional piece and have the season-ending debut be the piece of cheap comedy. This is a story that absolutely has to be big—on which they're openly and deliberately having everything ride—and they don't even bother to try making it big.

Instead we get poorly cast twins (that the director tried to cast with better actors only to be vetoed because Nathan-Turner, for what can at best be called no discernible reason and at worst viewed as part and parcel of other unsavoury tendencies that we'll get to in a couple of essays, decided it was crucial that the twins be boys), poorly cast everyone else, wretched sets, a stupid monster, flat direction, and a paper-thin plot. The story looks like it's aspiring to the Graham Williams era. Which is improbable given Nathan-Turner's views of that era, and anyway, the script completely lacks the self-awareness and sense of humor that the Williams era had. Say what you will about the Graham Williams era, but it knew enough to wink at the audience when it was being crap. Its only problem was that circumstances conspired to make it crap far too often.

Here, on the other hand, we have the show being crap without seeming to realize it, and on a story in which it's vitally important that the show not be crap. Miles and Wood offer the diagnosis that Nathan-Turner has, by this point, come to completely misunderstand how the series works. Certainly he seems to have simply internalized the assumption that "doing Doctor Who-like stuff" is the sole purpose of Doctor Who such that he hasn't bothered to think through the interactions of the material reality of production and transmission and the standard tropes of the series. That much is clear from the fact that he simultaneously went with giving Baker an orphan story to establish himself and using the post-regenerative trauma angle when one should have precluded the other.

But that doesn't explain the more fundamental errors. It doesn't explain how Nathan-Turner thought end-of-season filler was compatible with launching his new Doctor. Nothing does, really, save for simple incompetence—a complete failure to meaningfully think about how things were going to come off to the audience. And that's the really stark thing. I mean, let's imagine that we were to allow for everything we've already diagnosed. Let's allow that we're going with a deliberately unlikable Doctor, that we're going to have one story set the audience's impression of this Doctor for nine months, that we're going to have him act worse than normal in that story, and that we're not going to try to make it be good. I have no idea why we would allow all of these things, but let's do it, just for fun. If we accept that a cheaply made piece of fluff about an unlikable Doctor might somehow hook people and make them excited about the series, can we say that *Twin Dilemma* just might work?

No. We can't. Because even given all of that, it's impossible to suggest that the execution here is in any way workable. Baker's Doctor isn't just unlikable here. He's intolerable. He's an overtly bad person who any reasonable audience should actively dislike and want to see get his comeuppance. Whereas the series still visibly thinks he's the hero. It's not just that Baker's Doctor is prickly and hard to like, it's that he's a bad guy.

And I'm not just talking about the scene in which he strangles Peri. I mean, that's an appalling bit of bad taste. No, I'm talking about everything that comes after that. The Doctor reacting to it by declaring that he's going to be a hermit and effectively kidnapping Peri to spend the rest of her life tending to his needs. The Doctor's complete failure, at any point in the story, to actually apologize to her for it. To, in fact, declare instead that he's an alien bound to different values and customs and that he's who he is whether she likes it or not. And her grinning broadly at him as he says it, clearly okay with this abusive bastard who tried to kill her and not even caring about it.

Even if we do hold rigidly to the "no hanky-panky in the TARDIS" rule this is difficult to accept. The Doctor attempts to choke his heavily sexualized female companion (indeed, at this point in time the camera's tendency to linger on Nicola Bryant's cleavage is basically Peri's most distinctive character trait aside from her appalling accent). He physically and violently assaults her in a manner that is chillingly familiar as a real-world phenomenon that happens to far too many women at the hands of their male partners. Then he drags her against her will to what he says could be an entire life in which "it shall be your humble privilege to minister unto my needs." She readily forgives him and grins stupidly at his charms. It's not Nicola Bryant's fault—in this and every other story, she plays the material as well as it can be played. Nor is it Baker's fault. They try to make the scenes watchable, but nobody could possibly make this work. Peri is violently assaulted by a man who overtly sees her only purpose as being to serve him, and she happily chooses to stay with him. The show treats this man as its hero and expects the audience to tune in nine months later to watch his continuing adventures.

Of course they declined. Baker's Doctor is completely poisoned here. There's nothing whatsoever that can be done to make this character watchable to anyone who has seen this. And I speak from experience here. This is the story that killed my parents' interest in Doctor Who, and they're hardly alone in the judgment. To this day my mother refuses to accept the possibility that Baker might be good on the audios or in any other stories simply because of how much this story made her hate him. That's how bad this played to people. That's how you kill Doctor Who in under a hundred minutes. You make it about a battered woman idolizing her abuser.

Yeah, okay. I take it back. This is the worst fucking story ever.

## Pop Between Realities, Home in Time for Tea: *Max Headroom*, *Tripods*, *Robin of Sherwood*, *Box of Delights*

So what went wrong? I mean, the flaws are obvious enough in *The Twin Dilemma*. And it's easy enough to pin the blame. But what's the alternative? Throughout the Davison era, even when it was having its biggest disasters, it was at least relatively clear what the good parts of the show were. They may have frequently struggled to break through, but we could usually tell what good Doctor Who was supposed to look like. But the highlights of the Colin Baker era, though existent, are so few and far between that it's difficult to say what they should have done. For a long time the conventional wisdom was, "Don't cast Colin Baker," or, "Have a different concept of the Doctor," but as we'll see, Big Finish proves that Baker's Doctor can work. Still, the advance in storytelling techniques over the nearly thirty years since this era aired means that we can't just say, "They should have done what Big Finish did." The question is what Doctor Who in 1985-86 should have looked like.

The usual technique when we ask questions like this is to look at what else is going on in television at the time. But there are some important questions we have to settle first, namely what it's most appropriate to look at. We could look at sci-fi programs, for instance. In which case we'd have fairly slim pickings: *Max Headroom* and *Tripods* were about the only games in town, although there are some obvious choices if we want to look beyond them too. But let's start with those two, because the difference between them is suggestive. See, Doctor Who has always existed in a liminal space between children's television and science fiction. This may seem a bit of a strange claim given the rather obvious fact that a good deal of children's television is science fiction, but it's important to realize that these are two distinct traditions with a subtle but significant philosophical difference at their heart, and that Doctor Who has always had to do at least some active work to bridge them.

If one were to make a horrific overgeneralization about children's fiction, one of the least inaccurate ones available would be to observe that children's literature tends to focus thematically on the existence of a threshold between two worlds, whether they be mundane and fantastic or otherwise. The logic of this is not difficult to figure out—it's as sensible a metaphor for coming of age as exists. But at the heart of this approach is the fact that a children's story tends to be about obtaining some degree of mastery and sense over the strange second world. Put another way, the basic arc of children's fiction is that it makes the strange familiar.

Science fiction, on the other hand, when considered as a genre instead of as an iconography, does almost the exact opposite. Science fiction's main trick is to use the expanded possibilities of its iconography to reflect our own world back at us from an odd angle. So science fiction goes not for making the strange familiar, but for making the familiar strange.

These ideas are not impossible to reconcile, not least because science fiction can serve equally as a vague iconography that is easily made familiar, and because children's literature often involves making the world that its protagonist starts in a strange place while making the new world familiar. But there is a difference in approach here, and it's well illustrated by looking at the two of the major pieces of British science fiction television going around these days.

In one corner we have *Max Headroom*, which, prior to being a short-lived but well-remembered American sci-fi series in the late 1980s, was an hour-long TV movie on Channel 4 in the mid-80s. Max Headroom is an exceedingly early example of cyberpunk, a short-lived and hugely influential subgenre of science fiction that took the possibilities of technological progress extremely seriously while completely rejecting the idea that they would be connected to social progress. Focusing particularly on the rise of computers and information technology, cyberpunk tended to be at once high-tech and grungy. (Another way to phrase this is that the rest of the world abruptly realized that Philip K. Dick and J.G. Ballard existed.)

In practice, though, the original *Max Headroom*, entitled *Max Headroom: 20 Minutes into the Future*, which barely features Max Headroom at all, is basically an attempt to do a television version of David Cronenberg's *Videodrome*. The giveaway is the sequence in which we see someone explode from watching TV commercials, but the whole thing has similar themes. Both are centered on the physicality of the media—a sensible enough extension of the interminable debate about sex and violence, given that both sex and violence are intensely visceral acts. They imagine a world in which, essentially, media has won—where sexual extremity and extreme violence are widespread, and where the mass media itself has gained more physical and visceral aspects. And they end up creating a sort of oddly double-edged world—a "cool" dystopia that is at once nightmarish and oddly sexy.

In the case of *Max Headroom*, this seems exceedingly deliberate. Watching the pilot episode, one is struck by the difficulty that there's very little of the title character in it, and he's barely relevant to the plot. But that's because the TV movie isn't actually his debut. He was originally the host of a music video programming block on Channel 4, and was wildly popular, hence the idea to make an origin story. And even between his origin story and being picked up as a TV series in America he made appearances here and there in the popular culture. In other words, for all its dystopic trappings, it's clear that everyone involved in *Max Headroom* knew that their job was to make a character everyone was going to think was cool.

(Indeed, if you want to be one of those people who insists that only televised Doctor Who is canonical then it is notable that *Max Headroom* is canonical. Just ask anybody who was watching *The Horror of Fang Rock* in Chicago back in 1987.)

Implicit in the fact that any of this worked is proof that we have clearly reached a point where postmodernism is simply mainstream entertainment. Not the point where postmodern things can be popular, which has been true since David Bowie at the latest, but rather the point where the postmodern doesn't need any justification or explanation and can simply stride calmly onto the public scene without anyone noticing. (If you really want to dial it in, the switch is somewhere between this essay and *The Cleopatras*.) Suddenly the blending of different codes of reference and commentary on those codes of reference becomes something everyone can do.

Or, at least, everyone who's grown up. The rise of postmodernism left children's media relatively untouched, and to some extent continues to do so. This is on the one hand not surprising. There is an earnestness to children's media that cuts against postmodernism. And so in some ways nothing illustrates the gap that was opening up than comparing the BBC's only non-Doctor Who sci-fi program in 1984 with *Max Headroom*. That program, of course, is *Tripods*.

*Tripods*, I should stress, is not a bad show. Indeed, one can fairly reasonably call it timeless, in that its look, feel, and storytelling are almost but not quite impossible to distinguish from children's television for years on either side of it. It is an earnest action-adventure show about plucky youths and Orwellian mind control that, production values aside, could have fit just as well into the 1970s or the 1990s as it did into the 1980s.

That's not to say that *Tripods* is an overly simplistic show. It does a really nifty job of starting with a very pastoral view of the world and steadily making it a source of horror. It's a clever inversion, particularly given the fact that the idyllic pastoral world is, as a concept, intimately connected to idealizations of childhood. It's quite a good show, and clever. The fact that it's a fairly linear adaptation of books means that the transformation it makes between seasons is big and striking. One can absolutely understand why this was popular.

But look at the last time we looked at children's drama (as opposed to *The Adventure Game*), which was *Children of the Stones*. There what was striking was how astonishingly complex and intricate the children's show was. And if I'd compressed essays a little and done it alongside an adult sci-fi show, namely *Survivors*, what that essay would have been talking about would have been just how much more sophisticated the supposed children's show is.

Yes, this is a matter of selection bias—had I compared *The Tomorrow People* with *Survivors* the results would have been different. The big difference is that by 1985 *Tripods* was the only other piece of science fiction on the BBC besides Doctor Who, and so there's not any selection bias to be had anymore. There's just the uncomfortable gap that's visibly opening up between what children's science fiction does and what adult science fiction can do.

And this gap poses real problems for Doctor Who because, as I said, it has a foot in both worlds. On the one hand, Doctor Who has always been firmly science fiction with a clear mandate for estrangement. It's supposed to be a show about making its audience uncomfortable. On the other hand, its basic iconography is, as we've discussed, steeped in a vast history of children's literature. And this has always been reflected in its somewhat odd audience. It's not a children's show, nor is it a family show inasmuch as that term is defined as "a children's show adults don't hate to watch." It's a show that functions not just satisfyingly for both children and adults but independently for each population.

For much of its run this isn't that hard a balance to strike. The fact that adults like good children's television is well documented, and Doctor Who's tricks in terms of actively bridging the gap are relatively narrow—it mostly comes down to the fact that melodrama is a really effective way to suture the two audiences together. But around this period the gap starts to become very big. And this is something we're going to see with troubling vividness in the next season.

Simply put, on the one hand Doctor Who's cultural reputation is as a show for children. This is a problem for it in two ways. First of all, it may be thought of as being for children, but a substantial number of the people writing for it want it to be a serious and often satirical drama. This eventually leads down a rabbit hole of perversity when you have serious actors agreeing to appear in *Revelation of the Daleks* for their children, although to be fair, there are worse rabbit holes than the one that gets you Alexei Sayle. Second of all, the program's self-justification increasingly hinges on its fans, with stars and the producer alike milking the convention circuit. When these fans are easily caricatured as grown men who are obsessed with a children's program then you find yourself facing a bit of a PR problem.

On the other hand, the fact of the matter is that the next two seasons are going to work far better when trying to work for adults than for children. Doctor Who may be seen as a children's program, but that's a misperception. It's more than that. It's telling that in some accounts it was the cancellation of *Tripods* that justified bringing Doctor Who back after its 1985-86 hiatus. Because watching them, the two shows aren't even trying for the same audience. And when the series does, in the next season, attempt stories with a clear "for children" bent, it's some of the worst material of an already pretty dire season.

But equally, Doctor Who trying to be grown up is, if not cringeworthy, at least a bit embarrassing. In many ways the grotesque failures of *The Twin Dilemma* come from the series making a hash of an attempt at adult drama. This whole "make the Doctor abrasive and mellow him out" idea, even if taken seriously (and it is, I'll grant, the most sympathetic reading of the trainwreck), runs into the problem that you're trying to do angst-based character drama about a man wearing a willfully tasteless costume (that was apparently designed to serve as an Edwardian Hawaiian shirt) and fighting giant slugs with deely-boppers on their heads.

To put it another way, one of the problems the show is having in this period is that its gestures towards children and its gestures towards adults are becoming completely separate. But, crucially, so was the culture at large. Doctor Who is in a bizarre position of, between its ambitions and the expectations of it, trying to compete simultaneously with *Max Headroom* and *Tripods*. And it fails spectacularly at both.

Some of this, it should be noted, is a matter of money. Simply put, both *Max Headroom* and *Tripods* just plain looked a lot better than Doctor Who. A more illustrative gap is perhaps between Doctor Who and the UK's other big children's television export of the time, *Robin of Sherwood*. Created by veteran children's television writer Richard Carpenter for ITV, *Robin of Sherwood* is, very much unlike Doctor Who, one of the most iconic and influential children's shows of the 1980s—a beloved cultural touchstone and an unquestioned classic of its genre.

That said, the two shows are closer to each other than one might think. Obviously both belong to the tradition of television action serials, but it's worth noting that *Robin of Sherwood* is a distinctly fantasy-inflected take on the Robin Hood story, with frequent appearances from Herne the Hunter, various prophetic mutterings, and, perhaps most obviously, a first episode entitled "Robin Hood and the Sorcerer," with a proper and actual sorcerer as the villain. The presence of Herne the Hunter also highlights the fact that this is a take on Robin Hood that's very much invested in the character's larger position within Britain's mythology, which forms only a tacit connection with sci-fi like Doctor Who, but no less a genuine one.

All the same, watching them side by side is frankly embarrassing for Doctor Who. Much of this, to be fair, is just that co-producers HTV and Goldcrest (the latter flush with cash following the successes of *Chariots of Fire* and *Ghandi*) spent quite a bit of money on it. The show is done on film, primarily via location shoots, and is long on action sequences. It does these well enough that it's pretty obvious how the show ended up thrilling a generation of children.

Doctor Who, needless to say, isn't getting anything like this sort of treatment. Indeed, it's not even getting the sort of treatment it got during the Pertwee era, where it could put on better-than-decent action sequences when it wanted to. Doctor Who is a cheap studio-bound show. And the BBC had no interest in changing that, even as it increasingly expected Doctor Who to compete with *Robin of Sherwood* and its ilk. Indeed, perhaps more to the point, even as Doctor Who did compete with *Robin of Sherwood* and *Max Headroom*, working as a successful export in its own right.

But equally, one suspects that money was perhaps not the only problem. Certainly the BBC was still, in the general case, gifted at stretching a small budget. Indeed, so was John Nathan-Turner; whatever one might say about his tenure as producer, his ability to use the paltry budget he was given to maximum effect was unparalleled. And the fact that Doctor Who's ambition exceeds its means has always been one of the series' main creative energies.

In this regard, it's worth making a final comparison, this time with *The Box of Delights*, the BBC's six-part adaptation of John Masefield's not-actually-nearly-as-classic-as-the-TV-version novel. Among Doctor Who fans, it's best known for the fact that it casts Patrick Troughton as the mysterious Punch and Judy man Cole Hawlings, whose gift of the eponymous magical box to the protagonist Kay Harker gets the plot going. And Troughton is in many regards the best thing about it, not least because he manages to offer a performance of "immortal time traveller" that's entirely distinct from any previous characters he's played. The middle three episodes in which Troughton does not appear, truth be told, drag a bit.

But even when the series is flawed there's something strangely intriguing about it. It makes extensive use of video effects, in particular Quantel Paintbox, which would quickly become one of the go-to sources for visual effects in Doctor Who as well. Not unlike *The Cleopatras*, most of these effects feel intensely dated, but as with *The Cleopatras*, this is not exactly a criticism. For visual styles to date, after all, they have to look distinctly unlike anything before or after. There was, in other words, a real sense of daring to *The Box of Delights*—an interest in using the visual technology and means available to it in order to make something that was genuinely new.

Which is particularly significant when one considers why the series bogs down in the middle; without Troughton's star turn, it's stuck on Masefield's original plot, which is largely a hodgepodge of children's literature conventions and diffuse bits of British and European culture (Herne the Hunter appears here as well, which suggests there's a really interesting essay to write about English folklore in the mid-80s that doesn't quite fit into this volume because Doctor Who was busily completely ignoring this trend in favor of cannibalizing its own mythology). *The Box of Delights* is aggressively traditional in its content and tone, even as it's aggressively innovative in terms of its visuals and presentation.

There's a really important balance to this, and it's one that Doctor Who honestly never comes close to attempting anywhere in the 1984-86 period. You can see flashes of it in 1983 Doctor Who—the image of Edwardian ships in space from *Enlightenment*, for instance, or opting for a medieval period setting to introduce Kamelion. But it's something that really drops out of the program suddenly and unexpectedly, at least for the most part. (As we'll see, it is around this time that Doctor Who actually gets around to inventing the "celebrity historical" subgenre that is now one of its default modes, and it's difficult not to read this as at least tangentially related to the aesthetic implicit in *The Box of Delights*.)

And that really is down to the production team, and highlights a relatively basic problem that goes beyond mere BBC apathy towards the program. Simply put, it's no surprise that the program found itself behind the curve on innovation given that it kept its production team in place in 1984 instead of refreshing it. More than anything, what the show needed right now was someone to come at it with a bit of distance and provide a set of new ideas to try. The current production team has been around for three years, and, more troublingly, this is for Saward his second reinvention of the show and for Nathan-Turner his third. It barely matters how good you are at that point—you're almost certainly too close to the show to be able to see what the show needs to change. When you're reinventing your own reinvention you run into the basic and unavoidable problem that all of the flaws you're reacting against are ones you introduced, and thus ones you're the least likely person to be able to see.

The reality is that this needed to be when Saward and Nathan-Turner stepped aside, leaving Doctor Who's reinvention in the mid-80s to people with fresh ideas. If they had, the Nathan-Turner era would be remembered at least as well as the Letts era. For all that I pummeled them during the Davison era, the fact of the matter is that the slow motion disaster that's going to unfold over the next two months of the blog looms unfairly over the rest of their tenure. There have been problems over the past four seasons, but for the most part the good outweighed the bad.

But four years on a program with two reinventions is a long time, and after such, the fact is that one probably ought to move on. But it seems as though nobody seriously considered this. Nathan-Turner talked a little bit in interviews in the early 80s about wanting to move along after another year or so, but he always said that, and nothing came of it. And so you had a program that tried to keep one foot in two very different traditions without any real awareness of how they were diverging. The problem isn't even that Saward and Nathan-Turner are out of ideas. It's that the ideas they have are solutions to problems that don't exist and they seem to genuinely not see the problems that do exist. They're trying to recapture the nostalgic past of the show while television is pulling itself apart around them. If ever there was a moment in Doctor Who's history where "sod the past, whatever you do, come up with something new" was a good idea, it was 1985.

Equally, though, they have the misfortune of facing what is a genuinely hard problem in terms of coming up with something new. It would take a very, very good writer to figure out how to bridge the widening gap at the heart of what Doctor Who was. Even Robert Holmes, fresh from a classic, doesn't have the answer this time, as we'll see. It's easy to criticize the decisions made in the mid-80s and to pick over the gossip and assign the blame. What's harder is coming up with a realistic model of a show that can look like a contemporary *Box of Delights*, *Robin of Sherwood*, *Tripods*, or *Max Headroom* that doesn't rely on production and writing techniques from decades in the future or a budget wildly in excess of anything Doctor Who was ever going to get. Just because the production team failed spectacularly doesn't mean that the problem of how to make good Doctor Who in 1985 and 1986 was easy in the least.

## You Were Expecting Someone Else: FASA

The 1984 Doctor Who roleplaying game published by FASA is, as roleplaying games go, not hugely exciting or interesting. As Doctor Who merchandise it's slightly more exciting—and inadvertently hilarious at times, such as when it provides a character sheet for Peri that reveals her to be wildly less competent than a newly created player character would be. (So far as I can tell from a perusal of the rules she's spent exactly eight attribute points and three skill points. A new character should have 74-84 skill points and 38-48 attribute points. I assure you that if you knew what any of this meant it would be hilarious.)

But what's interesting about it, and why it gets more than a footnote in this project, is that it allows for an interesting look at the rather nebulous process of "identification" and its slightly saner cousin "empathy," both of which are concepts that have come up in the course of looking at Doctor Who and which I've taken idiosyncratic positions on. To recap, *TARDIS Eruditorum* generally takes a rather anti-realist and anti-escapist position on fiction that is not particularly fond of the idea of "identification" with fiction. In essentially all cases I strongly favor models of reading and viewing that openly and consistently acknowledge the fact that fiction is fiction, feeling that even if the resulting theories are a bit more complex at first glance they avoid the sorts of absurd contortions that are needed the moment you start digging into a model based around the idea of immersion, escapism, realism, or, yes, identification. Readings based on some flavor of "suspension of disbelief" require the reader to continually oscillate between a knowingly false premise ("this is real") and a true one ("this is not real"). In practice this is always going to be more complex than a system that sticks to one set of true premises.

Many years ago a professor expressed the problems of identification with the following example, which I don't know if was his originally or not. Imagine a horror movie with a female protagonist walking up a hill towards what the audience knows to be a haunted house, but that she does not. The girl is not afraid in this circumstance, but the audience is. Then, at the end of the movie, imagine her injured and battered, but having finally killed whatever monster lives in the house. At this moment the audience feels triumphant, but the girl feels traumatized, hurt, and terrified. Not only is the audience clearly not identifying with the protagonist here, were the audience to identify with the protagonist the story wouldn't work at all. In order to function, that kind of plot has to have the audience and the protagonist feeling almost the exact opposite.

To my mind, at least, everything one wants to get out of the concept of identification can be accomplished with far more sensible concepts like "investment" and "empathy." What's at issue in the hypothetical horror movie is not that we feel the same things as the protagonist but that we both understand what she feels and have an emotional investment in it that is rooted in similarities between her and her situation and things we recognize in our own lives. (Literary theory buffs will notice more than a whiff of Aristotle here.) This sort of structure lets us have all of the emotional responses that an identification-based structure lets us have with the handy side effect of actually making sense.

There are, however, two consequences to this line of thought that are worth looking at. The first has to do with Doctor Who. In *An Unearthly Child*, it is easiest to invest in and empathize with Ian and Barbara. One can invest in/empathize with Susan, but it's harder—on the one hand her basic position is familiar (a slightly rebellious young woman with profound love for her grandfather), but on the other she knows a lot of things the audience doesn't and she is, as the title points out, unearthly, which makes empathy harder. It's nearly impossible, on the other hand, to invest in the Doctor, who has unclear motives, knows scads the audience doesn't, and whose basic position is at best unfamiliar and at worst familiar but negative (he appears to be a runaway criminal).

Over time, however, this changes. The Doctor, by dint of having been around for decades, becomes increasingly familiar. Many of the key things he knew that the audience didn't—his origins, for instance—become progressively better known to the audience. His motivations crystallize and become predictable. Meanwhile, the companions cycle in and out. This makes us less likely to invest in them (we know they'll be gone, after all) and makes it so that we never get the chance to invest in them as deeply as the Doctor.

On top of that there is the fact that the universe of Doctor Who is teleologically configured around the Doctor. He's the only completely irreducible part of the show—it's impossible to have a Doctor Who story that the Doctor isn't at the heart of. Even in a story where he's absent like *Mission to the Unknown*, his absence becomes a tangible force that is at the heart of what happens: when he's not there, everyone dies. Heck, even if you decide to make the Doctor less well known and less famous, as Moffat obviously has recently, it doesn't mean that he isn't the center of the universe. It just means that not everyone knows it. In the end, he still is. This isn't, to be clear, some flaw in the show, despite various critics who foolishly blame it for whatever issues they have with it at any given moment, whether 1985 or 2015. The reality is that there is simply no way for a show that's been on for twenty-plus years not to go down this road. And so eventually the audience focus was going to be on the Doctor—not just in the sense of him unambiguously being the hero, but in terms of his reactions and character arc being the focus of a story. Simply put, the thing that most defines Doctor Who's setting is the fact that the Doctor arriving somewhere ensures that everything is going to go to hell in a handbasket, and, more specifically, that there's going to be some serious social upheaval. In this regard it really is the case that the universe revolves around the Doctor.

All of this is to say that the old truism that the companion is the audience identification figure is rubbish on two levels. First of all, as I said, screw identification. Second of all, the companion isn't even the figure the audience invests in the most. The role of the companion is to provide a consistent voice to people who aren't the teleological focus of the entire universe in the story—a population that includes most of the audience. That doesn't mean that their perspective is the one the audience is most invested in, though. I mean, if nothing else, the story follows the Doctor when the companions leave, not the companions. It's his story. The companions provide a moral grounding to the story more than they provide a narrative perspective.

The second major consequence of this line of thought about identification, on the other hand, applies to role-playing games, which are one of the few media in which identification does (or at least can) happen. This is because roleplaying games—and in this regard I would even separate them from video games—are in part derived from acting, and the fact of the matter is that the Method exists. The deliberate blurring of the line between self and character is something that happens in acting, and it's not surprising that in some cases it ports over to role-playing games. Indeed, I'd argue that much of what's interesting in role-playing game design since about 1991 has relied on this phenomenon.

But there's a problem here, and it's a problem that goes beyond what we talked about back with *The Adventure Game* in terms of "puzzle-solving" as a storytelling technique. Because when you take these factors in concert there's an obvious gaping problem with a Doctor Who roleplaying game, which is that everyone is going to want to be the Doctor.

The FASA game takes a relatively clever, if hilariously convoluted route to solving this by expanding the role of the CIA (the Time Lord one, obviously) to be a loosely knit organization of Time Lords in rackety TARDISes "liberated" from the scrapyards to go fix bits of space and time. Silly as this is with relation to the television show, it at least expands the milieu to where players can come up with interesting variations on "renegade Time Lord" and make the game something more complex than just communal fanfic writing. But the game can't quite control itself. It wants to open the door to the idea that there are tons of quasi-Doctors running around working for the CIA, but the rulebook keeps pulling back from this and continuing to concede that the Doctor has some ontological role in the universe, because, of course, it has to or else this is just a goofy time-travel game and not the Doctor Who roleplaying game.

But even aside from this, there's a larger problem, which is that any troupe is going to be configured as having one "leader" Time Lord character and a bunch of companions, despite the fact that the structure of the underlying show pushes everybody to invest primarily with the Time Lord and to view the companion not just as a "less cool" character but as a character who is by definition not who the story is about. Doctor Who isn't a narrative that lends itself to an ensemble cast. There's one very clearly defined lead, some kind of very important supporting role(s), and that's it.

This leads one to ask the relatively straightforward question—why the heck does this game exist? I mean, on a fundamental level a Doctor Who roleplaying game does not make a ton of sense. The show doesn't lend itself to this sort of storytelling at all. It's not a property that seems to beg for adaptation into this medium.

The answer is prosaic. Roleplaying games are the sorts of things that cult sci-fi properties have made of them. *Star Trek* got its role-playing game from FASA in 1982, and *Star Wars* got one from West End Games in 1987 (though Game Designer Workshop's earlier *Traveller* snuck in stats for Luke Skywalker and Darth Vader in one of its supplements). Marvel superheroes, *Lord of the Rings*, *Conan the Barbarian*, and

*Ringworld* also had games in the same general time period. So of course someone cashed in on Doctor Who.

In the US—and to be clear, FASA is an American company—this made some sense. Doctor Who's popularity in the US was at least substantively overlapping with fans of other science fiction shows. But this was more because science fiction had a relatively narrow range of things it could be in the US. The problem is that in this period, by all appearances, "cult sci-fi property" is what Doctor Who is aspiring for in the UK as well. Part of this is the over-arching tendency to focus on the export market for Doctor Who—as I've noted, there is a problematic tendency when talking about the series in this period and its hiatus to point out that the show was exceedingly profitable due to overseas sales.

But there's a more basic common logic behind the series in this period and the FASA game. Increasingly the series is acting as though there's a coherent world in which it takes place and that this presumed world is in some sense inherently valuable. American fandom coined the ghastly term "Whoniverse" for this setting. In practice, this is something the series never even came close to aspiring towards until the Bidmead era, and even there the uptick of references to other stories is less about establishing a single setting in which all of the series took place than about a continual exploration of a theme over multiple stories, with the stories referenced mostly being other stories in the same season. But of late, and obviously this is going to get miles out of hand in the next essay, there's been an increasing tendency of the show to act as though there is a single overarching setting in which its twenty-plus years of television has taken place.

In truth, though, there's not, and this is at the heart of why the idea of a role-playing game is so intrinsically strange for Doctor Who. Because Doctor Who is not a world, it's a type of interaction with a character. Doctor Who isn't about the world in which the Doctor travels, it's about the way in which the Doctor, when introduced to a world, deforms it.

And that makes it very much unlike something like *Star Trek*, where the Enterprise may be the shiniest ship in Starfleet but where the entire premise of the series is that the ship is part of an entire Starfleet of ships, each of which have their own ensemble casts. Or even *Star Wars*, a series where there's overtly a "chosen one" but where there's also a ton of effort made painting one big war in which there are necessarily going to be other stories going on. Or, most obviously, *Lord of the Rings*, which is in many ways a world in search of a story. (Or, actually, a language in search of a world in search of a story. Which is even better, really, where "better" is not actually a comment on quality or sanity in any meaningful sense.)

But Doctor Who, even if it is science fiction, doesn't work like this. In the aforementioned cases, the franchise is about a particular type of world and a main character who exemplifies the world. Doctor Who, on the other hand, is about a main character who completely screws up and destabilizes any world into which he's introduced. So glorifying the world just doesn't work. This is not, I should be clear, the somewhat clichéd attack in which fandom likes to complain about excessive continuity references in the series (which has always been, first of all, a bit perverse, and second of all, a reaction against a perceived reason for the failure of the Nathan-Turner era more than an actual reaction against the continuity). Rather, I mean it in the sense that a number of major ways in which most cult science fiction texts engage with their audience and create a paratext for themselves to increase profitability are only partially, if at all, open to Doctor Who. In some very simple ways, Doctor Who is very, very bad at being a cult science fiction show. The FASA game demonstrates some of these very thoroughly. More troubling, though, is the fact that the series itself is attempting many of the same things. Which brings us to...

## Things Which Act Against Everything We Believe In
### (*Attack of the Cybermen*)

It is January 5th, 1985. Band Aid are at number one with "Do They Know It's Christmas," a song that will have spectacularly unfortunate results for Doctor Who in a few months' time. They remain at number one through the story, with Wham! at number two with another Christmas song. Foreigner, Madonna, Paul McCartney, Tears for Fears, and Ray Parker Jr. are also in the charts, the last, of course, with the theme from *Ghostbusters*.

So in the news, since last we looked at a story, The Soviet Union decides to boycott the 1984 Olympics essentially in protest of the US boycotting the 1980 games four years earlier. So that's another thrilling series of events. The Indian government storms the holiest site in the Sikh religion to remove Sikh separatists, killing two thousand. Indira Gandhi, the Prime Minister of India, is assassinated by her Sikh security guards a few months later, which, you know, there's something to learn there. The other JNT, John Napier Turner, becomes Prime Minster of Canada. And is ousted three months later. The UK agrees to return Hong Kong to China.

While on television... The obvious putdown of *Attack of the Cybermen* is that it finally and demonstrably shows just how bad both Ian Levine and Eric Saward are, in that both of them take credit for this story instead of frantically trying to shift the blame onto each other. But denouncing *Attack of the Cybermen* is almost too easy. And anyway, I want to take a different line on Season Twenty-Two than all of that.

In writing *TARDIS Eruditorum* I have found that eras of the show tend to work in one of two ways. In the first case, there are those eras whose aesthetics are relatively straightforward, in which case readings of stories tend to be based on exploring the particulars of those aesthetics and pushing readings a bit further to find their conceptual breaking points. Much of the 1960s, along with the Hinchcliffe and Bidmead eras, worked like this. In the second case, there are what one might call the problem eras—chunks of the show where how the show works is contested and I have to spend a lot of time trying to figure out how to read the show in the first place instead of getting on with it. The Pertwee, Williams, and Davison eras were all like this, with essays having to go back and forth on questions like "What is the show actually trying to do here?" for large swaths of it.

The Colin Baker era is something else. Yes, it doesn't work. But its failures, though spectacular, are also so consistent and straightforward as to not require a lot of explanation. The era's flaws have almost completely been elucidated in *The Twin Dilemma* essay. And while this story adds continuity porn to the list, that's a flaw that also largely emerged during the Davison era. I try to write this series so that someone who isn't intimately familiar with the history of Doctor Who can follow it, but in this case there's almost no point. For every story this season you can safely assume that everything that went wrong in the Davison era happens about twice as much, and everything that went right happens at best half as much. You can take for granted that references to the past abound for their own sake, that the stories take active pleasure in violence and pain, and that Baker is interminably unpleasant due to writing that has the childish tendency to assume that less likable characters are inherently edgier and thus more dramatic. You can also assume that the switch to forty-five minute episodes was bungled and that the pacing is screwed to hell and back. And you can assume that the budgetary restrictions are poorly handled, with the show continuing to try ill-advised things instead of focusing on doing what it can do well. I'm mostly not going to reiterate any of that over the next five stories unless there's something particularly interesting about it. Take it as given that the stories this season are not very good and that most of the existing criticism of them is at least vaguely on target. So that's all sorted then.

Similarly, having done "The Agony and the Ecstasy of John Nathan-Turner" over the course of the Davison era, I want to put the travails of the production team aside for most of Season Twenty-Two, especially since the behind-the-scenes aspect has been hopelessly overdetermined with a wealth of partisan accounts. It won't be completely possible—you can't talk about *The Two Doctors* without some behind-the-scenes chatter, for instance—but for the most part I want to focus on what's on screen in Season Twenty-Two, not the sausage factory, which we'll instead return to in agonizing detail at season's end.

With *Attack of the Cybermen* there's an additional issue. I took my pot-shots at the last two universally despised stories, but as one of the things people say when they're saying nice things about *TARDIS Eruditorum* is that I come up with counter-intuitive and innovative readings of stories. So let's break the streak and ask a harder question, which is what a redemptive reading of *Attack of the Cybermen* would look like.

Interestingly, the angle of *Attack of the Cybermen* that most lends itself to redemption is also the one for which it is most infamous, namely its somewhat, shall we say, dense use of continuity. The most interesting aspect of this is the confirmation of the original role of Mondas in terms of the Cybermen. Much of the history of the Cybermen has, after all, been a matter of ignoring what they originally were, both in their role as Qlippothic others (this idea is unpacked in depth in Volume One, but to be very brief about it, "Qlippothic" describes a corrupted perversion of a real thing in which all the virtue is gone, leaving only a hollow husk of a once meaningful idea) and, more basically, in the sheer ludicrousness of their original premise as a race that drove their planet up alongside the Earth and then exploded. Mondas has been mentioned since then, yes, but the actual original event of the Cybermen has been largely obscured, simply because faceless robotic hordes are for the most part an easier idea to work with than whatever the hell *The Tenth Planet* was.

Except here it's brought back, and in its full and original weirdness. When, in 1966, Pedler and Davis posited a 1986 arrival of Mondas it was an understandable move—yes, it was sure to look silly in twenty years, but worrying about how your 1960s science fiction television was going to look in twenty years would have been ridiculous at the time; odds were it wasn't going to still exist anyway. (And hey, sure enough...) But come 1985 the little detail of when the Cybermen arrived on Earth would seem ripe for ignoring— as, let's remember, most details of the past are even in these continuity-obsessed days. Instead, however, the fact of Mondas's 1986 arrival forms one of the centerpieces of the story.

The whole story, of course, is about the evocation of the past. But in most of these cases the past is evoked, not used. The Cybermen lurk about in sewers, because that's classically what Cybermen do, or at least, what they did in *The Invasion*. We're back on Telos among the tombs because that's where Cybermen go, or at least, where they were in *Tomb of the Cybermen*. And, of course, we're in Totter's Lane for no reason other than the fact that we can be. There's a token attempt to link this all together into a "Whoniverse," a term I think I'll just repurpose to refer to the basic idea of even having that sort of coherence. But the real effect is a miasma of evocations of the series' past.

For all that one of its major influences is *The Invasion*, this story does little to take place in a London comprised of real and recognizable landmarks. It is telling that the shot the story slavishly reproduces is not the Cybermen marching down the steps of St. Paul's, but rather the Cybermen bursting from their tombs in *Tomb of the Cybermen*, a shot removed from reference to reality, for it was originally conceived of in terms of the genre tropes of mummy films. The only London landmark invoked here is an imaginary one—Totter's Lane. Haley's Comet may loom over the story along with 1986, but the world of the story is manifestly not ours. This is a story that takes place in the series' past.

Amidst the iconography of the series' past, the idea of the original Qlippothic Cybermen is unleashed. Not the things themselves, of course—these are the puissant action villains of *Earthshock* through and through. But the Qlippothic Cybermen are perhaps more unsettling as ideas than they are as actual presences. This story is consciously haunted by the 1986 run-in with Mondas, and thus the Qlippothic haunts it as well. This is asking for trouble. The flawed fetishization of the series' past risks obscuring the fact that this past has always held more power than its worshippers give it credit for. One is not on solid ground when walking amongst the rubble of Doctor Who's past, and the illusory terra firma of the Whoniverse presents little real protection against exposure.

Can we make a redemptive reading that still acknowledges the story to be rubbish? To some extent, at least, that's the plan for this entire era—a misbegotten wreck of television that nevertheless seems to crackle alchemically. In one sense, after all, we have the ultimate narrative collapse story here. The Cybermen oversee the sudden hemorrhage of a quarter of the viewership week over week, and then the series gets cancelled. There is no narrative collapse quite as thorough as the series actually getting taken off the air. And here are all the makings of that metatext. The Cybermen are allowed to run riot through Totter's Lane. It's fitting that this should come so early in the terminally long stretch of non-classics, particularly given that the next unambiguous triumph of the series will return again to this place with newfound alchemy.

All narrative collapses are averted at a price. It's tempting to say that this one's is that it comes too late—that the wound is mortal and an eighteen-month break in transmission, followed not long thereafter by a sixteen-year one, are inevitable. But perhaps a better option exists. It is notable that Doctor Who inflicts upon itself a symbolic wound right at the moment when, in a real, material, ratings sense everything goes off the rails. What, then, if we treat this era as a sort of Fisher King of Doctor Who? If Colin Baker's tenure is the cursed land ruled over by the wounded king created by this Qlippothic distortion of the very fabric of the series' identity?

The result is an era of exorcism. An era where the show rips itself to shreds in the name of excising its own weakness. In this reading, for all of *Attack of the Cybermen*'s flaws, it is in some sense a more interesting story than *The Five Doctors*, where all of Doctor Who's history seemed at last to be enmeshed in the grotesque stasis gestured at back in *The Space Museum*. This is, perhaps the price of escaping that. What follows *The Five Doctors*? What ideas come after Longleat? It's not an easy question, given that both events strove towards a totalizing, definitive statement of what Doctor Who was. There is a real sense in which all that can follow is destruction.

And so the price paid for the escape from this narrative collapse is, perhaps, *Attack of the Cybermen* itself—or, more broadly, the Colin Baker era. To unshackle the history of Doctor Who from the insidious chains of the Whoniverse may not be a task that can be undertaken by quality. After twenty years, perhaps the program has no way forward beyond tearing itself apart.

There's an odd parallelism to the overall cultural situation. As the miners' strike winds down to its crushing and deflated denouement, we reach a point where the phrase "creative destruction" seems glaringly apt. For all that the moral arguments stack against it—the firm insistence that one cannot simply dismantle communities for profit—there is eternally an allure to burning it all down. This is the odd alliance between Thatcherism and mercurial anarchy. At the end of the day, both want to tear down the world.

For all the horrors of Thatcher, it's difficult not to point out that in areas other than Doctor Who, Britain is in a bit of a cultural renaissance here. It's musically on top of the world, there are all-time classics of television being made in this period, and its comics are second to none, with Alan Moore making his famed leap to American comics in 1983. And much of this, albeit not all of it, is in direct reaction against Thatcherism. There's a compelling, if unintended, argument to be had here. This isn't the creative force the right wanted out of its creative destruction, but really, that's for the better. At some point we have to admit that hating Thatcher is something of a fetish—that she is the symptom that an entire and iconic era of British culture most enjoyed.

There is a moment of logical sloppiness here that we ought resist, however. The arc of history is not a moral force. That something happened and its consequences approached progress does not mean the thing was right or good. This howling exorcism of Doctor Who—this self-inflicted wound to claw the Whoniverse out of the concept of the show—is not a good thing. It is not a necessary thing, except inasmuch as it happened and so, tautologically, must have happened. But it is a thing—a price paid. To be clear, it is not that this is a bad story on the way to a good result. We'll save that defense for Season Twenty-Four, in the next book. This is something subtler—a bad story that nevertheless constitutes a plunge into alchemical depths and starts a process that will begin to remove the flaws it represents—flaws which predate this story by some margin. I sometimes describe William Faulkner's *The Sound and the Fury* by saying it is a book I love having read, even if I hated reading it. The Baker era was a disaster, but it was, perhaps, a disaster we ought love that the show went through.

At the heart of this is the character of Lytton, who rather unexpectedly finds himself thrust into the role of the story's moral center. The Doctor's final comment, taken superficially, is incoherently stupid—the fact that Lytton was working as a mercenary for the good guys surely does not constitute the worst misjudgment on the part of the Doctor, given that Lytton was previously and uncomplicatedly working as a mercenary for the Daleks. What, then, is the nature of this misjudgment?

Again, let us set aside what we know went on behind the scenes and take the events on their own merits, reading not what we know Saward meant here but what appeared. There is no way to seriously suggest Lytton's redemption from what is on screen. The alternative, then, is that working for the Daleks is not so bad. It is helpful here to turn back to earlier versions of alchemy, most specifically *The Ribos Operation*, which was an extended meditation on the problems of dualisms. A key part of that story was that differing levels of the system did not have 1:1 correspondence with each other. But this is the norm for alchemy: the true maxim turns out to be "As above, so below... more or less."

The Cybermen, of course, are the new Daleks, and always have been; the classic Cybermen stories of the Troughton era are primarily about the fact that Terry Nation took his ball and went to America. In this regard they are differing iterations of the same system (and so indeed, we can see the Cybermen as proper Qlippoths of the Daleks in this respect). But the Doctor's misjudgment of Lytton requires that we recognize a more significant difference between them. Working for the Cybermen would have been unforgivable, but finding out that Lytton only actually worked for the Daleks means that he's OK. This is not the only time this judgment is made in the Colin Baker era either—jump ahead and consider his monologue about the corruption of the Time Lords in *The Ultimate Foe*. He lists three monsters that are not as bad as the Time Lords—Daleks, Sontarans, and Cybermen—and delivers the line as if to suggest that being worse than the Cybermen is the real accomplishment here. Even in their first appearance, when we take them as the thing that persuades the Doctor that there are monsters that need to be fought, we are forced to realize that the Daleks were not sufficiently persuasive in this regard. The Cybermen have always been worse than the Daleks, both in the sense of being the second choice and in a diegetic sense.

The Daleks are merely the Doctor's opposite—the representation of death that threatens narrative collapse. But the Cybermen are the Doctor's corruption. They offer a living death—the possibility of continuing endlessly in a hollowed out, qlippothic state. In recognizing that Lytton is not *that*, the Doctor attains some measurement of knowledge—the ability to distinguish the qlippothic from the real. But this knowledge comes, in a sense, too late—the qlippothic has been unleashed amidst the core of what the program is. This, then, is the true nature of the Doctor's bad judgment—he's been so unable to differentiate the qlippothic from the real that he's allowed the very narrative foundations of the series to become infested. The only remaining option is an exorcism, and likely a painful one.

## Do You Think Anybody Votes for Sweet (*Vengeance on Varos*)

It's January 19th, 1985. Foreigner has decided that they are less interested in knowing whether it's Christmas and that they'd rather know what love is, asking the question over the two weeks of this story. Both Prince and King also chart, along with Tears for Fears and the gorgeously named Strawberry Switchblade. In real news, Ronald Reagan is sworn in for his second term. British Telecom announces that it will be phasing out red phoneboxes, relegating them to the same scrapheap as the Police Box (or at least trying to). A House of Lords debate is televised for the first time, and, three days after the end of this story, Thatcher is denied an honorary degree by Oxford University.

While on television, a story about television. *Vengeance on Varos* is for the most part the easiest story to like of Season Twenty-Two. This is not to say it is the best—the redemptive reading of *The Two Doctors* presents a story that is probably superior to this one. But where *The Two Doctors* is prickly and difficult, requiring effort to get at its redemptive version, liking *Vengeance on Varos* requires only a basic ability to appreciate satire and black comedy of the sort that ought be trivial for anyone reading *TARDIS Eruditorum*.

There is, of course, a negative reading to be had of the story in which it is simply an extended bit of nasty sadism and torture porn. But unlike *Warriors of the Deep* or *Resurrection of the*

*Daleks*, the embedded critique of the story's own violence is given some serious teeth. From the start, this story is solid on the fact that the Varosians' love of extravagant and sadistic executions is wrong.

But what makes *Vengeance on Varos* interesting, especially within the context of our chosen theme of the Colin Baker era as an exorcism, is the degree to which it wants to have its cake and eat it too. The story is overtly built around television as a medium, with active effort taken to make the Varosians' broadcasts look and feel like the BBC. Tat Wood observes that the fanfare for the governor is a dead-ringer for BBC home video, and the interactive "home voting" aspect would have been recognizable as a close cousin to the interactive television offered by Ceefax at the time. In other words, the line between *Vengeance on Varos* and what it's criticizing is deliberately porous.

More broadly, we're at a point in the history of television where the link between television and pornography is growing. A thread that's been absent for a few essays now is the rise of the VCR, which means that television is no longer simply a broadcast medium but a medium of storage and replay. Which means, of course, that it's possible to have pornography on it. In practice, of course, most of the pornography that could actually be obtained barely deserved the name—a motley of soft-core titillations. More common were cheap, dirty, and violent movies. But because the video market was mostly unregulated at first and major studios feared piracy, there was a flood of lurid schlock as all manner of grindhouse cinema wound its way onto the market. The term "video nasties" was bandied about a lot in the tabloids, and there was a good old-fashioned moral panic. So buzzing around in the culture was the idea that the television had, in effect, become an all-you-can-watch buffet of sex and violence. See also *Max Headroom*, as this story is the closest Doctor Who comes to playing on that field.

Now, *Vengeance on Varos* is a television program in which several of the characters appear on a television program and in which the audience repeatedly watches people watching television. And it frequently makes clever little cuts between these levels so that events move from being watched by diegetic characters to being watched by the audience. The best moment of this, and a strong candidate for best cliffhanger of the classic series to boot, is the end of episode one. The cliffhanger is a fairly standard bit—the Doctor is hallucinating himself to death—but instead of ending on the Doctor's danger we cut back to the control booth and the Governor watching the Doctor die before he says, "And cut it... there," as we sting our way to the starfield. Martin Jarvis, in other words, is directing the diegetic television program only to have his direction taken up by the real one. It's glorious.

But despite the program obviously engaging in self-critique, the script stubbornly resists giving up the very behavior it critiques. It's hard to blame the story for this, though. Last story, the Doctor was shooting at Cybermen. Before that he was strangling Peri. Not long before that was firing guns at Daleks. In two stories he'll kill someone with cyanide and make a lame joke about it. So when the Doctor, in this story, starts laying death traps and making fun of people for burning to death in acid vats (though it's not true, as some people claim, that the Doctor pushes someone into an acid vat. He just, you know, tries to. Followed by someone else pulling the guy in) it's not exactly an aberration. The series is clearly engaging in the exact behavior it critiques and daring the audience to draw some sort of line.

There's an added dimension to this, however, that is often overlooked. If we accept Tat Wood's observation that this story is in part a response to the "video nasties" moral panic then there are two enormously salient facts. The first is that the moral crusade against this "filth" was led by none other than our old friend Mary Whitehouse. The second is that among the things released on video around the time this story aired were *Revenge of the Cybermen, The Brain of Morbius,* and *The Pyramids of Mars*. In other words, three stories from the "teatime brutality for tots" era of the program. So when the program wades into a critique of television and violence here it does so in a way that, distantly, implicates its own history.

Indeed, we said way back at the end of the Hinchcliffe era that the run-in with Mary Whitehouse started the chain of decisions that brought the program down. Williams was forced to swing the pendulum back hard away from horror and towards comedy, and Nathan-Turner in turn reacted against that, trying to win back the fans alienated by Williams. And here we are today, seven years of reactions against Mary Whitehouse, and we're finally actually getting around to the obvious one, which is to do a Doctor Who story about it.

In one sense, of course, this is just the program sauntering up to a fight years too late, roaring that it's ready to take on Mary Whitehouse long after she's shuffled off to other things. It's not even doing it directly—there's no Mary Whitehouse figure here. If anything, *Vengeance on Varos* risks being accused of allying itself with Whitehouse in condemning brutality. But that accusation would be utterly off-base, of course. What's actually going on is that the program is showing that there's a distinction between torture porn and art, and it's not based on how violent the art is. *Vengeance on Varos* needs to be sick and nasty to work—it has deep roots in the avant-garde theatrical tradition of Brecht and Artaud. But it's turning those tools in a critique of dumb violence, and it's doing so with no shortage of sharpness.

A better description, then, would be that this is a program that has grown up and is returning to an old demon with newfound perspective. This isn't Doctor Who going and facing its schoolyard bully of seven years ago, it's Doctor Who reflecting on its past and the legacy of that past. It's Doctor Who looking at the question of "teatime brutality for tots"—and back in its good old Saturday viewing slot too—and saying, "OK, who benefits from the existence of a violent and sensational media?"

The answer, it seems, is the Right. *Vengeance on Varos* once again embroils itself in the imagery and symbolism of the mining strike, this time with evil corporate overlords cheating the miners of Varos. But this goes beyond a clichéd "evil corporate overlords sure are evil" bit of didacticism. Indeed, it goes further than the "everyone is to blame" position of *Caves of Androzani*. Had this been a Davison story, and thus not poisoned by the negative associations of the Colin Baker years, there's a fair case to be made that this would be even more popular than *Androzani*.

After all, this is a story in which the system that exploits the miners is shown to be all-encompassing. The televised executions, the almost hilariously crap rebels, the political system, and Sil's scam are all interrelated forms of oppression—a mutually supporting system. Everyone is to blame, but not in a cynical "because they're all corrupt bastards" way, which is, let's be honest, all *The Caves of Androzani* really got at. I mean, *Androzani* is great, but here we have a system in which visibly noble men and women—the Governor, Arak, and Etta, most notably—are made to act against their own interests and blind themselves to the fact that there's an alternative.

But in the midst of all this there's still something tentative here. Part of this is clearly deliberate, and is indeed part of what's so clever about the story—the decision to end on Arak and Etta having no idea what to do with their newfound future is a delightful bit of ambiguity that keeps this story from falling into the opposite trap of Holmes's utter cynicism, acknowledging the fact that the system of corruptions responsible for Varos was based on humans even as it exploited them, and that the next system may well be just as bad. In many ways it echoes the old complaints of *The War Games*—the fact that the Doctor leaves planets in a post-revolution haze and doesn't bother to put any work into making sure the revolution comes out well.

But more than that, there's an uncertainty about the program itself. Because *Vengeance on Varos* is constantly implicating the show in its own critique, it's never quite clear whether or not it views itself as part of the problem—nor, indeed, whether it's simply being part of the problem without realizing it. The fact that the Doctor is involved in much of the violence of the story brings it very close to the bit of the Hinchcliffe era that most validated Whitehouse, namely *The Seeds of Doom*. And more broadly, there's always a lurking sense that the tail is wagging the dog here—that the fact that there's a larger moral and political point to be made is being used to justify the violence of the story, as opposed to the story justifying the level of violence.

But this continues the exorcism theme that I'm increasingly staking the Colin Baker years on. All the stories this season, in their own ways, amount to the program taking stock of its own weaknesses. Not correcting them, at least for now, but acknowledging them and facing them. *Vengeance on Varos* ends on an unsettling note in which it's not at all clear whether the preceding ninety minutes actually stood up to their own critique. But given that the previous story would have failed unambiguously, it's difficult to call this ambivalence a fault.

## Time Can Be Rewritten: *Burning Heart*

The most interesting thing about *Burning Heart* is not actually what it is, but what it very nearly was. The book was originally pitched as a crossover between Doctor Who and Judge Dredd, which Virgin also had a license for, but was eventually reconceived of as a pure Doctor Who novel with an obvious Judge Dredd stand-in, a point emphasized by the cover, where a character is shown in a costume that is blatantly modelled on Dredd's.

It's perhaps worth noting who Judge Dredd is, for those who may have forgotten since the *2000 AD* essay last volume. Basically, he's a character from the satirical sci-fi comic *2000 AD*—an extremist law-and-order cop with no sympathy whatsoever for any lawbreaking. The central joke is that, despite being the structural hero of his stories, he's fundamentally unsympathetic; his first major story arc involves him violently putting down a revolution on the part of sentient robots who want to be free from slavery, and one of his most acclaimed stories featured his brutal opposition to pro-democracy protesters.

Moreover, that storyline began in 1986, during the hiatus between Seasons Twenty-Two and Twenty-Three of Doctor Who. Which highlights something important—I may have covered *2000 AD* back in the last book, as a lead-in for talking about a bunch of creators associated with the magazine being the first team on the *Doctor Who Weekly* comic, but in many ways this is the era it's actually closest to. The bleak satire of *Vengeance on Varos*, *The Two Doctors*, and *Revelation of the Daleks* has a lot in common with and owed to *2000 AD*, and Eric Saward's sensibilities would not have been remotely out of place in its pages. In other words, mashing the two up is a good idea.

That said, it's probably for the best that it wasn't a direct crossover, not least because Judge Dredd's reaction to the Doctor would be to shoot him in the face and get on with his life, and the Doctor's reaction to Judge Dredd would be to tear down his world and leave him powerless and humiliated. By replacing Dredd with "Craator," the hard-nosed Adjudicator who's motivated by a true and unwavering fealty to the law, author Dave Stone avoids the very basic problem of how to put an anarchic hero like the Doctor and a fascist anti-hero in the same story in a way that doesn't undermine one of them. Craator, unlike Dredd, can eventually mature into a force of reform, giving the book something of a compromise ending.

All the same, there's something bleakly unsettling about the book. The fascist government of Dramos ends up being presented as essentially morally neutral. The Doctor makes reference to future historical tragedies that undermine its moral position somewhat, but they're kept offstage and not really pinned on the Adjudicators. Instead, the Adjudicators are given moral cover by the existence of a group called Human First, which opposes the Adjudicators and is then is revealed to be a racist-as-hell group with obvious Nazi parallels, thus making the Adjudicators, who, at the end, start letting non-humans be fascist cops, look all very nice and reasonable.

Actually, "revealed" is probably a bit strong, since they're described as having a charismatic leader with impressive public speaking skills. It's obvious from the back cover, which refers to "the charismatic leader of Human First, a movement dedicated to bringing order out of chaos," that we're talking about Nazis. The only reason there's any sort of revelation to be had is the phrase that precedes that quote, namely "Peri falls in with." Because that's the entire plot arc: Peri acts like an outright moron, and is bailed out by a character eventually revealed to be a descendent of Bernice Summerfield, who gets the role of actually being intelligent.

Which is in many ways the other thing that's interesting in this book: it was published in 1997. Baker had been out of the role for a decade and receded enough into history that the passion with which his era was considered an abject failure had faded, and the stage was set for a reevaluation/reinvention of him. And indeed, a few years later Big Finish would provide exactly that. But here we get something altogether stranger—a failed rehabilitation. Not, to be clear, failed in the sense of being aesthetically unsound, although there are some egregiously inexcusable problems, such as having the most visible moment of the Doctor being a jerk coming in line that is basically a Holocaust joke with more than a whiff of "Jews are all greedy" to it. ("Tell you what, why don't we start with something easy and work our way up? Go back and assassinate Adolf Hitler as a child, maybe? The literary executors of Anne Frank would have the shirt off my back.") Rather, it's failed in that it's just not the direction fandom went.

Stone postulates that the Doctor blames Peri for the Fifth Doctor's regeneration, and that he's been taking this out on her, mostly subconsciously. It's an interesting enough move, except that it doesn't really follow from anything in the series. Baker's Doctor showed nothing but contempt for his predecessor, and the idea that Time Lords spend any time mourning past selves is more or less entirely unfounded.

But in many ways the real problem is Peri. By making her a gullible and naïve idiot who casually falls in with Nazis without even noticing, the book largely continues the ugly dynamic previously witnessed in the FASA game, where Peri's stats render her wildly less competent than a newly generated player character. There's a truly horrible tendency to denigrate Peri, treating her as a lesser companion. And, sure, Nicola Bryant's affected American accent and the generally dreadful scripts didn't exactly make Peri an easy choice for fan favorite.

But there's no path towards redeeming the Colin Baker era that doesn't go through repairing its treatment of the companions—a fact realized by Big Finish, whose new companions work quite well with him. But this still leaves Peri in an uncertain state; yes, she has plenty of good audios, but she's appeared considerably more often with Davison than with Baker at Big Finish.

Which is a nagging problem. So much of the problem with Baker's Doctor was the cruelty with which he treated Peri, most obviously in *The Twin Dilemma*. And when Peri is presented as a blithering idiot, the tacit suggestion is that the reason she got strangled is that she's the companion weak enough to let him. There's an implicit bit of victim blaming here—the suggestion that because she didn't walk off the TARDIS in horror when she got the chance, she deserved it.

It's never stated, of course. It doesn't have to be. All that's necessary is to leave her as the crappy companion—the incompetent, whimpering dunce. Sure, the Doctor strangled a companion, but it was only Peri. And as long as that sense is there, you can come up with all the clever explanations for the Doctor's behavior that you want. It's not going to change the actual problem with the era, which is that, on every level (including the John Nathan-Turner's treatment of Nicola Bryant), Peri is marginalized and belittled by the series.

So to summarize, *Burning Heart* is a novel that tries to engage with the satiric tradition of Judge Dredd only to end up endorsing fascism, and that tries to do complex character stuff with the Doctor that's derailed by the appalling treatment of Peri. In other words, it captures the era perfectly.

## Think I Don't Know My Own Mark (*The Mark of the Rani*)

It's February 2nd, 1985. Foreigner is still at number one, as they are on the albums chart as well. After one week, however, Elaine Paige and Barbara Dickson unseat them on the singles chart. Bruce Springsteen, The Art of Noise, and, just out of the top ten, Phil Collins and Bryan Adams also chart. In real news, the first British mobile phone call is made and nine miners are jailed for arson in the miners' strike.

Meanwhile, Doctor Who still sucks. Let us start with the Rani herself. The name is an odd choice, to say the least. On the one hand, she is clearly situated in the naming conventions that brought us the Doctor and the Master—in other words, having a title instead of a proper name, like other Time Lords. This is a meaningful distinction within the series—even among other exiled Time Lords, the Doctor, the Master, and the War Chief have a special status distinct from those who have retained their names. Those with names are either still on Gallifrey or appear merely to be expats—Time Lords who are on the outs with Gallifrey, but who are still living, if not within its laws, within its worldview. Whether it be that they take relatively menial positions in the grand order of things—i.e. Drax and Azmael—or that they retain outright distance from the world like K'anpo, even the named exiles seem to remain part of Time Lord society, albeit in defined positions as outsiders.

Then there are the outright renegades—those who have lost their names, and who live fundamentally at odds with the

Time Lords. This category, of course, includes the Doctor, and by extension his inversion in the Master. The precise nature of being a renegade is thus complex and inscrutable. But it's clear that there is a power to this group—one based on the old logic that the lowest and most debased part of something—that part of Time Lord society that has lost even their names—is inseparable from the highest point of it. (A point reiterated time and time again—when Borusa or Hedin attempt to engage with the likes of Rassilon or Omega, it kills them. Only the Doctor and the Master can walk out of Rassilon's tomb alive because, as lowly renegades, they alone are his equals.)

But the Rani makes a strange addition to this group. Described externally, at least, she's a joke. Where the Doctor and the Master have their deep and hidden reasons for joining the nameless, her reasons sound like parodic fanfic: her lab mice mutated, ate the President's cat, and took a chunk out of him too, leading to her exile. This is not the origin of a legendary character. Even her name is odd. The name means "the Queen," but is, of course, from Indian culture instead of British culture. Diegetically this is more difficult to explain than people give it credit for. We can allow that Time Lord names are translated into British English as a basic conceit of the series, but here we have one whose given name is presented in a different cultural context than all the others.

And, crucially, it's just her name. It's not like the Rani is built meaningfully out of Hindu mythology. That would be absolutely fantastic—if Doctor Who actually started doing real and serious engagement with non-Western mythologies—but that is not what's going on here. So the overall effect is much like that of how the naming of celestial bodies, after Greco-Roman mythological figures were all used up, finally turned to various other mythologies, as if all of the first pool of honorifics were exhausted so they had to start drawing from one of the secondary pools.

But if the Rani is conceptually a parody, she is in practice reasonably compelling. Kate O'Mara may be more than a little mockable, and yes, the Rani is desperately camp (indeed, the title of "Queen" has certain resonances in the rubric of gay camp culture) but in building her character the show has returned to what actually worked with Roger Delgado as the Master, hiring a ubiquitous and familiar supporting actor and letting them define the role, as opposed to hiring a reasonably good actor and telling him to just mimic someone else's performance. As a result she gets proper villainess moments, including a frankly wonderful one where she guns down of her two henchmen when they become inconvenient.

So the story ends up in the odd position of presenting a character who is, on paper, far less interesting than the Master and then allowing her to upstage him at every opportunity. Indeed, the Rani doesn't just get to upstage the Master, she gets to openly mock the conventions of his character and point out that he's being ridiculous at almost every turn. This is clearly intended to be the central pleasure of this story as well—hence bringing the Master in on a story otherwise designed to introduce a new villain. Ainley is actually in a supporting role here, with the Rani serving as the main antagonist. He's there to establish her credibility. It's a normal enough approach—a sort of villainous version of keeping UNIT around for *Robot*, but it's somewhat stranger to see it done by just shamelessly undermining the Master.

Let us pause here and observe the setting of the story, since it is focused on so intently, as the first episode opens with an exceedingly lengthy establishing shot of period Britain. We're back in British history again, and continuing on the theme of heritage theme-park Britain that we've been dealing with for the last few stories that were set in the past. Here the story is actually shot in heritage theme-parks to boot. But *The Mark of the Rani*, to its credit, resists that. It's in no way coincidental that we're having two stories about mining in a row here, and the "machines are coming in and putting all the miners out of work" themes of the industrial revolution echo directly with the "progress" underlying the modern-day pit closures. Unfortunately, of course, this story ends up simply endorsing progress and suggesting that the only reason anybody would oppose it is if they've been turned into aggressive brutes by the Rani, but, you know, you can't win them all.

(This may, in fact, be one of the most schizoid stories in the series' history when it comes to politics. On the one hand you have a story that revels in introducing a camp gay icon. On the other, it uncritically ends up endorsing neoliberal economic policies. It's like Doctor Who written by Roy Cohn.)

Our three Time Lords, accordingly, have their own position on this history. The Doctor, frustratingly, ends up being the arch-neoliberal who insists on maintaining the arc of history with no reference to any points other than "great man" theory. The Master, meanwhile, ends up as the mercurial anarchist who wants to destabilize history's flow seemingly for the sake of it. And finally we have the Rani, who seems almost completely disinterested in historical processes, caring only for her hazily-defined scientific project and, in passing, maybe ruling the universe a little bit. (Though even there she mostly rubbishes the Master's plan for seeming far more interested in killing the Doctor.)

And now we come to the peculiarities of the story's title. Admittedly Season Twenty-Two's titles are not the greatest. *Attack of the Cybermen* is a strong contender for the blandest title ever, *Vengeance on Varos* is suspiciously lacking in any vengeance, and it's not clear what, exactly, is revealed about the Daleks. Here, at least, the Rani does have a literal mark which she leaves upon her victims. But the term is perhaps more interesting in the context from which this essay derives its title, especially given the strange nature of names with relation to the three Time Lords of this story. What is interesting about the Rani, if you will, is that she has a mark but no name.

There is a lengthy body of postmodern scholarship that, when exposed to this observation, would promptly begin to giddily dance around. Let's extract a single line of thought from it, though—one closely related to alchemy. At the heart of alchemy is the idea of the symbol having some measure of power over the object it represents. But there are multiple types of symbols, and one major thread of postmodernism has involved the non-equivalence of different types of symbols and the interesting noise that comes out of this. The most obvious example—and by helpful coincidence the one relevant here—is the difference between speech and writing. A spoken word is fundamentally distinct from a written one—an observation that dates back at least to Plato. A written word is a geometric shape—a physical object (the usual jargon term is "grapheme") that we treat as the equivalent of a spoken one.

But there is a difference, and in some cases it's a significant one. Here the Rani has a mark—a grapheme—that is disconnected from a name. She is, in other words, capable of being symbolized in the material realm but is not capable of being spoken of except as an object or abstracted role ("the Rani"). Thus the loss of name experienced by this particular class of renegade Time Lord is revealed not as a punishment but as a form of power. The Rani is capable of marking history without ever being a definable part of it. History, as we've reiterated time and time again, is knowable only through memory and narrative. But the Rani cannot truly be a part of the narrative because there's no word for her.

And so in effect within this story we have three competing marks. The Rani's mark is based on science. But here, again, we have to pause and look at the science she engages in—most obviously her tree mines. These are, to say the least... interesting. They are landmines that, when stepped on, turn you into a tree. But it quickly becomes apparent that you do not become an ordinary tree, because one of the people to become a tree proceeds, at one point, to reach a branch around and grab/fondle Peri to save her from danger. So apparently one becomes a tree that still retains some level of humanoid movement and a functional set of desires, emotions, and thought. Biologically, of course, this is not possible—trees have neither muscles nor brains. So the Rani's tree-mines must work according to some other principle that extends beyond scientific empiricism.

But Doctor Who has always had some distinction between empiricism and science. Or, perhaps more accurately, science has never been reducible to mere empiricism within Doctor Who. "Scientist" is a social role, and has been since the Hartnell and early Troughton days when "But he's a scientist!" was the standard line trotted out to defend the character of someone. These days, of course, the sort of suspicion of unchecked science that the Rani represents runs rampant in the series, but it's still worth noting that the scientist is defined here by a quest for knowledge and certainty, not by their epistemology.

The Rani, then, is a force seeking to fix and transmute the material nature of things (she dismisses moral concerns over her transformation of people into trees by suggesting that all organic material is essentially interchangeable) with no regard whatsoever for its narrative. This is reflected in her basic concept—her narrative is absurd, but her material potency is considerable. Indeed, it's implied that the Rani has been invisibly sewing chaos throughout human history—that the social upheaval of the American Revolution and the Middle Ages were secretly her doing. For all that she's a ludicrous character, she's positioned as someone who has, without our knowing it, genuinely altered the material history of our world.

What, then, are the marks of the Master and of the Doctor? The Master is, in many ways, the inverse of the Rani here. He is materially impotent—a laughably ineffective villain—but symbolically powerful. He seeks to alter history with no concern for certainty—indeed, his schemes seem to have no endpoint beyond the desire for continual upheaval and transformation. This does not mean he lacks a mark, but it does mean that his mark exists within the mythology of the series. It's certainly the case that the Master has tangibly altered the overall structure of Doctor Who. But this alteration comes at the price of him being wholly unable to impact things. He cannot possibly affect the world. Where the Rani's lack of name makes her unspeakable (consider how the recurring joke about every mysterious female character in the contemporary series is that she might be the Rani) the Master's lack of name makes him uneraseable.

But when faced with these two polar opposites in villains, there's little room left for the Doctor. It's not just that he's stuck basically endorsing neoliberal economics. It's that faced with the Master and the Rani his position becomes, in effect, one of a referee. He becomes the character trying to maintain stability and order. He no longer has a mark, save perhaps the neon light logo of the series itself. By becoming a force of stasis—one who exists here to keep things as they are—he stops having a mark of his own and instead becomes something that is written upon. For all that Colin Baker defines the part with bluster and bombast he is, in a sense, more ineffectual here than his predecessor ever was, simply because there's no effect to be had. In facing these two mirrors of himself he stands revealed as the hollowed shell we feared.

## A Well-Prepared Meal (*The Two Doctors*)

It's February 16th, 1985. Elaine Paige and Barbara Dickson remain at number one, and stay there for all three weeks of this story. Kirsty MacColl, The Commodores, and Howard Jones also chart. More inspiring are the album charts, where The Smiths' landmark *Meat is Murder* debuts at number one in what is one of the most perfect thematic convergences of the music charts and Doctor Who in some time.

In real news, William J Schroeder is the first person to receive an artificial heart and leave the hospital. It doesn't go terribly well, admittedly, but it happens. *EastEnders* starts, and the day after the story ends the miner's strike ends. Oh, and Doctor Who gets cancelled. Right in the middle of *The Two Doctors*, its big celebration of its history this season. Damn.

When last we looked at this story back in Volume Two, the question was whether or not it functioned meaningfully as a Patrick Troughton story, and it was found wanting. Lucky for it, then, that its primary job is not to function as a Troughton story but as a Colin Baker story, a job that it performs markedly better at. Especially so under the model I've been approaching the series under—indeed, the "Baker era as exorcism" theory has, perhaps, no evidence better than this.

It can hardly be called a surprise. I said we'd have to drop the "no talking about the production team" rule for this story, so let's go ahead and point out that this is a Robert Holmes script. Holmes is always a nice writer to deal with as a critic simply because the authorial intent objection falls away. Holmes is a smart and clever enough writer to have intended much of what we'll find here, and it's only the alchemical embellishments that strike me as at all improbable.

The key detail is the part of the story everyone seems most ready to ignore—the Sontarans. Apparently Holmes was not terribly thrilled at the instruction to include the Sontarans, but was eventually mollified by Eric Saward when he pointed out that nobody had done them right since Holmes created them. This is certainly believable—appealing to a writer's ego is terribly effective. But this anecdote is, on the surface, difficult to reconcile with the fact that Holmes ends up treating the Sontarans as the most generic race of alien conquerors imaginable.

Here I must acknowledge my debt to Rob Shearman, whose guest analysis of this story in *About Time*, to which this essay is little more than an extended footnote, sets the standard to which all other redemptive readings of Doctor Who must aspire. The problem with assuming that Robert Holmes was going to restore his original version, just because he was persuaded to use the Sontarans on account of everybody else's take on them being terrible, is absurdly reductive. No, instead what we get is an aggressive examination of the nature of monsters.

This, in a nutshell, is the disagreement between Shearman in his guest defense of the story and Tat Wood's critique. Alongside the Sontarans are the Androgums, a race of food-obsessed aliens who are repeatedly treated as brute savages by all of the other characters. One—the story's main villainess—has been "enhanced" to where she is intelligent and acts like a human, to the consternation and horror of virtually every other character, particularly the Doctors. And the story over and over again stresses that you can't change or improve an Androgum.

Tat Wood objects, and not unreasonably, that this is ethically appalling. But where Shearman retorts—and to my mind clearly gets the better of Wood—is in pointing out that the only reason anyone finds the treatment of the Androgums problematic is that even in their unenhanced form they look human except for having funny eyebrows and a few pimples. Nobody, in watching the story, ever complains that the Sontarans are treated as generic and irredeemable monsters. The only difference is that one species has a potato face while the other just looks Scottish.

This, of course, is exactly what Holmes was trying to do back in *The Time Warrior*—to create a villainous character who happened to be a potato-faced alien. He created a generic alien culture for them—planet of the warlike people—but Linx was manifestly intended to be a character. The steady reduction of his concept to "generic war potatoes" was, as Saward guessed, a source of annoyance to Holmes. But he didn't fix the problem by redoing the Sontarans. He fixed it by creating the Androgums—essentially the same concept except with a food obsession as opposed to a war obsession—and having them be humanoid enough that nobody was ever going try to reuse them as generic monsters. And then, for good measure, having the story repeatedly and uncomfortably treat them like generic monsters even though they're clearly interesting characters. So basically, the Sontarans without funny masks.

That, right there, tells us an awful lot about how this story works. It's the one story that we can say with some confidence is meant to be an exorcism. This is a story that is overtly and consciously about the flaws of Doctor Who. And being Robert Holmes, it's not about fixing them. It's about screaming angrily at them. It's tempting to criticize Holmes here for his cynicism—to suggest that at some point bitching about the sad state of the world needs to come to an end in favor of doing something about it—but that's not fair. After all, the entire premise of this season is that exorcising one's demons is a form of progress.

This is a very important thing to realize about Holmes's critiques. It's not that he doesn't have a solution to the problems, it's that for a lot of them there isn't a solution that allows the series to still be Doctor Who. I mean, much as one can insist on some viewpoint where aliens aren't treated as generic monsters, for instance, the truth is that in an action sci-fi show there are always going to be monsters. This is an objection that was first raised by Sydney Newman back around week five of the program. Then the Daleks hit the scene and raised ratings to where the show could actually survive and these concerns fell permanently by the wayside. In other words, the idea that aliens aren't going to be treated like the Androgums and the Sontarans is absurd. (And indeed, thirty years later, when the series had an era in which the default setting was that the apparent monsters weren't actually villains, the show started getting criticism for not doing simple morality plays often enough anymore.)

This is true of most of what Holmes critiques here. Holmes is also visibly reacting against the role of nostalgia in this story. Given the task of bringing Troughton's Doctor back Holmes does what is more or less the exact thing that nobody who was obsessed with the nostalgia of the piece expected or wanted: he brings back Troughton's Doctor instead of "The Second Doctor." The difference between how Troughton plays the part here and how he played it in *The Five Doctors* is profound. Put simply, he looks much older here.

The thing is, he wasn't. *The Five Doctors* shot in March of 1983. This shot in August of 1984. And yet Troughton feels far older in this story than he does in *The Five Doctors*. But then, he feels far older in *The Invasion* than he does in *The Five Doctors* too. Troughton's Doctor always inherited more of the "old man" characteristics from Hartnell than people give him credit for, and his portrayal here is far closer to what he actually did on the series than the defanged clown he played in the anniversary stories. There are moments that jar— snapping at Jamie about his mongrel tongue remains indefensible—but for the most part Holmes actually writes the character that appeared in the 1960s. This character is still magnetic and charming—especially in contrast with Hartnell, who was, after all, the only point of comparison when people formed their impressions of him. But he's not nearly as saccharine as the character from 1973 or 1983.

This poses an interesting issue. For one thing, at least, it spares Colin Baker some of the ignominy that would otherwise exist. This is not a slight against Baker as an actor—it's just that his Doctor was not conceived of as a charming and fun figure. Putting him opposite Troughton is rough to begin with—Shearman observes that Holmes is working on a theme in which Troughton is the "old" Doctor whereas Baker is the younger, more "fun" Doctor, and even with Holmes's efforts to stack the deck in Baker's favor it's incredibly easy to love Troughton more. Had Troughton not been written back to his more... difficult version it would have been a completely impossible hand for Baker to play well.

But there's a larger issue here, which is an overt hostility to the very idea of nostalgia. With everything he brings back in this story, it's either in the form fans remember it with no regard for whether that's still worthwhile (i.e. the Sontarans) or it's with excessive fealty to the original concept so as to betray the false memories of nostalgia (i.e. Troughton). This culminates in his supposed continuity goof with regards to Troughton's Doctor and the Time Lords. Some amount of ink has been spilled on this, including a bit of my own, but for our purposes here suffice it to say that none of the options to explain how it is that the Time Lords can get in touch with Troughton or how Jamie knows about them quite work. This is, of course, a minor issue at best. But it's almost tailor-made to piss continuity-obsessive fans off.

That, I suspect, is the point. Holmes's interest in continuity has always been virtually null. He jettisoned everything we thought we knew about Gallifrey in *The Deadly Assassin*, and in bringing the Time Lords back as peripheral figures in this story he basically scraps all of that for a whole new set of technologies and explanations of things. Tat Wood accuses this of being the point where Holmes starts to believe his own reputation, but I think nothing could be further from the truth. This is the point where Holmes loses patience with being put on a pedestal. It's much like the classic story of comics legend Jack Kirby being told that someone was drawing one of his characters "Jack Kirby style" and remarking that "Jack Kirby style" would have been to create a new character. Likewise, the classic Robert Holmes style that fans so revere was never to do continuity-laden "Return of the X" assignments, but to come up with something new. It's a clear shot at the sorts of people who wanted *Attack of the Cybermen*—a reminder that the days of old that they were nostalgic for were not, in fact, defined by nostalgia.

This point also gets at the most controversial aspect of the story, the death of Oscar. I have little to add to Rob Shearman's analysis here. Oscar is a broad comedy character in the classic Robert Holmes style—and as such has always been safe within the overall shape of these sort of narratives. Killing him is thus shocking. But the brilliant part is that he remains a broad comic figure even as he's dying. Again, it's deliciously angry—a game of giving people what they want—a classic Robert Holmes comedy character—and then playing it more faithfully than they wanted it played, remaining funny even to his death. (After all, the other thing Holmes is known for is ridiculous body counts.)

So what we have is a story that savagely refuses to give the audience what they ostensibly want and that instead shows how those desires are corrupt and decadent. As I said, this is the one story this season where the exorcism seems deliberate—where the script really is about identifying and displaying the flaws of the series. And, more to the point, not just identifying them but performing them—enacting them and, in a perverse way, owning them. Again we have a story that is about its own flaws, where the thematic content of the story lines up oddly well with its deficiencies.

And here we have a rather damning example. Troughton's Doctor—the most alchemical and mercurial of them—is reintroduced into this milieu. More than any other Doctor, Troughton's was created by the actor. So much of his Doctor's nature comes from the fact that Troughton is an astonishingly good actor. There's a reason his character worked so rarely in books and other media that lacked Troughton himself—because so much of who his character is comes from him. And so his return is a genuinely powerful invocation—especially, in hindsight (as we've been taking much of this era), knowing that it's his last time in the role.

It is, then, a final credit to Troughton that he can pull off this last transformation of his Doctor. To have the character be so recognizable as Troughton's Doctor and yet remain unable to "save" this story (where salvation is defined, quite inaccurately, as avoiding its flaws) is impressive. Troughton has always carefully moderated his performances, but here they are more finely tuned than ever as he, in a sense, takes the bullet for the series. Because the point of the story is that an alchemic Doctor, a great actor, classic monsters, none of these things matter. None of them make the show good. With just a slight angling of the series' moral viewpoint—a tiny shift that brings its ethical problems to the fore—the rest comes crashing down in spite of them. No, worse than that—because of them.

And so it's fitting that the story that demonstrates that not even Patrick Troughton can save the series from itself is the one during which the plug was finally pulled. But equally, this is a confrontation the show needed to have. These are real demons within the series, and they needed to be seen, acknowledged, and named. This is how one shapes the conditions under which the show will revitalize itself. One can't just reinvent blindly.

In that regard, then, this is the archetypal Troughton story—one in which the spirit of his era is unleashed directly at its future. More than any other version it is Troughton's Doctor who is defined by a tendency to bring your world down around you, and who vanishes prior to rebuilding. The nature of mercurial anarchism is that one shapes the start conditions of the rebirth. In his last and most savagely brilliant gift to the program, the late, great Patrick Troughton does exactly that.

## By No Means the Most Interesting (*Timelash*)

It's March 9th, 1985. Dead or Alive are spinning right round. Like a record, baby. They continue to spin all story long, with Madonna, Prince, and Jermaine Jackson also charting. In the news, Mikhail Gorbachev takes over in the Soviet Union, and Mohammed Al Fayed takes over Harrods. Riots break out at the FA Cup quarterfinal between Luton Town and Millwall, presaging ominously the Heysel Stadium disaster that summer. While on television, *Timelash*.

Ah. Timelash. Its flaws are obvious—it's in many ways *The Horns of Nimon* only with Paul Darrow instead of Graham Crowden, and while Darrow's solution to the problem of the script is much the same as Crowden's, he lacks the sheer mass of cured pork necessary to pull it off completely. This isn't quite as awful as its reputation, but that's praising with faint damnation, and it's next to impossible to seriously argue that this works. Never mind that, though. I remain not terribly interested in discussing the quality of Season Twenty-Two directly. Instead let's talk about something in this story that's much odder than people tend to make it out to be: Herbert.

It's worth observing that the model of "the Doctor teams up with a figure from history to fight aliens" was actually invented by Pip and Jane Baker for *The Mark of the Rani*, then reiterated in the next story filmed, namely *Timelash*. Yes, the historicals involved meetings between the Doctor and historical figures, but those were just that—historicals. Given that King John was a duplicate in *The Kings Demons*, George Stephenson is actually the first famous historical figure the

Doctor has encountered since 1966, and the first ever outside of a pure historical. Nowadays "the Doctor teams up with someone from history to fight aliens" is a standard of the series, appearing at least once per season, but prior to 1985 this wasn't actually a category of story. And yet nobody remembers to put *The Mark of the Rani* and *Timelash* on their list of Doctor Who stories that changed the shape of things to come. (And both deserve credit, as there's no way to seriously argue that one inspired the other.)

The relevance of George Stephenson as a choice can probably be put down to the quirks of Pip and Jane Baker as writers, as it is largely consistent with their general aesthetic. More interesting, for my money, is H.G. Wells. Wells is lionized as a the father of modern science fiction, which is interesting given that almost nobody talks about any of his books following *The First Men in the Moon* in 1901. Indeed, Wells is an excessively sanitized character, the popular accounts of him largely treating him as a sort of pleasantly eccentric proto-steampunk figure instead of the aggressively socialist writer he actually was.

So what we have here is a defanged and largely pointless version of the father of science fiction appearing in a defanged and largely pointless imitation of scads of classic Doctor Who stories. It's sorely tempting to just declare the exorcism point made and end the essay there, but I shan't. Especially because there's another odd aspect of *Timelash*, which is the way in which the story is haunted by Jon Pertwee. And not just haunted by Jon Pertwee, but haunted by a Pertwee story that doesn't exist. This is not the first reference to an unseen adventure ever, of course, but it is in many ways the most substantive and deliberate. There's stuff like Planet 14 from *The Invasion*, but that can be explained away as a continuity goof. There's stuff like the Terrible Zodin, but that's clearly intended as a joke. And there's stuff like *Meglos*, but that story suggests a visit that was more tourism-based than a past adventure. The only previous story to have the plot hinge on an unseen past adventure was *The

*Face of Evil*, and even there the story specifically depended on the unseen story still being a Tom Baker adventure.

But what we have here is something altogether stranger—a continuity reference to nonexistent continuity. What, exactly, is its purpose? Typically we've assumed that continuity references exist as a sort of fan appeasement based on nostalgia. As we talked about last time, though, nostalgia is based on a lie. First of all, the remembered past is never based around the imitation of its own past. Nostalgia, by definition, wants something different than what the past was. Second of all, though, nostalgia is by its nature based on an idealization of the past with only minimal intersection with the actual material past.

In this regard, then, the nostalgia for the non-existent Pertwee story within *Timelash* is almost purer and more honest than normal nostalgia. At last, we have nostalgia that's honest about pining for a past that never existed! But this observation seems short of the mark. Nostalgia depends on the lie that it is accurate. Which is what makes *Timelash*'s invocation of a false past so strange. It's not even as though Pertwee is a particularly sensible era to choose here; indeed, of the past Doctors he's the least likely to have had a secret adventure like this, simply because he was the least likely to have outer space adventures in general. The only eras where stories like *Timelash* unfolded with any regularity were really the Hartnell era and the Graham Williams half of the Tom Baker era. The closest to this Pertwee ever got was Peladon, which, let's face it, is not very close.

In truth the selection of Pertwee is probably little more than another in a series of symptoms of careless and sloppy storytelling here. The cheap and silly filler episode has been a regular of the past few seasons, with only Season Twenty coming close to avoiding it (the one that's written as disposable filler—*The Kings Demons*—and the one that's shot that way—*Terminus*—are distinct). It's pretty fair to say that *Timelash* is clearly this year's entry to the group, and in that regard there's a pleasant improvement in that they avoided putting it after their climactic and thrilling action script—unlike *Time-Flight* and *The Twin Dilemma*. And so what is most interesting about Pertwee is probably the very wrongness of the choice—complete with asserting the existence of a second companion alongside Jo.

It suggests, and not entirely inaccurately (especially after Holmes's aggressive demonstration of what the actual past is like) that this era's investment in the past is indistinct even by the standards of nostalgia—that what is really desired at this point is merely the vague feeling that the series is of the past. That is to say, what matters is not the content of the past but the mere existence of it—that some past is invoked. Given what pragmatic arguments were being aired in the series' favor at this point in time, an issue we'll look at in more detail pretty soon, this is almost grotesquely appropriate.

Because what's interesting is that for all of its faults, *Timelash* pulls off a bleakly clever bit of thematic unity here. Just as the Doctor's past becomes a meaningless thing that is referenced vaguely and for its own sake, H.G. Wells is separated from almost all actual representation of his history. The list of historical howlers about Wells is huge—his accent is wrong, his hair color is wrong, he goes by Herbert instead of George, he's inexplicably well-off, he appears to believe in God...

Indeed, about the only meaningful trait Herbert displays in terms of him being H.G. Wells is that he'll supposedly write several books based on these experiences. But, of course, the plots of his books don't really resemble *Timelash* either. There's a few names he might have ripped off, but this story's suggestion that the events of *Timelash* secretly inspired the writing of H.G. Wells is a complete evasion of the actual history of science fiction in favor of a vague "history-ish" approach.

So yet again we have a story that seems to be about the horrible consequences that follow from itself, complete with a time-traveling robot that explodes midway through. But this one ends up playing with unusually inflated stakes. The use of

H.G. Wells is, of course, because of his role as the progenitor of science fiction, which isn't quite true, of course, but clearly we're not going to start worrying about that here of all places. And so the implication of the story is that really crap Doctor Who is the secret origin of all science fiction. *Timelash* thus positions itself, with hilarious hubris, as the logical endpoint of all science fiction—the point where everybody caught up to what H.G. Wells had really been doing when he invented the genre.

Unlike *The Two Doctors*, however, nobody at all seems to be in on the joke. This is in an odd sense the bleakest dystopia Doctor Who has ever produced. In a season known for its black comedy here we finally have a dark joke played so straight that it doesn't get itself. A piece of cruel absurdism that finally, mockingly asks, "So, then, this is what you want science fiction to be?"

It's not, of course. And *Timelash* clearly has no idea of this problem. If *The Two Doctors* was the story we could most readily believe was supposed to be an exorcism, this is the one it's most difficult to give any real credence to. Everything about this looks like poorly written knockoff Doctor Who— the *Meglos* of the mid-80s. It's by far the story that has the biggest problem with the forty-five minute structure, with a second episode that just gives up on any sort of structured plot in favor of just running an endless sequence of climaxes until the clock finally runs out. The clone Borad is easily the single most flagrant attempt to stretch out the runtime of something since *The Invasion of Time*'s Sontaran surprise.

And here we do get to the problem with this redemptive reading of Season Twenty-Two—one I copped to when introducing the approach. It's still based on the fact that the stories this season are almost all pretty bad. There are flashes of quality, and even, with *Vengeance on Varos*, a sustained attempt at it, but they feel like moments of lucidity in the midst of a protracted decline. Which leaves us again having to ask why we're even bothering with this process. What is it we think we can actually gain through this? It's only redemptive, after all, if there's some actual redemption. Otherwise we're just giving clever and metatextual readings of why stories suck.

The answer is that much of this era is about closing off dead routes for the series to take. Many of this season's stories are the last or nearly last time the classic series attempts something like this—and many of the ideas are ones that just flat-out didn't survive into the new series. *Attack of the Cybermen* is the last piece of vapid continuity fetishism; *The Mark of the Rani* is the last time the Master is used in quite this generic and leering a fashion; *The Two Doctors* does, in fact, spell the end of unproblematic "generic monster race" stories; this is the last time the series does a generic space dystopia. For all the egregious faults of these stories, they serve almost the exact purpose that they appear to in these readings. There's no clear future at this point, but that's not what this phase of the program is about. This is about purging the dead weight. Asking the question "So what's left after all of this?" is next season.

So let's take a look at the scorecard. Doctor Who has had the qlippothic force of the Cybermen unleashed within its basic premise. It's critiqued its own status as television entertainment, exposed the Doctor as an almost completely morally and philosophically bankrupt character, attacked the premise of monsters, and now, to top it all off, questioned not just the show's very history, but its standing as science fiction. There's only one thing left to do before we finish with our acknowledgment and naming of the show's demons and get into the business of properly expelling them—because it's just not a narrative collapse until you've got Daleks in it.

## Am I Becoming One of Your Angels (*Revelation of the Daleks*)

It's March 23rd, 1985. Philip Barley and Phil Collins are at number one with "Easy Lover." Madonna, Frankie Goes to Hollywood, Sarah Brightman and Paul Miles-Kingston, David Cassidy, and Nik Kershaw also chart. Lower in the charts, we have Billy Bragg, The Smiths, and The Damned. In real news, ummm... actually, all I've got, and I regret that I am not making this up, is that production of the Sinclair C5 electric tricycle is suspended. That's literally all the news that happened this week. Sorry. Let's move to television and *Revelation of the Daleks*.

What is most interesting about *Revelation of the Daleks* is that, other than the fact that it's rubbish, it's one of the greatest Doctor Who stories ever. This is, to some extent, just a restatement of our theme for Season Twenty-Two—that every story in it is a brilliant story about how terrible a story it is. Consider, for instance, the sequence in the first episode that pulls back from the Doctor and Peri to the DJ watching the Doctor and Peri, and then to Davros watching the DJ watch the Doctor and Peri. It's a thing of absolute beauty— one of the most narratively complex sequences in the classic series. And it's merely the cleverest of a bunch of intense clevernesses. This whole story is about passing control of the narrative around and about who does and doesn't have authority over what's happening.

The best Dalek stories involve unleashing the Doctor and the Daleks into someone else's story—a drama about a space colony, *The Forsythe Saga*, a World War II movie (I'm talking about *Genesis*, not *Victory*), or, more recently, a bunch of reality programs, *The Invasion*, and a mashup of *Torchwood*, *The Sarah Jane Adventures*, and a sitcom starring Catherine Tate that Catherine Tate is taking a week off from. Superficially, at least, *Revelation of the Daleks* mirrors that structure. Indeed, it's on the whole a very straightforward and competent execution of that structure, well-directed by Graeme Harper. Episode One shows us the world of Necros, Episode Two shows us Daleks slaughtering everybody on the world of Necros. But there's something ever so slightly wrong about this, and for that we need to look deeper at the notion of control over television.

There's an important technological shift to note in a discussion of control over television that happened over the course of the early 1980s, which was the mainstream adoption of the remote control. It's easiest to compare this to earlier television technology. When, in 1971, Doctor Who did a story with a bunch of very fast cuts among very colorful things and called it *The Claws of Axos*, the effect was that of a strange assemblage of imagery. That is, the somewhat confusing, rapid cuts around the Axon spaceship had the effect of creating an overall collage. This is because a 1971 television wasn't built to change channels quickly: you had to get up and fiddle with your physical set. And so the idea of switching between radically different things wasn't part of what television did. Television presented a continual transmission of a thing. If that thing was a collage, fine, but it was still clearly one collage, if you will, and the audience focused on the overall spectacle of the thing.

But the remote control, and forgive the obviousness of this observation, invented channel surfing. Suddenly another way of watching television—now arguably the default way—was to switch among different things. So when *Revelation of the Daleks* begins fast cuts among different parts of Necros it doesn't look like a collage of images from one thing, it looks like flipping among multiple television programs. All of which are, due to the structure of the story (and the obsession with surveillance states that flares up this season—note that this is the third story this season to involve lots of watching people watch people), about people watching the other television programs.

This is the key thing to realize about *Revelation of the Daleks* and about Necros. Look at how everybody is kept apart in the story—you have Natasha and Grigory's plot, Kara's plot, the DJ's not-actually-a-plot, and Jobel's plot. In the second episode you further spin off Orcini's plot from Kara's plot. None of these are recognizably part of a single milieu. The usual accusation is that this is a story that is far more interested in its world than in the Doctor or the Daleks, but that misses the point—there is no world to this story. There's just a collection of bits and bobs from other places. (This even extends to the physical world of Necros, apparently—the sets are mostly repurposed from other shows.)

So the Daleks aren't actually unleashed into anything as such. There's no "there" to Necros. But this can't be framed as some complaint about the inadequate fleshing out of Necros. Too much really clever effort has gone into making Necros not function as a coherent place. So this isn't the traditional Dalek story paradigm, but it's also not a failed execution of it. It's something else—an active inversion of the normal paradigm.

Given everything going on within Doctor Who at this moment in time, there's something frighteningly apt about having Doctor Who confronted with a vast assemblage of other television shows. The suspension of the program is going to take a large number of essays to unfold, but one of the major concerns underlying it was a shift towards a more overtly commercial BBC. (This ignores, of course, Doctor Who's overseas success. As I've noted, the question of how overseas success ought be considered by the BBC is complex at best. Similarly, at the time of the suspension crisis Colin

Baker hadn't yet debuted in the US: the assumption that he'd tank in the US as badly as he had in the UK was not entirely unreasonable, nor, for that matter, entirely wrong.)

So here we have a slightly absurd reiteration of the series' travails. Doctor Who is actually pitted against everything else on television here. Instead of the Daleks and the Doctor being injected into a half-dozen other television shows, we get a straightforward Dalek story that is invaded by those very same shows! This process ends up playing out substantially differently from the normal approach.

For one thing, neither the Doctor nor the Daleks actually do much in the first episode. The Doctor spends the first episode walking from the TARDIS to Tranquil Repose as various misadventures fail to happen to him. (There is that wall he climbs.) The Daleks, meanwhile, are almost entirely sidelined in the first episode, with Davros anchoring their aspect of the plot. Or, rather, his seemingly severed head in a vat. With all of them sidelined, the first episode is freed up to focus almost entirely on its other plotlines. And it's actually quite good.

This is a real problem. Whatever frustration one might have with the fact that the show is Doctor Who and that maybe the Doctor should be in it, the truth is that he's just about the least interesting thing on display in the first episode. And, worse than that, the bits with other characters are markedly more interesting than anything we've seen since Martin Jarvis was on screen ostensibly directing the cliffhanger to *Vengeance on Varos*. Yes, the deck is stacked against the Doctor here due to him having nothing to do, but really, the first episode of this is probably the high point of Season Twenty-Two.

However, just as the infusion of Doctor Who into another show does not erase the conventions of that show, the infusion of a host of other shows into a Dalek story does not mean that the conventions of a Dalek story go unobserved. And if you have a bunch of Daleks in the first act you have to have a bunch of exterminations in the second.

And so all of the cleverness that gets set up over the first forty-five minutes gets violently slaughtered over about twenty minutes of the second episode.

This is unfortunate, if inevitable. Because, frankly, the resulting Doctor/Davros confrontation and the Dalek civil war isn't nearly as interesting as most of what came before. The collapse of the DJ from omniscient narrator commenting wryly on events to a generic character hiding from the Daleks and then getting exterminated is particularly bleak, although if we're being honest, blowing up Daleks with rock and roll is possibly the most charming idea Eric Saward ever came up with. But for the most part this story amounts to the series confessing and demonstrating that, actually, even the Daleks can't measure up to the rest of television.

This, on its own, would serve as an adequate final admission in the course of the exorcism. Having explored all of the failings of the series, the series finally and conclusively demonstrates that it's behind the times and that the bits of other programs assembled to make Necros are far more interesting than even Dalek action. The supposed best of Doctor Who goes up against the rest of the televisual landscape and is found wanting. Clearly it's time to take a break and reevaluate things a bit.

Except it's worse than that. Continuing our alchemic themes, it is worth pointing out something significant that has not happened since *Day of the Daleks*, which is that the Daleks do not recognize the Doctor. There we read it as a commentary on the inadequacy of the earthbound format and the fact that the Doctor, in that story, isn't quite the Doctor. It's especially notable in contrast with *Power of the Daleks* where being identified by the Daleks was what firmly and truly defined Troughton's Doctor as the Doctor.

So within the existing grammar of the show, not being recognized by the Daleks is a cutting insult to this version of the show. It's a final pox. If the Daleks—who, let's face it, dominate the conclusion here, since it was never really that Davison's Doctor was ineffective so much as that the

Doctors when written by Eric Saward are ineffective—aren't able to stand up to the rest of what's on television, well, fine. At least they're still able to fulfill their function. The Daleks have never worked without the Doctor anyway, as Terry Nation spent the late 60s and early 70s discovering. So if they can't cut it in the televisual world of 1985, well, who's fault is that?

But let's be clear about this. Even the Daleks are doing better here than the Doctor. They may not be terribly interesting without the Doctor, but it's worth noting that they're still able to exterminate the rest of television, even if they're not up to the task of doing it in a compelling manner. So the Daleks don't need the Doctor to function, and television as a whole doesn't need either one of them.

The funny thing, if you want to call it that, is that this is wholly consistent with Saward's apparent intentions. He saw the Daleks as no longer interesting, and he genuinely believed the worlds the Doctor visited were more interesting than the Doctor himself. Yes, this is almost certainly a self-fulfilling prophecy, but, well, the prophecy is nevertheless fulfilled. The show is clearly not working even at the most basic level. It is, in fact, providing almost the exact opposite of compelling drama. Virtually all of the good bits of *Revelation of the Daleks* come in spite of it being a Doctor Who story, not because of it.

A central alchemical concept is the notion of putrefaction, previously dealt with in *The Green Death* essay back in Volume Three. At its most basic, putrefaction is the process by which death becomes a creative process. Here we have the process in spades. Our season of exorcism ends at a funeral home in which the dead are literally repurposed, most obviously into Daleks. (Physical death, of course, is strictly optional.) The Doctor is confronted with his apparent actual death—he even comments that it looks like this will be his last regeneration, which, to be fair, it very nearly was. The cliffhanger is him being crushed by his own death. In one sense, all that's missing from this story is a regeneration.

Instead we get something stranger—the putrefaction breaks free of this story and grabs the series in its own maw for the next two and a half years. The thing most obviously missing from this story instead appears vividly over the next eighteen episodes of the series, as well as over the next eighteen months of the calendar as Doctor Who grapples, in real time, with a simultaneous death and recreation. And when we get to the next season, well, that's where we'll pick up—the idea of *Trial of a Time Lord* as the productive decomposition of a series that was meticulously killed this season.

But for now, this ends the main thrust of the Colin Baker era. He does, of course, get another season. In fact, as a perusal of the number of pages still before you in this book will attest, we're going to spend quite a bit more time with him. But this is the main of it—the part that was able to play out exactly as Nathan-Turner and Saward had imagined it. (The next season, despite all the extra lead time given to it, is an ungodly mess.) And yet given all this, even at the end of it, it's not clear what the idea of this season was supposed to be. I admit that there's a bit of cheek to my "consciously demonstrating everything that's wrong with Doctor Who" theme to this season, but does a better explanation of what's supposed to be happening here exist? Behind the scenes, as any of the myriad accounts of this period will demonstrate, the show spent this era tearing itself apart. There isn't what can accurately be called a creative vision here, and in many ways it's a pleasant surprise that in the course of all of this that the program managed to articulate as clear a self-critique as it did.

Now, however, we have to turn to the question of what the series could have been in this era. There are a lot of parts to this question—what it materially was during the hiatus, what else was on television, what people have suggested it could have been after the fact, and what it nearly was at the time. So for the next rest of the book that's what we'll look at.

## Outside The Government: A Fix With Sontarans

For what it's worth, there is no evidence that either Jimmy Savile or Gary Downie raped Gareth Jenkins during the making of this, and Jenkins was too young for Downie anyway. Indeed, it's entirely probable that absolutely nobody was raped or sexually assaulted during the production of "A Fix With Sontarans." I mean, someone might have fended off an assault with a copy of the script at some point, but otherwise the odds look good.

None of this helps when watching it, though. I mean, Jimmy Savile's enough. Certainly he's single-handedly the reason this was hastily scrubbed from the DVD extras. And to be clear, even as a scholar with a tremendous investment in the preservation of the historical record, I understand that one. It's difficult to entirely comprehend the extent to which Savile marks a deep and excruciating psychic wound on British culture. Savile was omnipresent in British culture for decades, a fact that is central to how he also became one of the most shockingly prolific rapists in history.

What's most unsettling, in many ways, is the sense of collective culpability. As the extent of Savile's crimes emerged, so did the number of times he had almost been caught, only to slither away by threatening repercussions if anyone investigated him and threatening to sue any of his victims brave enough to speak out against him. Once it was public information, people teemed out of the woodwork to voice their suspicions in hindsight, as though knowing but remaining silent was somehow better than ignorance. (Colin Baker notes in hindsight that "his eyes were cold," for instance, though the only reason to single him out is that this is a Doctor Who book.) The result, and much of why this remains so hard to look at, is that Savile forms the visible portion of a deep and systemic rot that allowed him (and many others) to exist.

Which is perhaps to say that while I understand why this has to vanish from the DVD extras… it's going to come back. I mean, these things do. You can't actually scrub Savile from post-War England. If you could, he wouldn't be nearly as horrifying as he is. He's a part of British history, just like this is a part of Doctor Who history. These things don't vanish.

Of course, there is a second aspect that makes this piece deeply unsettling beyond Savile, albeit a stranger one: it's since emerged that there are some serious accusations of sexual assault to be levelled against John Nathan-Turner, or, more accurately, his partner, Gary Downie. Were it just Savile, this would become Doctor Who's awkward brush with a cultural storm. But the real problem is that Doctor Who has its own version of the problem, and it's impossible not to think about that while watching this.

This fact has been something of an oddity within Doctor Who fandom. It got a flurry of mainstream attention when it broke in 2013, with some news sites dutifully reporting on the allegations revealed in Richard Marson's authoritative *JN-T: The Life and Scandalous Times of John Nathan-Turner* biography, but the impact of it was strangely muted. Part of this is simply that *JN-T* was, for all the media attention, published by Miwk, an independent press that eschews ebooks and has no US distribution, which means that even with the *Daily Mail* trumpeting shocking revelations the book was unlikely to have much impact. Another part of it is that Marson, in addition to revealing the information, passes judgment, and mostly gives Nathan-Turner a pass. And given that he's among the victims, this carries some weight.

It shouldn't. Marson is of course perfectly free to forgive whomever he wants for himself, but as a moral assessment of the evidence he musters, phrases like "however reprehensible some of his behaviour" or "dubious and questionable behaviour" simply do not adequately cover the evidence Marson brings up, and his larger defense, which amounts to saying that Nathan-Turner wasn't as bad as Savile, so that's OK then, is simply appalling.

For the benefit of people who have not read *JN-T*, let's

take a horrifying moment to summarize the findings. First is Marson's personal story, which includes Gary Downie asking him, "Have you ever had two up you?" while he was visiting the set of *Resurrection of the Daleks* at the age of seventeen, and John Nathan-Turner calling him "fucking provincial" when he said he hadn't and didn't think he'd like to. On a subsequent visit to the production office he was sexually assaulted by Gary Downie, fled, and hid under a desk with a rolled up copy of the script to *Timelash* (Episode Two) in case he had to physically defend himself. Numerous people report efforts to get them drunk prior to making a pass. Elsewhere in the book is an account of Gary Downie tying someone's shoelaces to the table and then holding him down when he tripped as Nathan-Turner started to undo his belt. It's genuinely horrifying. (Likewise, while not directly related to this topic, the anecdote of John Nathan-Turner spitting in Nicola Bryant's face at an early 90s convention out of a mistaken belief she'd slept with a guy he fancied.)

Despite this, Marson mostly gives Nathan-Turner a pass. Bewilderingly, a few pages after describing how Downie forcibly tried to kiss him in an elevator while grabbing his crotch, Marson proclaims, "It would not be true to say that I've found anyone willing to testify to coercion or abuse," as though he had not just done so. Instead, Marson gets pointlessly caught up on the accurate but irrelevant point that there was an unjustly higher age of consent for gay sex than heterosexual sex, and that nothing Nathan-Turner and Downie did would have violated age of consent laws once the two were brought into line.

And there is some real significance to this point. One of the recurring themes in *JN-T* is the variety of ways in which Nathan-Turner's status as an out gay man hurt his career, with him being stuck on Doctor Who largely because the program was a bit of a joke within the BBC, and never granted much in the way of opportunities for promotion or other projects. All the same, Marson gets wrongly hung up on the question, "Was John Nathan-Turner a pedophile?"

instead of the rather more pressing question, "Did John Nathan-Turner serially sexually assault people?" To which the answer would appear at best to be, "No, he just did nothing while Gary Downie did." Which is still absolutely horrifying.

But does it matter? Or, rather, does this matter to how one reads the Nathan-Turner era of Doctor Who? It's a question that crops up plenty of places, from "Do the posthumous revelations about Marion Zimmer-Bradley invalidate *The Mists of Avalon?*" to "Does the fact that Heidegger was a Nazi undermine his philosophy?" And it's one of the most vexed questions in terms of art—how do you separate it from the artist?

Except we're not talking about *The Mists of Avalon*, a seminal book that was tremendously influential on the adolescences of thousands of people because it told stories from an underserved perspective in fantasy. Nor are we talking about one of the most influential philosophers of the twentieth century. We're talking about the John Nathan-Turner era. We're talking about *Time-Flight*, *Arc of Infinity*, *Warriors of the Deep*, and *Timelash*.

Which is to say that at some point the question stops being, "Do the personal failings of the people creating art invalidate the good aspects that art might have?" and starts being, "How far are we actually willing to go to try to redeem this?" Sure, you can cook up a redemptive reading for all sorts of stuff, and I've made cases for the dire throughout *TARDIS Eruditorum*, but at some point you have to ask... why? Why are we trying to redeem this?

For the Nathan-Turner era, at least, the answer is pretty obvious: because it's Doctor Who, and we are nostalgic fans. Even for the crap. We desperately want Doctor Who to be good, and are willing to go to some lengths to make it so. But this is the sort of attitude that leads to becoming someone like Ian Levine, who was perfectly willing to stand by for all the sexual assault (which he's bluntly said he knew about), but for whom casting Bonnie Langford was a bridge too far.

Perhaps it's sometimes worth making a case for good art

made by bad people. Perhaps it's sometimes worth making a case for deeply flawed gems. But somewhere in the midst of contemplating whether "its script makes suitable material for fending off someone who's trying to sexually assault you" is actually the best thing you can say about the second episode of *Timelash*, you just kind of hit the point where it stops being worth it.

Look, at the end of the day, the run of Doctor Who covered in this book is mostly dismal television. And then, on top of that, it was made by people who were deeply and practically morally compromised. That just doesn't seem to be true of anyone else who made Doctor Who. Yes, Terrance Dicks said some ghastly things about women in his day, and you can make whatever complaints you want about Moffat, but it remains the case that the number of major figures in the production of Doctor Who that are known to have spat in a woman's face is exactly one. Likewise, there's only one who allegedly stood over a man and started undoing his pants while his partner held him down.

Sure, there were worse at the BBC. Savile proves that. And sure, the blame goes deep, implicating an entire network of people who turned a blind eye. But we don't have to just reject the worst of the worst, and just because there's a litany of people who have already turned a blind eye doesn't mean we have to keep doing so. John Nathan-Turner was, by all appearances, complicit in numerous sexual assaults. Surely, at least, that means we can just say, "Fuck it, I'm not going to bother defending *The Mark of the Rani*." Surely we can just accept that this a bad, ugly time for the programme, on a number of levels, and leave it at that. Surely we can just have there be a dark period in the history that we don't much like to talk about. Or better yet, a dark period we do talk about. Because that's what you do with moral horrors. You face them. Corners of the universe that have bred the most terrible things and all that.

So let's not pretend this doesn't exist forever. Let's not bury this. Let's admit it. During a period where Doctor Who was run by someone complicit in numerous sexual assaults, it did a brief tie-in with Jimmy Savile. It happened. So let's put it on the DVD. With hard-coded production subtitles describing the accusations against Nathan-Turner and Downie. So when the Sontarans blast through the TARDIS doors, we can read about how Marson "froze, pinned against the side with Gary trying to thrust his tongue further in. Meanwhile, his other hand had released my nipple and slid between my legs, where it was forcefully investigating access."

Redeem that.

## Pop Between Realities, Home in Time for Tea: Doctor in Distress

Among those whose pathology animated the preceding essay, perhaps nobody is quite as infuriating as Ian Levine, who took to the red tops when the revelations in *JN-T* came out and proclaimed, "Things went on that were horrible, corrupt, too awful to discuss," which conveniently omits the fact that he knew about them all when they were happening and stood gamely by while suggesting that *Attack of the Cybermen* might be a good idea.

For all of this, however, there's something unpleasant about the degree of vitriol directed at Levine. At the end of the day, Levine in 1985 was a 30-year-old geek and acted the part. He was a poor spokesman for Doctor Who in the public eye, yes. But more than anything, one feels bad for him for being put there in the first place. His biggest problem, in many ways, was that he played the role that the cancellation crisis cast him in—slightly maladapted überfan—too well.

I'd also be lying if I said that, as a socially maladapted Doctor Who fan in my early 30s, I didn't have at least some visceral understanding of where Levine was coming from. Being an angry geek in 2015 is easy. There's a whole Internet for hard-headedly arguing on. And adamant as I am that one argues on the Internet for the entertainment of the lurkers, I'm not nearly daft enough to pretend that I don't like getting to vent obsessively on forums. Where do you think I learned to write two thousand words a day? I've been drawn inexorably into being a hard-nosed tit in Internet arguments too many times not to understand Levine. Time warp me into 1985 with no Internet to argue on and give me an in with the production office of Doctor Who and I'd probably smash a television as a publicity stunt too. And while I like to think I wouldn't stand by and say nothing about serial sex predators, let's face it: everybody who stood by and said nothing in 1985 liked to think that about themselves, too. At least Levine holds down steady employment, which is, let's face it, more than we can say for my overeducated ass.

And so to some extent one is left wanting to let sleeping dogs lie. 1985 was a long time ago. Ian Levine is nearly sixty now. At some point one has to stop blaming someone for dumb shit they did in their early thirties. And if nothing else, the 1985 crisis is a footnote in the history of a wildly successful show. Perhaps lingering axes to grind exist among those who were making the show—or at least those who are still with us—but it's tough to say that we the chattering public still have anything at stake in this fight. We're not so much beating a dead horse as beating the empty space where once a horse carcass lay before it was devoured by maggots and composted into the soil. These days Levine is mostly just another bloke with a Twitter who occasionally says stupid things about Doctor Who or DC Comics. So really, I'm one to talk.

And so I've avoided going too far into Ian Levine in this book. But he can't be avoided entirely. For one thing, he presents himself as a central player in this time period to this day. If he's going to continue grinding his axe by being one of the major interviews on the *Trials and Tribulations* documentary about the hiatus and the wreckage of the Colin Baker era, well, fine. He implicates himself in any judgment one makes on the evidence. I've occasionally entertained myself by noting, when Ian Levine has come up in passing on the blog, that he has personally told me to go fuck myself. The context of this is illustrative—I rather indecorously called him out on Twitter over his fearmongering in the wake of the whole *Private Eye*/shortened series kerfuffle with regards to the new series back in 2011 (I shouldn't have @replied him, for what it's worth—that was rude of me). Which is to say, if he's going to repeat the errors of 1985 and raise fearmongering panics over the future of Doctor Who, well, that, at least, remains perfectly fair game to criticize him for.

But perhaps most importantly, if most tragically, Levine serves as too useful a metaphor to let go of. He's not the only person to have views on Doctor Who like his. But he's got the highest profile. And he was at the wrong place at the wrong time. His views caused measurable, definable damage to Doctor Who. I think a very compelling case can be made that were it not for some of his actions, Doctor Who could have returned from its hiatus in a stronger position and that it needn't have gone off the air in 1989. Is he the sole architect of that failure? God no, and we'll sort out the particulars of that in the "Apportioning the Blame" essay that follows this. But he's inextricable from it. And because he, both through his own actions and through the actions of others, got positioned as the archetype of a particular type of Doctor Who fan, he serves as a symbol for a particular set of destructive impulses within fandom and their problems. Which is to say that our collective disdain for Ian Levine is largely self-loathing. All the same, just because it's self-hatred doesn't mean it's not deserved hatred.

At the heart of my criticism of Levine, at least, is the fact that he is a shining example of why conflicts of interest are dangerous. He is, within Doctor Who, the original professional fan. But his professional status was enormously contested. He was the continuity advisor to the early John Nathan-Turner era, but this was explicitly and deliberately an unofficial and uncredited role. In blunter terms, he was paid with access instead of money. This is just one example of what I've more broadly called the fan-industrial complex, but it's a real problem—Levine was simultaneously serving as the high profile voice of fandom while getting perks from the show. The result was that one of the go-to sources for quotes about Doctor Who fandom was, by and large, happy to serve as a mouthpiece for the producer.

What gives all of this an upsettingly cynical tinge is the fact that in the aftermath of the suspension crisis Levine was one of the large bloc of fandom that turned aggressively on Nathan-Turner. In Levine's account, the breaking point was the casting of Bonnie Langford, but the fact remains that the overwhelming bulk of fandom abandoned Nathan-Turner following the cancellation crisis and *Trial of a Time Lord*. (Indeed, there's still traces of a fan orthodoxy that viewed the McCoy era as a disaster. While it's overstating the case to suggest that anybody who dislikes McCoy is guilty of this, the fact remains that a significant thread of McCoy bashing has its roots in nothing more than the fact that fandom decided in 1986 that anything Nathan-Turner did was rubbish.) This is, in many ways, Levine's *modus operandi*, and it's a fair part of why he comes in for so much criticism—he's reliably among the first on the scene when there's some visible glory to be snatched, he has an astonishingly bad track record in picking what horses to back, and he's ruthlessly swift with blame-shifting once it becomes obvious that he's involved in a turkey.

As I noted earlier, there is perhaps no fact more revealing about Ian Levine than that he seeks to take the credit for *Attack of the Cybermen*. It is, after all, something of a rarity—the only other thing he actively takes a lion's share of the credit for is missing episode recovery, and there his contributions have pretty conclusively been shown to be overstated. He did indeed find a few, but fewer than he says, and his self-proclaimed role in stopping the junking ignores the tremendous role that Sue Malden played. This isn't to say, as some people attempt to, that he was uninvolved—he had some real contributions—but the legend exceeds the reality. Richard Moleworth's definitive *Wiped* suggests that the number of episodes Levine both actually discovered and returned promptly to the BBC instead of sitting on them for several years is six. Levine did serve as a clearinghouse—the people who did find the episodes often went through him in returning them to the BBC—but his actual find count numbers six. This is still a lot, but it's considerably less than he claims, and certainly not the largest haul anyone has ever had. More troubling is the fact that in several cases Levine sat on missing episodes for some time before returning them to the BBC. Ostensibly this is because of collectors who had missing episodes but would only trade them for other missing episodes instead of selling them. The problem with this assertion is straightforward: no episode has ever been recovered in that manner. Indeed, the only person who has ever been confirmed to have deliberately sat on a missing episode instead of returning it to the BBC is Ian Levine.

It is, of course, a mistake to suggest that Levine is purely or even primarily responsible for the series' continuity fetishism from Seasons Nineteen through Twenty-Two. But equally, the fact that Levine is actually eager to take the credit for *Attack of the Cybermen* points to the fact that he is as strong an advocate for such an approach as exists. Certainly all records of what suggestions he made over the course of his unofficial tenure as continuity advisor indicate this. And this gets at the heart of where Ian Levine, to my mind, starts to acquire some active blame for the series' cancellation. Because he believed the primary audience of Doctor Who to be Doctor Who fans, and at a key moment in the course of the suspension the production team, Ian Levine was used as their mouthpiece, doubling down on that view catastrophically.

Before any further discussion of the suspension crisis, however, it's necessary to try to square away exactly what happened. On February 27th, 1985, it was announced that Doctor Who would not be coming back for eighteen months after Season Twenty-Two. Central to any interpretation of what follows, however, is what we think this announcement actually meant. The conventional wisdom is that the eighteen-month delay was a front for an actual cancellation of the series. The reason this is widely believed, however, is deceptive: both Michael Grade and Ian Levine say it was, and since they're on polar opposite sides of this conflict everyone believes it.

It's undeniably the case that Doctor Who was not a popular program within the BBC at this point in time. For many reasons, that was why Nathan-Turner, a producer whom the BBC had little faith in overall, was put on it—and, more to the point, left on it. All the same, the announcement made was very clear that it was an eighteen-month break, not a cancellation. Is it possible, as both Levine and Grade imply, that this was a case of breaking the bad news into small chunks and that after eighteen months the show was still not going to come back? In theory, yes. But it's worth noting that Doctor Who wasn't the only show cancelled in this period. So far as I can tell, *Crackerjack* and the other shows cancelled around this time were not announced as delayed—they were cancelled outright. So the very fact that Doctor Who's suspension was announced as a delay suggests strongly that it was, in fact, a delay all along. To think otherwise is to assume that the BBC was capable of long-term conspiracy. Put simply, there's very little evidence they were that composed or competent at doing such things other than ignoring serial rapists in 1985. More to the point, it's just a strange tactic to try. Grade may have wanted to cancel it outright, but he very clearly didn't do it.

This raises the question of why Levine and Grade, who are otherwise proponents of seemingly irreconcilable positions, both insist that the show was really cancelled. The answer is much like the answer every other time, in the course of looking at history in this blog, we've found a fundamental alliance between two seemingly diametrically opposed positions: that there's another alternative position that both sides want erased. Because there's one tacit point of agreement between Levine and Grade, which is that Doctor Who was primarily for fans.

It's obvious enough why this position suits Levine, but one might fairly ask why it suited Grade. The answer is simple: Grade needed a pantomime villain to position his broader reforms of the BBC against, and Doctor Who fans were an easy target. Grade's mandate was to make the BBC more like a commercial broadcaster and less like the public service broadcaster it was. This is an unsurprising position to come upon in the height of the Thatcher years, where the idea of a public service broadcaster—particularly one that stubbornly refused to just be a mouthpiece for the government—was anathema. (And indeed, these days Grade is a Tory peer.) It was tremendously convenient for Grade to be able to position himself in opposition to a group as visibly pathetic as Doctor Who fans. Doctor Who was, after all, easily mocked. So Grade had a show he could rail against the production values of and have everyone acknowledge that he was right, then make a joke about how a small number of people stayed up all night in their parents' basement writing letters to complain, hitting a known stereotype of Doctor Who fans. And then poof: he's saving the BBC for the masses from the clutches of some entitled man-children. How very convenient. And this is what people should hate Michael Grade for—not for cancelling Doctor Who, but for using its fans as his own private Arthur Scargill.

But we know that, by all appearances, he didn't really want to cancel the show outright. Or, at least, he didn't try to cancel it outright in 1985. Which leaves us with the uncomfortable implication that it was the Levine-fronted fan campaign to save Doctor Who that gave Grade the opportunity he needed to make Doctor Who into his punching bag of choice. And here we begin to approach the erased alternative to what actually happened.

It is worth noting that there was, in fact, a massive wave of popular attention directed towards Doctor Who during the suspension crisis, with both *The Sun* and *The Daily Star* running "save Doctor Who" campaigns. The former is explicable enough—they were fed an almost certainly fictitious line about how the BBC was trying to bluff the government into giving them money and jumped on it as part of their standing hostility to the BBC. (Grade's politics make this unlikely, as noted.) But *The Daily Star* is not a particularly political paper, and even *The Sun*, for all its overt political agenda, won't touch something without a strong populist angle. That both would launch "save Doctor Who" campaigns, in other words, suggests that Doctor Who was still beloved by a wider public.

This is the position, of course, that's excluded from both Ian Levine and Michael Grade's account. Levine is so utterly obsessed with Doctor Who's cult fandom aspects that he genuinely doesn't seem to care about a mass audience. And this is why *Attack of the Cybermen*, though not even the worst story of its season, is nevertheless its easiest target—it's the one that doesn't even pretend that there's a reason to watch the show other than a Whoniverse fetish. And this is what's staggeringly absent from all of Levine's defenses of the program in 1985 and 1986—the actual defences of the program. Levine takes it almost completely for granted that Doctor Who is fantastic and wonderful, and just lays into the BBC for not appreciating its splendor. When, in truth, there were clearly a large number of people who wanted to like Doctor Who but who were, at this precise historical moment, failing to actually do so.

The issue here, and it's a big one, is that Doctor Who was never a cult show in the UK before 1985. It had its embarrassing fans, sure, but it was mainstream entertainment. Even in 1985 there's an odd tension between its return to Saturdays (its supposed "proper" timeslot, and one targeted at a family audience) and its descent even further into the cult-TV rabbit hole of the Whoniverse. Even in the US—where it actually was an obscure cult show—it didn't work like a traditional piece of cult science fiction. Certainly it was never the show Ian Levine wanted it to be, and the good will of the public that had sustained it for twenty-two years had nothing to do with any of the things Ian Levine liked about the program. In this regard Levine was the exact wrong face for the public campaign to save the series simply because the series he loved wasn't one the public wanted saved. If they had, they'd have watched it. They didn't, and the ratings showed that.

And this isn't, to be clear, a swipe at fans. Clearly Doctor Who had plenty of fans in the 1980s who knew what the public loved about the series. You can tell because, well, they're writing the show now, and the public loves it. Ian Levine was no more representative of fandom than he was of the general public. Levine represented a particular pathology, not fandom. And that position—that willful blindness to the quality of the show—is what set him up for the epic pratfall that was his public defense of it.

In this regard, it can't be ignored that the press campaign spearheaded by Levine was done with the explicit approval of Nathan-Turner, who, for reasons of obvious propriety, couldn't blast his bosses in the press personally. But equally, this reveals the show's "save Doctor Who" campaign for what it was—a "save John Nathan-Turner's reputation" campaign that adamantly denied that the series had gone off the rails in the first place. And what's tragic is that all of this was avoidable. It's not just Levine's failure, nor even just the production staff's—Jonathan Powell has been open about how there was no institutional will to reinvent Doctor Who.

But for that matter, its not all that clear that in late February of 1985 there was a sense in the BBC that Doctor Who needed a reinvention. Again we come back to the seeming fact that the suspension was never supposed to be that permanent. Yes, it was a vote of no confidence in the production team, but it clearly wasn't a full one or else there would have been an alternative in place. In reality it looks like budgets were tight for that year and so they took some long-running programs off the air to free up money for other things. (We'll talk about those other things in eventually, but it's worth noting that 1985/86 was a phenomenally good period for BBC dramas.) They always intended to put the program back, and accepted, broadly speaking, that it was going to be a program they thought was crap but that other people seemed to like. It was just a program they didn't care enough about to keep on the air when they were short on cash. And in this regard, going ballistic at the BBC over it forced the BBC's hand. At that point they had to defend their actions, and between the program's low quality and the gigantic bullseye Ian Levine was painting on his back, well, the defense of the BBC's actions wasn't hard—they blamed the low quality of the series.

Which brings us to "Doctor In Distress," Ian Levine's charity single to save Doctor Who. That the song and lyrics are appallingly bad has been pointed out enough that I have no need or reason to join the pile. Less often noted, but still significant, is that the song is yet another example of a too-perfect metaphor. Here are a bunch of pathetic C-list celebrities singing a terrible song about how good Doctor Who is. The result is confirmation of how bad Doctor Who is—so bad that it inspires crap like this from people like this.

But there's a larger and more interesting problem. Let's, for the moment, take "Doctor In Distress" seriously, if only because nobody else ever has. Inasmuch as the song forms an argument for the series' existence, what is the argument? Let's look at the first verse: "It was a cold wet night in November twenty-two years ago / It was a police box in a junkyard—we didn't know where it would go / An old man took two teachers into time and space / It started off a legend that no other could replace." What is telling here is that it is the legend, it seems, that is irreplaceable, not the show itself. This is reflected in the chorus—it is the Doctor who is in distress and whose SOS is being answered. Not the show that actually appears on people's physical television sets, but the imaginary person who is its main character. Similarly, the lines, "If we stop his travels, he'll be in a mess / The galaxy will fall to evil once more / With nightmarish monsters fighting a war," are puzzling in that they seem to suggest that the biggest danger of Doctor Who's cancellation is that imaginary species will run riot without him, as opposed to, say, that people who enjoy Doctor Who will be disappointed or that a British institution will be gone.

Indeed, what is strangest about the song is that the Doctor himself is curiously absent from it. The only point where he's described is in the line, "We learned to accept six Doctors with companions at their side," as if we've finished the Kübler-Ross stages of grief. (Which, given the Colin Baker era, is actually almost completely apropos.) The companions fare little better, with the line, "Each screaming girl just hoped that a Yeti wouldn't shoot her," suggesting an almost total extraneousness to a show that is really about monsters. And let's be more explicit—specifically about recurring monsters. The lyrics don't focus on bits of the show that are well-remembered by the public (or else Autons and maggots would appear) but on bits that have appeared multiple times. Indeed, the monster chosen for the line is the Yeti, who hadn't appeared in nearly twenty years apart from the recent 20th Anniversary special.

All of this bespeaks a larger hubris implicit in the song. It's overtly modeled the likes of "Do They Know It's Christmas" (released a few months earlier) and "We Are the World" (released a week earlier). But, well, "Do They Know It's Christmas" and "We Are The World" are about famine in Africa. There's something phenomenally, jaw-droppingly wrong about appropriating a format created to fight famine in Africa for the purposes of bitching that you have to wait eighteen months for the next episode of your favorite sci-fi show. And this blindness mirrors itself uncannily in the lyrics themselves—most obviously when the line "That police box takes him everywhere" is followed by "Oh! Bring him back!" in a way that oddly implies that the basic and expansive premise of Doctor Who—the ability of it to do anything—is antithetical to what its fans want, for if we treat Doctor Who over Season Twenty-Two as having gone through an exorcism, "Doctor In Distress" is the absurd moment when fandom looks at all of the putrescent material that the season exposed and shouts, "Yes! That's what we love! Bring it back, don't hesitate!" only to discover that the entire world is staring at them in abject pity. The song is, in the end, a monument to nothing more than fan privilege in such a distended and warped form that the very thing that it ostensibly calls for is excised.

And in all of this, it's difficult not to see the fan-industrial complex, and by extension Levine, as very much to blame. Because let's face it—*The Daily Star*, if not *The Sun*, were going to pick this one up either way. *The Sun* had fought to save K-9 only five years earlier. But had the campaign not been the one we had, with offensive charity singles and photographs of angry-looking men smashing televisions, it's easy to imagine a wave of populist pressure to reinvent Doctor Who instead of preserve it. Hints of it existed at the time. Jon Pertwee, for instance, went hilariously off-message in suggesting that they bring back past Doctors for a season each. Though this would probably have been disastrous, it again gets at the fact that there were other angles to take—that people wanted Doctor Who, they just didn't want John Nathan-Turner and Eric Saward's Doctor Who. The idea that they wanted Barry Letts's Doctor Who again in 1985 was ludicrous and self-serving, sure. But had fandom not been so blinded by the fan-industrial complex and the dishy access to their idols it granted them, one can easily imagine a fan response to the suspension that was based not on, "Bring it back now we won't take less," but on, "Can we please have a worthy program again with some proper writers?"

Instead we got the John Nathan-Turner Legacy Preservation Campaign. And by the time Levine stopped being a loyal attack dog and leaked the cut in episodes ordered for the return, an incident that seems to mark more or less where he and Nathan-Turner stopped getting on, the damage was irrevocable. Michael Grade had a convenient enemy, John Nathan-Turner had ensured his job and that he could just carry on as he had been, and we were all set for the disastrous reinvention that wasn't: *Trial of a Time Lord*. It would take just a year more for the show to begin its turnaround, and by 1988, as we'll see, it got to where it was a show that the public could plausibly have embraced. But by then it was too late. Public outrage had been squandered on defending the desiccated corpse of the series left at the end of Season Twenty-Two. The show was, as of April of 1985, finally and completely doomed.

## Apportioning the Blame

Loads of people have been blamed for Doctor Who's cancellation. This raises the obvious question, "Whose fault was it actually?" My position is that the show was doomed as of the hiatus crisis, with the final four seasons barely living on borrowed time. Which means that this is the period to look for people to blame. Here, then, is a rigorous and precise apportionment of the blame as divided among the major figures, listed below in alphabetical order.

### Colin Baker

An unpopular choice these days, and understandably. If nothing else, nobody can plausibly criticize Colin Baker's love of the show, commitment to fandom, or his enthusiasm for the part. In many ways, the fact that everything should have gone so abysmally wrong for Baker when the part was such a dream role for him is one of the saddest aspects of this story. And, as many people have pointed out, Baker opposed many of the most damning decisions (the coat, most obviously).

But however likeable Colin Baker is, his performance as the Doctor is fundamentally limited. As an actor, he is long on bluster and bravado and short on nuance. This amounts to a decision to move from the things that were compelling about the Fifth Doctor—the understated, intelligent performances—and revert to the things that were most frustrating about the Fourth. Except that Colin Baker does not have the preposterously magnetic charisma of Tom Baker, and can't actually anchor the show in the way Tom Baker did.

Even in the much-vaunted Big Finish era, where he distinguishes himself from the other Doctors by dint of actually reading the scripts before showing up in the recording booth, his basic limitations as an actor are visible: he doesn't have a lot of tools other than getting louder. His comic timing is strong, but that's not enough to make the role work.

But while he was the wrong actor for the role, he didn't cast himself, and he could hardly have been expected to turn such a role down. The fact that he just isn't much fun to watch as the Doctor is a problem, but he seems to have done the best he could with the hand he was dealt, and that counts for something. All told, he's 8% responsible for Doctor Who's cancellation.

## Michael Grade

The bogeyman, to be sure, and a popular figure of villainy, but his reputation has improved over the last few years. Russell T. Davies writes glowingly about him in *The Writer's Tale*, praising his strong sense of what makes good television. Past that, the decision to pull the plug for a bit and retool following Season Twenty-Two was a strong one. The Colin Baker era was giving every sign of being a rapidly crashing ship. Pulling the plug early on was an excellent call; had it been followed by sacking the production team and retooling the show, it might well have avoided cancellation entirely.

The thing is, not doing that wasn't his fault, as we'll see. No, Grade's prominence as someone to blame comes more from the degree to which he used the compromise to promote himself as a bold reformer. The use of Doctor Who fans for that was ugly, and it's hard to blame anyone resenting it who was around for that. All the same, Grade is notable as the only person on this list who you can plausibly argue made no bad decisions anywhere in the course of events. In the end, he's more of a scapegoat than a villain, and as such he's strictly 3% responsible for Doctor Who's cancellation.

## Ian Levine

Easily the person on this list with the most individual things for which he is blatantly at fault, as the last essay shows. But for all of this, the things he did that were stupid mostly aren't ones with obviously large consequences. As awful as "Doctor in Distress" was, it was also such a massive failure that hardly anyone actually noticed it outside of fandom. The continuity porn was frustrating, but as the modern series has demonstrated, it's not fannishness itself that's a problem. And his worst actions, like staying silent about Gary Downie's repeated sexual assaults, had nothing to do with the cancellation.

The crux of the problem with blaming Levine is twofold. First, he simply didn't have the power or influence to do much damage. A show cannot be killed by an unofficial fan advisor. Second, one has to remember that Levine acquired the power he did in part because he was the most tolerable of the extreme Doctor Who fans at the time. Some of that was that he was rich, as opposed to because he was a pleasant human being, but the fact remains: Levine is the only person on this list whose replacement, we can basically be certain, would be just as bad, if not worse. Between that and his basic powerlessness, despite being the single most loathsome person on the list, it's just not fair to give him more than 6% of the blame.

## John Nathan-Turner

The big one. Obviously, there's no accounting that doesn't end up with a fair amount of blame being put on

John Nathan-Turner's shoulders. He was the person at whose desk the buck stopped for several of the worst and most damaging decisions. He cast Colin Baker, he decided to do *The Twin Dilemma* in the slot it went to, he designed the ill-advised laundry list stories that plagued this era, he vetoed dropping the Myrka, et cetera, et cetera. Which of these were actually destructive as opposed to embarrassing is hard to tell, sure.

But the point remains: clearly one of the big problems Doctor Who had through this period was that it just wasn't very good. And John Nathan-Turner was personally responsible for some of its worst aspects. There's no way to escape that when apportioning blame.

For all of this, though, it's important to remember that Nathan-Turner supervised two very good stretches of Doctor Who on either side of the one that destroyed the series. That doesn't magically make him blameless for what happened here, but it's important context. So is the fact that the series probably would have been cancelled a lot sooner than 1985 were it not for Nathan-Turner's work. Unlike other people on this list, it's possible to imagine circumstances where Nathan-Turner could have succeeded. It's just that those circumstances weren't in play, and instead he was in circumstances where he was much more likely to fail, and indeed, to some extent, where he'd been set up to fail.

But fail he did, to the extent of being 18% responsible for the cancellation of Doctor Who.

## Jonathan Powell

An odd figure for the list, in some ways—he appears in most of the histories of this period, but generally he comes off as Grade's servant, not a major creative figure in his own right. And yet interviews with him are very clear that he had strong and passionate views about the program in the mid-80s, namely that it was complete shit. Significantly, then, it's Powell, not Grade, who was actually on the front line in terms of implementing any changes to the program, and Powell who was thus responsible for the decision to leave Nathan-Turner and Saward on it. Similarly, it's Powell whose contradictory notes on *The Mysterious Planet* drove Holmes to distraction.

In Powell's telling, there were two real factors here. The first was his animosity towards John Nathan-Turner, who he viewed as not good enough. This may seem a strange reason to keep him employed, except for the second, which is that he didn't think Doctor Who could work on a BBC budget anyway; he viewed it as an embarrassment. As a result, Powell was unwilling to put a new producer on Doctor Who because it would have meant moving Nathan-Turner to another show. Similarly, Powell is open about the fact that he didn't really have any ideas on what to do with Doctor Who and didn't really care. Given this aggressive indifference from BBC management, coupled with the decision to put the show on hiatus, it's unsurprising that things went so wrong. Accordingly, he is 29% responsible for the cancellation of Doctor Who.

## Eric Saward

Which leaves Saward. Ultimately, it is difficult to construct any solid defense of Eric Saward's contributions to the series. Nathan-Turner's lack of focus on writing meant that he was heavily dependent on his script editors. When he had good ones he was able to produce impressive television in genuinely trying circumstances, as he did in Season Eighteen and Seasons Twenty-Four through Twenty-Six. When he had Eric Saward, the program collapsed.

Saward's limitations as a writer are largely the subject of the next few essays, and to be clear, he remains a sympathetic figure in spite of his flaws. But the truth is, he's a subpar writer with a poor sense of what Doctor Who could do as a program, as evidenced by the tendency in his own scripts to not actually give the Doctor anything to do. His contributions are not wall-to-wall disasters, but they're consistently flawed, and his alterations to other writers' scripts were often troublesome as well. He had little eye for a good writer, and little ability to keep good writers once he had them.

And in the end, Doctor Who has had other periods where it's endured BBC hostility and problematic production. In every case, it pulled through because of genuinely clever and interesting writing that grabbed people. It's a very writerly show, and under Eric Saward, the writing was bad. It's hardly a surprise that this was a big problem. Indeed, it's precisely 36% responsible for the show's cancellation.

### Time Can Be Rewritten: *The Song of Megaptera*

Among the many services Big Finish provides for Doctor Who at large is the helpful testing of various pieces of fanlore regarding unmade stories. There are, for instance, people who wonder whether *Prison in Space* would really have been as unbearably terrible as it sounds. (Yes, as we saw in the Troughton book.) But there is perhaps nowhere this service is more valuable than in the Saward era. One of the less resolvable debates surrounding the Saward era, and one that will play heavily into the next two essays as well, is the nature of the writers. Simply put, there's some solid evidence of some very good writers having scripts rejected during this period while people like Glen McCoy and Anthony Steven had scripts made. It's one thing when Pip and Jane Baker, two writers who are at least fast and reliable, get repeated commissions. It's quite another when they're actively commissioned over Christopher Bidmead and PJ Hammond, as, in Season Twenty-Three, they were.

Of what I'd consider the big three of baffling rejections—PJ Hammond's *Paradise Five*, Pat Mills's *Song of the Space Whale*, and the twin rejection of Christopher Priest's *Sealed Orders* and *The Enemy Within*—two (Hammond's and Mills's) have subsequently been recorded by Big Finish. Since the fan lore has Hammond's rejection being down to Nathan-Turner and not Saward, whose influence I am more interested in tracking at the moment, let's opt for Mills's script, now renamed *The*

*Song of Megaptera.*

For those who don't obsessively memorize every detail I cover in *TARDIS Eruditorum*, Mills and John Wagner (who was a co-author on earlier drafts of this script) co-created Judge Dredd with artist Carlos Ezquerra, and co-wrote the earliest *Doctor Who Weekly* comic strips. The *Song of Megaptera* was originally a story for a Tom Baker comic strip, but Mills was persuaded that it was too good for that and instead sent it to the production office where it was, at various times, considered for Tom Baker, Peter Davison, and, finally, Colin Baker before finally being abandoned. In discussing its scrapping, Pat Mills has stated that one of the reasons Saward gave for objecting to it was that Saward didn't like Mills's decision to portray the ship's captain as working class, preferring the idea of a classless future.

Let's get one thing out of the way first—in a litany of poor creative decisions that can be laid directly at Eric Saward's feet, making *Timelash* over this is one of the most inexcusable. It is flat-out inconceivable how any remotely sane or reasonable script editor could look at *Timelash* next to this script and conclude that *Timelash* was going to work better. *The Twin Dilemma* was an aggregate of brain-searingly bad decisions, but I'm not convinced that any given decision, and particularly any of Saward's decisions about *The Twin Dilemma*, was prima facie worse than this.

It is not that *Song of Megaptera* is a flawless story. Its flaws are relatively evident: it displays an almost Baker and Martin level of obsession with cramming in new ideas, and like Baker and Martin it fails to explore most of them in the depth they deserve. This is, to be fair, simply the way Pat Mills is as a writer—his *2000 AD* work displays the same hyperactivity, as do his Doctor Who comics. Unlike the comics (which combine this with an at times puerile machismo), however, this script feels altogether more suited to Doctor Who.

It's also an example of politics done well in Doctor Who. The five-year incubation of this project coincided with the heyday of the "Save the Whales" campaign, and the year after its final abandonment marked the decision to put a moratorium on whaling that is still in place. This story is unrepentantly and unambiguously an anti-whaling screed. I've admittedly always been in favor of overtly political Doctor Who, but if there's been a season that's made that case for me more successfully than Season Twenty-Two it's tough to think of it—the three stories that have any reasonable claim to working are the three most political ones, and in each case their political edge is the thing that gives them any serious claim at quality.

But more than its politics, *The Song of Megaptera* has two things going for it that are significant. On the one hand, it wears its politics on its sleeve and builds outwards from them instead of building towards them. The question of whether or not the Doctor is going to oppose whaling is never seriously raised—of course the Doctor opposes it. This is refreshing. After all, a political story like this tends to telegraph its intentions early on, so holding off on having the Doctor's inevitable moral stand on the issue (in either direction—it's not impossible to imagine a story about defending a whaling vessel from ecoterrorists, after all) in favor of having that be the climax would have been dumb anyway.

But equally importantly, it does actually build from that. Yes, the story is anti-whaling, and yes, that's very blatant and up front. But because it takes that as a starting point it's actually able to go somewhere. The working class captain that Saward apparently didn't like is, in this regard, a fantastic character because one is able to understand why he's the way he is. Yes, he's the villain of the piece, but he's an utterly sympathetic villain. Because Mills is so up front about making whaling a loathsome practice, in other words, he's freed from the obligation to make anything else equally loathsome. There's no moustache-twirling villain in the piece. The captain is an over-aggressive Ahab because he's desperate both to prove himself and because he wants revenge on the company that he feels exploited him. The whaling practices take place not on anyone's overt command but out of a systemic failure of anyone to care about motives beyond profit. The sequences in which the Doctor impersonates an inspector making sure regulations are followed are fantastic largely because of the sheer banality of evil on display here and the way in which that banality makes for a far more nuanced game of manipulation than the basic "bad guys try to hide the plot from the Doctor." Instead it becomes a game of the villains trying to pull off a PR job on the Doctor, which is far more complex and involving.

The second thing the story does that's exceedingly satisfying is that it plays for willfully low stakes. For most of the story the dramatic tension hinges entirely on the survival of the space whale. Eventually there are a decent number of lives at stake, but we're still talking about hundreds of human lives and a herd of whales. This is an exceedingly small scale as far as Doctor Who goes—there's not even a planet at stake, and there's no iconic foe to artificially ratchet up the drama, either. The last time we played for such small stakes is the story that replaced this in Season Twenty, *Mawdryn Undead*, and even there we had the vast cosmic power of the Black Guardian lurking around in the B-plot. But on the whole this is refreshing—a reminder that Doctor Who's power comes in part from its ability to change scale and focus from week to week. When every single story is about massive danger that imperils the entire planet/galaxy/universe/species, well, frankly it gets a bit overwhelming. A story where what's at stake is "a whale" is nice simply because it's a reminder that Doctor Who can do more than cosmic angst. There are failings—the fungus monster who's also a stand-in for indigenous people who practice whaling is unfortunately under-explored in a way that's troublingly xenophobic. But on the whole this is a script with its heart in the right place that's trying to make the program do interesting things, and that constantly pushes to make sure there are exciting things happening in the story.

So why the hell was *Timelash* made and this rejected? We can posit personal and psychological reasons—and soon we will—but for now let's stick with aesthetic reasons.

It could simply be that the 2010 version of this is better than the 1985 version was. In the interviews at the end of the story Mills talks about changing scenes to work better on audio, and one of the highlights of the story (Peri's delirious ramblings when infected with the fungus) is one he specifically mentions adding. Perhaps this just wasn't that good a story back in 1985. Or perhaps nobody had the heart to point out that a giant whale is difficult to do on a BBC budget. At least some allowance has to be made for the fact that this is not the 1985 script but a polished 2010 adaptation.

It could also be stylistic. There is something odd about Mills's hyperactive approach. I'm more inclined to file it as an authorial idiosyncrasy than as a failing, but it would have stuck out like a sore thumb. Perhaps Saward favored the logorrhea of the Bakers or the lack of any distinguishing style or characteristics whatsoever of Glenn McCoy to this. There is something markedly different about this script compared to anything else from the time. That basic fact is, in some sense, a reason for rejection, even if the difference is that this script is actually good.

But I think the real issue is likely something very close to what Mills has said all along. The Saward era, even in Season Twenty-Two, was never fond of politics. Take *Vengeance on Varos* out of the mix and Season Twenty-Two becomes marginally more political than what had come before, but we're still basically left with Robert Holmes as the only solidly political writer of the bunch, with Saward himself poking at it (very) lightly in *Revelation of the Daleks*. Yes, it's impossible not to read *Mark of the Rani* as having political implications, but it takes pains to avoid having to make the connection directly or, more to the point, to avoid having anything to do with the material world. And Philip Martin recalls being warned off of politics rather angrily by Nathan-Turner prior to writing *Vengeance on Varos*. A script this political was out of step with the rest of the era.

A few essays from now we'll deal with the television

program that most flagrantly showed how foolish this approach was, but even here it's safe to say that it's a problem. As I noted, almost everything good about Season Twenty-Two came from its eagerness to engage more with the material world, a world so dominated by material politics that any piece of science fiction that turns away from it is at least somewhat problematic. This is where my long-standing opposition to escapism as an aesthetic goal becomes clearest. Escapism tacitly abandons changing the status quo in favor of purely imaginary pleasures. Whereas what the culture needed in 1985 was material change—a clear vision of something other than a Thatcherite hell. There is, I think, a direct line from the sociopathy of escapism to appropriating the methods of famine relief for complaining that you have to wait eighteen months for your favorite television program.

But at the end of the day, the why matters less in terms of understanding the program in this era than the basic fact that one of the central defenses of the program in this era—that better writers weren't available—just isn't true. Good scripts by proven writers were rejected while the litany of debacles goes on. There's an alternate Davison and Baker era where the stories that do work are accompanied not by *Arc of Infinity*, *Warriors of the Deep*, and *Timelash* but by stories from Pat Mills, Christopher Priest, PJ Hammond, and more scripts by Bidmead, Gallagher, Clegg, and Bailey. And if *The Song of Megaptera* is any indication, those scripts would have been better. For all the defenses we can mount of this era, it's difficult to ignore the fact that there were better alternatives right under the production team's noses and they hadn't the sense to use them.

## Time Can Be Rewritten: *The Nightmare Fair*

Once upon a time, I had a blog that was just starting to get some attention. And I came upon a story that, well, kinda sucked. And the thing is, it was a story that had a surprisingly good reputation, but the story itself was really, really rubbish. Plus there were some really uncomfortable racial elements to it, and it was the second story in a row to have those, and I wrote an entry that tore the story to shreds. And I was getting a nice build-up going writing it, so I went for broke in the conclusion and suggested that the story should be exiled from the canon on the grounds that it's racist and terrible.

So, funny thing, it turns out that if, right when people are just starting to take notice of your blog, you viciously slaughter a mildly sacred cow, this rapidly becomes one of the things you're best known for. It's not actually one of my most read posts, which I'm fine with, but to this day if I see a link in my referral logs from something I haven't heard about before and I click through, it still often turns out to be a link to that post.

And I stand by it. It is unmistakably the case that *The Celestial Toymaker* (or, really, the combination of that and *The Daleks' Masterplan* three entries earlier) is where my blog made itself. Because apparently nobody had really made the observation that *The Celestial Toymaker* was a piece of racist crap. If you want to read about it, it's back in the Hartnell book.

In any case, given this, you can imagine that it was somewhat comforting to open up Graham Williams's *The Nightmare Fair* and discover that someone actually had noticed this problem before I did. After referring to the Toymaker as a Mandarin for quite a bit, at about the halfway point of the book Williams drops all pretense and just becomes a wonderfully snarky jerk about the fact that watching Michael Gough pretend to be Asian is kind of horrifying. My favorite bit, for what it's worth, is, "Stefan carefully tore off the printed sheet and made his way towards the Mandarin, who was standing, listening attentively to a technician in a white coat who looked distinctly as though he had the better right to the eastern style wardrobe the Mandarin favoured." Oh snap, as they say.

This concludes the race and racism portion of our program. I don't think the Toymaker should have been brought back, but he was, or at least, was going to be. Given that, I'm at least pleased that his return openly acknowledged the most searing flaws of the original. And, more than that, it seems to attempt to address the more fundamental problems of the story, namely that there was nothing resembling a plot or a concept beyond "Michael Gough makes people play inane games." A problem that Graham Williams, who may have been many things, but who understood the basic standards of entertainment, would have noticed with the surviving episode immediately.

Actually, let's look at the basic phenomenon here. We'll talk about the oddness of Graham Williams being brought back in 1985 next essay (or, at least, about a closely related topic), but let's look more broadly at the fact that this marks the second reversal of John Nathan-Turner's rule against commissioning writers from before his time. The first, Robert Holmes, was largely down to Eric Saward's staunch advocacy of him, but it's difficult to imagine either Saward or Nathan-Turner demonstrating a deep and abiding love for Graham Williams's work.

It's telling to look at the planned scripts for Season

Twenty-Three as a whole. Four of them featured clear returns of past story elements, but one of these—*Mission to Magnus*—was at least partially Philip Martin reusing his own idea. The other three—*The Nightmare Fair, Yellow Fever and How to Cure It,* and *Gallifrey*—featured ideas created prior to Nathan-Turner's time. One (the certain-to-be-renamed *Yellow Fever and How to Cure It*) featured a writer revamping his own concept, but Holmes writing Autons fifteen years after *Terror of the Autons* in a story that also had the Master and the Rani in it is clearly another example of the kitchen sink script that he dealt with in Season Twenty-Two. The Bakers doing the Time Lords with *Gallifrey* is odder, but that script, from what is known about it, looked set to heavily revamp the basic concept of the Time Lords. Which means, in other words, that the two kitchen sink scripts in which a pile of pre-selected elements had to be cobbled together into a story were both given to extremely experienced Doctor Who writers.

This marks a change from past policy, when kitchen sink scripts were generally handed over to relatively new writers like Saward, Grimwade, or Byrne, the exception, obviously, being *The Two Doctors*. Given how poorly many of the past kitchen sink scripts worked, the decision to use writers well versed in Doctor Who was eminently sensible, and it marks a real improvement from how things were done in past seasons.

Ironically, though, the turn towards an older and more experienced writer meant that the resulting story was less connected with the original source material than the kitchen sink scripts of past had been. This is not to say that any of the kitchen sink scripts of the past had been wholly faithful, but *The Nightmare Fair* is much more of an overt reboot of the Toymaker concept than, say, *Arc of Infinity* was of Omega. There is, as I said, a clear sense that Graham Williams looked at *The Celestial Toymaker*, saw that it was nowhere near as good as people said, and began stripping the concept down until he found something that would work and went from there.

His resulting idea—Doctor Who does *Tron*—was timely, and the absence of an overt video game/computers story in the mid-80s is a strange gap for Doctor Who given that everything similar in the 80s did at least one, if not more. Williams doesn't necessarily have a huge number of new takes on it, but his ultimate resolution whereby the solitary nature of the lone video game protagonist fighting off waves of monsters parallels the Toymaker's isolation is genuinely clever.

The structure of the book also suggests a level of mastery over the forty-five minute episode that vexed so many of the Season Twenty-Two writers. The first half's insane evil carnival satisfies the "set in Blackpool" requirement of the checklist Williams was handed, while the second half contains the video game stuff and the actual plot. It's welcome in part because it keeps Williams from dealing with video games for long enough to have time to make any of the endearingly embarrassing mistakes that characterized the subgenre of "mid-80s video game/computers episode." Instead there are two distinct concepts, both of which are right up Doctor Who's alley, and neither of which are set to outstay their welcome. And with the location filming in Blackpool ready to make the nightmare carnival stuff relatively easy to do on a Doctor Who budget, there's a real chance that this could have been done well.

It's not, to be clear, revolutionary or brilliant Doctor Who. But the last piece of relatively straightforward Doctor Who to work well was *Frontios*, and even that aggressively broke the rules in places. The one thing that Doctor Who has been occasionally getting right lately is breaking radically from tradition and reconceptualizing what the show is. So to see that there was a real chance of Season Twenty-Three opening with what would have felt like good, solid, classic Doctor Who is heartening. And note that one of the big problems of last essay is alleviated here as well. This may not be an overtly political story, but the use of video games as a primary point of reference at least makes it directly relevant to 1986 in a real and cultural sense. This is Doctor Who that's about the viewer's world again.

The biggest problem, frankly, is the presence of the Toymaker. And not because of the racial issues, but just because, much like *Arc of Infinity*, the story clearly assumes that the audience is going to automatically care that this character from the past is there. Williams has necessarily had to reimagine large swaths of the Toymaker, giving him an origin story, establishing him on Earth, and changing what he does rather significantly. All of this is well and good, and the joke in which it turns out that the Toymaker hasn't been hanging around Earth to capture the Doctor, he's been doing it because he really likes Earth was, in particular, a delightful subversion of expectations.

But the point remains: what about this story would be made worse if it used a new villain? What's the argument against innovation here? Surely more of the audience is going to be perplexed as to why they're clearly expected to care about the Toymaker than is going to do so reflexively. And for all the reconceptualization it's notable that there isn't a scene in which the Toymaker is really well-justified as a threat. Not even his iconography works this time. Michael Gough in a Mandarin costume amidst a bunch of Victoriana was part of an overall aesthetic that was at least plausibly effective. Michael Gough in a Mandarin costume in Blackpool, on the other hand, has little to recommend it. It's just a guy in a funny costume acting menacing. The good ideas this story has—nightmarish carnivals and evil video games—are good ideas without an obscure villain from the 60s coming back.

And this gets at the real problem with this story as conceived. It demonstrates incremental improvement over Season Twenty-Two, yes. But incremental improvement in 1986 would surely have been too little too late. The decision to hire an experienced writer to handle the hellish continuity porn brief is sensible, but we're still left with a program more interested in servicing 1960s nostalgia than anything else.

We're still left with a program that's trying to polish the particulars of what it's doing in an era when the very center of the show was rotting.

It's unfair to expect the aborted Season Twenty-Three to be a radical reconceptualization of the show—incremental change is all that Nathan-Turner would have plausibly wanted to pursue. But equally, it's clear that something substantial was necessary and its absence implicitly justifies the need to put the series on hold. In the end, it's tough to miss these stories. That there were three stories planned that were bringing back concepts that hadn't been seen in over a decade is difficult to get excited about even if the writers were better. What we have here is mostly an argument for Graham Williams's skill—he makes something that works despite the nightmare assignment.

It's also worth reflecting on the fact that this is a novel and not a television episode. The novel works, but at least some of that is the fact that Graham Williams has a light and witty prose style. It's an open question whether the direction, which sandbagged no shortage of stories in Season Twenty-Two, would have kept the story as lively as Williams's prose does. In the end, about the best one can muster for this story is that despite being misconceived in some fundamental ways it could have turned out quite well.

## You Were Expecting Someone Else: *Slipback*

With Doctor Who off the air for eighteen months, everyone involved was interested in finding a way to get some new Doctor Who out. And so they ended up doing a radio series of six ten-minute episodes written by Eric Saward. The eventual landing place for this series was as part of a BBC Radio 4 children's magazine show called *Pirate Radio 4*. Since he was writing for an overtly children's audience Saward, to his credit, recognized that his usual space marine action approach was a no-go. Accordingly, he imitated Douglas Adams.

Wait, what?

Let's not forget that one of the foundational myths of the Nathan-Turner era is that the show was irrevocably broken by the Graham Williams era and its "silliness." Eric Saward was among those who piled on, accusing the Williams era of insulting the audience. Now, suddenly, he's trying to mimic the approach of Williams's final script editor?

The problem is that between the time when that myth was laid down—1980 or so—and 1985, there'd been a necessary reevaluation of things. In 1980 Douglas Adams was a comedy writer who'd had decent success with his radio play *The Hitchhiker's Guide to the Galaxy*, with a novelization coming out towards the end of his time on the show. Accordingly, he could be dismissed as having made the show silly. But by 1985 he'd gotten to the fourth book in the *Hitchhiker's* trilogy and was a reliably best-selling author. Suddenly he was a major point of legitimacy for Doctor Who—someone the program wanted to boast about its association with instead of leaving behind.

But more than that, there is something odd about the spectacle of Eric Saward writing light comedy. I mean, he attempted dark comedy on a regular basis—there's a great moment in the infamous *Starburst* interview when, pressed on the idea that Doctor Who isn't funny anymore, he pointed out that *Vengeance on Varos*, *The Two Doctors*, and *Revelation of the Daleks* are all comedies. Which is a true statement, and also clearly not what anybody who was complaining about a lack of humor in Doctor Who meant. This, though, is the only real instance of him doing an extended piece of straightforward comedy in Doctor Who on his own initiative (as opposed to in the course of a salvage operation).

It's not very good, but it's not very good in the same ways that *The Visitation* is not very good—a case of the whole being markedly less than the sum of its recycled parts. Many, if not most, of the ideas are genuinely funny, but the story is in many ways wholly encapsulated by the drunk ditz computer, a funny idea that overstays its welcome by a considerable margin. Still, it's nowhere near as bad as its reputation. Doctor Who has always faltered when people attempt explicitly "for children" versions of it. This is no worse than *The Pescatons* before it or *The Infinite Quest* after it, if we're being honest. Indeed, it's probably better than either.

No, once again we have something where the biggest factor in its critical reception seems to be what era it's a part of as opposed to a judgment of quality as such. Which is not to mount a defense of *Slipback* so much as to note that as Eric Saward's weakest bit of Doctor Who writing by far it acquires all of the excess hatred of Eric Saward. But what's interesting about it is that it provides a good window into Eric Saward himself, a figure who has been much contested over the course of this book (which roughly covers the Saward era, after all).

The trouble with Saward, at least from a critic's perspective, is that he's not quite as bad as would be useful. I mean, obviously we all want to find someone to blame completely for the train wreck of the Colin Baker years and the squandered potential of the Davison years. Certainly he's responsible for a lot of it, but there are some problems with laying it all at his feet, the main one being that Saward isn't that bad a writer. Yes, all five of his stories come in for some sharp criticism in this book, but only one of them is an abject turkey, and it might have been written by Ian Levine. The faults of Saward are maddeningly hard to pin down. Even the most obvious—that he's more interested in the violence around the Doctor than in the Doctor himself—doesn't quite stick after *Revelation of the Daleks*, given that the violence around the Doctor is so interesting there. Still, it's difficult to ignore the fact that the program takes a dramatic downturn that coincides almost precisely with his tenure as script editor. So what, exactly, is the problem if not that Saward is a rubbish writer?

Back when Saward first arrived on the scene I suggested that even from the beginning his work was best understood as a weak imitation of Robert Holmes. Now, with *Slipback*, we have the same phenomenon with a different source writer: a weak imitation of Douglas Adams. We can add to that the weak Evelyn Waugh imitation in *Revelation of the Daleks*. All of this begins to shape up as a pattern gestured at from the start—Saward's taste exceeds his talent. He tries to write like good writers and can't quite pull it off.

Or perhaps more accurately, Saward's taste exceeds his confidence. If anything, I think Saward's work and tenure on the series tends to demonstrate a real anxiety about other writers. It's easy to observe that for all of his complaining about having to use writers like Pip and Jane Baker, or Glen McCoy, the good writers he had found tended to vanish after one or two stories. The Lost Stories line shows that rejected scripts by Bailey, Bidmead, and Clegg existed. He shows a similar aversion to importing well-known writers from elsewhere. We've seen how good *The Song of Megaptera* actually was, and Saward's behavior in and around the Christopher Priest debacle is easy to criticize. (*About Time* quotes a letter replying to a fan who asked why the show didn't use writers like Priest that says, "The names of writers you quoat are novalists. Infact one of them has attempted to write a Doctor Who script with disasterous results. That is why we don't use novalists." Priest received a formal apology for this, apparently.) Equally, he was quick to ally with Robert Holmes, and clearly had respect for Philip Martin, so it's not as though he only surrounded himself with hacks. But equally, any suggestion that the writers just weren't there in the Saward era—as was the big problem in the Williams era—is, as we've seen, nonsense.

I am loathe to take the psychoanalytic tack when dealing with writers, but it is difficult to ignore the sense of Saward as desperate to prove himself the equal of writers he admires, terrified of being outshone, and unable to escape his influences enough to distinguish himself. But in this regard Saward is not so much the scapegoat on which to pin the era's failures but rather a tragic figure. Let's consider, first of all, Eric Saward's television experience prior to writing *The Visitation*:

Well, that was a short list. OK, let's move on to his television experience prior to becoming script editor: *The Visitation*.

If ever there was a case of promoting someone too fast, this is surely it. Even Douglas Adams had a few miscellaneous television gigs over the years before he got the job. If we look at *The Visitation* as what it is—the first produced television script of a writer—it's got considerable potential. Yes, it's a Robert Holmes knock-off, but it's mostly capable and he's ripping off the right stuff. It's just that nothing about it screamed, "This is the man who should be in charge of shaping the writing of Doctor Who for the next five years." It may have screamed, "Take this writer under your wing and in three years you'll have a good writer," but that's not what Nathan-Turner did.

We've also talked about the sheer size of the task the program faced in this era. With the family audience it had catered to for twenty years evaporating and science fiction making massive leaps and bounds as the doors opened by *Star Wars* are casually walked through on a regular basis in cinema, to make Doctor Who interesting and exciting in the mid-80s was a real challenge. But it was also a potentially fruitful one—the period was a heyday of alternative culture of the sort that Doctor Who had thrived on in the late 60s and early 70s, and the politics were exactly the sort of divisive and contentious field that science fiction was made to comment on. Doctor Who needed someone who could work towards what the show was capable of while simultaneously navigating the structural problems facing the production.

So yeah, the untested writer at the start of his television career couldn't cut it on that big a stage. But, I mean, this is hardly surprising. It's worth asking whether a writer we've mostly praised— Terrance Dicks—could have cut it in the mid-80s. There's a moment on the "Trials and Tribulations" documentary where Ian Levine accuses John Nathan-Turner of deliberately avoiding older Doctor Who writers who, as he puts it, could write Doctor Who in their sleep. It's true, but surely, in the mid-80s, when Doctor Who needed nothing so much as bold new ideas, the last people you want to write it are ones who can do conventional Doctor Who reflexively. The other writer Levine mentions—Holmes—certainly could do Doctor Who in his sleep, but we know that because sometimes he did, and those stories sucked. But Dicks, much as I love his writing, is a solid source of extremely traditional straight-up Doctor Who yarns. None of his skills would have helped in 1985 either. He was, in many ways, as fortunate to work on the program in the early 1970s as Saward was unfortunate to be working on it in the early-to-mid 1980s.

To Saward's credit, then, he was at least the sort of person the program needed—a fresh face who wanted to try ambitious stuff. The problem was that he was paralyzed by the anxiety of influence. We'll look next time at what topnotch BBC drama in 1985/86 looked like, but it's not nearly as far from what Saward tries to do with the program as his critics would have you believe. It's just that, well, Saward isn't good enough to pull off what Dennis Potter or Troy Kennedy Martin can do, any more than he can pull off Robert Holmes and Douglas Adams.

Unfortunately, between his meltdown criticizing Nathan-Turner in the aftermath of *Trial of a Time Lord* and his being at the helm for the hiatus, Doctor Who marked the end of his television career. And the thing is, *Slipback* really suggests that this is maddeningly unfortunate. Because for all of its multitude faults and sins, the reality is that *Slipback* is, much like *The Visitation*, a merely half-bad Douglas Adams knockoff. Which suggests that Saward has both taste and versatility. And, let's be honest, no small measure of talent. What he never got the chance to develop was experience and style.

Because frankly, crap scripts are what writers do early on. Robert Holmes had to get *The Krotons* and *The Space Pirates* out of his system before he became the Robert Holmes we all know and love. Does anyone seriously believe that if he'd been put in as script editor after *The Krotons* and had to mastermind the Pertwee era it would have gone off without a hitch? People have rough starts when it comes to writing.

In the end, Saward had very, very good instincts on who to imitate and what to try to do. He didn't have the execution down early in his career, and he was put in far too high a position far too quickly, and, crucially, before he'd had a chance to develop his own style instead of attempting mimicry. It's easy to imagine an Eric Saward whose career was allowed to develop normally and who became quite a good television writer in the mid-to-late 80s. But that's an Eric Saward who wasn't wildly prematurely tapped for one of the hardest jobs in television.

Saward, in the end, tried the right things. Better writers than him would have floundered as well. Yes, Saward's failings were exceedingly bad for the show. But of the two of them, Saward fared the worse, and we ought give him no small measure of sympathy for it.

## Pop Between Realities, Home in Time for Tea: *Edge of Darkness* and *The Singing Detective*

The weakness of Doctor Who in 1985-86 would be one thing if it were a weak period for British television in general. Instead, however, two of the most acclaimed British television productions of all time aired during the Colin Baker era. The first, at the end of 1985, was *Edge of Darkness*. The second, airing at the tail end of *Trial of a Time Lord*, one day after each of the last four episodes and then for another two weeks after, was *The Singing Detective*.

For those not reflexively versed in the nuances of British television, *Edge of Darkness* is a conspiracy thriller written by the creator of *Z-Cars* and directed by Martin Campbell, who went on to be a serious director who did such high profile work as the Daniel Craig *Casino Royale* and, less satisfyingly, the recent *Green Lantern* film. If "*Edge of Darkness*" sounds vaguely familiar as a Mel Gibson film, I'm very sorry for you, as that's Martin Campbell remaking the series as a film a few years back and it's very much not good. The plot concerns a police detective whose daughter is gunned down in front of him and the conspiracy that unfolds as he investigates her death and discovers that she, not he, was the target.

*The Singing Detective*, on the other hand, is one of the two things that people point towards when picking the masterpiece of Dennis Potter, the consensus best writer in British television history. It stars Michael Gambon as a writer with a debilitating skin condition (one that Potter himself also suffered from) who drifts between his stay in the hospital, the detective novel he's writing in his head (in which Gambon also plays the lead, the eponymous singing detective), and memories from his childhood.

Both are very, very good. Less clear is whether they're meaningfully comparable with Doctor Who. They certainly have wildly higher production standards. Indeed, in the case of *The Singing Detective*, the production standards were actually too high—Dennis Potter had wanted the hospital scenes shot on video to look like a sitcom, but he was overruled and the whole thing was done on film. And this is not, to be clear, just a special effects thing. Television is a visual medium. We Doctor Who fans are used to overlooking bad effects, but in doing so we can be prone to blinding ourselves to just how much good direction can matter. (Consider the degree to which *Revelation of the Daleks* was salvaged by Graeme Harper. Even in the new series, directors matter to a great extent—consider how much the relatively pedestrian script of *The God Complex* is elevated by Nick Hurran's revelatory direction.) It's not just that *Edge of Darkness* and *The Singing Detective* look ritzier, it's that they're fundamentally better and more complexly shot pieces of television. Doctor Who didn't have the money to let directors cut loose the way they can in these shows, and as a result the show struggled to get directors as good as these—one of the few claims in the infamous Eric Saward *Starburst* interview I have no trouble believing. As a result, yes, of course these shows look far better than Doctor Who. The long tracking shots that pop up throughout the start of *Edge of Darkness*, for instance, are just something that Doctor Who couldn't do.

So on that level, at least, looking at Doctor Who next to two of the legends of British television is terribly unfair to Doctor Who. But that's never been the way in which Doctor Who has compared to the highlights of British drama. Look back to the Troughton era, when Doctor Who was succinctly and thoroughly outshone by *The Prisoner*. Doctor Who in the

1960s never had an episode that looked half as good as *The Prisoner* looked, even ignoring the color issue. But Doctor Who in the Troughton era had several stories where the writing stood toe-to-toe with *The Prisoner*. In many ways this is the default mode for Doctor Who—production values far below other shows, but writing and (at least much of the time) acting that goes beyond it.

The central example here remains *The Ark in Space*, which looks incredibly bad but is played with such utter conviction that it works. And it doesn't just work; it thrives, to the extent that its most visible faults become virtues. When done right, Doctor Who is actually more likable for its shoddy elements simply because of the determination to make good television despite the limitations that they put on display. Because *The Ark in Space* cannot simply be casually good in the "impeccably well-made" sense, the ways in which it is good are even more vivid. And at the heart of why *The Ark in Space* works is the fact that it was written by Robert Holmes, a writer who, as the clichéd observation goes, never quite got that he was actually one of the best writers at the BBC.

So in this regard we can compare *Edge of Darkness* and *The Singing Detective* to Doctor Who. Because even if Doctor Who was never going to look like either production, it could at least be written like them. I mean, OK, maybe not quite as good Dennis Potter, but Troy Kennedy Martin, though a very good writer, is firmly the sort of writer that Doctor Who, in order to work, needs to be in the same league as; if Doctor Who's writers aren't going to be quite as good as Dennis Potter, they can at least contend for the open spaces in the ranking immediately below him. And more to the point, they have to. Doctor Who has always relied on having genius writers, whether they be ones capable of mass acclaim or more troubled, oddball geniuses who need a show like Doctor Who to excel.

Of course, Season Twenty-Two had two writers who were at least plausibly up to such a standard: Robert Holmes and Philip Martin. And it's telling that *Vengeance on Varos* is the one script in Season Twenty-Two that possibly belongs on a list of truly great Doctor Who stories. (Holmes, on the other hand, is clearly in open rebellion against the show as conceived at this point.) But on the whole, Doctor Who is not only lacking in writers who threaten to break out into genius at any moment (and even at its best it has only had enough of those for one or two stories per season), it's lacking in writers who can noodle along confidently at a level just a bit below genius.

And in the case of *The Singing Detective* one can even suggest that Doctor Who is trying to aspire towards it. The central conceit of *The Singing Detective* is that it switches among three distinct narratives, using ambiguous gaps among the narratives to allow the strands to blur together. It's worth pointing out, then, that both *Vengeance on Varos* and *Revelation of the Daleks* were overtly playing with similar ideas. *The Singing Detective* took it further, yes, but it's absolutely the case that Doctor Who is in the same context as *The Singing Detective* from a writing perspective. And slightly popularized, smoothed-out takes on the avant-garde is, again, one of the basic functions Doctor Who exists to perform.

So let's look at *Edge of Darkness* and *The Singing Detective* and ask what good writing in 1985-86 looked like. For the most part the two shows are very, very different. *Edge of Darkness* is a relatively straightforward thriller. It doesn't use any massively complicated narrative tricks save for some ambiguity at times over whether or not the main character is really seeing his dead daughter's ghost or just going mad. What is perhaps most notable about it is that there's next to no effort to spend a lot of time on exposition; the world has its rules and largely gets on with the business of storytelling within it. It's not until the sixth episode that people really start getting into lengthy philosophical speeches with one another, with the themes being allowed to build on their own terms until then.

*The Singing Detective* is less straightforwardly a mystery, but it also shares this style of letting its world unfold for the audience. The normal term for this is, I suppose, "show don't tell," but there's more to it than that. What's interesting about how *The Singing Detective* and *Edge of Darkness* unfold isn't just that they avoid clumsy exposition for the most part, it's that they carefully control the audience's knowledge and expectations without ever having to resort substantively to telling instead of showing.

This is a key approach for *Edge of Darkness*, because at its heart *Edge of Darkness* is a mystery. Over time we're meant to figure out the conspiracy behind the death of Craven's daughter as well as the nature of the world *Edge of Darkness* is set in (which, Quatermass-like, is almost but not quite our world). So it very much just depicts the world it's set in, in an ostensibly straightforward manner. It's not actually nearly as straightforward as it appears, but it's a method of storytelling that shifts an enormous weight onto the audience.

This is, to be frank, something Doctor Who has not come close to doing at this point. The *Edge of Darkness* approach requires a tremendous amount of respect for the audience—something Doctor Who hasn't had in a long time. I mean, the show has tremendous, even excessive faith in the audience's ability to remember who the Sontarans are and to think they're very cool. But there's very little respect for the audience's ability to fill in gaps on their own or, more broadly, think. It very rarely just introduces things without lengthy exposition sequences or infodumps. And that's a kind of gruesomely demeaning assumption to make. In reality, one suspects the audience was more than capable of understanding the basic outline of science fiction worlds, especially after twenty-two years of Doctor Who and at this point nearly a decade of post-*Star Wars* culture. The fact is that Doctor Who displays a distressing lack of confidence in the ability of the audience to understand the worlds it depicts without exposition.

The other thing that *Edge of Darkness* and *The Singing Detective* do that Doctor Who never really does in this period is focus the drama on the experiences of the characters. In both series the most powerful moments are those in which we watch uncomfortably as Michael Gambon or Bob Peck suffer visibly. Most of the best moments of *Edge of Darkness*'s first episode are those in which we watch Peck portray Craven's grief at his daughter's death. The show resolutely refuses to speed through it, instead showing Craven's bereavement in aggressive detail. Similarly, much of the thrust of *The Singing Detective* is capturing Gambon's humiliation and agony at his condition. Even as we delve into his psyche and understand more and more of why he's the way he is, the series is at its most powerful when we see the raw misery of his illness and the way in which he's callously marginalized and mistreated for it.

This is something Doctor Who never really does. It doesn't take the time to show an extended treatment of a single character's experience. And this is a real weakness. One of the best and subtlest moments of *Vengeance on Varos* is when we find out that Peri secretly wants wings. But what's powerful is that this is the one moment where Peri starts to be more than "generic human female" as a companion and to acquire some character traits. But the fleeting nature of it just exposes the way in which thought of actual emotional experience is sidelined. So much of what was horrible about the strangulation scene in *The Twin Dilemma* is that no space was ever provided to see Peri's reaction to it or to allow the audience to empathize with her. Instead she forgave the Doctor readily and the incident was brushed under the rug. For her strangulation to have any chance of working, an extended treatment of Peri and her reactions was absolutely necessary.

Again, this isn't something totally foreign to Doctor Who—it did it as recently as *Kinda* with the extended focus on Tegan's dreamscape. But it's been largely and conspicuously absent—most obviously in the failure to have Nyssa or Tegan ever react to the Master in a meaningful sense. And, to look ahead, as awkward as some of the Ace sequences are in the latter part of the McCoy era, they are major improvements simply because they're instances of the show trying to focus extensively on imagining the experience of being in the worlds it depicts. (Actually, it's worth remarking in the general case on the influence of *Edge of Darkness* on the McCoy era. Andrew Cartmel infamously declared in his interview for the position of script editor that his ambitions for Doctor Who were to bring down the government. Given John Nathan-Turner's visible resistance to overtly political Doctor Who over the seasons immediately prior to hiring Andrew Cartmel, the fact that he then hired Cartmel after that interview seems surprising to say the least. But it is worth remembering that Nathan-Turner was always a savvy viewer of television. He'd have been well aware that the overtly political *Edge of Darkness* was by miles the most successful piece of science fiction on the BBC in half a decade. And the hiring of Cartmel goes, I think, hand-in-hand with that.)

In the end, then, it's all too clear, comparing top-notch British drama in 1985-86 to Doctor Who, that there were serious problems with the show. The problems the series suffered are not, much as one might suggest, that it's badly of its time. Rather, it's that the series was hopelessly out of touch with what worked at the time. The simple, damning fact is that Doctor Who sorely missed a trick in this period. It's not that it wasn't as good as two of the best series the BBC ever made. It's that it wasn't even trying to be.

## You Were Expecting Someone Else: The Steve Parkhouse Strips

Following Steve Moore's departure from the *Doctor Who Monthly* comic strip (covered last book), writing duties were turned over to Steve Parkhouse, who worked at first with Dave Gibbons and then with a variety of other writers, most notably John Ridgway for a run of strips in the Sixth Doctor era that are widely regarded as one of the highlights of Doctor Who comics.

These comics are an interesting moment. It's in many ways difficult to connect them to the show at the time, which is unsurprising, given the aggressive contempt Parkhouse had for the series, which he described as "juvenile entertainment, where almost-famous actors delivered third-rate lines whilst avoiding the wobbly scenery," and as "power hungry aliens versus an emotionally challenged and sexually inhibited hero." Much of this was that Parkhouse was displeased with television as a medium—he's said in interviews that "television is run by people who are visually illiterate. They think a disused quarry is a great set for a show because it's cheap and it's just down the road." In contrast, Parkhouse took an aggressively visual style with the strip, focusing on giving Ridgway interesting things to draw.

The result would, obviously, not have worked on television, where the pleasures of the quarry as an alien planet were based more on necessity than desire. Had Steve

Parkhouse tried to write "Voyager" (his most acclaimed story) for television, one doesn't imagine he'd have gotten much further than "EXT. VAST FROZEN WASTELAND—NIGHT," and if he somehow had, "an ice-covered tall ship rests among the frozen peaks" would surely have been the end. Similarly, when you're only dealing with a writer and an artist as creative personnel it's not exactly the same challenge to get them all on the same creative page as it is to get a bunch of designers, musicians, costumers and actors on the same page as the writer, script editor, director, and producer, not to mention under a BBC budget.

All the same, it's easy to see the appeal. "Voyager" is an absolutely gorgeous and lush story full of creepy and haunting images. (I'm usually skeptical of the colorization of black and white comics, but IDW's color version is truly beautiful.) There's a long-standing train of thought within Doctor Who where the Doctor is cast into hallucinatory or surreal realms, dating back at the very least to *The Celestial Toymaker* and, I would argue, all the way back to *The Edge of Destruction*. "Voyager" is one of the most successful applications of this.

Much of its success comes from excellent taste in what images to use. "Voyager" is, like all great comics, focused in part on making sure the artist has impressive things to draw. Parkhouse conceives of situations where Ridgway will get to juxtapose vast, surrealist landscapes with sprawling starscapes. It's a subtle thing, but everything in the story looks uncannily large by virtue of Ridgway's decision to clutter his skies with planets, distorting all sense of proportion and making images like a lighthouse in space not seem like a small, tiny object drifting through the void but rather a towering monolith at the center of things.

Parkhouse also has a strong sense of contrasts, using period objects like lighthouses, tall ships, and Leonardo da Vinci-style flying machines alongside giant robots and the vastness of space. The trick is good enough to fuel an entire aesthetic subculture: steampunk. This aesthetic, in turn, is reflected in the plot, with a story that moves smoothly from serious epic menace to broad comedy. Even the basic setup provides these strong contrasts—for all the epic sweep of the story, it's worth remembering that the Doctor's comic strip companion for this era is Frobisher, a shape-shifter who has semi-permanently adopted the guise of a penguin "for personal reasons."

Without any budgetary restrictions, then, "Voyager" is able to be a story that looks like the nightmarish dreamscape that a lot of people always wanted Doctor Who to be in. But even this was, to a great extent, lightning in a bottle. After an intervening sillier, lighter tale, Parkhouse took another shot at the dreamlike and epic with the two-part "Once Upon a Time Lord." But this time his imagery is just bits and pieces of children's literature and fantasy, and the story has none of the eerie frisson of "Voyager" (although its four-page Rupert the Bear pastiche is pure charm).

And this gets at why the comics fall just a few crucial inches short of actually working. The underlying fundamentals are all there, but they don't quite add up to anything. The villain—Astrolabus—is conceptually a tour de force, a renegade Time Lord from the distant past pursued by a force of nature, with the Doctor getting caught in the middle of their struggle. But like a Baker and Martin script, all the actual good parts of these ideas are elided. In the final strip of the Astrolabus saga it's suggested that Astrolabus knows he's in a comic and has been the author of the Doctor's stories. (It's telling that this is also Parkhouse's last Doctor Who script.) This is a phenomenal implication, but it's been almost absent for the preceding nine stories.

More broadly, there's the exact same set of pitfalls that plague the Saward years. The conflict between Voyager and Astrolabus is stunning, but there's not really room for the Doctor in that dyad. The result is that the Doctor, in an almost overtly Sawardian fashion, is stranded on the margins of his own story. It's a fascinating story, but it's not entirely clear that it's a fascinating Doctor Who story. Indeed, it feels like the story of the old man with the secrets of the stars tattooed on his body running from a force of nature that, instead of being submitted to *2000 AD*, is being run in lieu of an actual Doctor Who story.

There's also an annoying failure of impact. "Voyager" builds Astrolabus up as a truly epic threat in a large part because of his mysteriousness. But there's no payoff to the idea of an ancient Time Lord criminal. All of the potential of the concept remains potential. At heart, Astrolabus is just a generic creepy old man figure, and his compelling origin is little more than a skinning of the general case concept. Astrolabus ends up being a villain that is more interesting to think about than to see in action.

But the larger point is that there's no exploration beyond the profusion of cool images. Parkhouse is so focused on being visual in a way that television can't be that he doesn't really think about anything besides the visuals: there's very little to these strips behind the images. In the face of the wall-to-wall weirdness it's surprising to note that neither the Doctor nor his companion are providing any sort of grounding or cues on how the audience should be taking things. More broadly, it has to be said that even putting the audience in a position to be looking to a shapeshifting penguin for their cues on how to respond to a story is, if not an outright bad move, at least high-risk. The strips veer dangerously close to the point where the Doctor's value is simply that he provides a recognizable lead character. Not, to be clear, one that the reader can invest in or learn about the story from—just a recognizable one. (Indeed, it's not entirely clear that Parkhouse even bothered to do anything like watch the series to see how the lead character changed in the various recastings.)

In other words, it's easier to love the idea of these Parkhouse strips than the execution. They're not bad by any stretch of the imagination, but they're not unambiguous classics. So why are they such massively influential pieces that they have left me with so many readers I'm no doubt bitterly disappointing right now with my rather tepid reaction?

Part of it is timeliness. The mid-80s were a heyday of demented Narnias. We're right in the period of *Labyrinth*, *A Nightmare on Elm Street*, *The NeverEnding Story* (a film far more upsetting than it gets credit for being) or, perhaps most relevantly, *Return to Oz*, in which the respected editor and sound designer Walter Murch takes the beloved *Wizard of Oz* and makes a horrifically dark and creepy movie out of it that is widely cited as one of the scariest things ever seen by anyone fortunate enough to have seen it as a child. (It is probably the only children's movie to take heavy visual inspiration from the book *Wisconsin Death Trip*.) In other words, a proper nightmarish dreamscape is one of the big things missing from the mid-80s of Doctor Who, and frankly *The Ultimate Foe* doesn't cut it.

In many ways this ties up some themes of *TARDIS Eruditorum*. I've talked a lot about how the best children's media scars children for life. And in the early to mid-1970s, Doctor Who was exceedingly good at this. To some extent, for all its violence under Saward, one of the biggest flaws of mid-80s Doctor Who is that it rarely manages to present children with anything that's going to permanently damage them. This is, actually, one of the reasons why the Colin Baker era doesn't feel very children-friendly. It's not that it's too dark and violent, it's that it's not nearly screwed up enough. And that is painful in an era where dark fantasy children's movies were a boom genre. Especially because that's a period that should have benefitted Doctor Who tremendously given how much it plays to Doctor Who's strengths. The show never took advantage, and so instead we have the Parkhouse strips.

There's also more links to draw regarding the British comics scene at large. The Colin Baker era coincided with the period where British writers and artists were really starting to flood across to America in the so-called British Invasion of Comics. And a lot of the best stuff from that movement took a complex dark fantasy take—one that would quickly come to heavily influence Doctor Who, both in its last years on television and throughout the Virgin era. The Parkhouse strips share cultural DNA with *Swamp Thing* and *Doom Patrol*—indeed, around the same time Parkhouse was working as the artist on Alan Moore's *The Bojeffries Saga*. And these are things that feed back into Doctor Who readily, and that, Parkhouse's disdain aside, come out of Doctor Who as well. (Consider the career of Neil Gaiman, for instance.) So the Parkhouse strips are the one part of mid-80s Who that feels like it has any connection to that strand of history. It's an important strand and one that people have a reasonable emotional investment in the idea that Doctor Who is involved with, and due to this, despite their flaws, the Parkhouse strips are considered classics.

But in the end, all of this is just another way of saying that part of what makes the Parkhouse strips so good is how bad the rest of Doctor Who was in these years. Yeah, they were the best Doctor Who on offer in the Colin Baker years, but let's be honest, that's faint praise.

## Time Can Be Rewritten: *The Holy Terror*

One of the truisms about Colin Baker in the modern era is that he has been redeemed by audio, which is to say, by Big Finish. This is a complex claim that I will ultimately duck out of actually agreeing or disagreeing with, but it is certainly the case that there are a number of very good Big Finish stories featuring Colin Baker. *The Holy Terror* is not generally agreed to be the first; Jacqueline Rayner's *The Marian Conspiracy*, which introduces the triumphant and audio-exclusive companion Evelyn Smythe, is widely beloved. But it is one of the earliest ones—Baker's fourth solo audio for Big Finish, coming out just a bit more than a year after the line started. And it is, perhaps more importantly, a very, very good bit of Doctor Who.

This is not down to Colin Baker. He's great in it, but as with many of his television stories, he's fairly sidelined for most of the action, figuring out the plot in the third episode and explaining it to people in the fourth, but mostly tagging along as other characters talk urgently other than that. Nor is it down to Robert Jezek, who entertainingly brings Frobisher to life and has some wonderful comedic bits, but who is in no way the main draw. No, it's that *The Holy Terror* is the Doctor Who debut of Rob Shearman, a minor but vivid figure in its litany of great writers.

All of Shearman's Doctor Who pieces are of a kind; they have deep roots in theatre, and especially in the absurdist tradition, putting the Doctor in fundamentally absurd places, generally prisons created by the very person they're imprisoning. And *The Holy Terror*, being the first, serves in some ways as the archetype. The prison is a literal prison, the constructed reality is actually a virtual reality, thus literalizing the metafictional aspects. Even the theatricality is slightly more explicit, with the script owing obvious debts to *Who's Afraid of Virginia Woolf*.

It is, of course, also absolutely brilliant, because "Doctor Who does *Who's Afraid of Virginia Woolf*" is simply an incredible idea. And it's an especially incredible idea for a neo-Sawardian piece, since the absurdist and dark comic theatrical traditions that Shearman comes out of were always explicit parts of what Saward wanted to do. It's not just Saward's debt to Holmes—a debt Shearman shares and makes no effort to hide—but the sorts of things Saward himself is doing in *Revelation of the Daleks*, and, moreover, the sorts of things that Philip Martin is doing in *Vengeance on Varos*. More broadly, we might tag the constructed reality of *Castrovalva* and the sly theatricality of *Kinda* and *Snakedance* to suggest that Shearman, though clearly drawing on influences from across Doctor Who (there's a near-explicit nod to *The Mind Robber* for instance), really is more at home with the Saward era than any other spot in the series.

Which isn't actually something you usually say about a good Doctor Who writer. And the fact that it can be said is significant; another crucial line on the "the Saward era could have worked" side of the ledger. Or, at least, and this is probably the fairer reading, a reminder that whatever its failings, the Saward era was, in one of its major influences at least, plugged into a significant and worthy literary tradition. Especially because that tradition is one of the few places where you can really create a sense of continuity and progress over the course of Doctor Who's history for which the Saward era is not, in some form, a massive interruption.

Because there is a narrative that works here. Prior to the Saward era you had the Hinchcliffe and Williams eras, which each gave their own perspectives on the absurdity of bureaucracy and the idea of petty tyrants as a source of vast horror. After the Saward era you have the Cartmel era, with its blunt logic of "you know what would be great? Blowing up Thatcher." And in between you have the Saward era, an era more inclined than any other to construct its worlds out of the very logic of bureaucracy, creating exaggerated, mad places that the Doctor must expose the ugly madness at the heart of. Which is, for one thing, actually a pretty sensible place to be at the zenith of the Thatcher era. But for another, "let's imagine a world constructed according to the logic of petty bureaucrats" is a reasonably coherent stopping point between "bureaucrats are horrible" and "we should blow them up."

Moreover, it's a good setting for Colin Baker's Doctor, whose rougher edges are, if not sanded off by such settings, at least given useful context. His bluster and bombast, in many ways, require an outsized opposite force, and grotesque absurdity is one of the few that has any proven track record in standing up to the storm. When Baker's Doctor is pushed into a quiet mournfulness he becomes considerably more effective, and Shearman does an excellent job of that, creating circumstances gruesomely mad enough for Baker's Doctor to work.

Of course, Frobisher helps here as well, slotting into a wonderfully idiosyncratic companion role. The beleaguered way in which he responds to being made a god and the automatic and self-evidently doomed way in which he goes about trying to implement a liberal democracy is the funniest thing in an audio that is long on humor.

All of which said, there's something acutely bleak about *The Holy Terror*. It joins *Warriors of the Deep* and *Horror of Fang Rock* on the list of Doctor Who stories that feature a complete wipe-out of the supporting cast, a grim "everybody dies" finale that, along with the repeated phrase "are you my daddy" makes the story a cynical and inverted antecedent to *The Empty Child/The Doctor Dances*. But in many ways *The Holy*

*Terror* goes further than previous "everybody dies" stories by having there really never have been any plausible hope that the Doctor could do anything. The setting of *The Holy Terror* is one that makes its ending entirely inevitable—the only "real" character (although the story actively calls that distinction into question) is hopelessly insane and suicidal, and everyone else is caught up in the machinations of a despotic torture machine. All the Doctor is left to do at the end is plead for a different outcome, pleas which are, obviously, not granted.

But, of course, even this is just pushing some of the usual criticisms of Saward-era Doctor Who to their endpoints, such that the key fact isn't so much their existence as the fact that, within *The Holy Terror*, they work and work well. It's not even possible to argue that this is a dead end—a thing that could only work once—given that Shearman uses elements of this to great success on all of his other Big Finish stories, and then adapts one of those into one of the most acclaimed stories of the first season of the revived series.

It is possible, however, to argue that this doesn't work as a primary model. Shearman does incredible things with Doctor Who—things that work particularly well with Colin Baker's Doctor. But they work because they're one of a variety of things that Doctor Who can do, not because borderline-nihilistic pieces of absurdism are the natural form for the series. Baker's Doctor and, more broadly, Saward's vision of the program can be done spectacularly, yes. Hell, if you want to argue that they're done spectacularly in *Vengeance on Varos* or *Revelation of the Daleks*, I'm not even going to hold it against you, even as I'll politely suggest that "spectacularly" might be overstating the case.

But that's not the same thing as being a viable long-running television show.

## Time Can Be Rewritten: ...*ish*

...*ish* is one of those pieces that is desperate for you to recognize how clever it is, which would be irritating if it weren't so damned clever. Indeed, it's sufficiently clever that a disappointing number of reviewers seem to think that this is a lot of clever presentation wrapped around an overly simple story. This, however, involves an unfortunate confusion of plot with story. The plot is standard Doctor Who fare: an expedition to an alien planet inadvertently collects something evil. It escapes back among the humans and threatens to cause untold devastation. After uncovering malfeasance among the people who went on the expedition, the Doctor stops the evil thing and saves the day. As basic as they come, really.

The only tricky bit, really, is that the "something evil" is, in fact, a word, and that the nature of the threat is the complete collapse of all language and meaning. The word, referred to as the "ish," destroys meaning itself—as, of course, does the suffix. The threat is that the ish will be unleashed into the Omniverbum, which is essentially the Word of "In the beginning was the" fame.

This tricky bit causes the story to extend considerably beyond the straightforward plot. It also, however, enables a mass of cleverness, some of which is oft-noted and some of which is less so. The most obvious thing to observe is that this is a story that required Colin Baker's Doctor. One of the key characteristics of Baker's Doctor is a degree of pomposity. Unfortunately, as Tat Wood rather cuttingly observed in *About Time*, this tends to manifest such that Baker comes off as a dumb person's idea of what a smart person is like. Which is to say that the writers had an irritating tendency to write with the thesaurus open such that Baker's Doctor displays a certain… ludicrous logorrhea, as Pip and Jane Baker, the worst offenders in this regard, would no doubt have it.

So for Phil Pascoe's *…ish*, a story that is about words and language, there was really only one Doctor to choose. And the story is littered with bits of wordplay and what is less continuity porn than continuity erotica—a bevy of jokes that are both terribly obscure and utterly artful. (An impossibly large encyclopedia volume beginning with DAL, for instance. Or a Delphon joke.) There's also a rampant set of jokes referencing post-structuralist literary theory—several bits of dialogue are straight lifts from major postmodernist thinkers. (I caught at the very least references to Lacan and Deleuze.) The timing is also a bit compelling: it's during the Sixth Doctor era in which the real breakout of postmodernism occurred, both in popular culture and in academia. So a story that is about postmodern literary theory is a natural fit—a story that on the one hand would never have been made in the era itself, but on the other still speaks to the cultural concerns of that time.

But there is one bit of cleverness worth dissecting in a bit more detail. At one point it's suggested that the renegade word is bigger on the inside. And more to the point, as soon as this is established, both the Doctor and Peri stop being able to remember the word "TARDIS." The obvious implication is that the ish has, at this point, consumed the idea of the TARDIS and rendered the very conception of the series meaningless.

Actually, calling this an implication is overstating the subtlety a bit. The narration has Professor Osefa, or, at least, a hologlyphic (not holographic, crucially) representation of her, describe the Doctor's wit and language, and to speculate as to what would happen if he met a foe that was *of* language and thus not susceptible to it. So the story is overtly in the realm of that old favorite genre of ours, narrative collapse.

To recap, narrative collapse works relatively straightforwardly. The story introduces a threat that not only endangers something like the universe or the Doctor's life, but that endangers the basic ability to tell Doctor Who stories in the first place. Then, once it appears that the basic storytelling of Doctor Who has collapsed, the Doctor figures out some clever way of cheating, breaking the rules, restoring order. But in order to do so, some sort of terrible price is extracted.

For some time we have been tracking the seeming price of a deferred narrative collapse. We have described Season Twenty-Two as an exorcism, a spasmodic execution of the program's accumulated flaws. And the major theme for next season is going to be the strange incoherence of the story— the bizarre incommensurability at the heart of *Trial of a Time Lord*. But there is a missing element here. We've been tracing the effects of a narrative collapse without seeing the collapse itself.

Instead what we see is a whacking big hole—the Season Twenty-Three That Wasn't. Or, as we may as well call it in the name of getting into the spirit of things, the Seasonish. Within this narrative space that is defined entirely by its absence, there is, by implication, a narrative collapse. But the collapse is wholly emboited.

Wait a moment, though. The "Charged Vacuum Emboitment" was the idea of a metaphor—a single unit that encompasses an entire universe. Here we have a strange inversion. Instead of the narrative collapse serving as a metaphor for the turmoil that led to the Seasonish, we have the Seasonish serving as a metaphor for an emboited narrative collapse.

In other words, one of the supposed fundamental principles of narrative has unexpectedly given way. We are used to narrative serving up metaphors for the real world. To see this inverted—for reality to begin actively to serve as a symbolic container for narrative effects—is uncanny. But not, crucially, unprecedented. The nature of television, as pointed out in the very first episode, is emboitement—the enclosure of a larger space within a small box. Television is itself the real symbol containing narrative effects. But typically that is what defines television—i.e. what sets it apart from everything around it. It's the real thing that emboits narratives.

But in the Seasonish it comes to confront an equally compelling concept: alchemy. The secret of alchemy is material social progress, but this is really just a restatement of the already asserted premise of alchemy: as above, so below. If we take Doctor Who as an alchemical television show then it is uniquely capable of the magic trick we're seeing here. If television emboits narrative space and Doctor Who is a narrative space defined by the principle that "as above so below" then Doctor Who is, in fact, a narrative space that can emboit anything. (As I said at the start, all stories are Doctor Who stories. Not for nothing is he the renegade Master of the Land of Fiction.)

The relevance of ...*ish*, obviously, is that it provides the lost narrative collapse by inserting itself into the Seasonish as one of the conspicuously absent stories. But in this regard it is key to note that ...*ish* is not a television story; it's an audio play. Television is an emboited medium, but radio/audio is not. Television encloses its narrative space, but radio expels it, pushing its narrative out into the world. And more to the point, it does so into a space that is completely unbounded. There is no physical box into which audio-based narrative is compressed. Instead, audio escapes from the box, spreading outwards. The only limiting factor to the physical size of the audient void is transmission itself—the length of the chain of molecules vibrated by the sound wave. As long as the text is reiterated it can grow infinitely.

And so ...*ish* provides the perfect vector for this

inversion of the order of things. By positioning the lost narrative collapse of the Seasonish in audio instead of television ...*ish* provides the means of Doctor Who's ultimate survival. If the preceding few years have been the story of how Doctor Who was driven off a cliff, the next four provide the story of how Doctor Who was put into a position where it would someday return, and return not as a reanimated corpse but as a genuine continuation of a particular line of thought and storytelling. If we attempt to treat ...*ish* as a component of the Seasonish—and the nature of the Seasonish is that it readily can include an ahistorical phenomenon like ...*ish* within it—then we find a moment that symbolically justifies Doctor Who's cheating of its actual narrative collapse of 1989.

I do not mean this only in terms of Doctor Who's sneaking out the back door of its own medium to survive in other forms and wait patiently for its return. I also mean that the issues that ...*ish* addresses are going to turn out to be crucial over the remaining sixteen Doctor Who stories in terms of how the series moves rapidly from the smoldering trainwreck of the Baker years to a concept that has real and serious legs. Taken as a rewriting of time, ...*ish* serves an explanatory function not in terms of the particulars of Doctor Who continuity but in terms of the basic conception of what Doctor Who is.

Another one of the basic premises of postmodernism is that all discourse is additive. The double negative may be logically equivalent to the positive, but as someone once said, logic is a new toy. On a more basic level, contradiction and rejection is still an additive process. "Not X" requires the conception of X in addition to its rejection. "Not Not X" extends this further, as opposed to regressing back to X. This is what laymen fail to recognize about deconstruction—it's not a plunge into nihilism but rather a plunge into a reckless surplus of meanings. By tearing something down into component parts and looking at the absurdities generated we do not mean to leave the thing taken apart and nonfunctional. Rather we mean to prompt the creation of further concepts—we mean progress. (The other thing people fail to realize about deconstruction and postmodernism is who we're trying to fool. Ourselves, mainly.)

It is telling, then, that the Doctor's specific cheat to defeat the ish is to employ the gaps and ambiguities of language as the Doctor and Peri attack it with the differences between American and British speech. In other words, the ish is finally foiled by the slipperiness between a word and its meaning—the very slipperiness that fuels postmodernism. Put another way, faced with a seemingly inescapable dualism between the word that would encompass the whole of creation into a single fixed thing (the Omniverbum) and the word that would destroy all meaning (the ish), and, more crushingly, faced with the prospect that these are actually the same thing, the Doctor's solution is to play word games. The Doctor survives through the idea that continued use of language is self-sustaining and always creates new things to escape both extremes of fixity.

And in doing so, symbolically, he makes the switch between the two ends of the narrative collapse—the grotesque exorcism of Season Twenty-Two and the chaotic rebirth of Season Twenty-Three. Which, since there's going to be a lot to do over the course of Season Twenty-Three, we may as well start setting up here. Season Twenty-Three does not make a lot of sense. Or, perhaps more accurately, it makes a wild excess of sense. Over the course of the fourteen episodes so many different things are implied, suggested, and gestured towards that the results are impossible to square away with anything at all, least of all *Trial of a Time Lord* itself. The result falls visibly short of "good," but is nevertheless such a massive chunk of concepts as to be strangely essential. Even though no televised Doctor Who stories since *Trial of a Time Lord* have once mentioned or referenced any of its ideas, it remains influential simply because of their sheer mass.

But it is terribly, terribly muddled and confused. And so, as a result, is the approach to it (hence this essay)—or, for that matter, the transition from it to the next thing that appears to be a coherent era of Doctor Who, the head-scratching nature of Season Twenty-Four, not to get horribly far ahead of ourselves. And so if the ideas on either side of it are a mess, one can only imagine what the inside of it must be like.

## Pop Between Realities, Home in Time for Tea: *Time*

*A commissioned essay for Thomas Hartwell.*

Just about the only claim more defensible than "*Trial of a Time Lord* was blatantly ripped off from the Dave Clark musical *Time*" is "*Time* was blatantly ripped off from Doctor Who," with Clark expanding on an earlier unproduced musical from David Soames and Jeff Daniels called *The Time Lord*, which was unapologetically a Doctor Who lift, albeit the sort of lift that's less a substantive use of ideas and more an inability to come up with a phrase better than "Time Lord," which is, let's face it, not exactly the product of Terrance Dicks at his creative height.

The subsequent lift on the part of John Nathan-Turner in developing *Trial of a Time Lord*, at least, is considerably more substantial. *Time* concerns a rock star, Chris Wilder, who is teleported to the High Court of the Universe and forced to defend humanity in an inquisition as to whether the planet should be destroyed before it can endanger other species. There are obvious differences, of course, to *Trial of a Time Lord*, but given that *Trial* was developed while this was debuting and that Nathan-Turner was a keen fan of musicals, the idea that he developed a story about Time Lords dragging people about the universe to put them on trial without thinking about the blockbuster musical going on in the West End is strained.

It is, of course, impossible, thirty years on, to know how *Time* was. It had a roughly two-year run on the West End, has never been revived, and doesn't have an actual cast album; the only existent album version is one Clark made with the songs sung by a variety of artists including Cliff Richard, Freddie Mercury, Stevie Wonder, and Dionne Warwick, of which only Richard was actually in the original cast. (Adding to the obscurity, the soundtrack only ever got a vinyl release, apparently because Clark disliked CDs, meaning it was basically out of print until a 25$^{th}$ anniversary iTunes-exclusive re-release.) There aren't a ton of photos or easy ways to reconstruct the show. But… it's an elaborate 1986 rock musical that had a wildly expensive hydraulic-operated stage, a filmed floating head appearance by Laurence Olivier (recycled for *Sky Captain and the World of Tomorrow*) and was made by someone who was opposed to CDs as a medium. I think we can guess its quality.

Certainly the music is largely wretched. If you imagine what a bad 80s rock opera is going to sound like, you're probably getting it about right. Lyrically, it consists of trite statements about the nature of love and warmed over New Age blather about mind over matter. There's an obvious disparity between its sense of its own scale and the actual content that tends to make every crescendo and climax in the soundtrack slightly cringeworthy.

The actual concept of the trial is similarly baleful. In one of the earlier songs, Melchisedic, the prosecuting Time Lord, describes himself thusly: "I am the Time Lord! Without father, without mother, without descent, having neither beginning of days nor end of life." Which is fine, except that two lines later the lyrics, unable to come up with a better rhyme for "ye who strive for power," he declares that he "strikes them by the hour," which is a curiously temporally limited perspective for an apparently eternal being. Sure, it's not actually much stupider than the Time Lords in Doctor Who are, but that's faint praise.

But the real problem is that, despite the conceptual flaccidity of the piece, it's insistent on extended pontifications about the world. One of its best-known tracks, due to becoming an inexplicable chart hit in Australia, is the "Theme from *Time*," a spoken word piece by Laurence Olivier on the occasion of humanity being granted the "Law of Probenation," explaining that people are the creators of their own universe because of free will, and that changing the world requires changing our thoughts. This is little more than a bland new age platitude, but it highlights the underlying banality of the piece, revealing the High Court of the Universe to be entirely anthropocentric despite its claims of eternity and cosmic grandeur, spouting recycled Maharishi Mahesh Yogi from an overly expensive hydraulic platform.

In some ways, it's tempting to make the snide comparisons to *Trial of a Time Lord*. And there's plenty of ways in which they're valid. "An overinflated sense of its own scale" describes the barely coherent morass of *Trial* perfectly well, after all. The sense of opulent spectacle is there in *Trial*, even if it can only really afford the opening model shot of the station. They're trying to accomplish similar things.

But this is slightly unfair. It is not as though the megamusical was not the style of the times, after all. *Cats* made its West End debut back in the early Davison era, and *Les Misérables* hit London in 1985. This was, in short, the age of the spectacle musical, and it's not as though it's a style without some genuinely classic stuff. *Time*, however, captures its worst impulses—a project with seemingly no ambition other than its grandeur. It's a monument to the sheer desire to make something big, for the very sake of bigness.

In this regard, at least, it's kind of the ultimate Thatcherite project, or, more fairly, the ultimate in the sort of 80s conservatism that took hold in Anglophone countries in general. And this is, in many ways, the same process that Doctor Who was caught up in. It was a sort of televisual Docklands, an aging bit of Britain that, in the spirit of the times, existed only to be bulldozed and modernized. It wasn't that the BBC wasn't spending money on things—*The Singing Detective* and *Edge of Darkness* show that they were. But the point of a prestige project, in the 1980s, was in part its newness. The cultural project of the 80s wasn't just the gaudy bombast of *Time* and Colin Baker's coat, but the destruction of the old in order to make room for gaudy bombast. Indeed, in many ways modernization was not a creative process at all, but rather primarily a destructive one, based more in the need to dismantle the old and "outdated" to make room for the new.

But given this, there's a certain irony to Nathan-Turner drawing inspiration from *Time*, given his own taste in musicals. The post-Doctor Who era of Nathan Turner's life is largely one of a sad and alcohol-fueled decline, punctuated by occasional stabs at projects that were, to an outside observer, self-evidently doomed. Nathan-Turner was a profound aficionado of light entertainment and the old music hall scene (what the US calls vaudeville, basically), retiring to Brighton and pitching things like compilation tapes of interviews with vintage drag acts.

There's something genuinely tragic about this, as there is with a lot of Nathan-Turner's later career. In many ways, the failures of Doctor Who in the mid-80s became a self-fulfilling prophecy with regards to Nathan-Turner. He was kept on the programme because he wasn't trusted with anything more important, a decision that was blatantly tied to the fact that he was openly gay. And in turn, as the program slowly collapsed in exactly the way it was intended to, Nathan-Turner's career declined with it. There were no shortage of self-inflicted wounds involved in this process, but it's also hard not to feel a real measure of sympathy for him.

In which case there's something profoundly and sadly touching about Nathan-Turner's last real throw of the dice in terms of saving Doctor Who being a rip off of *Time*, a bloated and ill-conceived spectacle whose production involved gutting the Dominion Theatre, constructed in the late 1920s, whose first big live show had been a Judy Garland concert.

As he desperately tried to reinvent the show he was stuck on, having been served with a brutal public humiliation in the form of the hiatus, he reached to the dramatic tradition he was most familiar and comfortable with, and tried to pull from what was immediate and present in it; the same instincts that he showed with the ripped-from-*Corrie* silent credits on *Earthshock*. But instead of getting gold, he got a plot ripped from what is at best an eccentric mediocrity. And the show kept sinking, dragging him beneath the waves alongside it.

# I Was Beginning to Fear You Had Lost Yourself (*The Mysterious Planet*)

## Part One: How To Write Colin Baker and Nicola Bryant

It's September 6th, 1986. Boris Gardiner is at number one with "I Want to Wake Up With You." A week later, The Communards replace them with "Don't Leave Me This Way," and stay there for the remaining three weeks of this story. Janet Jackson, The Human League, Frankie Goes to Hollywood, Run DMC/Aerosmith, the Eurythmics, and Cutting Crew also chart, while on the album charts it's the *True Blue* period for Madonna and the release of Paul Simon's *Graceland*.

In real news, and moving very quickly through the eighteen-month gap (which was really only seventeen months), the New Coke debacle happens and the ozone hole is discovered. The Heysel Disaster takes place, leading to a five-year ban from European competition for English clubs. A year later is the Hand of God goal, so really, almost as crappy a time to be an English football fan as it is to be a Doctor Who fan. The Nintendo Entertainment System and *Calvin and Hobbes* both debut. And finally, the Challenger disaster happens, as does Chernobyl. Whereas during this story, Desmond Tutu becomes a bishop, both the *Oprah Winfrey Show* and *Casualty* debut on television, and the Colwich rail crash happens, killing two and injuring a hundred more.

While on television we begin *The Trial of a Time Lord* with the segment of the story commonly referred to as *The Mysterious Planet*. But already we're in choppy waters as we hit "How many stories does *Trial of a Time Lord* count as?" Given that I've already argued that *An Unearthly Child* and *100,000 BC* should be thought of as two stories and that *The Daleks' Masterplan* should be thought of as at least three, I'm obviously unlikely to suggest that a run of episodes with four writers and three production codes should be treated as one story just because of the part numbering. And while there's a unity to the season that was missing from the previous season-long arc, as mentioned last time there's also a massive disunity to this season. So let's say not only four stories, but four very confused stories.

Within this mess there's a lot to talk about. But the trial-specific material will mostly benefit from being taken in the context of the end, so we'll save the bulk of it for the *Ultimate Foe* essay. Instead I want to start small, with the most visibly rebooted aspect of the series, namely the relationship between Baker's Doctor and Peri.

The intended structure of *Trial of a Time Lord* was based on *A Christmas Carol*, with the three stories shown as evidence representing the past, present, and future. And so *The Mysterious Planet* is intended to represent the past. Off the bat this is a little strange—it is, after all, an adventure with the then-current TARDIS crew seemingly set after the most recent televised adventure. The distinction between it and the succeeding story in terms of time is almost completely arbitrary.

Except that the present of *Trial of a Time Lord* is presumed to be the courtroom, and thus Peri's departure has already happened somewhere within the Seasonish. And so this story goes back to a past, yes, but to an erased past that never was.

It's not a new observation that *Trial of a Time Lord* can be read as a metaphor for the show's production difficulties in this time period. The Doctor on trial serves as a proxy for the show being on trial, with a demand that it prove itself worthy of being on the air. In which case this "past" section serves first and foremost as a representation of the show that was put on hiatus.

Given this, its rampant revisionism is understandable. After all, aesthetically speaking, Season Twenty-Two had been a bit of a disaster, and so representing the show as having been better than it was is a sound part of making the overall case that the show deserved to exist. But what's interesting is that this revisionism really focuses on a relatively narrow issue: the biggest visible change in the program, quite frankly, is that the Doctor and Peri get along much better.

Their opening scene wandering Ravalox is a small but distinct thing—the Doctor leaves Peri to make deductions, and praises her when she figures it out. When she accuses him of patronizing her, he reiterates his praise and confidence in her. And when he makes an egotistical joke in response to her asking about intelligent life on the planet ("apart from me, you mean?") it is with a smile that Peri returns. It's true that the tensions between them had cooled down by the time *Revelation of the Daleks* rolled around, but there's still a real difference in their relationship.

By and large this is an extremely positive thing. The spectre of abuse that has hung over the Doctor/Peri relationship since the debacle of *The Twin Dilemma* is a strong contender for "most toxic aspect of the Baker era," a competition with no small number of worthy candidates. But more to the point, Baker and Bryant are really quite good at this sort of warmth. It's the first time we've had a straightforward Doctor/Companion pair that got along since the fleeting few episodes of the Doctor and Nyssa, and the first time we've had it as the apparent status quo since the long lost days of Lalla Ward.

And to be clear, it's not that Holmes has simply jettisoned all tension. The sequence where Peri realizes that Ravalox is Earth and the Doctor is at once understanding of her emotions but unwilling to humor them at length may be the last great thing that Robert Holmes ever wrote. The combination of the Doctor's clear and genuine affection for Peri with his alien detachment from the emotions he understands but does not share is perfectly pitched, and indeed is what Baker's Doctor should have been pitched at all along.

## Part Four: The Unspeakable Screwedness of Nicola Bryant

But more on the particulars of the Doctor's acquittal next essay. For now, let's wrap this one up with the traditional "farewell to" portion for a departing companion. Because it's entirely possible that nobody has ever been screwed over by the series quite as thoroughly as Nicola Bryant. Let's first of all note that Nicola Bryant is quite a good actress. Her Peri can be awkward, but then again, putting Brits in American accents is almost but not quite as disastrous as putting Americans in British ones. And on top of that, anybody in that role would be awkward. It's a god-forsaken role.

The problem, at its core, is that Peri is clearly conceived in the oh-so-pure terms of "let's go back to the good old-fashioned girl companion." Her only character trait that goes beyond "generic girl" is that she's American, and they didn't actually bother to cast someone American for her. But the generic girl companion, as we observed back with Tegan, is largely an invention. At this point there had been exactly two Earth girls to travel solo with the Doctor—Jo and Sarah Jane. And both worked because they were extremely distinctive characters who were strong enough to carry the job of being 50% of the regular cast. They were anything but generic cookie-cutter companions.

Nothing of the sort can be said for Peri, who is the first companion since Victoria to be designed entirely and exclusively as a peril monkey. By all appearances they took Terrance Dicks at face value when he joked about creating Jo because the Doctor needed a dumb companion who would get rescued a lot. (And for all of Dicks's feminism problems, I think this is clearly a joke, simply because Jo was always, from her first appearance, more than that.) Almost all Peri gets to do is scream and be rescued.

And for a few brief and shining moments in the course of *Mindwarp*, it looks like she's going to get the opportunity to redeem that. First of all, Peri finally gets to do things over the course of the story because the plot requires the Doctor to be sidelined, meaning that several Doctorish jobs shift over to her. And, unsurprisingly, Nicola Bryant is quite good at it. Then she gets to, for a few lines, have her wish of playing a villain, and she's absolutely bone-chilling. The bald cap goes a long way, but Nicola Bryant absolutely nails it and is by far the most disturbing "possessed companion" to date.

And on top of that we get the tragic conclusion to her arc—a point bitter and cynical enough to almost redeem it. Because if you're going to have a character who exists only to get in trouble, frankly, you may as well kill her. At least it's honest. If Peri is going to embody rape culture as well as she does then this really is the right end for her: having her body completely taken over by a creepy old man. Given how often the series has gone out of its way to treat Nicola Bryant as a piece of meat, wringing tragic consequences out of it is the least it can do. It's not good. It's not nice. It's a crass fridging, not that this was a criticism that had meaning yet in 1986. But given the disaster that Peri has been turned into, it is the best available ending—one that at last acknowledges just how nasty and unpleasant the series has been. And Nicola Bryant goes out showing how good she was, and how wasted she was on this part.

Except we don't even get that. In the single trashiest and laziest retcon in the series history we get the pink-haze "she's a warrior queen of King Ycranos" scene. To which the Doctor sighs happily and leaves her. Note that this is not a voluntary companion departure so far as we can tell. The fact that the Doctor is kidnapped from Thoros Beta never gets retconned. By all appearances the Doctor never goes back for her, leaving her to Ycranos. With whom she never particularly got along, and who is a raging misogynist with violent tendencies. Indeed, it's something of a strain to get one's self to belief that "warrior queen" is a consensual position and not a euphemism for "woman King Ycranos claimed as conquest."

Combined with her battered wife syndrome when it comes to the Doctor himself, this paints an astonishingly ugly picture, especially given the series' apparent approval of the pairing. Peri is a helpless woman who not only is constantly left to the openly sadistic devices of men, but who apparently "wants it." And the series backs off making any critique of this, instead treating it as a happy ending. It is, moreso even than Ben, Polly, Dodo, or Leela, the single worst and most offensive companion departure in the whole of Doctor Who. And it's deeply depressing that all fandom ever wants to talk about is how screwed Colin Baker was by the handling of his character and era. Nicola Bryant was far, far more screwed. She deserved so much better.

### Part Two: Why on Earth Was This Made?

This brings us around to the larger disaster of *Trial of a Time Lord*, which is the ludicrous dropping of the ball involved in its ending. To some extent there's a litany of excuses we need to trot out here. Yes, Eric Saward walking off the job and taking his script for the final episode with him didn't help matters (regardless of how well it was or wasn't justified). But on the other hand, one has to wonder how something this messy even got made. With an extra year of planning time and the trial format supposedly agreed upon early in the process, how is it that a clear plot arc for the season didn't exist by the time they were making it? How did they get themselves thrown into such chaos in the first place?

This is something that the myriad words spilled on the production of this season never actually manage to get at. Yes, there was a ton of chaos at the end of the process, but the beginning of it—the actual conceptualization of the season—remains maddeningly obscure. Here they are doing a massive plot arc based on the model of a mystery/conspiracy thriller with tons of twists and turns and revelations, and by all appearances nobody at any point actually sat down and wrote an outline for the frame story. Yes, Robert Holmes's death was obviously a major blow, but for God's sake, how do you make it a year into working on a season-long plot arc and not have the ending worked out yet?

Because nothing about *Trial of a Time Lord* looks planned. And tempting as it is to blame this on Pip and Jane Baker, the fact of the matter is that *Terror of the Vervoids* is just where the season's flaws become readily apparent, not where they're introduced (the absurdities of *Mindwarp* not being visible until later, as discussed). The entire concept is misbegotten. It's not, to be sure, that doing a fourteen-week "event" season is a bad idea—such a run is, after all, a common thing on the BBC. Sure, fourteen weeks may be a bit long, but it's no longer than, say, *Knights of God*, which was made a year before *Trial* and aired a year after. (And which will be the first essay in the next book.) But again, if you're going to do something like that, you start from your big plot and work your way down. Instead it seems they had the vague idea of past/present/future/wrap it all up, and treated each of those elements as individual parts such that the "wrap it all up" story was going to be improvised. Even under Robert Holmes's original plan one doesn't get the sense that there was much of an actual idea underlying the season.

Throughout these essays I've been stressing the fact that the *Trial* was in part a metaphor for the series' own tribulations. (Something made clear from the opening few lines.) In which case there's something almost, but not quite, charmingly apropos about this awkwardness. "What's the reason why Doctor Who should survive its trial? We don't know either!" But the humor masks the fact that these were real questions. Other than "let's open with a really good model shot," there were seemingly no ideas on what to do next. It goes well beyond Robert Holmes's retreat to his old standards as well.

But it's not even largely unplanned—it's largely incoherent. Infamously, the BBC's *Open Air* ran a segment in which a trio of fans, including future series writer Chris Chibnall, ganged up on Pip and Jane Baker to complain that their work was clichéd and unintelligible. Much of the focus these days goes on Chris Chibnall, who looks like the geeky teenager he is, and the supposed irony of him going after Pip and Jane Baker given his own scripts. (While I think Chibnall is one of the weakest writers of the new series, the idea that he can somehow be equated to the Bakers is farcical.) This ignores, of course, the fact that Chibnall et al were largely right here. They complain that the *Trial* storyline lacked payoff and was a confusing and incoherent mess; it was. And not in a wonky "it violates what we know about Gallifrey" way, but in a "none of this actually coheres" way. So let's look instead at the Bakers, who are, I think, far more disturbingly revealing.

They make two arguments that seem on the surface to be contradictory. On the one hand they insist that they don't want to patronize the audience; they want to leave things for them to figure out. On the other, when Chibnall complains that the story was clichéd monsters and corridors stuff, Jane Baker rather icily notes that she thought Doctor Who fans liked traditional stuff. There's something really unsettling about this. It's difficult to see how feeding Doctor Who fans a steady diet of generic and traditional adventures could be called challenging. Indeed, "Here's the same thing you've been enjoying for decades done with no changes," seems the very definition of unchallenging and frankly patronizing television.

When compared with the Bakers' scripts, these comments become even more depressing. The festivals of hackneyed plot twists, cookie cutter characters, and bloviating dialogue that they pen clearly assume a barely sentient audience. The monsters are generic. The human villains' logic waffles between generic and incoherent. It's a mystery where no effort has even been made to secure basic facts and character motivations. It feels by and large like dumbed-down Pertwee-era stuff. They're writing for children and, worse, doing the thing that no good children's entertainment ever does: talking down to them. This would be one thing if the show were written for children, but the Bakers also clearly think the program is written for people who love classic Doctor Who.

And these are Nathan-Turner's favorite writers of this period. Yes, to his credit he clearly figures out that the ship needs to change course soon after this and doesn't force them on Cartmel beyond what they'd already been commissioned for, but Jesus Christ. Is this really what the show thinks of its audience now? Does it really treat them with such staggering, mind-wrenching contempt as to think that they're overgrown children who mistakenly believe themselves to be clever?

All of this is ultimately rooted in the fact that the show is still overtly going for a cult audience here with its big, sprawling epic. Even the name—*The Trial of a Time Lord*—plays overtly to fans with an investment in the series' mythology. To do that while so obviously disdaining cult audiences and their tastes is deeply, deeply ugly. (As, let's be honest, is the alternative explanation—that the Bakers really think they wrote a challenging and intelligent script.) For all that we talked back in *The Mysterious Planet* essay about *Trial* being part of a transition towards a better model for the series, it remains firmly rooted in the ugliness of the past few seasons.

## Part Four: Requiem for Robert Holmes

A narrative collapse, then. As ever, it's avoided—instead the program begins a creative renaissance, painfully tentative at first, but quickening in very short order. And as ever, there's a price. In this case, we can define it cynically and not even feel bad about it. *Trial of a Time Lord*: the story so bad it killed Robert Holmes.

If one were to make a list of writers most responsible for creating what Doctor Who is, then almost the entire soul of Doctor Who could be accounted for with three writers. David Whitaker, obviously, is the first. And these days it's clear that Russell T Davies must be there. But between them, responsible for much of the work of taking the show that David Whitaker created and developing it into a world-beater that could truly never run out of things to say, comes Robert Holmes.

It is not just that Holmes is wickedly, beautifully brilliant. It is not just the sheer number of concepts he introduced. It is not the diversity of stories he wrote, with outright comedies alongside some of the scariest and darkest moments of the series. First and foremost it is that he developed the true heart of Doctor Who. It may be Whitaker who made the Doctor a mercurial anarchist, but it is Holmes who took that to the next step and defined what the Doctor is opposed to. Whitaker may have created the idealism of the Doctor, but it is Holmes who created the raw fire of the character. It is Holmes who showed us what it is that drives the Doctor to fight.

There were always many possible answers to that question. Most of them were dumb and boring. If the matter had been left to Terry Nation the answer would have essentially been "Nazis," assuming he wasn't lazy and didn't say "space monsters." Terrance Dicks, for all his adventuring charm, would have picked a very generic sense of evil. Far too many writers would have picked something like "ignorance" or "superstition." But not Robert Holmes. Oh no.

Robert Holmes picked "bureaucracy." He set the Doctor against rules for their own sake. He set the Doctor against bullies and boredom and everything drab and dull. Robert Holmes decided that the mercurial hero who is the Doctor should, first and foremost, fight against the banality of evil. There are many things that are brilliant about Doctor Who—

the likeability of a clever and unpredictable hero, the flexibility of the format, several of the monsters and concepts. But in the end this is I think what made the show great: the fact that it is a profoundly delightful blow against the cruelty of "the way things are."

So it's at once ironic and fitting that Holmes goes down in the midst of a story that looks the rules of Doctor Who in the face and then suddenly throws them out. *Trial of a Time Lord*, if nothing else, turns out to have been the pragmatic deathblow to the Whoniverse. It is the story upon which almost any attempt to create a unitary narrative of Doctor Who breaks. (Although at least "between his twelfth and final incarnation" is now a preposterously vast window and not an impending continuity nightmare.) And more to the point, it's the story that marks the point where the television show abandons all thought of having any unifying narrative in favor of simply doing interesting things. It marks another passing of the alchemical baton, and the next generation of Doctor Who writers will take it and begin doing wildly and fascinatingly new things with the series—things that, even if they went out to a tiny and obscure audience, proved the cornerstone of the entire future of the series.

One of the things that is very clear about the next stable of writers is that they are people who grew up on Doctor Who but who are not, by and large, fans. Those who are proper fanboys still made their bones writing professionally elsewhere before coming to Doctor Who. And for every single great writer who works on the series after this point, one thing is going to be very, very obvious: whatever it is they think Doctor Who is, they learned from Robert Holmes.

## His Almost Gleeful Pleasure (*Mindwarp*)

## Part Four: How to Stage an Intervention

But if this explains the real reason for hastily convening a trial to dispose of the Doctor it does little to make sense of the ostensible reason for the trial. The Doctor is, as usual, accused of meddling and interfering—and it's explicitly stated that the accusation is the same as the one from *The War Games*. But we have to ask, at this point, what the hell the Time Lords actually mean by this.

Obviously some level of hypocrisy is in play here given the Time Lords' own actions, especially in this and the next story. *Mindwarp* is actually a particularly telling example, in that it clearly establishes that the Time Lords are still very much concerned with the natural order of things. Indeed, they seem more horrified by the fact that Crozier's experiments derail the course of evolution than they are by the prospect of an explosion that might destroy the entire universe. This is telling. The idea that the universe might be destroyed, fine. That had to happen eventually anyway, one figures. But the idea of evolution being disrupted—and Doctor Who has more than once dabbled in the idea that evolutionary and historical processes are related—that's a huge issue.

(It is of course worth discussing what the Time Lords do or don't actually do about Crozier, but that's another essay.)

But more broadly, the Time Lords are in favor of intervention in a number of circumstances. They interfere with Crozier's experiments, which seem to have happened with no help from them. (The Doctor's contributions seem minor at best, so we have to assume that Crozier gets there on his own.) And, more obviously, they interfere like mad with Earth. But their hypocrisy and corruption is more complex than just saying say they oppose interference while doing it anyway.

Indeed, even in their condemnation of the Doctor they seem to object more to the cavalierness of his interference than to the basic existence of it. The Valeyard faults him on Ravalox because people died, even though he saved the universe. (Though obviously, due to the nature of Ravalox, he does stress the idea that the Doctor should never have been there more than quite makes superficial sense, and this is meant to be a clue to something or other.) In other words, it's not that he interfered, but that he did so in a dangerous and careless manner.

This reveals a cruel tautology at the heart of Time Lord law. Interference is defined as intervention outside of the rules—as intervention that is not careful. In other words, it's only interference when it's not done from within the existing structures of authority. The morality of this is of course abhorrent—hence the belief that moving Earth is somehow an acceptable interference. But equally, there's a consistency to it. It's part and parcel of the idea of lords of time—the combination of the Time Lords' conception as the guardians of the arc of history and the cynicism that history is written by the victors. This is exceedingly Robert Holmesy, of course. In the end, it almost doesn't matter what the Doctor does. His real problem is that he's not one of the people who's in authority, and this alone puts him in perpetual danger. (In this regard it's telling that one of the disjunctions between the Holmes half and the Baker half of The Ultimate Foe is that Holmes plays up the Valeyard's obsession with rules and bureaucracy in the form of Mr. Popplewick, a thematic thread that the Bakers drop.) The biggest problem, Holmes seems to suggest, is the fact that the Doctor can never escape the existence of authority and rules. Taken in the context of the Trial being a metaphor for the program's tribulations within the BBC, the implication is clear and chilling.

**Part One: Bad Doctor, No Cookie!**

It's October 4th, 1986. The Communards are still alarmed about being left this way, but are unseated one week later by Madonna with "True Blue." The next week is Nick Berry with "Every Loser Wins," and he actually manages to stay there for two weeks. Paul Simon, A-Ha, The Pet Shop Boys, The Bangles, and Midnight Star also chart.

While in real news, *Phantom of the Opera* opens on the West End. *The Independent* begins publication. 1500 people die in an earthquake in El Salvador. Ronald Reagan and Mikhail Gorbachev meet in Reykjavik for disarmament talks, which end in failure. The Metrocentre, the largest shopping center in the UK and at the time the largest in Europe, opens in Gateshead. The president of Mozambique, Samora Machel, dies in a plane crash. And the day after this story concludes bus deregulation goes into effect in most of the UK.

*Mindwarp* poses an interesting problem in the context of *Trial of a Time Lord*. We'll deal with its overt narrative eccentricities later in the essay, but for now I want to look at its most basic issue, the question of whether or not the Doctor, or at least Colin Baker's version of him, is good. This is, after all, the story in which the Doctor most obviously errs and in which the Valeyard's criticism seems most applicable.

We are told, of course, that many of the events that we see are partially fraudulent. But as Tat Wood points out, there's not actually that much of the Doctor's behavior here that needs to be explained away. The explanation he gives— that it was all a ruse—largely holds. The usual story told about *Mindwarp*—that Baker couldn't get an answer out of anybody on what parts of the script were real and what parts were fabrication—speaks volumes simply because it is, in fact, ambiguous enough that the question comes up. But in a story that's set up to establish how disastrous the Doctor's actions are this raises some significant problems (even if the nature of the disaster is… confused).

All of this brings up a question that has been elided throughout this era—how much of the problem is just this version of the Doctor? To what extent is it just that Baker's Doctor is fatally flawed or miscast? As mentioned, the audios do suggest that Baker is, in fact a pretty good actor and that his Doctor can work, but then again, audio is a different medium. And it is, after all, Baker who was seemingly the biggest proponent of the misguided Mr. Darcy/peel-back-the-onion approach.

And in the end, that approach is what lies behind *Mindwarp*'s portrayal of the Doctor as potentially fatally flawed. So much effort was put into making Baker's Doctor unlikable that, well, it succeeded to a real extent. Even if the eventual redemption had played out, the fact remains that Baker's Doctor was always designed as being a bit dodgy and flawed. No amount of redemption, it should be noted, would have undone this. The idea that this Doctor was fatally flawed was written into the basic concept of the character. Even after a seven-season arc of redemption, Baker's Doctor would still be defined as the one that might have been bad.

It's revealing, in this regard, to compare the flawed nature of Baker's Doctor with the flawed nature of Davison's Doctor—something that was also stressed to tragic consequences, and, indeed, to tragic consequences that actually happened as opposed to ones that were retconned out a few episodes later. In the case of Davison's Doctor, though, the death of Adric was never pinned on his version of the Doctor. It was a critique of the Doctor in the general case that happened on Davison's watch, not a critique of Davison specifically. Indeed, Davison's Doctor is consistently treated as an unambiguously good guy no matter how much he screws up. Whatever critiques one might make of him as "the ineffective Doctor," the narrative sides with him consistently.

Whereas here the apparent death of Peri serves to complete an arc begun with *The Twin Dilemma*. Baker's Doctor's flaw was first defined by his utter callousness towards Peri. It's not merely that Baker's Doctor is shown to be flawed, it's that he's shown to be flawed first and foremost in terms of Peri. And so the idea that his flaws lead to Peri's demise is particularly stinging. It's a critique that cuts very deep, hitting the whole of his tenure.

But it also gets at another way in which the untrustworthy conception of the Doctor was a bad idea in practice. Simply put, it's difficult to imagine any Doctor other than Baker's in this situation to begin with. It's telling that throughout the trial the Doctor's sole defense tends to be yelling about the injustice of it all. He never actually goes about saying any of the sensible things, like, "You do realize that if I hadn't gone to Ravalox we'd probably all be dead," or, "Well, if you wanted Crozier's experiments stopped, why exactly did you pull me from Thoros Beta when I was just about to stop them, thus getting my companion killed?" Instead he just blusters on about the Matrix being tampered with (on the quite tentative grounds that he wouldn't do that) and objects to the entire idea of his being on trial. His reaction is defined by his egotism, and this sort of egotism is a trait unique to Baker's Doctor.

The cliché is that Baker's Doctor is in many ways a self-portrait of John Nathan-Turner. This is, I think, a bit strong, but there's a strong sense in which, in *Trial*, he's a too-accurate stand-in for the series itself. Conceived in the afterglow of Longleat, he is a fatally flawed idea too arrogant to admit to the possibility of his failings even enough to defend himself. That only Baker's Doctor could be in this story is, in some sense, the point.

## Part Four: Genocide and How to Cure It

But if this theory explains most of the idiosyncrasies of the trial, one stubbornly remains, namely the wobbly ethos of genocide. This goes well beyond the already discussed problems of intervention and of what the supposed goals of the trial are. It's made clear that the accusation of genocide is considered more or less absolute by the Time Lords. Indeed, even the fact that the genocide of the Vervoids was necessary to prevent a genocide of humanity is deemed wholly irrelevant to the judgment. And then a completely unrelated matter—the Doctor chasing his own evil self into the Matrix—is deemed reason to just dismiss the charges. (And not, as one might think, reasons to just have him executed on the grounds that he was, after all, also the one who tried to kill them all—so much for his defense of "I improve in the future," clearly.)

I am, in this case, not particularly interested in explaining away the moral reasoning behind this. We have, after all, already concluded that the court has no moral reasoning as such beyond a fealty to the regime that gets overthrown by the end of the story. (Though the fact that the Doctor just casually turns Gallifrey over to the Inquisitor is puzzling, given this assumption. One supposes that she showed more independence than anyone else involved in the trial, but surely someone who was actually involved in the popular uprising on Gallifrey would be preferable. Then again, perhaps the Doctor doesn't seriously think that his off-Gallifrey endorsement is going to carry any weight and is simply trying to appease the Inquisitor's obvious lust for power before slipping away from this nuthouse.) Rather, I'm interested in sorting out the larger question of what the show's ethics on this subject are.

Obviously the show broadly sides with the Doctor. So the fact that he wiped out the Vervoids is clearly intended to be acceptable. But this stands in contrast with, really, almost everything else the Doctor has ever done. The most obvious thing to contrast it with is the legendary "Have I the right?" speech from *Genesis of the Daleks*. But here the Doctor seems to not even consider the question, both at the time and in presenting the evidence, where he seems blindsided by the accusation of genocide.

There are moments throughout the Saward-edited era in which the Doctor seems to tip over into ethical danger zones. But for the most part these are isolated moments in which the series takes the wrong tone—the inappropriate banter at the deaths of Shockeye or the guards in *Vengeance on Varos*, for instance. So it's ironic that the moment after Saward's departure is the point where the Doctor finally does just plow over the line.

Admittedly, buried deep in the script is something approaching a reasoning for why the Doctor is in the right. It's stressed that both the Vervoids and the crew are acting on instinct, and before hatching his plan the Doctor suggests that this consists of breaking the cycle—that the Doctor's plan constitutes not raw instinct but a different approach. His plan is explicitly positioned as giving the Vervoids their entire life cycle at top speed. In other words, it's better than killing them because it's a natural process. (This gels well with the Bakers' love of the "science gone mad" theme.)

But even if the script seems to think this, the fact remains that it's out of line with the reasoning of the rest of the series. Especially given how much the Doctor stresses his empathy for the Vervoids and how they're only following instinct. Casual genocide is bad enough, but for him to engage in casual genocide a few lines after mounting a defense of the Vervoids is one of the most callous and distressing moments of the series.

Then again, let's remember what future these events seem to come from—one where the Doctor does, in fact, become the Valeyard. Given that we don't want to discard free will, we have to take this as a possible future for the Doctor. In which case there's a compelling, if inadvertent sense to all of this. The Doctor is, going into the Trial, on track to become the Valeyard, as evidenced by his failure to realize the horror of what he does in *Terror of the Vervoids*. And the rewriting of time that occurs at the end of all of this constitutes a turning away from this future towards something better. This is, at last, the moment of exorcism.

## Part Three: The First Law of Time

The First Law of Time is, we have been told, the prohibition on crossing your own timestream. Back in *The Mysterious Planet* the Valeyard accused the Doctor of transgressing this law. That line, as delivered, seemed to imply a different first law—the usual "meddling" accusation—but the line as written gives just enough wiggle room that it is worth entertaining the possibility of consistency with the past.

Certainly the irony of the Valeyard delivering that accusation is immense. Especially if we posit the First Law in the broader sense of being about the alteration of one's personal history (that being the first law of time that was ever revealed to the audience). The Valeyard's plan, after all, is nothing more than a massive rewriting of his own personal history. And we've already seen in reasonable detail how this can be spun as the seeming future of the show as it existed after Season Twenty-Two attempting to cannibalize the present to ensure its existence.

But to what extent is the Valeyard a meaningful future of the Doctor? This question becomes particularly vexed when he's taken in concert with the Master, who is already defined as an evil version of the Doctor and who largely makes much more sense. The Valeyard, a creature of rules, is a harder fit with the Doctor simply because the mercurial and anarchic nature of the Doctor is so strongly defined. The Valeyard outright hates who the Doctor is, seeming to view every aspect of the Doctor as an affront. It's difficult, throughout the story, to actually identify any common ground between the two or three aspects of the Doctor that could be said to become the Valeyard.

Fan lore typically has it as the Doctor's pride and anger that leads to the creation of the Valeyard in a very tiresome "we've been watching too much *Star Wars*" way, but there's no sign of this whatsoever in the course of *Trial of a Time Lord* itself. The claim that the Valeyard is a composite of the Doctor's every dark thought mostly seems to speak towards a terrible genericness in the Doctor's dark thoughts. And anyway—that's the Bakers' neutering of the Valeyard. Holmes's Valeyard—the creature of pure law—does not seem to extend from anything that can reasonably be described as the Doctor's dark thoughts. It just extends from standard issue Robert Holmes villainy.

The series' dark thoughts, on the other hand, might just work. The Valeyard is, as we've already discussed, the logical consequence of continuity fetishism. And if we treat him not as the Doctor's dark side in a psychological sense but in a meta-fictional sense he becomes a lot more comprehensible. But we still run into a big problem—if we do embrace this rules-based vision of the Valeyard, why on Earth is he so cavalierly breaking the First Law of Time himself?

The usual interpretation is that he fears death, but that's actively contradicted by the story itself. The Valeyard worships death as the ultimate reality. The Valeyard talks about obtaining his freedom, but there is no reason, for a Time Lord, that this freedom must be forward-looking. It makes just as much sense for him to obtain his freedom by rewriting the past and existing not as a mere historical endpoint of the Doctor but as the Doctor himself—as a living being. In other words, instead of becoming the teleology of the Doctor he wants to become the very historical process of the Doctor.

It is here that we should ask what the purpose of the First Law of Time is anyway. Is it anxiety over changing the past? Perhaps, but the law seems to be that one cannot even cross one's timestream—not that one cannot change it. But there is a distinct change that happens when one crosses one's own timestream. Let's think about it in terms of *The Two Doctors*. Nowhere in the entire course of Patrick Troughton's tenure on Doctor Who does it make sense to interpret an episode in light of the fact that Troughton will someday become Colin Baker. Troughton's Doctor—like all Doctors—are unaffected by the weight of the series' future. As all things are in the past. It is a fallacy to treat the present as a teleology that organizes the past.

But when one crosses one's own timestream, that gets violated. No matter what one does with *The Two Doctors*, no matter how faithful one tries to make it to the Troughton era, the one thing you cannot get away from is that it reconceives Troughton as an antecedent to the present—the one thing he could never possibly be in the 1960s themselves. A line from *The Mind Robber* is instructive here: "When someone writes about an incident after it's happened, that's history. But when the writing comes first, that's fiction." The First Law of Time, then, exists to prevent history from becoming fiction—to prevent history from simply writing the future. This is the freedom that the Valeyard seeks and is willing to break the First Law of Time for—to make all of Doctor Who lead to him. In a narrative such as Doctor Who, after all, this is what becoming real has to mean. The danger of the Valeyard isn't his existence: its his potential fictionality.

## A Far Greater Crime (*Terror of the Vervoids*)

## Part Two: Recycling the Future

*The Mysterious Planet*, of course, embodies the "past" idea in more ways than one. The story is an unrepentant "greatest hits" reel for Robert Holmes, plundering and reworking large swaths of his back catalogue. The underlying premise is *The Face of Evil*, with bits of *The Krotons* grafted on around Drathro. Glitz and Dibbler are, of course, just Garron and Unstoffe. The underlying notion of a Time Lord conspiracy is straight out of *The Deadly Assassin*. The restoration of a post-apocalyptic Earth is a reworking of *The Ark in Space*. Hints of *The Time Warrior* surround the Tribe of the Free, while the people in the tunnels feel, as much by set design as writerly intention, rather like *The Sun Makers*.

Of course, reckless plundering of the past has been the calling card of the series for some time now. But there's something very different about *The Mysterious Planet* compared to recent attempts to "do it like it was before" such as *Timelash*, *The Two Doctors*, and *Attack of the Cybermen*. Those were all concerned with plundering the actual signifiers of the past. But *The Mysterious Planet* takes a very different tack instead, by repeating the techniques of the past.

This is part of a general refocusing that goes on in the midst of the hiatus. Ian Levine's tenure as the unofficial continuity advisor comes to an end in this period. By his account, at least, it's the hiring of Bonnie Langford as Mel that was the last straw. Given this, then, it's interesting to note that the spaceship in Langford's first story, *Terror of the Vervoids*, is named the Hyperion. The first piece of concrete influence Levine had on the series was back in *State of Decay*, where he got the name of the ship changed from Hyperion to Hydrax on the grounds that the Hyperion had already been used back in 1972 for *The Mutants*. So the act of using the name again in the story that supposedly drove Ian Levine away seems almost a deliberate provocation, or, more charitably, a conscious break with Levine's particular relationship with the past.

Certainly it's true that from this point on the past will be engaged with very differently. It's not that continuity is dead—post-*Trial*, a solid six of the twelve remaining classic series stories are going to feature the return of past concepts or characters. But there's a marked change in the nature of it. Even in *Trial of a Time Lord* the Time Lords aren't brought back in the increasingly stale portrayal that has been crusting over them since *The Invasion of Time*. From here on out there's a change to bringing specific concepts back in order to reevaluate and reconceptualize them.

But in the midst of that transition we get this, a story that is in its own way more fetishistic towards the past than anything Levine ever involved himself in. To some extent this is just inevitability. We have here a production team ordered to reinvent the series for what is the script editor's third time, the producer's fourth, and the actual writer's sixth. These are not the right people to be heading an attempt to salvage the series, and the fact that one of the three will be involved in getting it right in a year is a small miracle. There was little this group could be expected to do but to turn to the past in a desperate attempt to redo what had worked before.

Where this is saddest, of course, is Robert Holmes, for whom this set of issues must have been depressingly familiar. When he quit the series under Graham Williams it was during a period when the show was being bounced back and forth between Mary Whitehouse-inspired directives to tone down the violence and objections that it was too silly, with his breaking point being the assignment to write the terribly overserious *The Power of Kroll*. Now he finds himself embroiled in the exact same issue, given conflicting instructions to make it more and less funny from Jonathan Powell.

It's not that Holmes's effort to salvage the series is anything less than sincere at this stage. Rather, it's that we've finally reached the limits of what he can do. With nowhere to go, Holmes turns to the past and simply dredges up everything he'd ever done before in the hopes that some part of it might work. It's a road that had to be attempted, really. Especially post-Levine, someone had to just knuckle down and attempt a straight up "go back to how it was done before" (as distinct from nostalgia). But what the program ends up finding is that the past isn't the future. Holmes's old tricks are just that—old tricks.

There's a way of looking at the program in terms of the shredding of its past—at the point where the creative personnel from past eras disappear. Tom Baker is the last Doctor to have stories written by people who worked on the Hartnell era. Colin Baker, on the other hand, is the last Doctor to have stories written by people who worked on the Troughton, Pertwee, Tom Baker, or Davison eras. And Sylvester McCoy's tenure, after his first script, does away with stories written by Colin Baker holdovers. Robert Holmes was the last real holdout of the long history of the series. And before the future proper could be moved into, there had to be this—a last, desperate firing on all thrusters of the tried and true techniques. They failed, as I think even Holmes knew they would. And so the program moved on.

## Part Three: Who's In Charge Here?

This disintegration of *Trial*'s coherence as a narrative is not limited merely to *Mindwarp*'s ambiguous reality either.

This is also where it really becomes difficult to make heads or tails of what the actual legal proceeding here is. We'll save large-scale observations and conjectures about the nature of the trial for later, but let's try for the moment to figure out what role the Inquisitor and the Jury have in this process.

It goes without saying that the Valeyard is corrupt and acting for his own purposes. It also appears to be the case that the Inquisitor has no knowledge of this prior to *The Ultimate Foe*. On the other hand, the end of *Mindwarp* suggests strongly that the entire courtroom knew about the Thoros Beta incident. After all, the Valeyard implies a thoroughly reasoned intervention on the part of the Time Lords regarding Crozier and his experiments. The Inquisitor goes along with this, whereas at other times she overrules the Valeyard. And on top of that we know that the psychic energy of the Jury was used to summon the Doctor. We'll trace the big implication of that next essay, but surely if they're pulling the Doctor from a specific point in space and time they have to know something about what's going on at that moment in time.

Except that we're eventually told that what they see on the screen is complete bull. And yet they buy it. It's tempting to suggest that all of them are in on the Valeyard's conspiracy, but the Inquisitor's later actions seem to completely disprove this. This is a real pity, because it would provide this sequence with a much needed dose of making a damn bit of sense. As previously noted, the Time Lords seem to go out of their way to screw things up here, including preventing the Doctor from stopping Crozier while simultaneously blaming him for it. Similarly, the accusation that the Doctor abandoned Peri when they apparently kidnapped him and kept him from saving her is simply bewildering.

And though we previously took the potential danger of Crozier seriously, it does have to be noted that all Crozier is doing is something that would put him in the same league as the Wirrn, Sutekh, Solon, and a host of other Doctor Who villains. I mean, seriously, mind transference is now a threat that requires drastic intervention? This is utterly unconvincing. Given all of this, it would be so much easier to simply believe that the Inquisitor and the Jury are in on the conspiracy and know that this is a misrepresentation of the Doctor's actions simply because it would save us the trouble of figuring out how on Earth they're supposed to believe any of this or take it seriously.

The easiest explanation is that they're stooges who were picked because they could be trusted to arrive at the correct conclusion regardless of the evidence. That is, they know that the story they're being given makes no sense, but they have enough loyalty to the High Council to do their job and arrive at the result expected of them. This is a particularly bleak portrait of post-Revolutionary Gallifrey, but it does seem the simplest explanation by some margin.

But this, in turn, opens a different can of worms. After all, the flagrantly false account of how they summoned the Doctor is not what jolts them or the Inquisitor into acquitting the Doctor. Something in *The Ultimate Foe*—and it's never entirely made clear what—eventually flips them out of their designated roles as party stooges.

## Part One: Mel: Huh?

It's November 1st, 1986. Nick Berry remains at number one with "Every Loser Wins." A week later Berlin's love theme for *Top Gun*, "Take My Breath Away," unseats him. Cliff Richard and Sarah Brightman, the Pretenders, Duran Duran, Europe, Bon Jovi, and Peter Gabriel and Kate Bush also chart.

In real news, the US begins having a whole lot of fun with the Iran-Contra affair. The deadliest civilian helicopter crash in history happens just east of Sumburgh Airport in Scotland. Efforts begin to find two more bodies from the Moors Murders, which you may remember from twenty years ago on this blog. Sir Alex Ferguson, then only Alex Ferguson, takes over at Manchester United, which is rather a thing.

While on television the *Trial* goes irretrievably off the rails. The final six episodes are 83% Pip and Jane Baker, with all that entails. There's a lot of ways in here, but let's start with the big one, which is the spectacular mislaunch of Bonnie Langford as Mel.

As legendarily hateable as Mel is (she is one of the most roundly mocked characters in all of Doctor Who), she's not nearly as misbegotten as all that. We'll talk in a moment about the strange decision making behind Doctor Who's *Trial* relaunch, but the logic behind it is not entirely unsound. Bonnie Langford was a big name. As a former child star viewed as being a bit overly precious she was not, strictly speaking, a well-loved name, but it was attention-getting casting of the sort that the series needed.

On top of that, she actually turned out to be quite good. She was never given very much to work with, saddled continually with scripts that condescended to her character. The oft-told story that she was instructed to scream in a particular key so as to lead into the theme music better for the cliffhanger at the end of her first episode is instructive. On the one hand, there's a real and charming level of professionalism in that, and the effect is about the only good part of that cliffhanger. On the other hand, it seems to have been all the production team thought Langford capable of.

But as poor as much of the writing for Mel is (and it does improve considerably when it's not the Bakers writing for her), the larger problem is that she's a companion with a strangely swallowed origin. John Nathan-Turner quasi-famously wrote an origin story for her in his book on the companions that had her teaming up with the Doctor to stop the Master from an audacious computer hacking attack on the world's banks, which, let's be honest, probably would have been terrible. But it's still preferable to what we got, which is slightly less than nothing.

There are people who act as though the Mel chronology is easily resolved. It's true that there is a fairly entrenched bit of fanon that explains it all based around Mel being pulled from a moment where the Doctor has left her on vacation, but the idea that this fits well with what's on screen is tenuous at best. The core problem comes from another thing we'll deal with in a moment, which is that *Terror of the Vervoids* is ostensibly a future story of the Doctor, so Mel is introduced as already travelling with the him. Then, in *The Ultimate Foe*, she's brought to the trial.

But look at her dialogue in *The Ultimate Foe*. She asks the Doctor what he's been up to. The implication is that she hasn't seen him in a while—i.e. that she's brought from a time after she's already left the Doctor. Two major problems with this exist, of course: she doesn't recognize Glitz, and she doesn't think anything of the fact that the Doctor isn't Sylvester McCoy. Then, when she and the Doctor depart at the end of *The Ultimate Foe*, the clear implication is that they're resuming their travels together—note that Mel is putting the Doctor back on his exercise routine, and the Doctor acts weary about the constant barrage of carrot juice. Everything about that final scene is keyed to look like the Doctor and Mel resuming a standard course of adventuring—not like the Doctor is going to return Mel to where she got plucked out of time so she can meet up with a later version of him, or indeed like he's never actually met her before.

Put another way, it's clear that the show doesn't care a jot about cleaning up Mel's origins. They're left to be utterly incoherent, and this seems, if not deliberate, at least consciously acknowledged. But more to the point, any interpretation of how Mel meets up with the Doctor—especially if we take *The Companions* as part of her story (and much of fandom does, for some reason. Though to be fair, I have an enormous emotional attachment to the book—the fact that someone randomly gave it to me as a gift is what prompted me to start watching the show, since I had no reference point whatsoever for what the heck the book was)—is going to jar with something. We can reconcile the basic facts, but there's no way to reconcile the larger story.

## Part Two: Fucking Valeyards, How Do They Work?

Yes, at long last, it's time to deal with the Valeyard. Considerable effort has been made to explain the Valeyard in various media, and we'll deal with a major chunk of them in the next run of essays, but those in many ways have an ambiguous relationship with the actual story. Speaking strictly in terms of what we see on screen, then, what sense can we make of this character?

First and foremost, it is telling that Robert Holmes clearly writes the Valeyard's obsession with law and order in the *Trial* itself as an actual trait of the character and not as an act. As previously noted, the fact that Popplewick goes on at such length about the importance of rules and bureaucracy makes it clear that the Valeyard is a creature of rules. And this is so utterly consistent with Robert Holmes's larger ethos as to be, if not impossible to ignore, at least flagrantly unwise to ignore.

The larger arc of Robert Holmes's career also implies an answer to the obvious question of how, exactly, the Valeyard is supposed to work in terms of the Doctor's life and how regeneration works. That answer, of course, is, "Shut up, fanboy." And really, fair enough. There's not a lot about regeneration that's clear enough to make any explanation of the logistics clear. Except... the claim is that the Valeyard exists somewhere between the Doctor's twelfth and final incarnation.

These days that's a phrase with limitless possibility, but in 1986 it's altogether stranger. The Valeyard exists right at the point Robert Holmes idly gave as an end date for the series back in 1976. In a story that openly begs to be read as a discussion of the series' potential cancellation. From a writer who last season was loudly and openly denouncing the direction of the show in his script, with particular venom saved for continuity obsessives. And the evil side of the Doctor is shown to be defined primarily by an obsession with rules and law.

This all fits together too perfectly to ignore. The Valeyard is the desire to follow the rules of the series to the point of the series' own destruction. Coming from a point where the series is, in fact, necessarily doomed he proposes to rewrite the remainder of the series so as to lead to that point. This makes far more sense than the alternative—that the Valeyard is seeking to extend his life—since presumably transferring regenerations from one's past into one's future would be difficult. It's far more likely, I should think, that the Valeyard is seeking to secure the inevitability of his existence—to force the Doctor to become the creature of laws that he is. And his defeat constitutes a rejection of that logic.

But it's also worth paralleling this story with *The Deadly Assassin*, especially given how much *The Ultimate Foe* overtly mirrors that story. The Valeyard serves as the reunification of the renegade with the rules. He is the Doctor, but he is the Doctor in a way that has completely reintegrated himself with the structures of authority. His primary concern is the rules. This even manages to carry through to the Bakers' script through the absurd line about the catharsis of spurious morality. The choice of the word "spurious" is interesting, implying as it does an unnecessary or disingenuous morality that ought not be taken seriously. This is a contrast from the "your evil is my good" routine of, say, Sutekh or the Black Guardian. To the Valeyard, good and evil are wholly extraneous. There is only authority.

What the Valeyard threatens, in other words, is authority freed from concern for any morality. The law as something that exists entirely for its own sake, as an end in itself. Within Doctor Who terms this is, indeed, the ultimate foe—something sufficiently terrifying that even the Master would turn away from it. The only question, then, is how we could possibly say that this constitutes the evil portion of the Doctor.

## The Catharsis of Spurious Morality (*The Ultimate Foe*)

## Part Three: The Nature of Earth to Gallifrey

In the course of Holmes's mad recycling of the past, however, Holmes fires off one of the most fascinatingly problematic concepts in the history of Doctor Who, namely the idea that the Time Lords eventually yank Earth and its constellation out of place in the galaxy and plop it down elsewhere.

The use of the word "constellation" is interesting. It's a chronic foible of Holmes that he seems to use the word as a synonym for "solar system," but the error is almost the perfect Holmesian error. The nature of a constellation, after all, is that it makes sense only from a set physical vantage point. The constellations of one solar system are not the constellations of another. And yet the Doctor routinely identifies Gallifrey with reference to its constellation.

Tellingly, though, the constellation he names—Kasterborous—cannot be a Gallifreyan one, since constellations are merely happenstance arrangements of stars in the sky of a given planet, and thus one cannot see a constellation that one is a part of. So when Gallifrey is said to be in the constellation of Kasterborous, what can this possibly mean?

Clearly, and this ties in alarmingly well with Gallifrey as we understood it back in *The Deadly Assassin*, the Time Lords' understanding of themselves is defined primarily by reference to an external observer. They are, after all, seemingly a race governed not by the recorded facts of history but by the material memory of history. Their entire civilization is based around the Matrix, known to be a collection of memories. So it's not a surprise that even the location of their planet is defined in terms of an external perspective. The only question is whose.

By far the most sensible answer, within Doctor Who, is Earth's. Yes, there's a sort of dreary cliché to the idea that the Time Lords are future versions of humanity, but it's also difficult to avoid the fact that it makes a lot of sense. Not, as Miles and Woods sneer, because the sorts of people who like this idea are the sorts of people who want the Doctor to be Anakin Skywalker's father, but because some version of this is already true. The series is hopeless at making up its mind whether the Time Lords consider Earth an obscure backwater or whether they see it as a vitally important planet, but it's difficult not to observe that Earth has been the obsession of every single renegade Time Lord in the series from the Monk on.

Part of this may simply be geopolitical. Clearly there comes a point where Earth is the dominant force in the galaxy. In that regard, the Time Lords would, in any conception of them, have a lot of investment in the precise fate of humanity. But the Time Lords seem almost wholly unconcerned with, say, Draconia. None of the other vast conquering species besides the Daleks raise much of an eyebrow. The Time Lord fascination with Earth exceeds mere local politics. After all, we remain at least somewhat committed to the idea of the Time Lords as guardians of the arc of history. But if pressed on whose history, exactly, we'd be forced to confess that we are ourselves the most likely suspects here. This is inevitable—after all, it's humans writing the series, and so a human conception of history that drives things. And indeed, if we really want to be particular about it, this is inevitable simply because its true. The Time Lords really do exist and understand themselves only through our eyes.

But let's pull this thread a little further. The Time Lords at large seem at best marginally aware of Earth in *The Deadly Assassin*, which is strange given that their politics are flagrantly a reenactment of the Kennedy assassination in that story. But renegade Time Lords are all obsessed with Earth. Something about renegade status, in other words, seems to involve an awareness of the fact that the Time Lords are inherently linked to human perspectives. (If we take the meta-fictional truth of this seriously then it is perhaps telling that *The Mind Robber*, along with implying that the Doctor is an exile from the Land of Fiction, inadvertently gestures forward and implies the Master's presence there as well.) But on Gallifrey itself this seems to be more secret knowledge.

But let's return to *Trial of a Time Lord* specifically. Of the many bits of dodgy explanation to be offered in the course of the story, the Time Lords' supposed logic in moving Earth around is by far the strangest. Surely options less extreme and scandalous existed to deal with the seemingly minor problem they were actually facing. Moving a planet in lieu of chasing down some thieves whose location is already known is just strange.

Here it's worth thinking again about the fact that Earth's entire constellation is moved. In other words, the shape of it within the Gallifreyan sky is maintained with a seemingly slight positional change. But from an Earthbound perspective the difference is more significant—the entire sky would change. And the Earthbound perspective is how the location of Gallifrey is understood. In other words, moving Earth's constellation would be nothing short of a covert redefinition of the entirety of Time Lord culture—the most fundamental social revolution imaginable, done as a complete secret. No wonder the coverup was such a big deal.

## Part Two: The Story That Didn't Happen?

Indeed, in the end the only escape the story can muster from its own critique is the idea that it never happened. This is emphasized twice over. First of all, we're told throughout the story that the Doctor's actions are being misrepresented. Second, we're told at the end of *The Ultimate Foe* that the story's grand crescendo, Peri's death, was all a fabrication and that Peri is fine. (…ish. But that's for later in the essay.) What we're left with is an oddity in Doctor Who—a story defined primarily by the fact that it never happened.

This is a pity, as what's actually going on in *Mindwarp* is quite good. Philip Martin, predictably, brings the politics, and *Mindwarp* ends up being, among other things, a pleasant bit of anti-capitalism (or, at least, anti-the-capitalism-of-the-1980s). In terms of its own storytelling, it's far and away the highlight of Season Twenty-Three. (Of course, in another sense, the idea that the Colin Baker era would render one of its best stories non-canon is almost too fitting.)

But what's really interesting here is the idea of a story that is televised Doctor Who (and thus "canonical" by even the strictest of definitions not to be willfully silly) that nonetheless never happened. Doctor Who has not previously engaged in the idea of an unreliable narrator like this, and it won't again until *Love and Monsters*.

This requires some thought about the narration of the program in general. Tat Wood has what is probably his most unfortunate essay on this subject, in which he proceeds to try to posit some actual diegetic reason why the actions of a Time Lord are being sent to the BBC for transmission. But even if this take is overly silly, it's worth noting in the general case that the psychic impressions taken by the TARDIS of events around it are edited with careful choice of camera angles and cuts. And the implication is that this is not simply the Valeyard making choices, as the Doctor's objections in *Terror of the Vervoids* are merely to the truth of the evidence. Had he served as film editor in preparing his defense, one imagines his objections would be phrased very differently. Similarly, the fact that the Doctor struggles for an explanation as to how the emphasis of the evidence in *Mindwarp* might be misleading suggests that he hasn't thought about editing. If nothing else, the fact that the Doctor is not allowed to review any sort of master tape from which this edited evidence is extracted suggests that, no, the Matrix really is recording information as though it's a television program. (Recall that in *The Deadly Assassin* we posited that the camera and the Panopticon are fundamentally related concepts.)

But by and large this fits with our larger understanding of the Time Lords. Of course their sense of events are narratively constructed. How else could they possibly see the world? Even the Doctor doesn't question it. Indeed, there's something altogether consistent about all this—remember that the Doctor's mental impressions of *The Evil of the Daleks* were also edited like a television program. Not for the first time it appears that the Time Lords have no conception of events except as narrative. Indeed, even the Matrix is just a collection of stories. (Perhaps explaining how something that is apparently just a collection of Time Lord brains is capable of providing nightmarish virtual reality to entrap people—it's just fragments of the narratives contained within it.)

Above all, however, it is fitting that this happens in the segment of the story designated as "the present." *Trial of a Time Lord* exists in place of the Seasonish, and the one story that ostensibly exists within its timeframe is itself ished and left ambiguous as to its very existence. This is, in short, the point where *Trial* begins to fall apart as a coherent narrative.

## Part Three: What Is The Future?

As *Terror of the Vervoids* descends into an incoherent mess, however, there are interesting interpretations to be made of it. The biggest bit of intensive wonkiness to come out of the story is the idea of the Doctor reviewing the events of a future adventure. But as bits of head-scratching incoherence in Doctor Who go, there are few bits more generative of strange implications.

Let's start big here with predestination. Doctor Who has typically been pretty strongly on the side of free will. Even in the new series, when things get intensively timey-wimey, the show constantly stresses the ability to change and reshape time. So given that, it's difficult to even begin to make headway into the idea of the Doctor casually reviewing his future adventures. And presumably he did have to review a decent number—I mean, one doubts he just plunged into his future, grabbed an adventure at random, and thought, "I'm sure this will do." So how, exactly, can this be squared away with the series more general embrace of free will? I mean, it's one thing for the Doctor to know vaguely what his future incarnations look like and how one of his adventures might play out. It's another to systematically peruse them to find evidence in a trial.

But wait, there's a bigger issue here. The Matrix contains the minds of past Time Lords. We've been told repeatedly that we're watching the psychic impressions of the TARDIS. So why the heck does the Matrix have access to this adventure in the first place? Short of completely abandoning the idea that Time Lords have any sense of the present—a viewpoint that is irreconcilable with everything else we've ever seen of them—there's no way to figure out how this would work.

Unless, of course, these aren't the Doctor's Time Lords. After all, the presence of the Valeyard does necessitate that the Doctor is out of his own personal timeline here. The question is purely whether the Valeyard is meddling with the past of Gallifrey or whether the Doctor is being yanked around by a future Gallifrey. The fact that the Doctor's future adventures are known to these Time Lords suggests very strongly that it's the latter: that this is a Gallifrey from several incarnations in the Doctor's future.

Indeed, future events in the series even make it fairly easy to peg when in the future it is. We're jumping the gun a little bit here, but one thing we'll notice when we get around to the new series is that the Time War is in part a metaphor for the program's cancellation and the resulting loss of a unified or master text. Given this, and given *Trial*'s necessary engagement with the Seasonish, there's every reason to treat *Trial* as an early echo of the Time War.

So what we have is, in effect, the future of the series attempting to rewrite its past. Or, more accurately, its present. And by necessity, at least some of this rewriting takes. The Valeyard may be defeated at the end, but that doesn't mean that the Doctor's narrative doesn't shift. Aside from handily resolving the mess of continuity errors introduced by *Trial*, this has the exceedingly useful benefit of providing a diegetic reason for the increase in quality that (slowly but surely) begins after the *Trial*. The future goes to the weakest point in the program and demands that it justify itself. And in response, the program begins to retune itself towards that future.

## Part One: A Courtroom of Renegades

It's November 29th, 1986. Berlin remain at number one, and are unseated for the final week of this story by Europe with The Final Countdown. Erasure and Debbie Harry also chart. Lower in the charts—we've not looked in some time, after all—are Genesis with "Land of Confusion," A-ha, The Eurythmics, Simple Minds, and The Damned. Which paints a rosy picture, but we could also have done that by saying Bucks Fizz, Kenny Loggins, and Rod Stewart were in the lower charts, so, you know, let's not get carried away.

In real news, the first case of bovine spongiform encephalopathy, or, as we cheerily call it, Mad Cow Disease, is diagnosed in British cattle, and preparations are made to offer shares of British Gas as the British natural gas industry gets privatized.

While on television, *Trial of a Time Lord* finally wraps up. Throughout the preceding three essays we have been pursuing various theories as to what is actually going on in this suite of stories. And for the most part we've been relatively fortunate, in that the thematic implications of the *Trial* have managed to explain the on-screen events surprisingly well. The infelicities of Holmes's cosmic terminology play off of our established understanding of the Time Lords perfectly to produce a political situation where the apparent malfeasance of the trial makes sense. The implications of the Doctor perusing future adventures perfectly sets up the bizarre contradictions within the story. We're clearly miles out of line with what anyone writing this intended, but we're nevertheless finding ourselves with a fairly easy interpretation of the entire trial as belonging to some hypothetical future period of the show that is at least partially averted by the revamp of the show that occurs in the *Trial*'s wake.

What remains, then, is understanding what this future timeline is like. Given that it is a future timeline, my readership will forgive me for actively cross-checking it with future stories, since I try not to discuss stories I've not covered yet at length. In any case, very few details present themselves. The Master is still in his Tremas skinsuit, suggesting that it predates the McGann movie. But we've also posited that this could be as far forward as the Time War, in which we know the Master was brought back to life, so presumably any version of the Master could do there. A better clue comes from the Inquisitor's claim that the Doctor was deposed as Lord President.

This clue is admittedly trickier. At first glance it seems to suggest that we are, in fact, in the Doctor's present. But that is just about the only thing in the entire Trial that points towards that, so let's instead suggest that it merely implies that the Doctor has been deposed by the time in Gallifreyan history that the trial is taking place. That tells us that it post-dates *Remembrance of the Daleks*. (This is, of course, assuming that time is not excessively rewritten by the events of the *Trial*—a topic we'll come to shortly.)

But past those vague guideposts we're left without much mooring in terms of the when—which is, admittedly, unsurprising given that Gallifrey post-*Five Doctors* is a complex topic to say the least. But it's sufficient to observe that the Trial seems to take place somewhere in the hiatus—a period that, as I've already remarked, necessarily coincides with the Time War.

Moving on from when, then, let's look at what. The first and most obvious thing to point out is that the setting of *Trial* is strange. On the one hand it is clearly aboard a space station distant from Gallifrey. On the other the space station is clearly a place important enough to be the location of the Seventh Door to the Matrix. To be blunt about the question, then, where the heck is this place?

The more interesting thing to point out, however, is that nobody on the station seems to have a name. Even the seeming representative of Gallifreyan authority, the Keeper of the Matrix, is a position we have never seen referred to before held by someone who lacks a name. We observed back in *The Mark of the Rani* that there is an existent if inadvertent distinction within Time Lords between named exiles and nameless renegades. And so it is of considerable interest to note that according to this logic, the trial is comprised entirely of renegades: the Inquisitor, the Valeyard, the Keeper, et cetera.

What is strange about renegades (as opposed to any other group of Time Lords) is that they are at once the lowest and the most powerful sorts of Time Lords. On the one hand they are wholly separate from Gallifreyan society, on the other they are continually uniquely privileged within it. The fact that the Doctor is put on trial by renegades speaks volumes and is one of the most intriguing details of the story. Especially when one thinks about how the renegades are privileged. For one thing, the only people we have ever seen to have a TARDIS in all of Doctor Who are renegades. Now we see that a space station full of renegades has one of the doors to the Matrix. And let's further note that in *The Deadly Assassin* entering the Matrix from Gallifrey is a dangerous and dodgy process involving machines. Similarly, communion with the Matrix in *The Invasion of Time* requires no end of danger and equipment. We've never seen anything like a door to the Matrix on Gallifrey, and prior to this story it was never viewed as one of the functions of the Key to Rassilon. The implication is that not only do the renegades have privileged access to the Matrix, they are in fact the true keepers of it.

To be a renegade, in other words, is to be in a position of true authority—to be the driver of the eye of the Panopticon. And the Trial consists of them turning the Panopticon and all of their authority onto the Doctor in what we now understand as an explicit attempt to rewrite his history. At this point, then, we must finally turn to the question of who's doing this.

### Time Can Be Rewritten: *Peri and the Piscon Paradox*

One of the fundamental benefits of rewriting time—something you can readily point to and say, "This is why doing audio dramas nearly a quarter-century after the actors stopped playing their roles is worthwhile"—is the ability to pick at the wounds of the past, or to try, belatedly, to heal them. And one of the fundamental benefits of Big Finish's *Companion Chronicles* line is that it encouraged bold and experimental takes, as opposed to the often blandly conservative preferences of the main line. Add to the mix Nev Fountain, one of the most reliably inventive writers at Big Finish and the idea of *Peri and the Piscon Paradox* seems exceedingly appealing.

The gist of this one's simple—it's a two-disc adventure (double size for a Companion Chronicle), the first of which features Peri and the Fifth Doctor dealing some fish aliens. In the course of the adventure, Peri meets her future self, who appears to gun down a more or less innocent alien for little reason. The disc ends with Peri leaving, aghast, and the Doctor making a very touching speech about how he's always terrified of meeting his future self because he knows how he can change. There's a final line about heading to Androzani Minor, and that's the disc. Then the second disc tells the same story from the perspective of future Peri, who is a talk show host. It turns out the fish alien wasn't a fish alien at all, but the Sixth Doctor in a rubber suit (the reasons are complicated), and that future Peri didn't kill him after all, it was all an illusion. And in the course of this, Peri's final fate is squared away. It's all quite a clever idea.

And on the first disc, at least, it's very good. Peri is engagingly fleshed out as a character, there are some genuinely funny jokes, and the whole thing sets up a promising engagement with the big problems of Peri. Bits of it feel as though they anticipate *Dark Water/Death in Heaven* in terms of the plot and Peri's characterization. Even in the second disc, things are mostly engaging, although the gimmick of going through the exact same plot from a second perspective does lead to some unfortunately tedious stretches of waiting for what you know is going to happen. It's all very smart, right up until the point it falls apart.

It's tempting to say that the point where this happens is when a Time Lord shows up more or less out of nowhere and explains Peri's fate, especially given that, although it's come up (and is tacitly raised throughout by the existence of an earthbound future Peri), it's not as though this has been a story about what happens to Peri. And it's true, that is unsatisfying, not least because it really just describes things happening to Peri, which is to say, it goes against the tone of the entire story up to that point. And, as amendments to the past go, it's not an altogether compelling one—by its nature it doesn't actually fix anything for the character or increase her dignity in any way.

But the real problem comes moments earlier, in a sequence that comes breathtakingly close to being good only to fail utterly at this. See, at the start of the first disc, Peri muses on her boyfriend that she'd left at home before heading off to Lanzarote and, subsequently, all of time and space, going back and forth on whether to return to him. He seems, in her description, like a nice if utterly banal guy, and when she meets her future self she asks about him and is told that she eventually marries him. Then, at disc's end, she realizes her future self lied about this, and angrily declares that it was not marrying the guy that set her future self on this wrong path. When the story circles back to this moment towards the end of the second disc, then, we get future Peri's take on it, and it's revealed that she did not in fact lie; rather, it's that the guy was violently abusive, resulting in a line about how nice guys can suddenly turn violent, which is a very pointed meta-comment on the Fifth to Sixth Doctor regeneration and the events of *The Twin Dilemma*.

On the one hand, this is satisfying, in that it marks an actual acknowledgment that the Doctor's conduct in that story constitutes outright abuse, and addresses the way in which Peri is characterized as a battered woman in the Sixth Doctor era. Except for, well, several problems. First, of course, is that it's still implicit. The story is passing judgment on *The Twin Dilemma*, but the events never explicitly come up. In fact, the story goes somewhat out of its way to never have a version of Peri who has any knowledge of or experience with the Sixth Doctor appear: the future Peri has suffered a Jamie/Zoe-style mindwipe so that she only remembers *Planet of Fire*, and the Fifth Doctor version of Peri is, well, with the Fifth Doctor. It goes right to the edge of actually trying to talk about it, but then... doesn't.

The second problem is a more general one, which is that the really awful thing about future Peri's abuse is that it's left her infertile. Indeed, this comes up over and over. Apparently Peri's fondest desire in the world is to have children. This has no real antecedent in the series—it's wholly an invention of the audio. And it's a crassly stereotypical move, made all the worse by the sense that somehow the domestic violence isn't bad enough on its own merits.

And then there's the third and perhaps broadest problem, which is that the entire revelation comes out of nowhere in the course of a story that had previously been a broad comedy with a lot of jokes about plastic surgery. There's a character in it, Beretta, who's described as having so disfigured herself with plastic surgery that she basically looks like a fish, and who is routinely mocked and humiliated by the plot, in no small part because she's an idiot. It's a broad joke about the American "white trash" stereotype, and I suppose it's vaguely funny in some way, but even within Doctor Who, where the juxtaposition of comedy and drama is part of the point, it's a bit of a tough ask to put a ridiculous caricature like Beretta in a story that suddenly turns around to make a Very Serious Point about domestic violence.

But this gets at, perhaps, a larger point: the entire story is laced with absurdity and irony. I mean, that's pretty implicit in the "monster turns out to be the Doctor in a rubber suit" plot twist, but the whole thing basically goes this way. There's loads of nudge-nudge wink-wink jokes about Doctor Who and its ostensible lack of quality, loads of snark about plastic surgery and the present day—basically, loads of ironic detachment.

Obviously I am not opposed to comedy in Doctor Who. Nor am I opposed to Doctor Who engaging in serious issues. I'm not even opposed to it doing both at once. But look, I want to be clear: I am not ironically detached from *The Twin Dilemma*. I am not ironically detached from what was done to Peri in Doctor Who. And I am not ironically detached from the Nathan-Turner era. Bad things were done. Things that I think it is legitimate to be angry about. In fact, things that I think deciding you care about Doctor Who *requires* you to be angry about.

And ironic detachment in the face of that is not, to my mind, productive or valuable. I don't want to see two versions of Peri who haven't experienced the strangulation in *The Twin Dilemma* go through a plot that obliquely and metaphorically criticizes it. I want to see Peri confront the Doctor, and for the Doctor to actually admit that what he did was irredeemably awful. This jokey pastiche of plastic surgery jokes and puns about warrior queens doesn't cut it.

In many ways, it's the presence of the Sixth Doctor, and specifically of Colin Baker that does it. Because any criticism of the character is muted by the fact that Colin Baker's on the audio loving the hell out of shouting into a ring modulator and pretending to be evil. The presence of the Sixth Doctor as a loveably funny old coot who keeps getting outwitted by the Fifth without the Fifth ever realizing that it's him means that the criticism of the strangulation stops being connected to any actual character. Sure, future-Peri declines the offer to travel with him, partly out of disgust over what's been done to her timestream, but it doesn't matter. The story that finally brings some form of narrative justice to Peri simply cannot also be one about enjoying the Sixth Doctor, let alone full of ironic detachment that serves to suggest that none of this matters.

If we're going to take the classic series seriously, let's take it seriously. There's no point trying to rewrite time if you're not going to try to get it right.

## Time Can Be Rewritten: *Jubilee*

The first and most obvious thing to say is that the Sixth Doctor does, in fact, work. More than anything else, we ought to acknowledge the fact that Rob Shearman, with *Jubilee*, makes it so that Colin Baker has an unambiguous classic of Doctor Who under his belt. Baker has a lot of good audios, actually, but this is one that is blatantly a classic. So before we get into anything else we ought look at what it did with Baker's Doctor that finally got the character to work.

I would argue that there are two things. The first is a trick the show should have picked up from Jon Pertwee, who was so often at his best when his confident and at times outright arrogant Doctor was put on the back foot or the defensive. Baker's Doctor is helped enormously by the scenes in this story in which he gets to play the Doctor driven mad by a hundred years locked in the Tower of London. Seeing his Doctor so weakened and afraid has the same effect it does for Pertwee, on top of letting Baker show off some acting ability that he was rarely given the opportunity to on television. Indeed, the mad Doctor in the Tower is in many ways an idea perfectly suited to Baker's Doctor, whose bluster and confidence can be subverted with a wickedness that the Doctors on either side of him couldn't hope to match.

The other major trick that *Jubilee* manages to improve Baker is not Shearman's invention, but a brilliant idea nevertheless: Evelyn Smythe. Evelyn is an interesting concept for a companion—a fifty-five-year old history teacher. OK, so actually, that's more accurately described as the original concept of a companion, despite Evelyn being a good twenty years older than Barbara was. But it's a compelling move away from the horribly sexualized peril monkey Peri was stuck playing that doesn't go straight to comedy as Mel, by dint of her casting, did.

The result is a companion who can actually stand up to the Doctor in such a way as to make him no longer seem nearly so nasty. Again, this is largely lifted from the Pertwee era. Pertwee worked because he had Jo Grant for three years and she, no matter what Pertwee did, could smile winsomely and reassert herself with a moment of sheer pluck and charm. That meant that Pertwee's character was always kept in check. It's the same thing that made Tom Baker's grandstanding in the latter days of his tenure bearable—the fact that Lalla Ward could hold her own. And in Evelyn Smythe, Big Finish created a character who could stand up to Baker's Doctor in that way and thus keep him charming instead of overbearing. She was in many ways the companion he should always have had, although realistically the basic premise of a senior citizen companion was never going to fly in the era of aiming the camera at Nicola Bryant's bosom "for the dads."

This, at least, explains the infrastructure changes that *Jubilee* enjoys. It starts at a higher baseline of quality and potential, and that makes it easier for it to achieve greatness. It doesn't, however, explain why *Jubilee* is great. And this question sets up an interesting opportunity for us. If we were only covering *Jubilee*, of course, this would be an essay for talking about all the terribly clever things that Rob Shearman does with the Daleks. But if I do that I'm going to have very little to talk about when I get to *Dalek*, in two books' time. So instead I'm going to do something that hardly anybody has done for the much-acclaimed *Jubilee* and talk about all the brilliant bits that get overlooked for the Dalek stuff, and keep the Dalek bits to a minimum here in favor of talking about them with *Dalek*, a story that, while also very good, doesn't have all the other clever stuff that *Jubilee* does.

In practice *Jubilee* is a piece of snarling political leftism of the sort that I'm predisposed towards liking. Let's start with its title, an oft-overlooked detail. It's not called *Foo of the Daleks* or anything like that. It's called *Jubilee*, a title that focuses attention away from the Daleks and towards an act of celebration, specifically celebration of history and the anniversary of a monarch's reign. But what's crucial to *Jubilee*, and what the whole of the plot and theme revolves around, is the fact that a jubilee is not a piece of history itself but merely a ritualized celebration of it.

*Jubilee* is, of course, tremendously skeptical of this logic. Actually, more than skeptical, it's outright hostile to this logic. It openly accuses the celebratory commemorations of history of being tools of oppression that sustain and justify imperial horrors. It's a remarkably compelling piece in that regard, echoing later obscenities like the fact the Queen's Diamond Jubilee was used as an occasion to force people to work an unpaid fourteen-hour shift and to sleep under a bridge. Or the fact that the Olympics were being used as a reason to install missile batteries on residential buildings and to have London patrolled by helicopter-based snipers. Or the fact that a government preaching austerity and slashing benefits for the poor endorsed both of the above, because these "celebrations" are, after all, absolutely essential to Britain. (Not that my country is any better on any of these fronts. Celebration capitalism knows no national boundaries.) The sequence where Rochester dismisses the idea of spending money to rebuild houses demolished as part of an aborted redevelopment of London on the grounds that the jubilee is more important is particularly chilling in light of the Olympic-instigated levelling of swaths of East London.

So right off the bat we have a story that's baring its teeth and going for the political throat—something the Saward era, even when doing pitch-black comedy, tended not to do in such a materialist sense. And it's a flat refutation of the idea that this sort of approach requires being heavy-handed or obvious. Yes, *Jubilee* goes on a bit about how people shouldn't be like the Daleks, but as we'll see even that's more complex than it appears. But nobody complains about the excessive anti-imperialism or anti-capitalism of *Jubilee*. It's not a heavy-handed allegory. It's a damn good piece of drama.

Part of this is down to the quality of its cast. When the lion's share of the dialogue for the non-regulars is going to Martin Jarvis, Rosalind Ayres, and Nicholas Briggs doing some stunningly disturbing Dalek voices, you have a strong baseline. On top of that, Shearman doesn't take the "moralizing polemic" approach in the first place. He takes the Robert Holmes "deeply uncomfortable joke" approach, letting the characters take on comedic roles and then pushing the comedy past the point where it's funny in order to make it disturbing and upsetting.

But the other tremendously interesting thing about *Jubilee* is that it uses the history of the program as one of its weapons. The story is one that only works because it has Daleks and all of the history they imply. What's key is that the Daleks play a double role in the story. On the one hand they are themselves nostalgic fetish objects—the subjects of their own jubilee. (Indeed, this is Big Finish's Dalek story for the 40th anniversary.) They're repeatedly treated as the silly pieces of history that, in the larger culture of the show, they are. (There's a choice line about how slapping a picture of a Dalek on anything increases sales.) But this jubilee purpose is continually subverted by an alternate version of the Daleks—one in which they're a genuine, terrifying menace.

Here's where *Jubilee* differs from *Dalek*, then. *Dalek* is entirely about establishing the Daleks as a credible threat. *Jubilee*, on the other hand, depends on the fact that the Daleks continually move back and forth from being jubilee monsters—empty signifiers of nothing more than the series' history—and seriously disturbing threats. These two positions aren't even presented as opposed to one another. The Daleks are dangerous in part because of their history, and, more specifically, because of the way that history is obscured by their jubilee nature.

The big moment in terms of this comes in the phenomenal scene in which the Dalek orders Farrow to cut Lamb's head off, leading to Farrow nervously asking whether the Dalek knows the history of the Tower. In response the Dalek thunders that it *is* the history of the Tower. This is a wonderful concept—the Dalek is claiming to be the gore and violence and horror that constitutes the material history of the Tower of London. The Daleks, in other words, are reconceptualized as the erased material remnant of history— as the very thing that the jubilee serves to obfuscate—while simultaneously being presented as the jubilee itself.

This is what stands at the heart of the Dalek's concluding paradox whereby the Daleks, to conquer the universe, must never conquer the universe. It's not a drab "blow up the computers with a paradox" ending, but an acknowledgment of this fundamental tension at the heart of the Daleks. The Daleks are dangerous precisely because of the jubilee's erasure. The entire threat of the Daleks is based on the fact that they are the horrific consequence of reiterated history.

This also gets at what's actually going on in the Doctor's rather overlong and unconvincing speech to the people. The Doctor is, in fact, going about it the wrong way—a point reiterated by the awkward echoing effect given to his speech, making it sound like every bad commencement speech you've ever heard. He's trying to persuade people to not be like the Daleks. But the rejection of the Daleks is, in fact, the problem. The fact that everybody has pushed the Daleks into the darkness of an erased history is what's dangerous about them in the first place and where their power comes from. Or, to put it another way, the fact that the Daleks are mythic wildly enhances the threat posed when their visceral horror reasserts itself.

This is a relationship with the series' past that is, in 1986, still a bit ahead of what the series can actually do. It's not until 1988 that the ideas underlying *Jubilee* even start to emerge in the program itself, and it takes time for the techniques to develop to where something as conceptually radical as *Jubilee* is possible. But we do, here, have a very different sort of take on the idea of continuity and the past. Here the excess of history that the program has is one of the tools it uses to make its point. The irreconcilability of the program's continuity is where its power comes from. The fact that the Daleks are simultaneously ontologically defined as the most dangerous thing in the universe and obviously nothing more than homicidal salt shakers is used as a concept not in spite of the contradiction but because of it.

And, fantastically, deliciously, this feeds back into the story's point. The story makes much of its anti-imperialism. On the one hand, this is prescient—the story came out months before the invasion of Iraq and all of the sublimated dreams of empire involved in that. On the other, "the British empire was really bad" is, while undoubtedly true, a bit of a bland point to be making in 2003. But under Shearman's approach the degree to which "imperialism is bad" is a banal cliché is exactly what makes it dangerous. The fact that we all know that imperialism is bad and have relegated it to the past is what allows it to sneak out and rear its ugly head again. (Compare to how, in the US, the victories of the Civil Rights movement of the 1960s and Obama's election are used to obscure the continuing existence of racism, and indeed, how Obama's election worsened racism in America.) The same processes through which the Daleks gain their potency are the ones through which real-world structures of oppression disguise themselves and their intentions.

## We're Doing Something No One Else Would Dare Do: An Interview With Rob Shearman

**Phil Sandifer**: I want to start with the Davison portion of the sort of Eric Saward era, since I know that was very much your era growing up.

**Rob Shearman**: Yeah, hugely, yeah.

**PS:** I know you praised Christopher Bailey's two stories a lot, and quite rightly, but what else about the era stands out for you?

**RS:** The first proper Doctor Who story that I watched was *Castrovalva*.

**PS:** You got in at exactly the right place, really.

**RS:** I got into Doctor Who partly because I suddenly realized there was a history to it, and the history appealed to me. They'd shown on BBC only a couple of months before *Castrovalva* went out, the big *Five Faces of Doctor Who* season.

**PS:** Right, that's actually one of the first essays in the book, so.

**RS:** So, just to explain, I'd always grown up with the idea that

Tom Baker was the Doctor; I was four years old when *Robot* went out. And I'd never really watched Tom Baker because every time I tried to I was scared stiff of it. My younger sister, who was braver than me, would watch it. I would honestly be scared even by the time-tunnel and the theme music. And I do have vague memories of things which of course in later years I can now identify as bits of *The Sun Makers*, bits of *Creature from the Pit*, and reacting to them with and absolute dread which is in no way borne out. It would frighten me simply because it was Doctor Who at all. And it was only when I had my interest piqued by the notion that there was a longer history to the program than simply this sort of strange series of scares on a Saturday night that I began to find it intriguing. I was lent by a friend at school a copy of *The Making of Doctor Who*, and I just loved the fact there was a list of all the stories! It was very odd. Within about two months—because I didn't see any of the *Five Faces of Doctor Who* completely, but I would still catch bits of those episodes, so I saw bits of *The Krotons* and a bit of *Carnival of Monsters*—

**PS:** Right, because those aired on consecutive days of the week, so those were basically running Monday through Thursday.

**RS:** Yeah, and I was thick, I didn't realize that, I thought it was a weekly thing, so I remember catching only bits but never a whole story. So what really happened was that by the time *Castrovalva* went on I had gobbled up a couple of reference books—this is actually how much of a nerd I am and how much I like the whole academic approach. My first Doctor Who books were *The Making of Doctor Who*, the *Doctor Who Programme Guide, Volume One* by Jean-Marc Lofficier, which I memorized, so I knew all the titles of Doctor Who stories before I actually knew what they even were about, and *Doctor Who Discovers: The Conquerors*, which was—

**PS:** That is the first that I have heard of that book.

**RS:** There was a series of books published by Target—it basically had Tom Baker as Doctor Who dropping in and telling you about characters from history or science. So you'd have him meeting Napoleon, but it wouldn't be a story, it would just be a sort of very stupid children's reference book with no real information, which they were trying to make seem a bit more palatable by putting Tom Baker on the cover. So, I read those books before I read any Target novelizations, and by the time I'd seen *Castrovalva* I'd read maybe a dozen novelizations? I remember steeling myself for others. I remember the first novelization I bought was *Image of the Fendahl* and I bought it specifically because it had the worst cover.

**PS:** (laughs)

**RS:** And I couldn't believe anything really scary could be in it, because of this dreadful cover.

**PS:** How did that work out for you?

**RS:** Yeah, it was fine, I mean, it was terribly short. I was quite a smart reader. Reading novelizations was a retrograde step for me. I was reading Charles Dickens at that point! And here I am reading Terrance Dicks, and I get sucked into this whirlpool of reading maybe things that weren't quite as proper as Dickens for a few years. My parents were very disappointed. I wasn't the genius they'd hoped for! So *Image of the Fendahl* was a very quick read, and I enjoyed it, and I could see it was a bit scary but it wasn't really going to do anything bad to me. And once I'd had the courage to do that I was able to read others—I think it's ironic actually, I had just begun to read Season Fifteen novelizations without at that point quite realizing that they were of the same season. So I remember reading *Horror of Fang Rock* soon after that. And then *The Invisible Enemy*. I began to get this impression that every single book was going to feature the Doctor and Leela and maybe a K9 who didn't do very much. Which is quite strange.

**PS:** Yes.

**RS:** And so by the time *Castrovalva* started, I was also a Doctor Who fan—it was odd, I described myself at that point, watching my first complete story, as a fan. And it meant that as a result when you got all that sort of continuity references in Episode One and Two, you know, with the Brigadier being talked about and Ice Warriors and Ogrons get a mention, I thought "Ahhh," I knew exactly what that means and it made feel very very proud, though of course I had never seen any of it.

This is a very roundabout way of trying to explain where I was with Doctor Who, which means when I came to it, all of the Davison era to me was like a sort of blank page upon which I was learning to understand what Doctor Who was. The novelizations were fine, but they didn't give me a taste of that television language that Doctor Who had, for a long while I thought of them as completely different ways of storytelling—I knew *Doctor Who and the Cave Monsters* had once been on telly, but only theoretically; I couldn't quite see how that would work. (I was so excited when *The Visitation* was released as the first Davison novel, because I wanted to see how the same story could be told on screen and on the page!) And as a result, Season Nineteen, the first Davison season, which I think is a remarkable piece of work, constantly wrong-footed me by never offering the same tone any story running. And for me that's one of the reasons that I love the Davison era so much, is that I think for that—really for the next four years, even with Colin's first season, you do get the sense of a show which feels quite schizophrenic, and I think very intelligently so. And I think it is deliberately wrong-footing. I remember when I watched *Four to Doomsday* being a little bit nervous that this was now going to be a show about spaceships after all. I didn't want it to be. I wanted it to be about people trapped in weird paintings. That first run of

Davison stories confounded me—from the show's reputation, and from my scared childhood memories, I thought it was all about monsters in corridors shooting people down with ray guns, which didn't actually happen until *The Visitation* Episode One.

**PS:** Oh, okay.

**RS:** So all those clichés that I thought Doctor Who was, all those years, were never being given to me. What I was getting was something which felt infinitely richer. I mean, I would never have expected Doctor Who could have been *Black Orchid*. I never thought it could be *Kinda*. *Kinda* was the one and only time that as a genuine watcher of Doctor Who that I was scared. I was twelve years old—

**PS:** I actually watched your interview with Bailey to prep for this, and I remember you said the opening of the Box of Jhana terrified you.

**RS:** The opening of the Box—not the one which is the cliffhanger, which is the bit everyone remembers at the end of Episode Two, which is wonderful, it's a great cliffhanger with Nerys Hughes screaming—the scene that frightened me was earlier in the episode. And it just felt so cruel and it still does actually, I think it's wonderfully directed, it's the bit where Sanders is in the TSS machine and he comes across Karuna in that weird jungle, and she passes him the Box, and then her face contorts into a strange victorious smile as he opens it and his own face turns red. Watch it, it's wonderful! Oh, I didn't understand it one little bit. I was utterly baffled by it. And I was baffled, and it thrilled me, and I couldn't not love it.

I was caught between my expectations of the show and what it was actually doing week by week, and it was that disjunct that made me become a really passionate fan. And I think the irony is that if I'd seen it only a few years before, if I'd caught the stories that I now genuinely admire from the Hinchcliffe years or from Graham Williams, where Doctor Who has its own house style it repeats consistently week by week, I think I'd have been far less interested. What really amazed me about the Davison years is just how random and freewheeling it seems. And just how experimental it is. And I know that it is not at times the most artistically consistent show ever made, but even that actually really really thrills me. I mean—some people see it as a tremendous flaw, that you can follow the likes of *Caves of Androzani* with *Twin Dilemma*, or, I know it's controversial for you, but the likes of *Earthshock*—which I'm very fond of—with *Time-Flight*.

**PS:** I enjoy *Earthshock* more than I like it. If that makes sense.

**RS:** I actually really do like *Earthshock*, I think it's a very clever sort of piece of work, and I think it's actually a sensitive piece of work as well. But we shall come to that, no doubt. But again, part of that is sort of the way in which other people now criticize JNT and even at the time—I joined the Doctor Who Appreciation Society terribly quickly, and fans were there moaning at the way you could never trust it to be consistent—you'd get this sense that you could get stories which would be questing and smart followed by something which felt really rubbish—and you couldn't ever be quite sure you could trust the show not to suddenly give you episodes that would make you cringe a bit. I remember watching *Terminus*, and—which actually I quite like, now—

**PS:** I'm fond of that one too.

**RS:** Yeah, I mean, *Terminus* has big problems, but I think it's a very ambitious piece of work, and I think *Mawdryn Undead* and *Enlightenment* on either side of it are actually quite stunning pieces of work in their own way. I remember at the time watching *Terminus* thinking, "But two weeks ago there was something really weird going on about explorations of identity and time travel and nostalgia, and now we've got this weird looking... dog... that seems to be walking around a spaceship in a very slow, uneventful story," and yet that actually still appealed to me. I think one of the great joys of the Davison years, in particular for me, is that it has a certain strange confidence in just trying things that the show would never have done at any other point in the show's history. Maybe because it was actually in some ways almost accidentally trying things out that no one else should have tried. I mean, those stories where you just know no one else would have wanted to have commissioned. And not all of them worked, in fact most of them in some ways don't work, but it's so much braver than that sort of typical story typified by those Target novelizations where you could actually see the rigid structure of the four-part story—

**PS:** Right.

**RS:** I began to notice the way that a Terrance Dicks novelization would be twelve chapters, and the end of Episode One would be the end of Chapter Three, and the end of Chapter Six would be the end of Episode Two, but what you'd actually expect is simply a group of characters who'd all be killed one by one as a sort of Agatha Christie-like format. Except the Doctor Who I was watching with Peter Davison in! It was never doing that. And I found that really engaging. Yeah. I'm not perhaps explaining it very academically—

**PS:** No, I think that makes a lot of sense. I remember you answered a question on Tumblr a while back where you said that you didn't think that the Seventh Doctor was a character you could write well. What about the Fifth? Could you write Davison's Doctor if you wanted?

**RS:** No, I don't think so.

**PS:** Why not?

**RS:** I think mostly because it really is my nostalgia, I mean Davison's Doctor is the only Doctor that I kind of feel somewhat stymied by. I don't think I can recapture that same childish excitement now.

**PS:** Right, because I considered pointing out that you sort of had written a Seventh Doctor under a pen name for BBV but that just felt too obsessive.

**RS:** Yeah. Although I don't think that I did, really, I mean, only because—actually more because I think that what—*Punchline*, it was called *Punchline*, wasn't it?

**PS:** I admit I only read about it on Wikipedia, I found that fact today while brushing up for this, so—

**RS:** I think *Punchline*—I've not heard *Punchline* for sixteen, seventeen years—I remember when I wrote that, I wasn't writing—I mean, I was specifically writing something in which he wasn't the Doctor. Even if he were the Doctor it'd be like he had his brain wiped, so what I was really writing was a sort of perverse version of a 1970s sitcom. It was actually quite easy to write because I was not writing the Doctor up until maybe the final scene.

So Davison's Doctor, to answer your question, I think the problem is he's the only one that—and I don't mean it sexually necessarily!—but he's the only Doctor I find to be truly beautiful. I find him to have a sort of... just this wonderful, frustrated exasperation... and there's a kindness to him. It all means that I don't want in any way to muddy that pool by dipping my toes into it myself. I found that even when I was watching *Time Crash* years later, when Davison pops up and he's wearing—you know, he's a bit fatter than he had been, bless him, not as fat as me many years junior to him, mind you!—I just found myself thinking, "Even now I've slipped back, I've got that Davison Doctor feel I've missed since I was fourteen years old," and he just makes me terribly happy, nostalgic, and I don't think it ever really pays to write terribly nostalgically.

When I was writing Colin Baker's Doctor for Big Finish, I think we all were kind of bouncing off the awkwardnesses of the time and trying to reinvent it, and when you're writing, say, Paul McGann's or Chris Eccleston's Doctor, in both those instances, or when I was dabbling around with Matt Smith briefly, at that point it's a completely new Doctor. And in fact you are inventing the Doctor. For Davison, there's nothing to invent. You know, it's a funny thing, Davison's Doctor is the only Doctor that I really feel that way about. He's not even my favorite Doctor in an intellectual way, I don't think he's the best example of what makes the Doctor such an interesting character, but for me he just takes me back to between those years of being twelve and fourteen years old, when his presence on the screen made me feel... not only very happy but also challenged and excited by the possibility of what stories might be told to me.

And it's something which I've spent an adult lifetime reading books and watching other television shows and watching movies—I've spent an entire adult life trying to recreate that sort of magical feeling I got when I would open up the Radio Times and see that another Doctor Who episode was about to come on, and it's another title with Peter Davison as the Doctor, and not knowing whether I would love it or merely find it something that I would watch fifteen thousand times on VHS afterwards.

**PS:** (cackles)

**RS:** So... that's part of my trouble with the Davison years, now, is that those were the stories I watched over and over and over again. I mean, I remember the first one that I could afford to keep a videotape of, the earliest one was *Arc of Infinity*. A three hour videotape could hold seven episodes, and the year before I'd had to wipe over the stories every few weeks to get something new—how annoyed was I at the end of Season Nineteen and the only complete story I'd got was *Time-Flight*! But the next Christmas I was given four or five videotapes, so I could keep them all, and *Arc of Infinity* is not necessarily the best one to start your collection with! And I found myself—

**PS:** I think *Arc of Infinity* may be the Davison I have the most instinctive revulsion towards.

**RS:** I mean, it's a weird thing, because actually, because *Arc of Infinity* is also, I think, a very brave story, and it does a lot of terribly clever things, which come across rather incompetently, but… there isn't a Davison story that I don't actually have a great deal of respect for, because even the ones that don't work, I feel that they are sincere, and actually they are in their own way quite intellectually questing. I know that that's not a very common viewpoint, but actually I think Eric Saward is a terribly unregarded editor, mostly by himself, bless him—I saw Eric a few years ago back when I was doing *Dalek*, and we had a long chat. I was going to a party and I suddenly found out that it was Eric Saward's. It was just a coincidence. I was accompanying my wife, and we went to this place and the house belonged to this chap called Eric and his partner Jane and I was like, "Oh my god it's Eric Saward!"

**PS:** (Laughs)

**RS:** And I told him at the time that I was writing a Dalek story, and bless him, he was delighted someone else was having a go at writing for them! And we talked on and on about it. So I asked him at great length about all of his stories, and he was so dismissive, he said, "I just failed at everything." He said, "I failed every single time." And I said, "You really didn't. They are very interesting." And even the ones which don't work, I really feel that I'm grateful that they were made. And that even goes for things like *Timelash*. You know, *Timelash* doesn't work at all, but there's still something…

actually, I do find it rather hard to defend *Timelash*. But that's not a Davison story so that's okay. I can certainly defend *Time-Flight*, and certainly *Arc of Infinity*, and *Warriors of the Deep*, and even *King's Demons*, which is probably my least favorite Davison, because I think it's just stupid! But even so, the thing about that stupidity, it's so off the wall that I can't help but feel a sneaky admiration for it, it's a very strange thing. Anyway, I'm rambling now.

**PS:** The rambling fascinated me, so it works out. Tell me about what it was like to actually experience the Davison to Baker regeneration? I mean, not just in the sense of going from *Caves of Androzani* to *The Twin Dilemma*, which must have been a hell of a transition to actually live through, but just the entire transition from Davison to Baker. Because in the show's accepted mythology that's when it goes hopelessly off the rails, and I suspect that wasn't what it was like for you.

**RS:** No it wasn't. I was still hugely excited. And I didn't think *Twin Dilemma* was very good; I didn't see it either as the death knell of the program. I think *Twin Dilemma* in its own way is doing something extraordinarily brave and is actually a bit braver than most of the rest of the season. I think Season Twenty-One of Davison, which is the one that at the time fandom seemed to think was a return to form after the disappointing Season Twenty, is the most pedestrian season of the eighties. I think Season Twenty is magnificent, actually. I think it's a terribly clever season, in an anniversary year, which revolves about this rather sad realization that nostalgia can't work. I don't think it's necessarily intentional. It just runs through all the stories. *Snakedance* is full of it and *Mawdryn Undead* is heartbreakingly full of it, it's wonderful that there's this perfect reason why the Brigadier is just a faded schoolteacher, it's amazing—I know at the time lots of fans felt very betrayed by that, and I thought, "It's about that betrayal! In the anniversary year, this most iconic character has sold out, has even forgotten what *Doctor Who* is." It's wonderful.

Anyway, that's not answering your question. So the thing about *Twin Dilemma*, everyone says, "Well, he really shouldn't have been strangling Peri." I thought, "No, he really should be strangling Peri, it's so interesting," that actually you get the idea of regeneration, which has become right through the Davison years such of an almost over-familiar term—most Davison stories find a way of constantly mentioning yet again that he's one of many incarnations and regeneration is a possibility, and certainly every Colin Baker story does. There's the bit in *King's Demons* when—it's bizarre, actually, that you'd actually have a bit dialogue about this—you have Anthony Ainley suddenly saying to Davison, "Oh, you're getting old, Doctor, it's time you regenerated," and you think, "When else in the show's history would villains suddenly turn around to Jon Pertwee and say, 'I think it's probably time you turned into Tom Baker?'"

**PS:** Jon Pertwee could have used that during *The Mutants*.

**RS:** Yeah, absolutely! It's a funny thing, but what *Twin Dilemma* felt like to me, it was like a huge payoff at the time. Regeneration was something which had become something which felt like a sort of safe "get out"—I think one of the things Steven Moffat has done really cleverly with the show is confronting that head-on—since regeneration has become something that you now have as a staple of how the show presents itself. You recast the lead actor every few years, and how exciting that is, and there's a big hoopla in the press about it, but now maybe there's one in the middle that you didn't actually know about, did you?

**PS:** (laughs)

**RS:** And things like that are wonderful and clever and a really brave thing to do. In a funny way there's a similarity going on when you get *Twin Dilemma*. It's about the idea of someone suddenly saying, "This thing which you are beginning to feel is a safety valve, and which you had rammed down your throats because last year was the anniversary year, with so much evidence of previous Doctors walking around—it's not as safe or as pleasant as you thought." And all of the merchandise at the time stressed the existence of previous Doctors—the program guide had on the cover every Doctor, you know, William Hartnell to Peter Davison, and we never got that in Tom Baker's time, because that's not how the program worked. At the time Doctor Who went out, back then, the history of Doctor Who was an irrelevant consequence of the fact it had been on air for so long. That all changed under JNT, and for me in a very positive way, because that's what got me into it—here was an acknowledgement and celebration of the fact that this was a long running show. It's easy to forget that by the time *Five Doctors* went out, we knew Davison was going.

**PS:** Yeah.

**RS:** I mean, it was well known. And we also knew that Colin Baker would be taking over. So by the time you get to *Twin Dilemma*—rather like, I suspect, in a funny way, leading to Matt Smith after a year of waiting for him, it feels a bit like a foregone conclusion.

**PS:** Or Peter Capaldi for that matter, he had about a year's lead time, too.

**RS:** Yeah! That's right. So what's necessary is taking that foregone conclusion and subverting it. And I think what's so clever about *Twin Dilemma* is it says, "Okay, here's a new Doctor!" And the process of creating a new Doctor, that death and rebirth, breaks him. You know, you're going to have this Frankenstein-like imagery of him looking at a mirror and recoiling. Because that isn't what he wants to see. Sylvester's reaction to regeneration is there only for the comedy, all that confusion has no edge to it at all. What I find interesting about the comparison between *Twin Dilemma* and *Time of the Rani*, you know, and some say it's a comparison I make every day because that's what I do with my spare time—

**PS:** (laughs)

**RS:** —so when you've got in *Time of the Rani* Sylvester going through the wardrobe and putting on costumes and saying, "Old hat." You start an entire new Doctor's tenure by suggesting everything's aleady stale! Whereas in *Twin Dilemma*, what Colin is doing is playing the birth of a new man and the death of an old one, and despising the man he was, and fearing the man he's becoming, and it's something which I think—although it's a hard story to like, it's very brave! I mean what he's doing, I think it's mistimed, it's something to do at the start of a season, not at the end of it. I've always had a big problem with regeneration anyway. Back when I wrote an audio—not to make it about my story—but back when I wrote *Jubilee*, which—

**PS:** Which we'll talk about eventually, I have questions about it.

**RS:** Yeah! There's a bit in that when I kill off Colin Baker's Doctor, I kill off one of them—

**PS:** Yeah, yeah, because you have two roaming around at that point.

**RS:** People wrote me at the time to say, "But why doesn't he turn into Sylvester McCoy?" And I said, "Because... he doesn't!" Because regeneration was never ever meant to be something which was just an automatic consequence of death, because if that's the case, it takes for me all the heroism out of the program. I always think about that bit in *Terror of the Zygons* where you've got a relatively newly regenerated Tom Baker who takes two bits of ganglions in the spaceship and puts them together, thinking, "I wonder if this will electrocute me?" He does it anyway, because the risk of death is never enough to put him off being a hero. He doesn't say, "I wonder if I'll move on to my next regeneration." All those times Tom Baker risks his life for the good of all, the stakes have to be higher than he'll merely sacrifice an incarnation. In some ways the promise of regeneration turns the show into a computer game, if you die you just move onto another life. I find that rather tedious. And I think that even in *Androzani*—which I obviously adore, as, you know, as a Davison fan you can't not love *Androzani*, it's beautiful—but at the very end of that, amongst Davison's final lines is, "I might regenerate, I don't know!" It's the last time it never seems an obvious thing, and then you go into *Twin Dilemma* from that, and I mean, I think that's just—I find that really remarkable, when so quickly afterwards regeneration becomes something which is just a means of counting the number of Doctors. Which I think is a bit of a shame. But, you know. I think it's also the inevitable consequence of a show that runs for as long as it is.

**PS:** On a similar note, I've always loved the retcon in *Time of the Doctor* that says that Matt Smith is suddenly the last Doctor in his regeneration cycle, because I love how it retcons the entire Matt Smith era as—he knows for a fact every single threat is the one that's going to kill him, and it doesn't change him at all!

**RS:** Yes, quite, quite.

**PS:** I love how this thing that fandom built up into this massive piece of mythology, you know, what will the Thirteenth Doctor be like, what will he be like when he's out of regenerations, and the answer is—there's only fifteen minutes of that story where he actually is officially on his last regeneration, and I thought that was a beautiful way to do away with that.

**RS:** True. And that's what the show has to do, that whatever Doctor Who becomes, you must challenge the whole mechanics of how it's perceived. All the different Doctors, that's now part of that public perception. I remember when I first heard about the John Hurt Doctor coming in, and I had half an hour of confused fanboy headbursting, because it upset—

**PS:** I remember you were still a little skeptical about it during the buildup.

**RS:** But I couldn't find a good reason, actually, I mean the only reason I could find for being upset by it—was because my anal numbering of the Doctor's incarnations was being threatened. If the only thing that was wrong about it was because I'd just found out that David Tennant was actually not Ten but Eleven—

**PS:** And Twelve for that matter!

**RS:** Actually, it's also one of those things that we conveniently—I mean, that isn't how we number them, and Steven is enough of a fan too to say, "Yeah, but he's still the Twelfth Doctor, Peter Capaldi, because John Hurt wasn't 'The Doctor'," and I think in a funny way we can still do that. Everyone knows that when you're referring to the Twelfth Doctor you're not referring to Matt Smith, because if you started doing that you're just being irritatingly pedantic. I was actually talking recently with a writer friend who had been commissioned for the show in the early Eighties, and he had this idea that the TARDIS was powered by a strange monster. I thought, "No, no one would ever have done that, because it would have upset too much the rhythm of what we think Doctor Who should be!" And that's the point. Things like that ought to come along and upset the rhythm of what Doctor Who can be.

**PS:** I think "the TARDIS is powered by a strange monster" probably would have been better than *Journey to the Centre of the TARDIS*.

**RS:** I'll be honest, the only time Doctor Who ever frustrates me, and it's true now as it was back then when I was a child, is when it doesn't feel like it's trying to do something new. Did you like Peter Capaldi's first season? Everything in that, every story, felt so brave and clever.

**PS:** Oh yeah, I think the first year of Peter Capaldi is just about my favorite stretch ever of watching Doctor Who, and I've said that the reason for that is because I turned it on and saw something new every week. And especially after writing the entirety of *TARDIS Eruditorum*, that is literally all I want out of the program is to see something I haven't seen before.

**RS:** Yeah, right, absolutely. This is actually what I thought. What's so astonishing about Peter Capaldi's first season—and, I gather, from obviously the very little I know, will be continued into the second year—there was a new sense of freshness, even down to the little things. We now have a blackboard in the TARDIS console room! I love that it's just there, as if it's always been part of the show, as if blackboards are just what *Doctor Who* does. I know people who found that really objectionable because it seemed the equivalent, for example, of *Timelash* (poor old *Timelash*) suddenly having seat belts on the TARDIS console, and you think, it's really not quite the same thing. There's a sense of strange reinvention even to the simplest things that actually feel like they are important, and certainly the way that every story is—I mean, episodes like *Kill the Moon*, which I think is given a terribly, terribly hard—

**PS:** It's my favorite of the season, I think it's one of the best episodes ever.

**RS:** Yeah, I think *Kill the Moon* is astonishing, actually, I think it's a really good episode.

**PS:** I'm actually interviewing Peter Harness just for fun next week, so, you know, I'll tell him you said so. (Note: I completely failed to do this.)

**RS:** Oh Peter's great.

**PS:** Yeah.

**RS:** I think Peter knows, because Peter and I are friends, but tell him anyway, because the wonderful thing about Peter is that he's such a kind and humble man, he really is, he's one of the humblest writers I know. There's a part of him that when I tell him how much I like *Kill the Moon* he probably thinks I'm just being nice.

**PS:** I have the awful feeling that the main reason Peter Harness sort of stumbled on my blog and liked it was just that I was the only person who was being nice to *Kill the Moon* at the time, and everyone else was, you know, reading it as an anti-abortion parable and complaining that the moon was an egg.

**RS:** Yeah, yeah, but actually, the whole *Kill the Moon* thing… which other show could possibly have a sequence where you stand on a beach and watch the moon explode and then a creature flies out of it? And when I say it to people, they say, "Well, that's why it shouldn't have happened." And I say, "No, it's kind of why it *has* to!" It has to happen, because no one else would dare go far enough to do it. Other shows would hit a reset of some sort, and I suppose you can argue that the laying of the second moon is a reset of a sort, but it isn't actually. It kind of annoys people to know that when you've got the Second Doctor and Jamie and Ben and Polly dancing upon the moon in *The Moonbase*—

**PS:** It's not the real moon!

**RS:** Yeah!

**PS:** I love that!

**RS:** Yeah, I think that's wonderful, actually, and I don't care—I admire hugely the actual bravery of the show to say, "We are doing something no one else would dare do." Star Trek wouldn't dare do it. I'm not looking to judge, don't misunderstand me, but Star Trek needs to conform to a basic homogeneity, because that's what Star Trek is. Doctor Who constantly contradicts itself, because that's the nature of what the show is, I always believed. This is much an indication of everything in Doctor Who—anything that happens this week on Doctor Who, because of the vagaries of time travel, anything else that's happened before is suddenly up for grabs. I think that's great.

I've tried to point out to people this before, you know, about my episode, *Dalek*, which can't actually now really have happened. Later episodes contradict it! My episode relied upon the fact no one would recognize a Dalek—by the end of David Tennant's time on the series, in a story set before mine, everyone on Earth has met them! Some fans at a convention pointed this out to me, bless their hearts—I've been erased from history! But you know what? It's still available to buy on DVD, and if you want to watch it you still can! I think that's wonderful. It doesn't bother me at all. It never has bothered me that I can watch *The Ambassadors of Death*, with its own take on Mars, and think, "But only five stories before we had an Ice Warrior story, and now they've been ignored!" Because it's a different Doctor, and it's a different style of program, we actually forget that *Seeds of Death* and *Ambassadors of Death* are only a season apart, and it feels like nobody involved in one has any clue about what happened in the other! And I don't think that we ought to care too much except when it suits us. And I think that's wonderful. I love the way *Doctor Who* can, if it wants to, reinvent entire histories of anywhere in the universe if the story is good enough.

**PS:** You said, while setting up the interview, that you have lots of awkward respect for the weirdness of Colin's stint. By which I assume you mean the same sense of "anything can happen" that you were praising in the Davison era.

**RS:** With Colin's first season, I think Colin's first season was really brave. I think it's trying to find on certain different levels a new way of telling Doctor Who stories. It doesn't get it right in every story, God knows, because it's learning on the hoof, the pressure of production means it's trying it by piecemeal. It is the first season which is trying to tell stories in a forty-five-minute format, and it often does that pretty well. The whole new structure of storytelling is an experiment. Some people might think *Revelation* does it badly, but using episode one as a weird prologue for a story that has the Doctor in it in Episode Two is so clearly deliberate. It could never have worked before. I adore *Revelation*, actually, I think it's one of the most interesting Doctor Who stories ever made. When I told Eric Saward that he looked bemused.

**PS:** (laughs)

**RS:** But it's structured in a way not unlike new series structure, where you say, "I think there's two very different tones to a story week by week," and in fact keeping the Doctor out of the main story for forty-five minutes feels like a really interesting structural look, as opposed to, as people often say, that Saward doesn't know what he's doing. It's so clearly not the case. It's not an attack on Colin Baker's Doctor, it's not self-indulgence—it's setting up the rules of a black comedy setting that next week Doctor Who is going to crash. *Varos* is structured terribly cleverly, *Attack of the Cybermen* is structured so both episodes—I don't think *Attack of the Cybermen* is very good!—but it doesn't change the fact that those two episodes feel so different. It's clearly not just a standard story cut in two halves, it feels that there's a completely different tone and pace per episode, and I find that remarkable.

At the same time, leaving aside structure, what you've got—and it really inspired me at the time, I mean, this is something I wanted to try as a fifteen-year-old now wanting to be a writer—what you've got is this sudden welter of tremendously sharp black comedies. They aren't afraid to be sick, disturbing, and push hard enough at the walls of good taste to see where those walls are. And I'm a huge supporter of things which are offensive, for the sake of it! I think in art, once in a while, you have to find out how far you can go. That's the air of Season Twenty-Two—rather than an aging show resting on its laurels, it's asking itself how far it can go. It makes mistakes. It's in the nature of bold experimenting that you make mistakes. If there aren't mistakes, you aren't trying hard enough! Colin's coat is a mistake, I think no one would really want to defend Colin Baker's coat, but there's still something within that costume choice that's saying, "This is now a tasteless take on Doctor Who. How tasteless can we go? Is it going to be justifiable that we have a sequence in which Shockeye eats a rat and murders an old woman? It's always been a violent show, it's a show of fantasy and extremes. Let's find out."

Which is a bit unpleasant, but it's not stupid—I mean, *Varos* is all about the actual tastelessness of what we're watching in the first place—when I was reading the Target novelizations as a child, things like *Planet of Evil*, where basically I was just reading the book to see who'd get killed one by one. And I was enjoying that. I'd say, "Hurrah, another one's got killed by that antimatter monster." Is that not really just the same as, in *Varos*, watching to see the next elaborate death? And it is, I think. And I think *Varos* addressing that in its own way seemed not only very timely to me, but right. And at the same time very, very funny.

Season Twenty-Two is for obvious reasons very maligned and quite controversial, it doesn't help that halfway through suddenly the BBC said, "We don't like this and, well, we're going to pull it," because that's never going to make you feel it's a success story. But it manages, in this fourth season of the JNT/Eric Saward era, to feel like it's attempting to reinvent itself. It still looks the same. It still has the same directors, it still has the same composers of music, largely, it doesn't feel stylistically very different in a way that you get subsequently. And… it doesn't fully work, and there are stories which I think are quite remarkably rubbish within it. Yet it's even doing new things within the way it treats writing historical stories!

**PS:** *Mark of the Rani* and *Timelash* basically invent the celebrity historical as we know it today. The idea of "the Doctor teams up with a famous person from history to fight monsters" is basically an invention of Season Twenty-Two. And now it's standard, pretty much.

**RS:** Okay, if *Mark of the Rani* just did it on its own, you might think it's a coincidence. You get George Stephenson popping up in Episode Two of *Mark of the Rani* and think, "Oh my goodness, it's the real George Stephenson," as opposed to playing this sort of funny game with what's always happened in Doctor Who for years, you keep on missing Leonardo da Vinci because real historical figures haven't appeared in *Doctor Who* since Hartnell. But suddenly you've got George Stephenson, and then a few weeks later H.G. Wells pops up too! I mean, it's actively intentional. It seems to me—I'm not saying it's actually revolutionary, but there is a sense the series is trying to do all these new things. I mean, I would also argue, as a contrary position to my own argument there, with what we know of the season that was to have followed, it doesn't look particularly innovative!

**PS:** (laughs)

**RS:** I don't think the likes of *Nightmare Fair* and *Mission to Madness*, and *Ultimate Evil*, seem to have that sort of balance of black comedy and sort of new style that I was enjoying the year before and that's a shame.

**PS:** I have a soft spot for *The Nightmare Fair*, actually.

**RS:** Yeah, I mean, I have no problem with the idea that it might have once existed. It just doesn't seem to me to be particularly interesting. The only things I find funny about it, and of course I'm sure you do as well—because I don't think we had dissimilar views with *Celestial Toymaker*—

**PS:** No.

**RS:** It's the way that *Nightmare Fair* is being commissioned in response to the popularity of a story that didn't exist, and that therefore no one noticed was bloody awful! It's as if *Celestial Toymaker* was actually watchable, and someone actually commissioned twenty years later a sequel, how bizarre is that? That's really bizarre. It's almost, like, no one actually involved had even seen it, which is truly—it's such a weird thing! I don't hate *Nightmare Fair*, it's just that to me, what I got from Season Twenty-Two in particular was that wonderful sense of quite brave black comedy, I think that *Revelation* is genuinely one of the sharpest, funniest of his scripts—

**PS:** Right, you've got *Revelation*, you've got *Vengeance on Varos*, and you've got *The Two Doctors*. Obviously *Holy Terror* and *Jubilee* both fit into this black comedy tradition as well.

**RS:** Yeah.

**PS:** Why do you think Colin Baker's Doctor works so well in bleak absurdist comedies?

**RS:** I think because his Doctor is a bit of a joke, and I don't mean that in the way that Colin might read it and be offended, either.

**PS:** Well at least we're not putting it in a list.

**RS:** It isn't necessarily a sort of a subtle thing, Colin's time on the show, but there's also something quite vivid and quite angry about it, and I think that sometimes, if you're going to just be very brash, it's actually not a bad way to communicate something darker—I think that it's a very good way of communicating *invective*, and I think there is an awful lot of anger to the Colin Baker years—there is a sense—it might just be artistic frustration some of the time, which you'd really get with the characterizations of *Varos* and *Two Doctors* and *Revelation*, there's something which is... I don't know... the bright colors and the brash comedy, something which actually lends itself to allowing something much, much nastier to be addressed. I'm not really answering the question, am I?

I'm not sure actually that Colin's performance—it think it's something to do with the way that when he... once you've got that sort of bright light studio thing that Colin's costume seems to demand, which means you can't really do subtle shadow anymore, what you've got left has got to be so bright that you might as well be very angrily satirical as opposed to being subtle and emotional. There isn't an awful lot of sentiment to Colin's time in the TARDIS, but what you have got as a result gracing it is something which feels very inventive. Sometimes I sort of play a game, I sometimes just think, "Can I really imagine Davison responding to those stories?" And actually I can't really, even though Peter could have done them, and in fact many were probably being designed for him, I know that *Vengeance on Varos* would have been, but it suits far better Colin Baker's tone. *Two Doctors*, which I know I've got myself a bit of a reputation for liking, because I was asked to step in and give a sort of defense review in the—to Tat Wood, in the—

**PS:** *About Time*, in which I think you already—you made a really impressive defense of that story.

**RS:** And I believe—I don't think *Two Doctors* is necessarily the best thing ever made, either—

**PS:** I think the funniest line of yours, of the essays, is where you say that it's "Robert Holmes's finest hour but unfortunately there's two-and-a-half of them."

**RS:** It's a funny thing—I mean, as a writer, it's a script I really love because I feel there is a joy to it, though it feels... this sounds like a very stupid comparison, I'm really not comparing *The Two Doctors* to the best work of William Shakespeare, because that would be weird, but a few nights ago I went to see *Hamlet*, with Benedict Cumberbatch.

**PS:** How was it?

**RS:** It's not very good, actually. I think it's badly directed, it has some really quite poor guest acting in it, and it's saddled with some really strange direction which I think saddles Cumberbatch, who, when he's allowed to be quite insular does a wonderful job. It's a shame. He's great. The production around him, not so much. But anyway.

The thing which I think makes *Hamlet* so interesting is that it's not a play that makes an awful lot of sense. Because it's Shakespeare—suddenly, I believe—discovering his own genius. And he's just—it is the most self-indulgent thing Shakespeare ever wrote. And as a result it's freewheelingly brilliant without necessarily always making, from scene to scene, consistently plotted drama. I mean, the famous "To be or not to be" speech in Act Three doesn't in any credible way fit. It's not where you leave Hamlet emotionally before he gives it at all. It's almost as if Shakespeare said, "I love that speech, great bit about slings and arrows, arrgh, I can't find a place for it. Sod it, I'm putting it in here."

But what it is, it's a writer utterly in love suddenly with being able to write. Criticising *Hamlet* because it doesn't feel like meat and potatoes drama is to crassly misunderstand the genius of *Hamlet*. And I think what *Two Doctors* is, it seems to me, it's Robert Holmes—I think from the success of *Androzani*, a freshness from his time away from the show, and also I'm sure responding to the adulation that Eric Saward is giving him—it's Holmes being allowed just to be as funny as he wants to be and go as far as he wants to go. And—

**PS:** I have a theory about Holmes in general, that there's a particular type of script he occasionally writes when he's just pissed off about the assignment itself. He does it with *The Space Pirates*, he does it again with *Power of Kroll*, where you can tell he's just really angry that he has to write this. And I think there's a way in which in *The Two Doctors* he finally learns to enjoy the really shitty assignment.

**RS:** Well, I don't think he thinks it is shitty. I don't actually get that sense. Yes, one wants to criticize Nathan-Turner particularly for the shopping-list Doctor Who commissions, which is pretty much what all Doctor Who is, it certainly was when I was on the show, and it has been ever since. This is actually how the show works: it's about throwing things together and seeing if you can actually make an interesting mix out of them. So I don't know if he is reacting badly to the idea of, "Oooh, now put some Sontarans in." He possibly is, but the impression I get is that when he's pissed off he gets bored, and *Power of Kroll* is only months past *Ribos Operation*, one of the most dazzling things he ever wrote.

**PS:** I think *The Ribos Operation* is one of the best stories, period, yeah.

**RS:** Yeah, so do I. I think it probably is Holmes's best script, *Ribos Operation*. But at the same time we all know it's a script which, as you would not expect from someone who has worked on the show editing it since the end of the Pertwee years, comes in massively over length. Because he's just having fun writing it. And I think *Two Doctors* is a bit like that. I think *Two Doctors* is—as we know, it's a storyline that he tried to get made years ago and was told it was too silly and too dark and a bit too weird, and now he's doing it again, and he's not being stopped. And he's pushing himself to see how far he can go with it. And there's something I think truly wonderful about it.

I think there were certain set pieces—and you don't get them in Doctor Who very often, you don't often get many set piece of just people having good dialogue, but the whole sequence in Oscar's restaurant in the final episode, it's just amazing writing! And it's amazing writing not because it's Tom Baker talking to Davros, it's not *that* sort of great writing, it's someone just having wonderful fun having people just talk to each other, and getting the most comedy out of it he could possibly have. And to end it with having him just killed, because that's not where you think the joke is going to go. And that's what it is to me, it's about somebody saying, "I can surprise you, with constantly changing tone away from what you think Doctor Who ought to be." The sequence that I really love in *Two Doctors*, and I know I've mentioned this before, but I really truly love it, is when you see Troughton kill somebody!

**PS:** Yes!

**RS:** And he's playing it, Troughton, with such glee! He kills that man as if it's such a lovely prank!

**PS:** He's playing it as though he's chasing Jon Pertwee around at a convention with a water pistol.

**RS:** Yes, precisely! He's actually playing it a little bit like the sort of over-the-top sub-Troughton Doctor we saw in the anniversary episodes, because he has to up the Troughtonism to make it into a stereotype, and suddenly we see how dark that can be—also there's that wonderful comedy bit where he's turned into an Androgum and Shockeye pulls the cover off his face, and then Troughton just starts listing dinners, and the way Troughton does it is just amazing, he gets to the end of it and wonders, "Why am I talking about food?" And then Shockeye explains it to him and the look of absolute childish delight on his face is gorgeous! That's why I love *Two Doctors*, it's something which is just—it's bonkers. It's actually a bit like *Kill the Moon*. It's the 1980s' *Kill the Moon*. It's doing something where you just say, "Just to be able to do this, even if for instance it's two-and-a-quarter hours long and it probably really shouldn't be—" although you know what? It's not that over-long. I mean, there's a lot of running around haciendas and things. But actually, I think that extra space gives it a feel utterly unlike any other Doctor Who story of that period or indeed of any period, actually. It's the first sort of six-parter that we've had since *Armageddon Factor*—

**PS:** Yes.

**RS:** —or will arguably ever have again.

**PS:** The only time it comes close is the *Utopia/Sound of Drums/Last of the Time Lords*.

**RS:** Yeah, I was thinking of that.

**PS:** And I don't think that's a three-parter. I've never liked calling Utopia "Part One of Three."

**RS:** Yeah... but that's also one of the clevernesses of what Russell and now Steven do, is that they rather like the idea that—and I think it comes out of the idea of not calling things Part One, Part Three, whatever—they rather like the idea of saying these episodes, which are Part Two of a two-part story, potentially, feel like they're completely different to the Part One. Tonally.

**PS:** I admit, one of the things I'm really excited about—

**RS:** —We'll get a lot more of that this year.

**PS:** Yeah, one of the things I'm really excited about with

Series Nine is the idea that it's not even going to be clear what is and isn't a two-parter.

**RS:** Yeah, precisely. And I think one of the joys about the *Utopia/Sound of Drums/Last of the Time Lords* trilogy is that it isn't clear at all whether it's a three-part story or a one-parter into a two-parter, and even the two-parter—

**PS:** Yeah, those two episodes are as wildly different from each other as *Utopia* is from *Sound of Drums*.

**RS:** And the setting, and it's set, what, a year later? And, I don't know, who does that? To actually have someone say, "Anyway, it's a year later." When has Doctor Who ever been as bold with its storytelling structure as it has been?

**PS:** *The Romans*.

**RS:** That's a good answer. *The Romans* is great.

**PS:** I love *The Romans*.

**RS:** Right.

**PS:** Changing gears, slightly, *Holy Terror* also brought back Frobisher, who is a wonderful character, but since I'm also a comics blogger I have to ask, what are your thoughts and memories of those Steve Parkhouse/John Ridgway strips that actually introduced Frobisher?

**RS:** Well, I mean, I wasn't a big comics reader, actually, and what lured me in to the Colin strips in some way was the absence of new material on TV. So, again, this sounds silly, but when you've got that sort of eighteen months abstention, I went back to the old magazines and found myself reading the strips to get some extra stuff. And I read things like *Tides of Time*, *Tides of Time* was the big Davison story, and then the—

**PS:** *Voyager.*

**RS:** Yeah. And you find yourself thinking, "This is absolutely nothing remotely like the actual tone of what Doctor Who is at all."

**PS:** I'm pretty sure Steve Parkhouse never watched a minute of 80s Doctor Who.

**RS:** Wouldn't surprise me at all. And yet that's actually one of the things that makes it so brilliant. What I love about Colin's stuff, in particular, is that in some strange way the sort of brashness and tastelessness of what Season Twenty-Two was doing forces the show to find a different way of talking about different things. It makes it into a strange satire, because it can't do subtle anymore—the same thing but differently is happening in the comic strips. So suddenly you explode with such invention—into having a companion who is a private eye who likes wearing a penguin body. Which you can't imagine happening, really, except at a time in the show's history when almost everything feels like it's all up in the air. And that's one of the reasons I find the Colin Baker time so interesting, is that I don't feel that the characters like Frobisher—it's enormously out of step with what the TV show is doing, but it's not, in a funny way, *artistically* out of step with what the TV show is doing at the same time, it's actually saying, we have now gone into a very weird place. And—

**PS:** I think there's zero doubt that if you would have offered John Nathan-Turner a penguin he would have put it on screen.

**RS:** You think?

**PS:** He did with Kamelion.

**RS:** But that's completely different. And actually, that's part of the trouble, is that Kamelion and Frobisher are so different. I mean, Kamelion clearly has no character, or indeed sense of humor, or anything except being this insipid robot.

**PS:** That doesn't actually work.

**RS:** Frobisher, though, is a character I could never see Nathan-Turner using. I really enjoyed writing Frobisher—he doesn't see himself as being a Companion. At the time, I always thought, growing up, watching the show, the characters began to define themselves as if they were Companions or not, and that's weird because in real life you never actually do that.

**PS:** Right.

**RS:** I mean, *Castrovalva*, which I adore, as you know, is the only Doctor Who I can think of where you get a scene where you've got floaty Davison in the Zero Room basically assigning them all companion roles, and you think, "Really?" It's like turning it into a sort of—you know, rather like seeing Donald Trump, or in this country, Alan Sugar, treating them like they're on the Apprentice. It's a weird thing. I don't have a problem with it, actually, because at the time watching it I didn't realize how weird that was. And I think that Frobisher, more than any other character, just sees himself as the lead character! Which is what you would do! We always think of ourselves as the lead characters in our own lives. And I find it tremendously funny that a talking shapeshifting penguin sees himself as the lead, and the Doctor as his sidekick.

**PS:** And I think you put to great use in *Holy Terror*, I think that Frobisher buckling down and trying to teach them about liberal democracy is one of the funniest moments in Doctor Who.

**RS:** Well thank you! It's not something I actually remember very well, I don't spend much of my time listening back to my own work. That way lies embarrassment! And self-indulgence. People know that I've never seen *Dalek* properly, I've only ever seen *Dalek* to give commentary on it, so I don't—I mean, therefore, I know what happens, but I talking over it, I've never actually wanted to sit and watch it, and I've never listened to the audios beyond working on them. I remember hearing *Holy Terror*, and thinking that it came out pretty well, that Nick Pegg did a great job directing it, that I was very lucky with the cast, that it had a great sound design. One of the cliffhangers was very good, I thought that the cliffhanger at the end of Episode Three, probably, where you reveal the actual true nature of who that child is, was rather good.

**PS:** Yeah, that's a good one.

**RS:** Yeah, that was rather chilling, I thought. I really wanted to do one chilling *Doctor Who* cliffhanger, everything else was gravy! But it's a funny thing, I don't actually remember what happened in *Holy Terror* very much! I mean, I remember what I was tonally trying to do; I remember what I thought *Chimes* was trying to do, so that's why I wrote *Chimes* that way; I remember what I thought *Jubilee* should do, *Jubilee* in some ways was like it's trying to be the sort of wayward brash angry Colin Baker story that you get, thinks he's in Season Twenty-Two—

**PS:** I was actually going to ask about *Jubilee*, what sort of came first with that one? Did you start with the Daleks there, or did you start from wanting to do a Sixth Doctor story, or were you somewhere else entirely with that?

**RS:** It was an odd thing, actually, *Jubilee* came about because I was asked to do one of those, what do you call them, webcasts—

**PS:** Yeah.

**RS:** So they'd done *Death Comes to Time*, and Gary asked if I would come up with a story which would feature the Daleks and Colin Baker, and it was in animated form and over six ten-minute episodes or something. And I went, "Sure! Alright." And I went away, I had a few days to do it, to come up with something, and I came up with the idea of a lone Dalek being tortured at the Tower of London. And I ran out of time, I realized I couldn't write it in time, I'm quite a fast writer but only when I've got the story sorted out, and I hadn't yet! So Gary went away and wrote *Real Time* instead...

Later, he said to me, "Why don't we get you to do it as a regular four-parter for me? When you've got time." Because I was working on a TV show at that time, I was—Chris Chibnall was my boss, I was doing *Born and Bred*. I managed to get a few months later a couple of weeks off *Born and Bred*, and I thought, "I must write this audio." And suddenly what would have been a very tight sixty-minute story became this sprawling angry story, partly because I was frustrated with being on *Born and Bred*, I knew it wasn't a series that quite suited my writing style, and I wasn't feeling very confident on it.

So *Jubilee* was just me letting rip, and doing my own stuff, and overwriting and getting carried away and it was enormous fun to write, I remember, it felt like being on holiday, and compared to *Chimes*, which I had found a real slog, it was hard work at times... *Jubilee*, let's face it, I think is a very undisciplined script, and I think that it doesn't have an ending, and I think it probably, looking back, it's probably the weakest Doctor Who thing I've actually done, as a script, but god it has some fun things in it.

**PS:** I think the defense you offer of *Two Doctors* works pretty well for *Jubilee* as well. Undisciplined as it may be, you're just having so much fun with it!

**RS:** Yeah, and there's a point to it, I mean the thing about

*Jubilee*, as with *The Two Doctors*, is that I think that there's a certain anger to it, I mean I always say about *Two Doctors*, and I don't know this is actually true, it's simply my own take of it—it's one of the things we do with art, but one of the things that people attack *Two Doctors* for is the Androgums. And I always felt what was interesting about the Androgums was that the response the Doctor has to them seems entirely racist, if it's… if frankly, they're just a bunch of people who look exactly human with silly eyebrows. It's as if Robert Holmes has written a race of aliens that all the *characters* think look like inhuman monsters, but we don't—and it holds up that rather uncomfortable way we treat any race that's unlike us as not worthy of feelings of complex sympathy. It fed into what *Dalek* was about.

**PS:** My wife always says the same thing about *Dalek*, because the Eccleston season was her first ever season of Doctor Who, she knew nothing about it, she was thoroughly confused when David Tennant showed up, and similarly, what really worked about *Dalek* for her was that the Doctor looks completely and utterly unhinged in it, if you don't know what the Daleks are.

**RS:** Yeah, exactly, and there's a way in which… Terrance said, you know, "The Doctor is never cruel or cowardly, except of course to the Daleks, who are fair game!" And you think, "Well why are they fair game?" Anyway, yeah, but that's what *Jubilee* does. It's trying to be dissonant, being angry and a bit random and seeing what ideas come flying out. Had someone ever said to me, "This script you are now writing will be the basis one day for the first Dalek story that's on television in the 21$^{st}$ century," I would have been a lot more cautious!

**PS:** (laughs)

**RS:** But I could never have known that would ever have happened. You know, back then. It's a funny thing, even now, ten years on, I still don't really believe it happened. I don't believe I could write for Doctor Who, that just seems stupid to me!

**PS:** I do love your quote that—your claim that all of Doctor Who is canonical except for the bits you wrote.

**RS:** Yeah, absolutely! I mean, I have to think that way. I love Doctor Who, in all of its strange, contradictory at times, ugly, tonally weird ways, I think that *is* Doctor Who, it's constantly reinventing itself and bending itself into shapes I could hardly imagine it bending itself into, so I'm constantly fascinated by it. I also really like the *TARDIS Eruditorum*, it's about that, it's about the fact that how can all of this really be the same show. Because if you're looking for any tonal consistency over fifty years, that would be insane. And as a result, I don't want, really, to see the mechanics of what I was doing interfering with it too much! So I can't take *Dalek* seriously. It just doesn't make sense to me that *Dalek* is really part of Doctor Who. I'm very glad that other people think it is, it makes me happy that apparently that was the real show, good on them for thinking that. I think what I was doing was something like a childhood present to myself, that I was allowed to write that. And then they went and broadcast it! It was unbelievable.

**PS:** It was like being on *Jim'll Fix It* or something.

**RS:** Well that's the funny thing, I mean, back at the time I got the job, I made lots of *Jim'll Fix It* references—

**PS:** (cackles)

**RS:** —in the press. People say, "What's it was like doing this?" And I said, "You know, it's like being on *Jim'll Fix It*." Had I only known.

**PS:** So, one final question. You obviously have a particular style of Doctor Who story you're inclined to—and I'm not saying that as a criticism, I know it's something you've said as well—

**RS:** I like strange fictional self-contained universes. I just love that. And it goes back to *Castrovalva*, I just think, I think that's really cool. I just do.

**PS:** And I think that style works particularly well for Colin Baker's Doctor, so just broadly speaking, because you know he still has the reputation as "the problem Doctor" in a lot of ways, how do you go about writing Colin Baker well? What's the trick to writing a good Colin Baker story?

**RS:** You respect the character, is the simple answer. You don't see that you need to write it as an apology, you don't see that you need to write it as a kick against what's come before, you understand that Colin Baker himself is a very intelligent and very reasoned actor, and you give him something that he will find intellectually stimulating, and you give the audience something which you feel will also give them reason, as the story goes on, to be questioning what it is that they think they're listening to. Which I think is, again, you know, is basically the whole nature of drama, but it's also the nature of what good Doctor Who is. I always think that really good Doctor Who is when we're watching it and we're trying in some ways to—trying to decode it. That's why I always liked your blog so much, that you were attempting to find ways of trying to decoding what it was that we were watching, and I think sometimes all that decoding that goes on, and I think some of the duller blander stories are things that we are sort of not imposing on the narrative but… it's actually more that we're trying to decode the time and way in which it was made.

**PS:** Yes.

**RS:** I think interesting television invites you to try and decode how this story is told. What I love about Colin's Doctor is that because it's such a sort of strange, brash, confusing Doctor, you can really write stories in which you start at Point A and then you move your story to a distant Point B, and you want at the end of that story for people to listen to the end of *Holy Terror* or *Jubilee* and say, "How did we get from that first scene, tonally, to this?" And that's what I love doing. And I think Colin's Doctor in particular, because it's such a strange, awkward, confusing mixture of styles and things, allows that far more than say writing for Peter Davison—who of course I adore as a Doctor—would have allowed you to do. Because Davison's Doctor feels to me very exact. Colin's Doctor, because it feels like a sort of strange truncated experiment of styles and ambitions that weren't allowed to be paid off, kind of allows you to be a lot more freewheeling about telling really interestingly structured stories. Does that make sense?

**PS:** Yeah, that's a great answer, thank you.

**RS:** I hope that makes sense.

**PS:** I think it'll work well.

**RS:** Yeah. Well, I haven't even explained to you why I like things like *Kinda* and *Snakedance* and *Earthshock* and stuff, we haven't really discussed Davison at all, have we?

**PS:** No, this is mostly a Colin Baker interview.

**RS:** Yeah. Which is perfectly fair. But I will still say that *Snakedance* is the best Doctor Who story ever written, and I'm going to stick to that forever. Even though most people who like it prefer *Kinda*!

**PS:** Yeah, I mean—actually, Jack Graham agrees with you on that one, I don't know if you're familiar with his blogging as well, but he—

**RS:** I'm not, really.

**PS:** He's the Marxist rabble rouser of Doctor Who blogging. Which Doctor Who blogging needed.

**RS:** It does a bit, doesn't it?

**PS:** It really does. He's the unabashed Doctor Who critic who, you know, we always really needed, and I made a commentary on *Kinda* with him and we disagreed. He's in your camp of thinking *Snakedance* is the better story.

**RS:** I mean, I think that they're both great, don't get me wrong. I mean, I just—I think I like metafiction, and I really, as I said to you earlier—

**PS:** You *think* you like metafiction? Have you read your work? (laughs)

**RS:** Yeah, well, as I come to the end of my latest book, which is very, very weird metafiction stuff, which is kind of fun, which I hope people actually like, it's, yeah, I think—that's why I love Season Twenty, you know? Season Twenty is so much about the disillusionment of anniversaries. It's weird. *Mawdryn Undead* is heartbreaking.

**PS:** Oh, it is.

**RS:** It's so good. It's an amazing piece of storytelling. And the fact that it follows *Snakedance*, which is also about people having these sort of empty hollow celebrations of things they no longer understand.

**PS:** I don't think I've ever heard anyone say that about Season Twenty before, so, you know, that's... I'm not sure I'm really sold on the claim, but I like the claim.

**RS:** Yeah, I mean, *Arc of Infinity* as well. Look, *Arc of Infinity* doesn't work, does it, but Episode Two is very good. Episode Two is actually surprisingly good. I mean, it isn't maybe isn't as good packaged with Episodes One, Three, and Four, but

Episode Two is bizarre.

**PS:** I should put on *Arc of Infinity* Episode Two and just watch it in isolation.

**RS:** Episode Two is the really weird episode which is all about the Doctor being led off for unfair execution, while Nyssa tries to save him.

**PS:** Oh yes!

**RS:** It is pretty self-contained. And everything good about *Arc of Infinity* is all about his sort of acceptance of that sort of self-sacrifice even though he thinks it might not be allowed to happen, and the way in which Nyssa breaks into the council room with a gun, only to have the Doctor say, "Please give me the gun," is beautifully well done.

**PS:** That's a great scene.

**RS:** And basically that's the entire episode. Okay, you've also got Tegan's weird cousin being hit by a giant chicken, and being zapped and stuff around that time as well, and that isn't very good, but actually *Arc of Infinity* does some really interesting things which we inevitably—it's one of the reason why Toby and I, when we were doing *Running Through Corridors*, the whole joy about doing those books was the desire to free individual episodes from being trapped from the story surrounding it sometimes, because, because... *Terminus* Episode One, it's brilliant! It's really good television, Episode One, it's just isn't so good afterwards. So to have at Episode One and actually celebrate it is usually impossible because we get bogged down by the sort of knowledge of what happens afterwards. We're finding that when we're doing things like *War Games*—*War Games* is a story which is so, so good, but the revelations of what happens at the end of *War Games* have always, for fans anyways, seem to have cast a long shadow and we forget just how amazing some of those earlier episodes are, because we're that far away from them by the time we get to the Time Lords turning up. So you have things like *Arc of Infinity* and you get some genuinely great things which are overshadowed by the stuff that we know is critically more what we should discuss. It's a strange thing.

Doctor Who is sort of kind of cursed by the way that, when it was first broadcast as we know it, it was seen as being a sort of an ongoing adventure in space and time, and of course it was in different stories, but actually the way it was being absorbed by us was as a sort of non-ending series—they'd usually go somewhere else. Once you get in the late Hartnell time onwards, the breaking up of stories into individually titled stories with episodes one, two, three, and four, it changes inevitably the way that we see those stories. But it doesn't really change the fact that we're watching this sort of weekly thing going out. Which just runs into each other.

And actually that's the thing that I found particularly with Davison: *Black Orchid* only works because it's there to lull you into a false sense of security before you get *Earthshock*. You see the obvious reason why *Black Orchid* is made. Because we are trained to see *Black Orchid* as an individual story, we sneer at it, but actually, the job it's doing is extraordinary. *Earthshock* wouldn't work without *Black Orchid*, I think, I mean arguably it doesn't work for a lot of people now anyways, but it's a funny thing, stories around the Davison period where they start actually to have these sort of strange lead-ins into each other, which often don't entirely work, they often feel a bit forced, but it's an attempt to try and make things not feel as if they're actual real breaks between things—that actually, in some strange way, these stories are part of a single unit. And I think that makes it really interesting, it means as a result you can actually assess episodes on their own much more easily.

When Toby and I were doing the book on the Seventies, the Seventies book is when stories really do feel terribly rigid in the way that they're told. Pertwee stories have a real established rhythm to them, which actually makes it quite hard to write an essay about Episode Four of a six-part story, because so what? It's Episode Four of a six-part story. It's not doing anything different than Episodes Three and Five, really. Whereas Davison's stuff and in fact JNT's stuff generally, episodes are doing completely different things sometimes within the same story, and it's fascinating. And they work in part because they are—*The Visitation* feels, if you pluck it off the shelf and watch it, it feels really weird and bland. It's not, actually. It's a really strange story because of where it comes in the season and how it's earned that place. To suddenly be doing a historical in which no characters have any names, even, is a weird decision. But it is a decision being made, and it's partly because it's still trying to get Tegan home—it's sort of like this new Doctor and these new companions are learning actually how to see things. And you take them on this history thing where of course nobody is actually allowed an identity, it's very, very odd. Anyways, sorry, I'm just rambling on.

**PS:** No, you're rambling fascinatingly. That said, I should probably let you go. But thank you very much for this.

**RS:** You're totally welcome, Phil.

**PS:** I think this will be a great addition to the book.

**RS:** That's okay, and I look forward to seeing it! Because, yes, I suppose you must be doing that—it's quite, I suppose it's time, isn't it? Because I've got your Graham Williams one—

**PS:** Yeah, I'd like to be doing them faster than I am, but it seems to take—

**RS:** Well it's hard work.

**PS:** It is, and I've got to produce new stuff as well, so, sitting down with the old stuff isn't always as high a priority as I wish it were.

**RS:** But many congratulations upon finishing *TARDIS Eruditorum* in the first place—

**PS:** Oh thank you.

**RS:** —which I think is actually a genuinely monumental achievement in Doctor Who academia, I really do. I think it's a wonderful piece of work.

**PS:** Thank you. That's very kind of you.

**RS:** And, no, not at all, I really really think it's extremely impressive. It makes, certainly, when we get to the edits for the *Running Through Corridors of the 80s* book that much easier.

**PS:** (laughs) Well, you made the Hartnell/Troughton years easier with Volume One, so I'm glad I can repay that.

**RS:** Thank you very much!

## Time Can Be Rewritten: *Business Unusual*

Last time we dealt with Gary Russell, back in the Pertwee book, we found ourselves reflecting heavily on the notion of fanwank. Broadly speaking, at least, I'm hard-pressed to complain too heavily about fanwank in the novel lines, particularly the Missing Adventures and Past Doctor Adventures, both of which by their nature appeal almost entirely to dedicated Doctor Who fans. When you're dealing with an audience of dedicated fans the extent to which you can rely on existing work increases dramatically. There is a fundamental difference between writing novels for a fan audience and writing television for BBC1.

But having navigated the Saward era and its continuity fetishism, there are some new issues to consider around this. The mere fact that there's nothing wrong with fanwank is not equivalent to fanwank being inherently worthwhile. There are things that you can do when working in the margins of existing work that you can't do any other way—a fact that is responsible for no small part of my interest in things like Doctor Who and superhero comics. But the margins aren't interesting in and of themselves—a problem that plagues Gary Russell's work, and that, in a few paragraphs, is going to prove the undoing of *Business Unusual*.

But let's back up and look at the larger situation. At the heart of the problem is still the Seasonish and the way in which both Season Twenty-Threes—the transmitted one and the erased one—create a tangible gap in the history of Doctor Who. Colin Baker is the only Doctor to lack a regeneration story, a fact that coincides with Mel being the first companion since Susan to lack an origin story, and then there's the deeply unsatisfying nature of the Valeyard, an idea with far more and deeper implications than the series was willing to actually explore, with all of this slotting into the already confused gap introduced by the hiatus.

The result is a period that is the subject of a massive amount of fan theories. And so, having at least determined that the flaw is not inherently Colin Baker, let's tie off the last issue: was there ever anything interesting to do here? Are the gaps of this era—gaps that we cannot, given the absurd turmoil behind the scenes, chalk up to any deliberate ambiguity—ones that can be interestingly filled? In other words, is the era we've just been witness to fatally and irrevocably flawed, or is there actual quality to be had here?

So that's what this triptych of Time Can Be Rewritten essays is going to focus on—three books that fill the holes in and around the gap between *Trial of a Time Lord* and *Time and the Rani*. And first up we have Gary Russell with *Business Unusual*, a novel that proposes to introduce Mel. And give Colin Baker his "missing" Brigadier story. And serve as a sequel to *The Scales of Injustice*. And bring back the Autons.

I almost wrote "so no shortage of ambition" after that list, but no, that's wrong. The problem here is that there is a profound shortage of ambition. The goals of the book are to check off some supposedly needed boxes in Doctor Who and to advance a couple of pet projects from the writer. In many ways it's the inclusion of the Brigadier that's the dead giveaway. Like the obsession with the idea that Pertwee should have a Cybermen story, it sets the defining characteristics of an era as being nothing more than attaining a pre-existing set of goals. And what's key about these obsessions is that they comprise a list that can never be added to. Only things old enough to have been in the Hartnell era can be one of these bucket list items. Their nature is to constrain the show, limiting what it can be to what it already has been. It's the Whoniverse logic at play once again. (It's perhaps thankful that the list has dwindled in size, with Eccleston, Tennant, and Smith all not getting Brigadier stories and Eccleston not getting a Cybermen story, leaving the Daleks as the only plausibly necessary element for an era, which is just about right.)

But this checklist approach is particularly visible when it comes to Mel. We've already discussed how Mel is oddly torn between her description in John Nathan-Turner's *The Companions* volume and what appears on screen. *The Companions* makes much of the fact that Mel is a computer programmer. This information plays into what we see on screen exactly three times, though—twice in *Time and the Rani* it's mentioned that Mel is good with computers, and then once in *The Ultimate Foe* she identifies something as a "megabyte modem." But there's a larger problem, which is that Bonnie Langford comes nowhere close to playing a tech-savvy career woman of the mid-1980s.

I don't mean this as a criticism of Bonnie Langford at all. It's just that if "1980s crack computer programmer" was what the show was actually going for, then having Bonnie Langford written by Pip and Jane Baker was an absurd idea. Bonnie Langford played the role she was obviously hired for—Bonnie Langford as a Doctor Who companion—quite well. But there's a massive disjunct between that and the character described in *The Companions*.

However, Gary Russell has clearly decided that he's going to try to write a Mel story that builds off of *The Companions*. And so despite the fact that the Mel that appeared on screen could easily have had any origin, she is dutifully a computer programmer. Even the detail of her being involved in an attempt to stop the Master from taking over the world's banks is preserved, with Russell going out of his way to make sure that can be reconciled with the fact that Mel doesn't recognize the Master in *The Ultimate Foe*. The trouble is that we're left instead trying to imagine Bonnie Langford delivering the line, "Be thankful I don't play loud Gothic music, try to sell *Socialist Worker* to your WI friends or have a drawerful of thirty-five different-flavoured condoms in my bedroom."

In other words, Mel's origin story is, to a fault, exactly what the readership would expect. But when the answer to "What goes in this gap?" is "Exactly what you'd expect to go in that gap," then narratively speaking there's not much of a reason to fill it. Mel's origin story is, it seems, a completely generic piece of Doctor Who that tells us nothing new about Mel and makes little effort to reconcile or resolve any of the existing mysteries surrounding her.

Indeed, the story is bizarrely dislocated from any actual impact. I'm not one to nitpick bad writing about computers, in no small part because I have a not-terribly-secret love for it, but on the other hand, if you're writing in 1997 and setting your book about computer technology in 1989 then there's not really a lot of excuses for glaring anachronism. And yet the book has the idea that Sony and Sega are preparing "a 32-bit CD-based system for release early next decade" that the fictional Maxx 64-bit CD system is going to be miles ahead of, a claim that flubs the release date for the Sega Saturn and Sony Playstation (both were, by any reasonable definition, mid-decade) and dramatically overestimates the impact that the 64-bit Atari Jaguar had, given it actually came out in the early 1990s. Similarly jarring is the Brigadier knowing who Sonic the Hedgehog is, which is bizarre first because it's anachronistic for 1989 and second because it involves the Brigadier knowing who Sonic the Hedgehog is. Yes, this is all just a nitpick, but equally, if you're going to write a story about computers and corporate culture in the late 1980s there's something to be said for not screwing up the details on the setting. It's not like 1989 is a particularly difficult time period to research in 1997, after all.

But really, I harp on this issue because it's so indicative of what this book is about, or, more accurately, what it isn't about, which is telling its own story. Heck, even the underlying premise—corporate machinations and the Autons—is just a ripoff of an Alan Moore comic that Russell could barely be bothered to change the name of. There are interesting Doctor Who stories to be done about computer technology—something we'll see when we get to the New Adventures. There are interesting Doctor Who stories to be done about corporate culture—something we saw in the Baker era itself. But this isn't trying to be either. It's just interested in being The One That Introduces Mel, The One Where Colin Baker Meets The Brigadier, and The One Alan Moore Already Wrote.

What's more interesting is that this effort to just fill in blanks and correct Doctor Who leads to some bewildering tonal lapses. Ostensibly, Russell's goal is to, as he says in his introduction, "write a sixth Doctor story that I thought Colin Baker would have liked to be in," a vision that, based on the book, he sees as a character full of bombastic charm. Certainly this is plausible based on Baker's acting. But this more charming, fun version of the Doctor who gives plastic toys to children in restaurants becomes grotesquely jarring when later scenes in the book gruesomely describe a twelve-year-old boy being murdered by his toys.

Like the murderous policemen of *Resurrection of the Daleks* or the lifting of the deleted "Kill me Vera" sequence from *The Ark in Space* for *Revelation of the Daleks*, this seems largely to be a case of doing something that the show couldn't have gotten away with, in this case riffing on the alarm at the killer toys in *Terror of the Autons*. It is, in other words, the exact sort of thing that the Saward era so regularly got wrong. It's almost as though the empty recitations of continuity points and a sort of blithe nastiness go hand in hand.

In a way, this even makes sense—when drama abandons being about people in favor of being about obscure points of sci-fi continuity it becomes ugly like this. Certainly it's an argument that works well with the overall themes of this blog—when Doctor Who becomes nothing more than a commodity and a brand it loses all of its power. Because this is market-tested Doctor Who—a case of writing a story not because there's anything dramatically interesting about the story but because it's something fans are known to want and thus will buy. (Ironically, this is exactly what the Autons were designed by Holmes to critique. They're the ultimate capitalist Doctor Who monster.)

But all of this paints me into an interesting corner as a critic. I'll confess that in picking books to cover in the Time Can Be Rewritten essays I have tended towards ones that have continuity ramifications. Part of that is simply the premise of the essays—the point of these little side jaunts is to look at later conceptions of the era, so the ones that have metafictional implications are naturally more interesting to me. But the implications are somewhat questionable. It's fair to ask whether, instead of spending three Colin Baker books on the mess surrounding *Trial of a Time Lord* I shouldn't have done the oft-recommended *Killing Ground*, or *Synthespians*™, a story that would actually give me an eighties Auton story that attempts what this story should have (and has what is surely the most logical extension of the Auton concept, killer breast implants).

Because this is a bad book pointlessly filling a continuity gap in a bad era of Doctor Who. It's a book that comes perilously close to indicting the entire concept of the Time Can Be Rewritten essays—for given what we have in *Business Unusual*, it can be unnervingly suggested that perhaps the gaps and margins left in the past of Doctor Who are best left alone on the grounds that they are, by definition, not going to be functional pieces of drama.

## Time Can Be Rewritten: *Millennial Rites*

More than anyone—even Gary Russell or Lance Parkin—the late Craig Hinton has a reputation for fanwank. For one thing, he coined the term. But the fact that we're dealing with that list in the first place is interesting. On one extreme we have Russell, who I confess to having relatively little regard for as a fiction writer. On the other we have Parkin, one of the consensus best novel writers. So once again there's clearly not a direct correlation between fanwank and quality.

It's tempting to try to chart out some sort of principle based on the fact that *Jubilee* works and *Business Unusual* doesn't: *Jubilee* deals with the past of the program in broad strokes, for instance, while *Business Unusual* gets bogged down in tedious and pointless details. But I'm hard-pressed to buy that as a logic—there's something desperately unsatisfying about the idea that the details not only don't matter but necessarily cannot matter and are fundamentally opposed to good storytelling. (For one thing, it would pose an uncomfortable existential challenge to the logic of *TARDIS Eruditorum*.)

We're at a point of transition in the arc of *TARDIS Eruditorum*, moving from the decade-long deflation of the series that stretched from *Horror of Fang Rock* to *Revelation of the Daleks* to the invisible reinvention of the series once it moved out of the public eye. One of the things that's going to happen over that period is, both within Doctor Who and outside of it, an evolution of how storytelling works in what we can broadly describe as genre fiction. We'll watch this unfold over the next volume, but one of the basic principles of the new way of doing things is that the high concept genre ideas are parallel structures to character-based storytelling.

And that's the difference between Lance Parkin and Gary Russell: Parkin writes in a form that recognizably behaves like that, while Russell writes more in the style of the Saward-era continuity writers. And the thing is, even though Craig Hinton's level of fanwank exceeds both of them, he's a Parkin-style writer. And so we have *Millennial Rites*, a story that is on the one hand a massive celebration of minutiae and on the other is actually a reasonably functional piece of storytelling in its own right that has an actual point to it.

On its most basic level, *Millennial Rites* is a story about the Doctor's fear of the Valeyard and what that does to him. All of its big dramatic beats come out of that, from the Doctor's realization that his treatment of Mel is putting him on the road to that future, to his temporary transformation into the Valeyard late in the novel. Even the smaller details work towards that, with Ashley Chapel and Anne Travers both serving as figures that in their own way grapple with obsessions, paranoias, and temptations, thus backing up the theme.

It's difficult to overstate how big an improvement this is over *Business Unusual*. Put bluntly, there's actually a point to this book. Indeed, it does relatively little of the stuff that was so frustrating about *Business Unusual*. It's not a book that sets out to answer lingering questions about continuity. It has some hints about how the Valeyard fits in with the larger mythology that the Virgin line was spinning in this period, but most of the hints are exactly what everybody had been assuming anyway. Mostly, though, it's serving either as a straightforward sequel to stories—not necessarily a great idea, but not an inherently doomed one—or it's grabbing concepts either for a passing joke (a la the chronic hysteresis drinking song in *Cold Fusion*) or because they contribute usefully to the ideas it's playing with.

Let's take Anne Travers as an example. In terms of her,

*Millennial Rites* is just serving as a sequel. It's picking up the character at the most recent point anyone has seen her (actually, even more recent—the book makes heavy allusion to the then-unreleased *Downtime*, teasing its contents as a sequel) and telling the next story in her life. The most obvious thing to point out here is that this isn't a gap. There's a difference between sequels, which, while potentially ill-advised, at least pick something up and go forward, and prequels, which are very rarely good things unless they were actively planned for from the start. (Do we want to go with *Prometheu*s as the example here? Or *Before Watchmen*? Or perhaps *Star Wars*, where, contrary to popular belief, the first movie was not originally targeted as "Episode IV?" You're spoiled for choice here. But contrast with *The Hobbit*, which was always planned for.) More to the point, Anne Travers has a story about the way in which her past experiences have left her jaded and bitter, and about her eventual redemption from that.

Of course, Mel and the Doctor are not the most recent versions. But this isn't a story about Mel, in the end, and inasmuch as it is one about her it's structured like a sequel to a story we've never seen. Mel returns to Earth and checks in with her old friends from college. Since Mel's return to Earth is a blank slate, this works. Unlike in *Business Unusual*, which is about setting up a prior status quo from which Mel will move to the character we know, *Millennial Rites* is about setting Mel up with a previously unknown status quo and moving her to one we also know nothing about, as we don't know what her relationship with Julia or Barry will turn into. (Admittedly we didn't know about Mel's relationship with her family either, but *Business Unusual*, inasmuch as it was about Mel, wasn't about that relationship. Whereas here the bulk of Mel's plot is about her old classmates, not about how she met the Doctor.)

The Doctor, on the other hand, is actually in a position to have sequels—something he shared only with McCoy in 1995. Baker's Doctor never got a regeneration story—he got a lame excuse at the start of *Time and the Rani* instead. Unlike

Mel, who is primarily a McCoy companion, we never see Baker's Doctor on screen again after *Trial of a Time Lord*. His story is open-ended here, which allows for something that the Missing Adventures can rarely do: tell a story about a past Doctor that fundamentally changes that past Doctor. Which fits well with a story about the Doctor's relationship with the Valeyard, another concept that is not a gap but an outright dropped thread in the series.

So *Millennial Rites* has an actual idea underpinning it, and one that is distinctly a story. The Doctor is forced to confront the apparent fact of the Valeyard and to come to terms with the idea that he might go bad. It's not something we've seen before, and it's a story in which characters have things happen to them that readers can empathize with. This is closer to drama than almost anything we've seen in several seasons, in fact.

On top of that, *Millennial Rites* manages to do something that the continuity-minded era of the program was rarely able to do, which is to simultaneously call on Doctor Who's history and Doctor Who's ability to do anything. It trucks along for half a book seeming like a fairly straightforward continuity-heavy technothriller (an unfortunately existent subgenre of Doctor Who) before suddenly and with minimal warning turning into a cyberpunk sword-and-sorcery epic, and then, to boot, finishing its story in a sensible fashion given this turn.

Let's consider for a moment the virtues of this. For one thing, it's a case of playing to both of Doctor Who's strengths—the fact that it can do anything and the fact that it has a titanic history of doing just that. It's easy to treat the debate over fanwank as a debate over creativity and doing new things, and Hinton, in one gonzo move, demonstrates that no, in fact, such a distinction constitutes a false opposition, for you can easily do both. As with much of what we've talked about here, this is a train of thought picked up straightforwardly by the new series. ("Let's bring back the Emperor of the Daleks. In a story that also features a *Big*

*Brother* parody.")

For another thing, it demonstrates a solid sense of how good the idea actually is. The truth of the matter is that cyberpunk sword-and-sorcery is an idea that sounds cooler than it is. I mean, it has some precedents, most obviously *Nemesis the Warlock* in *2000 AD*, but for the most part it sounds like the sort of thing someone excitedly describes before never getting around to actually writing it. And no surprise, really—this is true for the exact same reasons that it's true that this is a better book than *Business Unusual*, namely that "an idea that's cool to vaguely imagine" and "a good story" are two distinct things.

But in the scope Hinton uses the idea—about half of a book—it's perfect. This is one of the oldest tricks Doctor Who has, really. It establishes a cool-sounding premise, pokes at it for a while, hits the highlights, and then either beats a retreat before it wears out its welcome or suddenly and without warning switches to a different premise. Here Hinton comes up with an outlandish conceit, plays with it for about the amount of time the idea remains cool on its own merits, and then gets out. It's proper, vintage Doctor Who.

This is not to say that the book is unambiguously and straightforwardly belonging to the future of Doctor Who storytelling. It's awkward in several ways, most of them related to its consciously limited audience of hardcore Doctor Who fans. There's an odd bum note in the book I want to look at, not because it's a big moment, but because it's a revealing one. Mel is told by two characters about a birth defect their child suffers from. The mother, it is mentioned, smokes. Mel, in response to being told about this, says, "I hope you gave that up while you were pregnant." This is not the key moment, though. The moment is what comes after: "The looks that shot between Barry and Louise indicated that she hadn't just touched on a nerve, she had wired it into the mains."

This is very strange. It's not that the book doesn't realize that what Mel says here is inappropriate, but it seems to have no real sense of how inappropriate or why it's inappropriate. The book seems completely blind to the idea that shaming a mother to her face about her responsibility for her child's disabilities is not inappropriate merely because it touches a nerve but because it's a completely appalling thing to do. Which, not to plunge headlong into gender politics, but... there's something painfully confirmatory about every stereotype that Doctor Who fandom is overwhelmingly male here. The scene reads like it was written and edited by people who just have no awareness whatsoever of the conversations that surround motherhood, pregnancy, birth defects, or any related issues. It's painfully limited and blinkered.

And I highlight it not to stamp my feet about gender in Doctor Who but because it's indicative of a larger problem with the book, which is that it has the basic shape and approach of a good story but doesn't quite stick the landing. The Doctor confronts the possibility of becoming the Valeyard, but he never quite does anything with the confrontation. There's no resolution.

Part of the problem is that Hinton is trying to weld together two concepts that don't quite go together. He's trying to link the Valeyard to the later image of McCoy's Doctor as the master manipulator and as "Time's Champion," with the idea that this darker figure McCoy embodies is a step on the road to the Valeyard. But these are two different concepts, and they don't actually go together that well. The idea of McCoy confronting the Valeyard really doesn't work (even if you do try to take Perry and Tucker's *Matrix* into account—note that it hinges on the idea that the Seventh Doctor isn't part of the Valeyard). The Valeyard is, in the end, a concern of the Sixth Doctor, and the seams between the two ideas in this story never quite work.

But the larger issue is that, frankly, the Valeyard is just damaged goods as a concept. Because *Trial of a Time Lord* is so incoherent in introducing him, there's no way out—his character doesn't make sense. Like cyberpunk sword-and-sorcery, he's a cool idea in search of an actual story. And so he proves to be the weak link in the chain for Hinton. There's really not a satisfying solution to the Valeyard problem. The general consensus solution—ignore it—is probably the best one. And yet so many people, Hinton included, can't bring themselves to. Which brings us to the last part of this little triptych…

## Time Can Be Rewritten: *Time's Champion*

*Time's Champion*—probably the single least findable thing I'll cover within *TARDIS Eruditorum*—is an unlicensed novel by Craig Hinton and Chris McKeon published as a charity endeavor in 2008. The provenance of it is interesting—Hinton pitched the novel to BBC Books, but it was rejected—instead they published Gary Russell's *Spiral Scratch* to fill basically the same purpose of giving Colin Baker a regeneration story. Separately, the American writer Chris McKeon pitched a story to Big Finish about the Valeyard which was also rejected. McKeon and Hinton got in touch, and Hinton gave McKeon permission to turn his outline of *Time's Champion* into a full novel, which, following Hinton's death, McKeon did.

It's fair to ask why I chose this one over, for instance, the officially published *Spiral Scratch* or what would be the most obvious choice these days, *The Last Adventure*, Big Finish's take on the Sixth Doctor's regeneration—which, in typical Big Finish fashion, is actually four adventures, three of which take place much earlier in the Sixth Doctor era. And in some ways, the question is its own answer. The Sixth Doctor regeneration story borders on a distinct microgenre of Doctor Who at this point. Given that, if I'm only going to do one, it's going to be the most pathologically weird one. Everything there is to say about the idea of Big Finish doing a Sixth Doctor regeneration story in 2015 is ultimately just the same things I said about BBC Books doing a first Mel story in

1997, except with a few more jokes about its excessive length. But there's really no year in which *Time's Champion* wouldn't be a shockingly, breathtakingly strange book.

Let's get one thing out of the way: it is a fascinating book, but not a good book. McKeon, who is by far the more involved writer, is a weak prosesmith at best. On top of that, the plot elevates fanwank to a profound art, relying heavily not only on Hinton's previous novels *Millennial Rites* and *The Quantum Archangel* but also on references to scads of other stuff. This is not in and of itself a problem, except that it seems to be the entire point of this book—to try to fit as many existing pieces of Doctor Who together as is absolutely possible.

I'll attempt something resembling a summary of the plot. The Doctor visits Sergeant Benton's 70th birthday party, which is also visited by some characters from *The Quantum Archangel*, including the human component of Kronos from *The Time Monster* and his pregnant wife. Meanwhile, in 1908, a writer is attempting to write a book called *Time's Champion* that turns out to be written in quantum mnemonics, the magical language from *Millennial Rites*. And in 9908 another man with the same name as the 1908 writer is writing a computer virus called Abbadon. Eventually it turns out that both are being manipulated by Morbius's children to launch an attack on Gallifrey, which coincides with the birth of Kronos's child.

So all hell predictably breaks loose, the Doctor runs to Gallifrey where he meets up with President Romana, a character from another Hinton book, and several other named Time Lords, then goes into the Matrix where the Keeper turns out to be the Valeyard, who is later revealed to be the Doctor's stolen regeneration energy caught in a time loop created by the gods Pain, Hope, Time, Life, Death, and Fate, as a substitute Doctor because Time wanted the Doctor as her champion but was denied by the other transcendent beings, thus creating the Valeyard as a compromise. Then there's a bunch more stuff, but it ends with the Doctor taking complete control of the Matrix by temporarily becoming Lord President of Gallifrey, then letting the TARDIS get eaten by a sentient computer virus and using quantum mnemonics to blow up the computer virus outside of the universe, but only after unregenerating in order to trick the Valeyard and destroy him, and then has to become Death's Champion to save Mel, but cheats and sacrifice himself using the powers of Time's Champion to force a regeneration, and what is this I don't even.

Despite all this, underneath the hood—deep, deep underneath it at times, but underneath it nevertheless—there is a glimmer of the thing that distinguished *Millennial Rites* from *Business Unusual*. For all the book's flaws, this is striving to be a story about characters. It's the final and definitive redemption of Colin Baker's Doctor, the story where he and he alone defeats his own dark side (and let's be honest, the nature of *Trial of a Time Lord* means that the Valeyard has always specifically been the dark mirror of Baker's Doctor, "twelfth and final regeneration" business or not), and earns a meaningful, real place in the arc of who the Doctor is. It's a hot mess, but a hot mess that's trying to be something interesting. (In this regard, it's considerably more interesting than *The Last Adventure*'s take on the Sixth Doctor's relationship with the Valeyard, which, no doubt in part because it had to actually be a story Colin Baker would agree to do, is wildly more flattering to the Sixth Doctor, largely ignoring the Virgin-era idea this book is based on, in which the Sixth Doctor is the specific path to the Valeyard.)

But let's look at this mess again, setting aside McKeon's clunky prose to focus on the plot. It's absurdly over the top, yes. Nevertheless, there is something irritatingly, compellingly... cool about it. I mean, look, I'd be lying if I didn't say that there was something kind of intriguingly awesome about the entire basic idea of this story. How could I possibly say otherwise? I must be at least a half million words into a massive exegesis of everything involved in Doctor Who. Like I'm going to pretend taking Doctor Who apart and putting it back together stops being interesting or valid just because it has a plot?

One can't even easily mount the main distinction I've previously sought to make regarding continuity and how there's a difference between a unitary "Whoniverse" explanation and just playing around with possibilities. But this is a fan-published novel that goes out of its way to leave other stories, even *Spiral Scratch*, in place. This isn't some horrific land grab to collapse the possibilities of Doctor Who. It's the exact sort of thing that one opposes those land grabs in order to allow: some fans expounding their pet theories. So is there any basis to object to this book beyond poor execution?

One possibility, at least, is based on the contested nature of the epic. The epic, especially within sci-fi/fantasy, is a common trope that's been plaguing Doctor Who since The Key to Time. I'm certainly not going to criticize epics in the general case, but there is something troubling about the idea that they're the pinnacle of the genre. The epic, by definition, is defined by its scope and scale—by the fact that it is a big, definitive story. Indeed, within a serialized narrative an "epic" is the biggest story around—one that asserts gravity on everything around it.

Epics, in other words, impose a master narrative on everything around them. By their very nature they imply unity and singular vision. Even a hypothetical epic like this has those implications—that nagging insistence that this story ought be the one through which you look at every other story. That infuriating belief in absolute, fixed truth.

To some extent this is a conflict embedded in the very fabric of Doctor Who. Doctor Who's debut came in a period where Britain was coming to terms with the fact that post-World War II it was a supporting player in global affairs instead of a superpower. In 1963 that was a difficult proposition, not least because Britain still had an awful lot of empire. But fundamentally, Doctor Who was science fiction coming from the perspective of a country that was giving up the idea that it had a singular vision of the world.

But that anti-imperialism, in Doctor Who, always contrasted interestingly with the fact that Doctor Who's central character was an obvious heir to the same Victorian tradition that oversaw the height of the British Empire. The Doctor, as we've said before, is ultimately the Victorian inventor. But he's the Victorian inventor recast and reimagined for a post-empire era. He is at once of the imperial past and rebelling against it, an attempt to salvage a secret history of the Victorian era that provided a way forward from its apparent dead end.

This is a tradition that still exists in Doctor Who. The whole "little people are the most important people" ethos that runs through the Davies and Moffat eras comes directly from this aspect of the show's history. The Doctor, to start at least, was interesting not because he was a prime mover of history but because he was a cranky old man who couldn't fly his spaceship. He was consciously designed as the opposite of the traditional "great man" of history—indeed, under Troughton he became a figure who had clearly chosen to rebel against greatness in favor of the mercurial.

Unfortunately, he was in a genre that the Americans, drunk on their newfound status as the world's superpower, had recrafted to suit a new sort of cultural imperialism. A genre that was rapidly obsessed with hero's journeys and interstellar manifest destinies. A genre, in other words, that fell in love with epics. And to some extent we can just set this up as a tension that plagues Doctor Who. It constantly gets pulled towards epics when what it does best is something else. No, more than that—when its soul, its original concept, is a reaction against epics.

But dammit, they're fun! Epics are fun! They're big, ostentatious fun. And more to the point, there are things you can do in epics that you can't do otherwise. Epics allow for circumstances where the normal rules of business are suspended, which allow for stories that throw out the rules. In this regard epics are why Doctor Who is still around—because they had the idea of doing a big story where the

Doctor died at the end and then casually carried on. Whatever hostility to epics might be built into Doctor Who, there's also a dependence on them.

It's worth looking, though, at the sort of epic a regeneration story is. Its epic nature hinges on the fact that the Doctor dies. It's a narrative collapse—a story that appears to threaten the end of Doctor Who and then doesn't, albeit at a substantial cost. This is the first type of epic that Doctor Who ever did. I mean, it faked and blustered its way to an epic with *The Dalek Invasion of Earth*, but its first real epic was *The Chase*. Where the whole point turned out to be that taking Doctor Who and adding an epic flight from the Daleks to it was absolutely horrible.

Put another way, Doctor Who epics can and do work, but when they work it's because the absolute, orienting power of the epic is undercut by the fact that such an ordering power is antithetical to the structure of Doctor Who. They work by threatening a narrative collapse. Or, as with The Key to Time, they work by wedding the epic structure to something profoundly non-epic and relishing in the tension this creates. These are the two main structures for Doctor Who epics. We can, if we want—and I certainly do—even label them. The narrative collapse is the Whittakerian epic, the epic of minutiae the Holmesian epic. Or we can describe them as alchemical principles. The Whittakerian epic is "solve et coagula," the Holmesian "as above, so below."

And this, in the end, is the problem with *Time's Champion*. It's neither of those things. The Valeyard isn't a narrative collapse. He's an evil twin. That's still an epic trope—but there's none of that glorious focus on the minute that characterizes the Holmesian epic. Nor does it tear apart the principles of Doctor Who, especially since the Doctor has already had an evil twin for some time now in the Master. So *Time's Champion* isn't falling into either epic shape. It's just being a big epic that tries to explain everything. Even if it goes out of its way not to erase any other stories, it still tacitly demands that it be allowed to serve as the key that interprets them. It's exactly the sort of sci-fi epic that Doctor Who resists.

It's not that it's fanwanky. There are great stories to be told out of the minutiae of Doctor Who history. It's that it's a bad story—one that goes against the aesthetics of Doctor Who and, in doing so, goes against the ethics of Doctor Who as well. The problem isn't that it tries to present a grand unified theory of Doctor Who. It's that the theory *Time's Champion* advances is more boring and more limited than Doctor Who. The show that *Time's Champion* is a story about, well, it just isn't as good a show as the one I love.

As for me, my favorite epic theory about Doctor Who remains that Graeme Harper and Robert Holmes are both, as *The Brain of Morbius* suggests, pre-Hartnell Doctors, and that the making of *The Caves of Androzani* is itself a multi-Doctor story that explains how the Doctor got around the twelve regeneration limit (the first time; as for why he's at twelve again by *Time of the Doctor*, the answer is obviously that John Hurt regenerated into Rowan Atkinson, went through the entire plot of "The Curse of Fatal Death," then regenerated from Joanna Lumley back into John Hurt, and that the "Tenth Doctor regenerated into himself" explanation was just the Doctor not wanting to get into the finer details of Dalek bumps with Clara just then), namely by sneaking out of the narrative and cheating the rules. A Whittakerian epic starring Robert Holmes that actually took place over the 20th Anniversary (which fell in the midst of shooting Androzani). What more do you want out of Doctor Who?

## Now My Doctor: Colin Baker

He's not, of course. I mean, I can't lie. There are those willing to defend the Colin Baker era as an unfairly maligned work of genius, but I'm not among them. And yet. I remember, in my Doctor Who days, getting the news that my grandparents in Texas's PBS station had started airing Doctor Who, and that they'd started taping it for me. They didn't know a thing about the program, and so I got the excitement of a VHS tape in the mail that contained an unknown piece of Doctor Who. Into the VCR it went, and I found myself watching *Vengeance on Varos*. And it was wonderful. So was every subsequent tape that arrived as KERA worked its way through the Colin Baker era. New Doctor Who was new Doctor Who, and sure, I may have preferred something else, but it was still exciting. Which is to say that it's not as if I don't understand the arguments for Colin Baker, even if I can't quite bring myself to buy them.

 Let's start with trying to figure out where he works best, then. For all that Season Twenty-Two is a deeply flawed thing, and for all that there are concrete improvements to how the Sixth Doctor works in Season Twenty-Three, I am inclined to suggest that the stories where Baker's Doctor works well are generally in Season Twenty-Two. (And, of course, on Big Finish.) As I suggested in the *Holy Terror* essay, the dark comedy and absurdism is a good fit for his Doctor. And I think, at the heart of this, is the fact that Season

Twenty-Three, for all that it fixes some problems with the character, is also endlessly obsessed with apologizing for him, whereas Season Twenty-Two takes him on his own terms. And I think that fact is key to understanding the appeal of Colin Baker's Doctor: you can't apologize for him.

Perhaps the most interesting thing about passionate defenses of Baker's Doctor is who they come from. It's certainly by no means a hard and fast rule, but there's an observable tendency for Baker's Doctor to be vocally embraced by fans who are neuroatypical, and specifically fans who are somewhere on the autism spectrum. (Just to announce my privilege: I have never been diagnosed as neuroatypical, and do not identify as such, although these are both statements that are deliberately distinct from "I am neurotypical.")

This makes some sense. Much of what the majority of viewers found off-putting about Baker's Doctor was not just his initial cruelties to Peri, but his continual and overt lack of social graces. He's unrepentantly arrogant and bombastic. Yes, this is what makes the Peri-strangling so awful; it's not that having the Doctor's post-regenerative trauma actually be that scarring and debilitating is a bad idea. Rather, it's that the Doctor never really has any moment of meaningful repentance or atonement for it. But that same lack of repentance becomes, to a certain eye, charming when applied to the Doctor's very nature.

Put another way, the Sixth Doctor is socially awkward, gives zero fucks about it, and is a hero anyway. And that's an appealing portrait for someone who's neuroatypical. Significantly, it's not even presented as a defense of the ways in which the Sixth Doctor routinely violates social conventions. Rather, it's presented as a complete refusal to even engage with the debate. It isn't, to be clear, "It's more important to be true to yourself and wear the bizarre coat that makes you happy than it is to worry about whether other people will think it's ugly." Rather, "Here is a man who wears a ridiculous coat and isn't a great listener, deal with it." And that's remarkable. Most narratives about the neuroatypical seek to justify their existence, a patronizing and infantalizing exercise at best. The Colin Baker era doesn't.

Of course, there's a limit to this. On the one hand, the Sixth Doctor's heroism serves to highlight the arbitrary and often capricious nature of social norms. Which are real; one of the things you quickly learn when interacting with neuroatypical folks is that social norms are very hard to explain in terms other than the instinctive and largely unspoken ways in which neurotypicals grasp them. On the other, how much this matters changes with context. "You shouldn't wear that hideous coat" and "you should be held morally accountable for an action you took while in the grips of a severe and debilitating mental illness" are statements that are, from a variety of reasonable perspectives, equally irrational. In practice, however, blustering by without discussing them plays out very differently.

But there's a larger issue here, and one that requires a lot of care. Readers of this volume will have noticed a certain degree of intense and seething hostility towards a certain style of fan engagement with Doctor Who. And within Doctor Who fandom, there's a stereotype of the list-obsessed fan, the sort of person who's better at listing every story in which the Cybermen appear than they are at carrying on a conversation. What often goes unspoken, however, are that these methods of fandom are ones that are appreciably reflective of neuroatypical perspectives. People on the autism spectrum often develop what are called special interests—topics with which they engage passionately and deeply, often quickly developing a tremendous depth of understanding and knowledge about. This is one of those places where remembering that "fan" is short for "fanatic" is probably useful. And even among sci-fi programs, Doctor Who offers a wealth of pleasures as a special interest due to its lengthy history. This certainly isn't any sort of universal rule; not all people on the autism spectrum have special interests, and not everyone who is capable of rattling off the list of pure historicals in reverse order off the top of their head is neuroatypical. (*Black Orchid, The Highlanders, The Smugglers, The Gunfighters, The Massacre, The Myth Makers, The Crusade, The Romans, The Reign of Terror, The Aztecs,* and *Marco Polo*, I think, and I expressly forbid my copyeditor from checking that.)

There's a lot of care to be taken, in other words, with this connection. The neuroatypical tendencies of fandom have often been the cited reasons for vicious anti-autism hate speech and, more generally, for bullying that isn't explicitly based in anti-autism bigotry but that is targeted and focused in ways that are hard to ignore. And yet there are some issues here. A fair way to characterize what went wrong during the Colin Baker era, for instance, is that things like *Mark of the Rani* and *Attack of the Cybermen* were pitched almost exclusively at the sorts of people who wanted to make lists about them.

But equally, dear reader, you're currently reading the sixth volume of an exhaustive critical history of Doctor Who, and I'm currently writing it, and I'm going to go out on a limb and suggest that we both probably have some inherent sympathy for socially awkward geeks. That's not some crass claim that we're all a little bit neuroatypical or anything. Quite the opposite. My point is that you can't explain the awkwardness of fandom entirely in terms of "Doctor Who's long history makes it attractive as a special interest." There's a chicken and egg problem at the heart of this; aspects of geek culture make it an attractive safe haven for neuroatypical people, and neuroatypical people have, consequentially shaped geek culture. I'm not usually inclined to suggest that there's a wrong way to be a fan, but I think there's an exception to be made here: if your fandom doesn't instill a measure of empathy with neuroatypical people, you're doing it wrong.

And that's really my point. Baker's Doctor isn't just a good fit for neuroatypical people. Indeed, I have zero belief that anybody involved in crafting the character spent even a moment thinking about him that way. The appeal of his

Doctor to neuroatypical people is a two-step coincidence. His Doctor is a product of a moment when the show was heavily shaped by its fandom, and specifically by some of the aspects of fandom that happen to make it a welcoming place for neuroatypical people. But it is, in the end, this link to fandom that is what matters and defines him. There's a joke that the Sixth Doctor, with his garish shirts and brash personality, was conceived of as a pastiche of John Nathan-Turner, and that's surely a true statement. But it's also a true statement that he's a pastiche of Ian Levine, and, more broadly, of fandom. He may not be my Doctor. But there's no real way to deny that he's our Doctor.

And yes, there's a lot of soul-searching reflection that comes from that. The Sixth Doctor era demands that we confront some of the most problematic tendencies of sci-fi media, of fandom, and often, of ourselves. But there's also, I think, a sense of joy. There's not a fan alive who hasn't been, at times, a bit too brash, a bit too visible, and a bit too loud. Condemn his era and prefer other Doctors. I certainly do. But this is part of who we are, and the problems of its excesses don't erase the beauty it's capable of. If we're going to love our show, and moreover, if we're going to love ourselves, we have to love Baker's Doctor, not in spite of his rough edges, but because of them. And while there are many occasions to rue the consequences of those edges, there are, I think, no real occasions to apologize for them. Not even for the coat.

**About the Author**

Philip Sandifer lives in Connecticut and writes about many things besides Doctor Who, including *The Last War in Albion*, which is what happens when he looks at British comic books and thinks "what if I wrote something more sprawlingly detailed than *TARDIS Eruditorum*?"

In terms of stuff that isn't British, he is the co-author of *Flood*, along with S. Alexander Reed – an overview of They Might Be Giants' landmark 1990 album for Bloomsbury Academic's 33 1/3 series, and of *A Golden Thread*, a critical history of Wonder Woman.

He blogs at eruditorumpress.com.

Printed in Poland
by Amazon Fulfillment
Poland Sp. z o.o., Wrocław